ENGLAND: BEFORE AND AFTER WESLEY

WESLEY PREACHING FROM A CLIFF PULPIT
TO TENS OF THOUSANDS IN GWENNAP AMPHI-
THEATRE, CORNWALL

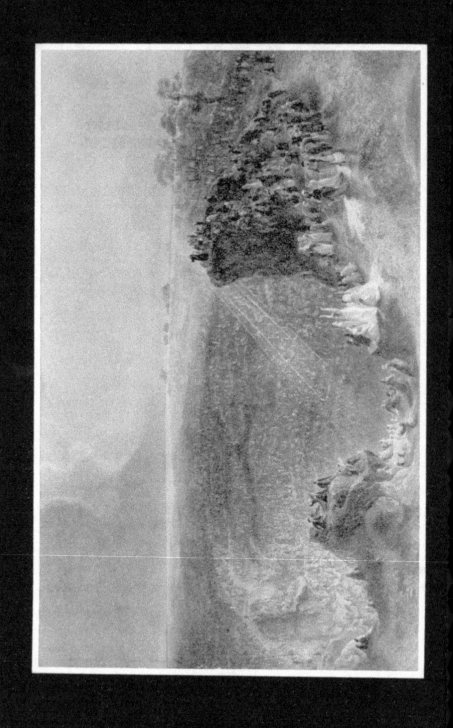

ENGLAND: BEFORE AND AFTER WESLEY

The Evangelical Revival and Social Reform

by
J. WESLEY BREADY

Ph.D. University of London

B.A. Queen's University, Canada ; M.A. Columbia University, New York City ; B.D. (Church History) Knox College, Toronto University, Canada ; B.D. (Religious Education) Union Seminary, New York City

REGENT COLLEGE PUBLISHING
Vancouver, British Columbia

First printed	•	-	-	1938
Reprinted			-	1938
Reprinted	-	-	February,	1939

DEDICATION

TO

SYDNEY WALTON, C.B.E.

who sowed the germinal idea of this work in the
Author's mind ;

TO

THE VERY REVEREND GEORGE C. PIDGEON, D.D.,
PROFESSOR FREDERICK TRACY, Ph.D., LL.D.
AND
JOHN JENNINGS, K.C.

who, as Administrators of the Research Trust Fund
created to make possible the long studies and investigations behind this book, have proven themselves patient,
loyal friends ;

AND TO

THE RT. HON. R. B. BENNETT

who, at a critical juncture, rendered gracious assistance.

England: Before and After Wesley by J. Wesley Bready
Foreword copyright © 2021 Michael Tymchak and Abraham Ninan

Originally published in 1939 by Hodder and Stoughton, London

This edition published by
Regent College Publishing
5800 University Boulevard
Vancouver, BC V6T 2E4 Canada

Regent College Publishing is an imprint of the Regent Bookstore (www. RegentBookstore.com). Views expressed in works published by Regent College Publishing are those of the author and do not necessarily represent the official position of Regent College (www.Regent-College.edu).

ISBN: 978-1-57383-594-7

CONTENTS
PART I

PART II

A BAPTISM OF FIRE

PART III

SOME FRUITS OF FAITH

LIST OF ILLUSTRATIONS

FOREWORD

FOR THOSE OF US deeply immersed in the dominant and contested social and political discourse of our own day, J. Wesley Bready's *England: Before and After Wesley* is a must read. Its re-publication by Regent College could not be more timely. Admittedly, the underlying thesis of the book is not a modest one and is likely to come as a bit of a shock to both faith-oriented and secular readers alike, namely, that "In these words are focused the very essence of the world's elemental problem today: John Wesley and Karl Marx, unmistakably, are the two most influential characters of all modern history."[1]

Ideas have consequences and, as Bready so eloquently argues, the nature and character of these ideas will be manifested in their social expression. In our view even a casual reading of this book will convince readers that in the eighteenth and nineteenth centuries, at least, evangelical religion—as found in the life and teaching of John Wesley—had profound consequences that were anything but an opiate of the people (contra the teachings of Karl Marx). Instead, "vital religion" proved itself to be powerfully transformative, not only in the personal lives of its converts, but also in the deepest fibre of their social and political lives.

J. Wesley Bready's careful documentation of the profound social and political influence of John Wesley's preaching and teaching will, for many readers today, prove to be a convincing demonstration of the transformative power of the gospel of Jesus Christ. The power and scope of this evangelical Christian influence was extraordinary: from education to health care; from the needs of the poor and orphans, to prison reform and the founding of democratic institutions; from the promotion of good reading to an end to cruelty to animals (and founding of the RSPCA). All of these, and more, are the hallmarks and outward manifestations of a vital Christian faith. Nothing could illustrate more convincingly that "faith without works is dead" and, contrary to Marx, that the gospel of

---

1. J. Wesley Bready, *England: Before and After Wesley—The Evangelical Revival and Social Reform* (London: Hodder and Stoughton, 1938), 451.

Jesus Christ more typically serves as a sharp awakening rather than an opiate of the people.

In our view a fair-minded assessment of the impact of John Wesley's life also has much to say about the contested space of Christian faith in society today. We acknowledge that its critics would prefer to understand and portray faith in a very negative light, for example, as aiding and abetting colonialism, or promoting the oppressive hierarchies of the status quo and its elites. Bready's book runs completely contrary to this analysis. Instead, he forcefully argues that the influence of "vital faith" was consistently ameliorative and emancipatory.

On the basis of careful and fair-minded historical argument, Bready seeks to document and illustrate the profound social changes that derive from Wesley's life and teaching. He demonstrates that not only are its influences broadly based and expansive in their scope, but they also burst the boundaries of any single denomination (e.g., Methodism). In like manner, vital faith maintains its transformative influence from one generation to another, extending itself well into the following Century (i.e., the nineteenth). Following this argument, we see the contagion of Wesley's influence on members of the Church of England in the century that follows, evidenced by reformers like William Wilberforce and his battle to end slavery, or the Earl of Shaftesbury's valiant efforts to bring educational opportunities to the poor (e.g., ragged schools), as well as his political activities expended to emancipate the working people of industrial England (e.g., in the matter of child labour).

Some readers will be a little surprised (even shocked) by the scope of the inspired movements that are cited: consider, for example, the thoroughly "converted" Keir Hardie and his role in the founding of the Labour Party in Britain: "His conversion . . . unified his every faculty, intensified his humanitarian zeal, and made him a dynamic leader of men. Henceforth he was to be an apostle, a crusader, an evangelist proclaiming a Message; and that message centered in the Fatherhood of God, the Brotherhood of man and the things appertaining to the Kingdom of Christ on earth."[2]

Or, again, consider William Wilberforce, an evangelical Christian (and a Tory) who, when it came to the matter of prison reform, was will-

---

2. Bready, *England: Before and After Wesley*, 397.

ing to collaborate with the "Philosophical Radicals." These Benthamites were well known for being rationalists and, as such, thoroughly inimical to faith. From the perspective of the desire for social change, however, the gospel's influence on both Hardie and Wilberforce appears to serve more as an amphetamine with respect to their strategies and behavior than as a sleep inducing "opiate" (again, contrary to Karl Marx).

Bready's book will not be comfortable reading for commentators at ease with the typical politico-religious discourse of our day, content as they are with shallow and superficial stereotypes. Admittedly, the issues are complex and there is more than enough room for adherents of the Christian faith to repent of their impact on some issues of social affairs. We are called to repent of our errors of omission as well as commission. The complicity of churches in the goals and practices of Indian Residential Schools in Canada, for example, must be painfully acknowledged and the need for reconciliation heartily embraced.

This complicity, however, should not be the sole (or any) basis upon which "vital religion"—embodied by the impact of John Wesley in the eighteenth and nineteenth centuries—contributed to the progressive, humanising and reforming social movements of the eighteenth and nineteenth centuries and, by extension, into our own day. As Bready argues, the West, and by extension the world, owes a great debt to the gospel of Jesus Christ for so many of the emancipating movements familiar to our own day, including human rights, amelioration of oppressive social conditions, and the mitigation of so many of the evils existing, for example, in England prior to the preaching of John Wesley in the eighteenth century.

Thankfully, the limitations of the current socio-political discourse of our day and its (typical) orientation to Christian faith is coming under critical scrutiny. An awareness that, at the deepest level, rather than a fundamental evil, Christian faith has made a highly positive contribution to social and political reforms, and many of the rights enjoyed, not only in the West, but throughout the world. Even in the areas often cited for the demonstration of the evils of colonization (such as India), an awareness is beginning to surface that recognizes that the real picture—and the true representation—is more nuanced and complex. Admittedly there were evils, but there was also great good and much for which to be thankful. As we write, for example a group of thinkers and leaders from various disciplines in India is beginning to coalesce for the purpose of considering a discourse that differs in significant ways from one that is merely "anti-colonial."[3] Yes, there are colonial evils to be reckoned with, but that is not the whole story. For these thinkers, any serious and fair-minded study of the socio-political impact of Christian faith will admit, even for "colonized" India, a narrative that is not merely negative, but one that is also emancipatory and ameliorative.

Those of us with an Indian perspective (i.e., the majority world) see the Christian movement, impressively, coming alive with the resurrection of Christ. Thereafter, it became a force for good in the Mediterranean world. The Acts of the Apostles tells the story of how the church grew with the preaching of the gospel. Most notably, the first Christians lived communally and fostered a welfare scheme that cared for the poor, the widow, and the orphan.[4]

Later, in the first centuries of the Christian era, when Europe was decimated by measles and smallpox epidemics, Christians nursed many of the victims back to health. As a result the church grew, and society was transformed.[5] Bready's account stands in this tradition, that of Christianity as a catalyst for transformation.

Bready convincingly documents the salutary effects of Wesley's preaching and the reforms it fostered in Britain. But when it comes to dealings with its colonies, Britain has been rightly chastised for the negative impact of its imperialistic tendencies. It must be said, however, as we have already suggested, this is not the whole story. The truth is more nuanced and more complex. Although some of those involved in the colonial enterprise, particularly those charged with governance, treated their subjects badly, others worked for the uplifting and betterment of Indian society. It is, for example, evident that the scions of the Wesleyan movement in India established schools, colleges, orphanages, and hospitals. Educated Indians, who took their cues from a variety of sources, including the Judeo-Christian worldview, contributed to nation-building

---

3. It should be noted that already, more than a decade ago, Vishal Manglwadi wrote a trenchant reassessment of the impact of Christian faith on Western society (with contrasts to India) in his highly significant *The Book That Made Your World: How the Bible Created the Soul of Western Civilization* (Nashville: Thomas Nelson, 2011).

4. Acts 2:44, 45; Gal. 2:20.

5. Rodney Stark, *The Rise of Christianity* (Princeton: Princeton University Press, 1996).

by crafting an enlightened Constitution, creating a parliamentary democracy and promoting a modern judiciary.

Although they represented a small minority, it can certainly be argued that the Indian church benefited the nation in many ways. Moreover, in recent times we note that a particularly serious effort has been made to address the socio-cultural and political implications of the gospel. It may also be recognized that the social conditions in India, including the economic disparity between classes, are in some ways very similar to pre-Wesleyan Britain. At the same time, no doubt, some challenges such as features of the caste system, are peculiar to India. It may be argued, therefore, that a renewed and enlightened Christianity, similar to that which resulted from Wesley's efforts in Britain, could go a long way toward fostering positive change. And what is true of India, by the same token, may be seen to hold great promise for other postcolonial countries. Bready's book documents the beneficial effects of a revitalized Christianity and so, for us, an opportunity to learn from, and emulate, Wesley and his spiritual heirs.

Admittedly, Bready's book does not read in the manner or voice of balanced and sophisticated historiography that we are familiar with today. However, there is another way of looking at things. Can we see this book not as an early and somewhat crude version of something that later becomes more sophisticated but rather as belonging to a different genre altogether? Beyond the work of the historian, do we not find in his writing something of the court lawyer and apologist, and even the Methodist preacher? Here we may also wish to recall that the prophetic role and voice is sometimes a little embarrassing. One thinks of Ezekiel's "siege works" play-acting, or Hosea's recovery of his (adulteress) wife. Consideration must also be given to a long tradition of rabbinic teaching (by sharp metaphor), for instance, Jesus enjoining his followers to "eat his flesh and drink his blood" or to cut off their hands and pluck out their eyes—designed to shock its hearers into attention! Speech of this kind belongs to a genre intended to make a strong, arresting statement; it is not cautiously nuanced scholarship. As such, this voice must be understood as being heavily contextualized: prophetically, it speaks to its generation clearly and emphatically, with no holds barred.

Furthermore, despite the fact that the title of Bready's book suggests that its significance is limited only to students of English church history, the types of reform he documents and highlights so vividly and so well can be easily seen as having a truly global significance in our contemporary world. The path to globalized impact, however, can only be blazed by Wesley's kind of Christian faith and commitment, marked as it was by intense vigour, comprehensive vision, and sound implementation. Bready's book republished today is a strong reminder of our own need to rise to the occasion, as Wesley did, all those generations ago.

Michael Tymchak, PhD
Abraham Ninan, MBBS, FRCPC

PREFACE

WHEN, a dozen years ago, I concluded my Doctorate researches in social history at the University of London, I had been driven to conclusions far different from those held five years earlier, at the beginning of that research, and far different also from certain basic assumptions common to most historians, whether general, political or economic. I was forced by pressure of much evidence to the conclusion that the democratic and cultural heritage of the modern English-speaking world is much more a spiritual than a political or an economic achievement ; that the positive impact of the French Revolution and its philosophy upon British and American developments has been vastly over-rated, or unduly taken for granted ; and that the much-neglected and oft-lampooned Evangelical Revival, which began with Wesley among the outcast masses, was the true nursing-mother of the spirit and character values that have created and sustained Free Institutions throughout the English-speaking world.

Twelve years of further study and research have but deepened and strengthened these convictions. My books, *Lord Shaftesbury and Social-Industrial Progress*, and *Dr. Barnardo : Physician, Pioneer, Prophet*, are segmentary studies within this vast orbit of moral and spiritual influence. To understand the epic victories of Shaftesbury, " the British Abraham Lincoln," or of Barnardo, " the Emancipator of the Outcast Child," aside from the permeating influence of the Evangelical Revival, which inspired and nurtured their characters and crusades, is utterly impossible. Exactly the same is true of the character and achievements of Wilberforce, Howard, Raikes, Carey, Asbury, Ryerson, Lincoln, Harriet Beecher-Stowe, Florence Nightingale, Frances Willard, General Booth, Keir Hardie, President Wilson, and a hundred other vital leaders in an unparalleled spiritual succession of mighty emancipating movements. Such men and their causes were the spiritual progeny of the purging Baptism of Fire mediated by that matchless practical prophet, John Wesley.

In 1932, I had the memorable privilege of a lecture tour for Canadian clubs, colleges and societies, from Atlantic to

Pacific, across Canada. Following this, a group of prominent Canadians conceived the plan of creating a modest Historical Research Fund, which would enable me to return to England and complete the whole cycle of research within which my *Shaftesbury* and *Barnardo* books are but limited and particular studies. Some two hundred subscribers supported this fund. My sincerest thanks are due to them all ; for without their practical help, the researches for this wider study could never have been achieved. The Research Fund was raised on the anticipation of three years labour ; the study has commanded more than five years of the most arduous toil ; and, at a critical juncture, the gracious interest of the Right Hon. R. B. Bennett enabled the task to be carried, unbroken, to its conclusion.

Concerning the plan of the book, I expect criticism ; some readers certainly will think Part I too long and detailed. I believe, however, the plan adopted best fits the subject. This is not merely a life of Wesley ; it is the history of an epochal movement, of which Wesley was the master-figure. That movement, indeed, represents a water-shed in Anglo-Saxon history ; and to appraise the intensity and sweep of its repercussions, we must first see clearly its incredible social and moral backgrounds, then proceed to the origin and evolution of the movement itself, and finally examine the fruitage of its maturity in different spheres of cultural attainment on different continents ; hence the *three* parts. The title, *England : Before and After Wesley*, suggests the water-shed significance of the great Spiritual Awakening to Britain. Its impact, however, upon the United States and upon various parts of the British Empire has been not less pronounced. In this year, therefore, which marks both the Bicentenary of Wesley's Conversion and the Quatercentenary of the Open English Bible—a year with much demonstration of militarism and paganism around us—it surely behoves the English-speaking peoples to study seriously the debt of their free and voluntary institutions to this peerless Revival of vital, practical Christianity. Such a study this book has attempted.

My thanks, in the preparation of this volume, are due to Professor Fred Tracy, L.L.D. ; the Very Reverend Dr. George Pidgeon, first Moderator of the United Church of Canada ; Dr. Charles J. Bready, of the United States ; and Dr. Donald Soper, all of whom have read the completed book in manuscript. For cheerful assistance in specialised aspects of the work, I thank Mr. Sydney Walton, Dr. Benjamin Gregory, Mr. Edmund Lamplough, Dr. Thomas P. Potter, Rev. Percy Boyling,

Dr. Frank Murray, and Dr. M. Dorothy George. Nor should I omit my indebtedness to the various officials in different departments of the British Museum, or to the secretaries of several societies, both English and American, who have rendered ungrudging assistance. But, above all, my gratitude goes out to the patience and encouragement, the assistance and criticism, of Ruth, my wife, who has supported me at every turn.

My book, *Lord Shaftesbury*, contains a long and organised *Bibliography* (pages 415-435). That, together with the numerous foot-notes in this study, will sufficiently indicate the source materials upon which I here have drawn.

PREFATORY NOTE TO THIRD IMPRESSION

In the few months since this book was published nearly 300 Press judgments have appeared. They have come from all continents ; from every large city in England, Ireland, Scotland and Wales ; from every quarter of the British Empire, and from every part of the U.S.A. ; while also they have appeared in Spanish, French, Dutch, Norwegian, Danish and Swedish. Yet almost daily they still arrive, some being three and four pages in length. Together they represent organs in all schools of political and economic, of secular and religious opinion.

The all but unanimous approval with which this study has been greeted, together with the fact that a second impression had to be issued in the month of publication, persuades me that the exacting years of research behind it have not been in vain. The data and documentation of the book have been unchallenged. The sole serious criticism which a few reviewers have raised is that the study is over much in black and white. The period into which the converted Wesley stepped, they argue, was not quite so decadent and the effect of the Evangelical Revival not quite so far-reaching as here depicted. My *apologia* is this : The severe curtailments incidental to the limitations of a single volume prohibited much minor colouring, and bold outlines were therefore obligatory. Many attempts have been made to justify and even to " whitewash " the early eighteenth century, the resulting volumes being known to every student of the period. Yet, despite all, the stubborn fact remains that at this period the trend of affairs was directed by materialism, self-seeking and blatant paganism in high places. The age was one of moral and spiritual eclipse. As for the *results* of this Spiritual Renaissance, they were, of course, often hidden as leaven in the lump of life's manifold expression. But it is my increasing conviction (strengthened by reviewers of this book) that the results of the Evangelical Movement, in its interdenominational impacts, were more—not less—far-reaching than is indicated by my documentation. No other movement has a comparable claim to be known as the moral watershed of Anglo-Saxon history.

Greatly am I encouraged by appreciations of this book from eminent men. Professor James Moffatt has written : " It is one of the rare historical works which breaks new ground." Jack Lawson, M.P., writes : " This book will lead to the re-writing of much nineteenth and twentieth-century history." Lord Stamp says : " It should be carefully read by all moulding opinion throughout the Democratic world." Dean Inge avers : " This book has proved that Wesley was not only a very great man but a real saint." Some other judgments are :

The Rt. Hon. General Smuts : " Wesley certainly was a *landmark* in English History ! " Rt. Hon. W. L. MacKenzie King : " It is a work of great significance." Rt. Hon. R. B. Bennett : " This book may have a most profound effect upon the history of our time." Rt. Hon. Sir Thomas Inskip : " It is an invaluable book." Bishop Francis J. McConnell (New York) : " There is no other work that covers just this field. In design of arrangement and cogency of treatment, it is fascinating." The Bishop of Birmingham : " A most interesting volume. I am much impressed by its marshalling of facts." The Bishop of Chelmsford : " The best of all the *modern* books on Wesley. Probably the best of *all*." Bishop Blake (Michigan) : " The greatest book in Wesleyan literature." Lorne Pierce, D.Litt., L.L.D. (Editor, Ryerson Press, and *Canadian Bookman*) : " A magnificent work. It will change our judgment of an entire age." President H. Sloane Coffin (Union Seminary, New York) : " A vast amount of valuable material. The book is fascinating reading." Professor C. E. Raven : " I owe much to Bready's *Shaftesbury*. This volume is of even greater importance." The Hon. H. J. Cody (President, Toronto University) : " I read this book through with the greatest delight . . . a valuable contribution to Sociology." Dr. J. Fort Newton : " A superb piece of work." Canon V. F. Storr (Westminster Abbey) : " The fruit of ripe, sound judgment . . . an *indispensable* book." The Dean of Liverpool : " A grand book, a rare achievement." Lord Daryngton : " Very able . . . of great value and should be widely read." Dr. Salem Bland (*Toronto Star*) : " A work that has never been done before and need never be done again." Dr. Scott Lidgett : " A very great service to English history."[2]

Principal R. Newton Flew (Cambridge) : " A compendium of research which should be in every public library." The Very Rev. George Pidgeon : " One of the best bits of work done in our time." Mildred Cable : " It is a unique volume of historical research, a book for to-day, (Read it.)" Nellie McClung, (Canadian novelist) : " It will do much to stiffen the muscles of professing Christians everywhere." Chancellor E. W. Wallace (Victoria University) : " It puts beyond shadow of question the tremendous influence of Wesley upon the social, moral and religious conditions of Great Britain, the Empire and the world." The Very Rev. T. Albert Moore, D.D., LL.D., (Ex-Moderator and Ex-Secretary, United Church of Canada) : " The more I read it, the more I admire this wonderful book."

Scores of further judgments from well-known men and women are equally encouraging.

J. WESLEY BREADY.

94, Tressillian Road,
    BROCKLEY,
        LONDON, S.E.4,
            ENGLAND.

February, 1939.

PART I

BEFORE THE SPIRITUAL AWAKENING

CHAPTER I

TRIPLE TRAGEDIES

" THE foundation of democracy is the sense of spiritual
independence, which nerves the individual to stand
alone against the powers of this world, and in England,
where squire and parson, lifting arrogant eyebrows at
the insolence of the lower orders, combined to crush
popular agitation, as a menace at once to society and
to the Church, it is probable that democracy owes more
to Nonconformity than to any other single movement."

PROFESSOR R. H. TAWNEY, D.LITT.

Religion and the Rise of Capitalism. p. 272.

B

TRIPLE TRAGEDIES

In 1738, the year of Wesley's " conversion," Bishop Berkeley in his *Discourse Addressed to Magistrates and Men in Authority*, declared that morality and religion in Britain had collapsed " to a degree that has never been known in any Christian country." " Our prospect," he averred, " is very terrible and the symptoms grow worse from day to day." The accumulating torrent of evil, " which threatens a general inundation and destruction of these realms," Berkeley attributed chiefly to " the irreligion and bad example of those . . . styled the better sort." Then, pleading with all State officials to mend their ways and consider well the future of their country, he continued : " The youth born and brought up in wicked times without any bias to good from early principle, or instilled opinion, when they grow ripe, must be monsters indeed. And it is to be feared that the age of monsters is not far off."[1]

Berkeley's place in history is that of philosopher rather than moralist. He disliked both enthusiasm and exaggeration ; he was accustomed to weigh well the purport of his words : and in 1738 his influence was at its height. If, however, his fears seem extreme and we turn to the writings and records of his contemporaries, a host might be cited to the same end. Wittingly or unwittingly, and from vastly different angles, Fielding, Defoe, Swift, Bolingbroke, Pope, Steele, Gay, Addison, Butler, Sterne, Walpole and Johnson offer evidence of the moral and spiritual eclipse with which the earlier half of the eighteenth century was seriously threatened. Historians, too, of widely divergent schools, on this particular issue are singularly agreed. Examine Lecky, Stephen, Ranke, Macaulay, Rogers, Green, Overton, Abbey, Robertson, Trevelyan, Halévy and Temperley, and it will be found that none would seriously dispute either the justification for, or the relative accuracy of, Bishop Berkeley's verdict.

The fact then of a phenomenal social and moral degeneracy at this period is indisputable. The manifold causes of that

---

[1] George Berkeley, *op. cit.*, p. 41f.

degeneracy, though interrelated, are more elusive : three nevertheless, being unmistakable, are of vital importance to the unfolding of our subject.

(i) The Anti-Puritan Purge

First among these three causes was the anti-Puritan " Code of Persecution "[1] passed between 1661 and 1665. Charles II in his *Declaration*, signed at Breda before his return to England, had promised a general amnesty, including liberty to " tender consciences." The ensuing carnival of triumphant royalism, however, swept all before it. In April, 1661, the King's coronation was solemnised amidst scenes of wild excitement and elaborate pomp. Adroitly, too, a General Election was staged almost to synchronise with the coronation pageant, thus exploiting its exuberant and flamboyant passions. Hence the Cavalier Parliament, now overwhelmingly elected, consisted chiefly of " hot Royalists and hot Churchmen," whose dominant idea of religion was a revengeful, aggressive hatred of everything even savouring of Commonwealth association or influence.

Already the bodies of Cromwell, Bradshaw and Ireton had been torn from their graves and gibbeted at Tyburn. The Solemn League and Covenant was burned by the common hangman in Westminster Hall. More than a dozen " regicides " were executed and large numbers of prominent Puritans were cast into gaol, while the royalist squires, lawyers and bishops, not to be outdone even by the mob spirit which they had stimulated, proceeded by legislative enactment to exterminate, root, stem and branch, the " monstrous heresy " from every department of the nation's life.

The first legislative thrust in the Cavalier " purge " was directed toward municipalities and was designed to kill all Puritan influence in the sphere of legislation ; for the members of municipal bodies controlled the election of Members of Parliament. By the *Corporation Act* (1661),[2] all holders of municipal office had to swear a solemn oath that they would not " on any pretext whatever," take up arms against, or resist, the King. They had to repudiate the *Solemn League and Covenant*

---

[1] J. R. Green, *History of England*, Vol. III, p. 375.
[2] 13 Chas. II, St. 2, cap. 1. All the statutes of Chas. II are *dated* as though he had immediately succeeded his father. On this point, G. M. Trevelyan (*History of England*, p. 446), quaintly notes : " Lawyers pretended, after their fashion, that Chas. II was King from the moment of his father's death."

and to pronounce it an illegal document, while also they had to receive the Sacrament according to the rites of the Church of England.

The Corporation Act, however, was but a prelude to the really deadly assault. The Act of Uniformity, the Conventicle Act and the Five Mile Act stabbed at the very heart of Puritan religion, Puritan ideals, Puritan education and Puritan culture. Taken together, they represent perhaps the most nefarious and most thoroughly un-British legislation ever placed on the Statute Books of England.

In preparation for the *Act of Uniformity* (1662) the Prayer Book was revised by Convocation in an anti-Puritan direction to the extent of several hundred alterations.[1] Then, the stage being set, every clergyman and schoolmaster, by the clauses of this Act, had to " declare his unfeigned assent and consent to the use of all things in the said book contained and prescribed, in these words and in no other." One clause of the oath reads : " I (A—— B——) do declare that it is not lawful upon any pretence whatever to take arms against the King. . . . And that I will conform to the Liturgy of the Church of England, as it is *now* by law established." He had to repudiate, and pronounce illegal, the *Solemn League and Covenant* and to pledge himself *not to seek* to make any change in the Constitution of Church or State. And so through twenty-nine quarto pages this stupid, vindictive Act blusters on, even stipulating that the nation was to act toward any who refused to subscribe, " as though the person or persons so offending, or neglecting, were dead."[2]

The immediate result of this Act was that nearly 2,000 rectors and vicars, whose consciences were not subservient to the dictates of State, were turned adrift from their livings without compensation[3] : among whom were such eminent pastors and scholars as Baxter, Howe, and Calamy. Among them, too, were Dr. Samuel Annesley and John Wesley, the grandfathers, and Dr. Bartholomew Wesley, a great-grandfather, of the famous eighteenth century evangelists.

This expulsion represented one-fifth of the entire English

---

[1] Warner and Marten, *Ground Work of British History* (Part II, p. 410) place the number at six hundred.

[2] 14 Chas. II, cap. 4 (a). It is significant that the *Statutes of the Realm*, as published during Charles II's reign, simply leave a blank for all Commonwealth legislation. These contemporary publications may be examined in the State Papers Room of the British Museum Library.

[3] It must, of course, be remembered that about an equal number of " Laudian clergy " had been ejected during the Puritan era. See G. M. Trevelyan, *History of England*, pp. 417–18.

clergy : " Men whose zeal and labour had diffused throughout the country a greater appearance of piety and religion than it had ever displayed before."[1] The famous historian, J. R. Green (himself an Anglican clergyman), says of this expulsion : " No such sweeping alteration in the religious aspect of the Church had ever been seen before . . . the rectors and vicars who were driven out were the most learned and most active of their order.· . . . It was the definite expulsion of a great party which from the time of the Reformation had played the most active and popular part in the life of the Church." " The Church of England," says Green, " stood from that moment isolated and alone among the Churches of the Christian world . . . it sank into immobility . . . With the expulsion of the Puritan clergy all change, all efforts after reform, all natural development, suddenly stopped."[2]

But the 2,000 expelled pastors were not the kind of shepherds who forsake their flock when the wolf raids the fold. Most of them were compelled at once to seek new means of livelihood ; nevertheless they continued to meet with their people in private houses and there to conduct worship according to the dictates of conscience. This " audacity " was answered by the *Conventicle Act* (1664) which " punished with fine, imprisonment and transportation on a third offence, all persons who met in greater numbers than five " for any act of Dissenting worship. Transportation at this time moreover might well mean literal slavery ; for in 1685, following Monmouth's Rebellion, the 800 victims sentenced by Judge Jeffreys, under James II, to transportation were " presented to various courtiers, who *sold them to slavery* in the West Indian plantations."[3]

Then, in 1665, came the Great Plague which mowed down in London alone 100,000 citizens—one in five of all her population. This ghastly visitation was enough to strike terror into the stoutest hearts. Parliament was hustled off to Oxford and large numbers of London clergymen, joining the popular exodus, fled the city for country air, thus forsaking their flocks and leaving them without religious rites. Expelled Puritan divines forthwith stepped into the gap, ministering to the sick, burying the dead and consoling, as best they could, the mourners of deceased loved ones. Not a few went further : believing

---

[1] J. R. Green, *op. cit.*, Vol. III, p. 362 ; Leopold Von Ranke, *History of England*, Vol. III, p. 375ff.
[2] Green, Vol. III, p. 361ff. For some remarkable social reforms initiated by the Commonwealth, see *Property : Its Duties and Rights* (composite authorship), pp. 143–46.
[3] Warner and Marten, *op. cit.*, Part II, p. 416.

that, at such a time, the Spiritual Law superseded all State enactments, they entered the Churches whence they had been expelled and conducted services for their quondam parishioners.[1] The fear and fury now " roused by the revival of a foe that seemed to have been crushed," registered itself in the *Five Mile Act* (1665)—the crowning infamy of the Anti-Puritan Code. This Act presented a re-hashed and highly-spiced statement of the bitterest clauses in the foregoing legislation ; and, on the expelled clergymen refusing to subscribe—as apparently all did—they " were forbidden under penalty of £40 *and* six months imprisonment, to approach within five miles of any corporate town, or borough, or of any parish in which they had previously taught or preached."[2] The Act was applied to schoolmasters as well as clergymen. Hence, torn and tortured by persecution, Puritanism was almost completely severed from its spiritual and cultural roots. Not for twenty-five years, till the passing of the *Toleration Act* by William and Mary, did Protestant Dissenters enjoy even the semblance of corporate liberty ; and even then the measure granted them was small.[3] Remembering that for a considerable period more than 4,000 Quakers and Baptists—to say nothing of Presbyterians, Independents, etc.—were in gaol through the fury of this Anti-Puritan Purge, is it surprising that in a later and more industrialised age, Puritan Dissenters often carried the doctrines and dogmas of *laissez-faire* too far ?[4]

Professor G. M. Trevelyan, commenting on the results of this Code of Persecution, points out that Puritans were not only " excluded from the Universities and from their natural share in social and political influence," but were actually " driven out of polite society." The loss inflicted by this Code upon " Puritan Culture," Professor Trevelyan thinks, " was never completely made good."[5] Puritans, for a generation, were as Babylonian Captives in their native land.

The spirit of the whole Cavalier Purge is reflected by the fact that even Milton, for a time, was hurled into prison. Dire difficulty was experienced in procuring publication for *Paradise*

---

[1] *Political History of England*, Vol. VIII, p. 69f. (Richard Lodge, L.L.D.) ; Green, Vol. III, p. 375.
[2] Dr. Lodge, *op. cit.*, Vol. VIII, p. 70.
[3] William & Mary, St. 1, cap. 18. Even still, marriages were only legal when performed by a clergyman of the State Church. See, too, Elie Halévy, *A History of the English People in 1815*, p. 352.
[4] A special Act was passed against Quakers, and the *Licensing Act* (1662) was designed to muzzle the Puritan press. The Quakers' religious aversion to all oaths made them specially-marked victims of such repressive legislation.
[5] Trevelyan's *History of England*, p. 450f.

Lost : it was ordered to be burned by the common hangman ; and Milton, finally reduced to a state of penury that compelled him to sell his library, could get but £5 for the copyright of the immortal Puritan epic.

Such was the outcome of Charles II's promise of " liberty to tender consciences " in the *Declaration* at Breda.   A century later, John Wesley, on reading Wodrow's *History of the Sufferings of the Church of Scotland*, wrote : " It would transcend belief, but that the vouchers are too authentic to admit of any exception.   O what a blessed Governor was that good-natured man, so called, King Charles the Second !   Bloody Mary was a lamb, a mere dove, in comparison of him ! "[1]   Admittedly Charles II was not directly responsible for this persecuting purge.   A pensioner of France, he had his own secret, sinister schemes in hand, which partly were thwarted by the Anti-Puritan Code.   Nevertheless mercy to Protestant Dissenters held no place in his ultimate plans, and the unparalleled licentiousness of his Court put all purity and virtue to rout.[2]

(ii)   *The Expulsion of Non-Jurors*

The second tragedy takes us to the years 1689 and 1690.   It was not pregnant with such fatal consequences as was the *Code of Persecution* ; nevertheless it left behind it a cruel scar, not to be healed till several generations had passed.

Though James II had ingloriously fled the country, the whole Jacobite party contended that the Crown " could not be forfeited " ; and among the most vehement spokesmen of that party was a group of ultra-High Church clergy who claimed that James II was still " the Lord's Anointed " and therefore that William III's title to the throne was " pretended."   Among these ecclesiastics, moreover, were several prominent bishops and many zealous " old Catholic " priests.   William's position at best was difficult.   He wanted to grant liberty of worship to the oppressed Puritan Dissenters, and so offered to excuse the National clergy from taking the Oath of Allegiance, if the Church dignitaries would agree to the abolition of the Persecuting Code.   To both hierarchy and squirearchy, however, this proposal smacked of treason.   The Oath accordingly was administered, though to make it less objectionable the words

---

[1] John Wesley's *Journal*, entry of January 11th, 1768.
[2] In his *Short History* (p. 608) Green says : " In mere love of what was vile, in contempt of virtue and disbelief in purity or honesty, the King himself stood ahead of any of his subjects."

" rightful and lawful," as previously applied to the sovereign, were omitted. The upshot of it all, was that eight prelates and over 400 clergy of the extreme right wing refused to subscribe. Hence on August 1st, 1689, they were suspended ; and on February 1st, 1690, all were deprived of their livings.[1]

Among these *Non-Jurors*—as the new outcasts were styled— were such courageous leaders as Sancroft, the Primate, and such saintly souls as Bishop Ken, the hymn writer, while, on the accession of George I, they were joined by the famous mystic, William Law. Among them, too, were the chief exponents of the patristic, sacramental and old Catholic conception of the Church, as distinguished from the Protestant, prophetic and more directly New Testament conception. In brief, 400 spiritual sons of Laud suffered in 1690, for conscience sake, the same fate as the 2,000 spiritual sons of Luther suffered in 1662[2] : and the latter expulsion, like the former, bore poisoned fruit.

With this second tragedy the Church found herself shorn of both left and right wings. Zealous priest and flaming prophet were now cut off. The " moderate," " reasonable " men, the time-servers, self-seekers and pluralists—these all were left : but the wings of faith were gone. Had the " National " Church studied how best to extinguish all spiritual fire within the realm and to crush all crusading initiative, she could have devised no better plan than these two tragic expulsions. The ability to quarrel was stimulated ; the ability to aspire was stultified.

A quaint instance of the deep-rooted feelings associated with the Nonjuring expulsion was later to manifest itself in the Wesley parsonage at Epworth. Though a moderate High Churchman, Rev. Samuel Wesley (John's father) in family devotions prayed regularly and fervently for William III, as King. Shortly before William's decease, however, he discovered to his dismay that Susannah, his wife, was not saying " Amen " to these particular petitions. Taxing her for the reason, out came the truth. The daughter of Dr. Samuel Annesley—that expelled Puritan, often styled " the St. Paul of Nonconformity " —was now at heart a Non-Juror. Unrepentently she asserted that William at best was regent—not King. Samuel Wesley consequently left the house in a huff. He would not share the bed and board of a " disloyal " wife, and for some months, apparently, they lived apart ; then, conveniently, William died

---

[1] William & Mary, cap. 8.

[2] C. J. Abbey and J. H. Overton, *The English Church in the Eighteenth Century*, Vol. I, p. 3 and p. 58f.

Encyclopædia of Religion and Ethics (Non-Jurors).

and with the accession of Anne, the Epworth parsonage was again harmonious. Jacobitism, the " Divine Right of Kings " and the Nonjuring expulsion, divided many parsonages besides that of Epworth. The Succession issue, in fact, divided the nation.

(iii) *The Suppression of Convocation*

The third tragedy is so closely associated with the second that it might almost be said to have sprung from it. Yet it can only be understood in its relation to a broad stream of influences flowing down from Commonwealth days.

From the Restoration to the Revolution of 1688, Squirearchy and Hierarchy dominated the national outlook. " Church and King " was the watchword of the ruling oligarchy. Prince, priest and politician believed that the Civil War and the Commonwealth had demolished the Constitutional framework of the country ; so they set about to rebuild it according to their hearts' desire, taking due pains that their own interests, together with those of the classes and orders they represented, were not overlooked. " Divine Right of Kings " was an assumption inherent in all this new programme. But the shameless personal conduct and profligate Court of Charles II, through twenty-five disappointing years, were not easy to reconcile with any Christian conception of " Divinity." Moreover, it was not pleasant for the " Highest " Churchmen[1] to recall that Charles II, as Father of his Country and Sovereign Head of the National Church, had, on his death-bed, blessed the kneeling prelates and a little later, in fear of the Last Enemy, had " smuggled " into his chamber a Roman Catholic priest, at whose hands he secretly received the Last Rites.

When, therefore, James II, after the " Bloody Assize," by treating the Judges of the realm as his puppets, by violating the rights of Oxford and Cambridge Universities, by dissolving Parliament and preparing to " pack " a new one, by planning openly to re-establish Roman Catholicism as the National religion, and by overriding the Constitution, asserted seriously and imperiously the " Divine Right " of his kingship, grave misgivings were expressed in unexpected quarters. The episode of the Seven Bishops defying the King's second *Declaration of*

---

[1] " High Churchmen " at this time, indicated a high view of the *authority* of the State Church in politics and society, support of Divine Right of Kings, and a strong antipathy to both Dissenters and Romanists. " Low Churchmen " meant " broad," " liberal," " latitudinarian," and had *no* *Evangelical* significance. (G. M. Trevelyan, *op. cit.*, p. 453.)

Indulgence, and drawing up a protest against it, gave warning that the " Divine Right " prerogative could be carried too far, and that " Passive Obedience " had its limitations, even among the High Church clergy.

Hence when William of Orange was invited to come over " to save the Constitution of Church and State," many High Churchmen and squires acquiesced in his plans ; and not a few supported his efforts. But to the thoroughgoing traditionalist, whether peer or priest, William and Mary were regents, not sovereigns ; for by his doctrine " the Crown could not be forfeited." Loyalty therefore to William, even from the beginning, in Tory quarters, was halting and cold ; but when in 1689 he granted the barest toleration of worship to such Nonconformists as would subscribe to a specified thirty of the Thirty-nine Articles, the resentment of hot-headed reactionaries was all agog. Their fury against Puritanism was stronger than their fear of Rome. Then, too, the Non-Jurors, as a body, were firebrands. True, Ken and some others conducted themselves without malice and with much charity. But such proved the exception. The zeal of most of the Nonjuring party soon turned sour and expressed itself in Jacobite plotting and scheming. To Non-Jurors as a group the National Church, on their expulsion, was " schismatic " and her prayers " immoral." They alone could bestow Apostolic Orders, and through their Sacraments alone, flowed Divine Grace.

After Mary's death, too, William's position became increasingly difficult, and during the latter years of his reign " continual plots " were hatched against his life.[1]

Anne owed her accession to " the Revolution Settlement " ; but at heart she was a sentimental reactionary, with a warm attachment to the " Divine Right " theory. During the whole of her reign the strife of parties, political and ecclesiastical, was violent[2] ; but during its latter part the national cauldron seethed ; and in the raging animosities engendered, a series of co-related events gathered such momentum as to make the third tragedy inevitable.

In November, 1709, Dr. Henry Sacheverell, a High Churchman of little judgment and less charity, was invited to preach in St. Paul's Cathedral. With venomous rancour he assailed both the Revolution Settlement and the Toleration Act, whilst

---

[1] *Dictionary of National Biography* (William III) ; *Chambers's Biog. Dict.* ; Traill's *William III.*

[2] Cf. Daniel Defoe's satire, *Shortest Way with Dissenters* (1703), which won for him a spell in the pillory.

Dissenters he depicted as little better than wily serpents. " We must watch," urged Sacheverell, " against these crafty, faithless and insidious persons, who can creep to our altars and partake of our Sacraments, that they may be qualified more secretly and powerfully to undermine us." [1] The Whigs, already unpopular, instead of letting Sacheverell stew in his own broth, decided to impeach him before the bar of the Lords ; and by so doing, made mob heroes of him and the ultra-High Church party behind him. " God save the Church and the Doctor," cried a half-drunken mob around his carriage en route to Westminster, pausing now and then " to wreck a meeting-house " and to knock down all who refused to shout, " Sacheverell and High Church." In the wake of the " Sacheverell Riots " the Tories were hurled to power and, new fuel being added to already raging fires, the cauldron, now boiling, was soon to overflow.

In 1711 came the nefarious *Occasional Conformity Act* with its bitter persecution and fierce fines upon Dissenters. [2] In 1714 followed the *Schism Acts*, striking at the Educational institutions of Nonconformity by " forbidding anyone to teach without a bishop's license." Meanwhile, too, numerous Jacobite schemes were hatching underground. Queen Anne, the Duke of Ormonde, Bolingbroke and the Duke of Buckinghamshire, to say nothing of a large fry of politicians, squires and Non-Jurors, were working " double-shift " to secure the succession of the " Pretender." But all ended in the old story of " the best laid schemes o' mice and men." The arch-intriguer Bolingbroke, despite his brilliance, over-reached himself. He had just succeeded in shelving Harley, his one-time Tory colleague, when the Queen died—too soon for the realisation of his schemes. " The Earl of Oxford (Harley) was removed on Tuesday, the Queen died on Sunday ! " moaned Bolingbroke to Swift : " What a world is this, and how does Fortune banter us ! " [3] Had Anne lived even a month longer, the moulds of succeeding English history might have assumed a different shape. [4]

In 1714, George I, a stranger to the British people and knowing not a word of English, was peacefully crowned King. His

---

[1] Abbey and Overton, *op. cit.*, Vol. II, p. 379f.

[2] The purpose of this Act was to stop Nonconformists from receiving the Sacrament in the Church of England and then worshipping in Meeting Houses.

[3] Swift's *Correspondence* (letter, August 3rd, 1714).

[4] See G. M. Trevelyan, *England under Queen Anne* (the Plan of the Protestant Succession), Chap. XVII and Epilogue ; also W. E. H. Lecky, *Hist. of England in Eighteenth Century*, Vol. I, p. 161ff.

coronation dealt a deadly blow to the " Divine Right " tradition. Political idolatry was now increasingly transferred from the Sovereign to the Constitution. But the Jacobites were in no mood to accept defeat. In 1715 came the Old Pretender's Rebellion, and the year following appeared the posthumous publication, *Constitution of the Church of England and the Nature and Consequences of Schism*, by the bitter Nonjuring bishop, George Hickes, in which with pontifical infallibility he excommunicated all and sundry, save Non-Jurors. Hereon the versatile latitudinarian, Bishop Hoadly, entered the fray. His *Preservative against the Principles and Practices of Non-Jurors* was a speedy and able reply not only to Hickes, but to all hierarchical assumptions. A little later (1717) Hoadly preached before the King his famous and provocative sermon, *Nature of the Kingdom, or Church, of Christ*, wherein he claimed that Christ had not delegated His authority to any ecclesiastical system, and that the spiritual, Invisible Church was the only true representative of Jesus Christ.

The fat was now completely in the fire. The ensuing Bangorian Controversy soon broke into side-issues ; the Lower House of Convocation literally howled for the official censure of Hoadly, and much *odium theologicum* was loudly expressed. Whereupon the Whig politicians, having their own axe to grind, and glad of a plausible excuse to silence High Church politics, called upon the King to prorogue Convocation by Royal Writ. The request was granted ; the prorogation really spelled suppression : not till the middle of the nineteenth century was Convocation again permitted to transact business.[1]

The Triple Tragedies were now complete. Not only was the " National " Church shorn of left-wing prophet and right-wing priest, even her vocal organs were torn from her. And the famous Queen Anne's Bounty, which meanwhile had greatly augmented her endowments and income,[2] was destined to swell the loathsome system of pluralities and sinecures which so grossly vulgarised and paganised the eighteenth-century Church. These Triple Tragedies, with their co-related events, contributed lamentably to the moral and spiritual stagnation which Bishop Berkeley, in the year of Wesley's conversion, so deeply deplored. In that same year (1738), Dr. Thomas Secker, then Bishop of Oxford and soon to be Archbishop of Canterbury,

---

[1] *Encyclopædia Britannica* (" Convocation," " Bangorian Controversy ") ; *Ency. of Rel. and Ethics* (" Convocation ").
[2] For an acute analysis of the meaning of Queen Anne's Bounty, see Nathaniel Micklem, K.C., *A Note on the Disestablishment of the Welsh Church*.

complained that " Christianity is now railed at and ridiculed with very little reserve, and the teachers of it without any at all . . ." [1] But neither Secker nor any other Primate of his century seems to have fathomed the underlying causes of that ridicule ; and certainly none gave any vigorous lead towards the rekindling of spiritual life.

[1] Abbey and Overton, *op. cit.*, Vol. II, p. 20.

DEISM AND ITS AFTERMATH

" Thus God and Nature formed the general frame,
And bade self-love and social be the same.

All Nature is but Art, unknown to thee ;
All chance, direction, which thou can'st not see ;
All discord, harmony, not understood ;
All partial evil, Universal Good ;

One truth is clear—whatever is, is right."

PoPE's *Essay on Man* (1733)

" To make society happy, it is necessary that great
numbers should be wretched as well as poor."
BERNARD MANDEVILLE, *The Fable of the Bees* (1723) p. 194.

CHAPTER II

DEISM AND ITS AFTERMATH

ANTHONY COLLINS, author of *Priestcraft in Perfection* and *Discourse on Free-thinking*, on being asked why, holding such deistical opinions, he sent his servants to Church, answered : "That they may neither rob nor murder me!"[1] Lord Bolingbroke, a confirmed Deist, considered Christianity "a fable," yet he held that "a statesman ought to profess the Doctrines of the Church of England."[2] Sir Leslie Stephen in his *English Thought in the Eighteenth Century*, referring to the later Deistic period, says : "Scepticism, widely diffused through the upper classes, was of the indolent variety, implying a perfect willingness that the churches should survive though the Faith should perish."[3] It is more than a coincidence that following the Restoration and the "Triple Tragedies," a soulless, superficial Deism, emerging gradually into open scepticism, came increasingly to dominate the mental outlook of potentates in Church and State. Nor was it till after the dawn of the nineteenth century that this influence was completely dethroned.

(i) *The Origin and Trend of Deism*

On the earliest manifestations of the Deistic outlook, as exhibited in Lord Herbert of Cherbury's *De Veritate* and *De Religione Gentilium*, this treatise need not pause. Neither need we examine the philosophy of Thomas Hobbes, tutor to Charles II : for great as was the influence of his materialistic rationalism, with its uncompromising reduction of religion to a department of state and its cool pronouncement of the "sovereign power" as "absolute and irresponsible," Hobbes's position was but indirectly related to Deism. Paradoxically, it was the sincere, if latitudinarian, Christian, John Locke, who

[1] Mark Pattison, *Tendencies of Religious Thought in England*, 1688–1750 (in *Essays and Reviews*, p. 301).
[2] *Chambers's Biog. Dict. ; Dict. of Nat. Biog.*
[3] Vol. I, p. 375.

opened the door to popular Deistical speculation. In 1795 appeared Locke's famous thesis, *Reasonableness of Christianity*, destined to be the chief text of Christian apologetics for almost a century. The following year came John Toland's *Christianity not Mysterious*, the first popular Deistic treatise—based obviously on Locke, but pointing unmistakably toward the uncompromising scepticism of David Hume.

Locke, an eloquent apostle of religious toleration, was actuated by a sincere and laudable desire to free Christianity of all encumbrances and restore it to its " original simplicity " : a task which he thought could be achieved by mental clarification alone. His only creed would be the acceptance of Jesus as the Messiah ; and pure reason he would make the touchstone of all religious solutions. But this to Locke did not mean the denial of revelation, which he considered a natural, harmonious and necessary expansion of human reason. " Reason," taught Locke, " is natural revelation whereby the eternal Father of light and fountain of all knowledge, communicates to mankind that portion of truth which He has laid within the reach of their natural faculties : revelation is natural reason enlarged by a new set of discoveries communicated by God immediately, which reason vouches the truth of, by the testimony and proofs it gives, that they came from God."[1]   Locke's position, therefore, like that of Archbishop Tillotson, may be defined as one of " supernatural rationalism." Religious questions he divided into three categories, those *above* reason, *contrary to* reason, and *according to* reason.[2]   Toland, Locke's young Irish disciple, pushed still further the natural, rational position, and minimised the supernatural. To him Locke's category " above reason " was quite superfluous, and all matters appertaining to religion, morals or life in general, were either " according to " or " contrary to " reason. Toland did not actually deny " revelation " ; but to him nothing was above the comprehension of the natural man ; nothing was too profound for the human intellect to penetrate.[3]   The spiritual sense, therefore, of mystery, awe, reverence and gratitude was dulled. Reason was isolated and deified. Toland was a herald of that genus of " rational " knowledge which, parting company with modesty, imagined it could lay bare all the secrets of heaven and earth.

Anthony Collins, with his contempt for the " vagaries of priests " and his pert assertions regarding the perfection of

---

[1] John Locke, *Essay on Human Understanding*, Bk. IV, chap. xix (4). See also his *Reasonableness of Christianity*, p. 257ff.
[2] *Essay* . . . Bk. IV, chap. xvii (23).
[3] Principal A. C McGiffert, *Protestant Thought Before Kant*, p. 202.

" natural religion," carried the Deistic position beyond Toland. He took the stand that " unless the Bible prophecies can be proven to have been literally fulfilled," then Christianity is false ; but " they have *not* been so proven," he argued ; " therefore Christianity *is* false."[1]

Thomas Woolston, the most scurrilous of Deistic writers, in his six *Discourses on the Miracles of Christ* (1727–29), maintained that the Gospel narratives taken literally, were a " tissue of absurdities." The miracles of Jesus, he contended, were in most cases " foolish, trivial, contradictory, absurd, unworthy of a divinely appointed teacher, and characteristic rather of a sorcerer or wizard." With coarse wit, and jibing satire, he sneered not only at the works and teaching, but also at the character, of Christ.[2]

Then in 1730 appeared Matthew Tindal's *Christianity as Old as the Creation*, a work soon acclaimed as " the Deists' Bible." This book, being more sober and restrained, represents a higher level of argument than that of Collins or Woolston, and at certain points marks a definite contribution to thought. So trenchantly, for instance, does Tindal assert the moral evil of ecclesiastical systems demanding, in the name of religion, the acceptance of dogmas and the performance of rites in themselves morally indifferent, that in places his words recall the chastening and withering indictments of certain Old Testament prophets. The avowed purpose therefore of Tindal's work was to free " pure and natural religion," itself a " perfect," " unalterable " thing, of all obscuring accretions and thus liberate society from the deception and tyranny of " priestcraft."[3]   His thesis, on its face, seemed both plausible and laudable ; but the assumptions on which it was based were colossal.   As his title implied, he assumed that everything genuine in Christianity was derived directly from natural religion and consequently had existed from the time of Creation ; the obvious deduction, therefore, was that traditional and organised Christianity was at best superfluous, while at worst it represented a conglomeration of intolerable superstitions and bigotries. He assumed, too, that mankind, at all times and in all places, were for religious purposes exactly the same, for human nature he pronounced " unchangeable " ; while again he assumed that the Moral Code was a static and definite " natural law " planted equally and universally in the native reason of all peoples alike.

[1] Sir Leslie Stephen, *English Thought in the Eighteenth Century*, Vol. I, p. 216.
[2] Woolston was fined and imprisoned for blasphemy.
[3] Matthew Tindal. *op. cit.*, chaps. vi and xiii.

Tindal prated very solemnly about rationality, morality, benevolence, universal love and the like,[1] but the logic of his thesis forced the conclusion that everything is natural, that God is nature, and that, therefore, *whatever is, is right*. This last deduction, moreover, was smugly expressed both by Pope and Bolingbroke, while even Burke, who sneered at the Deists, and scoffingly asked, " Whoever reads them now ? " came at times dangerously close to this soulless and morally paralysing fatalism.[2]

(ii) *Controversial Victory Masks Spiritual Defeat*

The published answers to the Deists by contemporary theologians are to be numbered in hundreds ; and if meta-physical acuteness, classical scholarship and poignant phraseology had decided the issue, the Divines easily won the debate. Sir Leslie Stephen, himself a rationalist, describes the theologians as " finished scholars" refuting mere " dabblers in letters " ; while the Deists, in general, he depicts as a " ragged regiment, whose whole ammunition of learning was but a trifle when compared with the abundant stores of a single light of orthodoxy."[3] Again, in " speculative ability," says Stephen, " most of the Deists were as children by the side of their ablest antagonists." Many critics would endorse Stephen's verdict ; yet even if the result was as sweeping as he and others suggest, it represented but a barren victory. The Christian apologists, with one or two exceptions, met the Deists on their own ground, " natural religion," and fought them with their own weapon, " reason " : but natural religion soon proved to be slippery ground, and reason a two-edged sword.

Collins, exposing himself to the stinging satire of Dean Swift, was so overwhelmed by the contempt poured upon him that he found it expedient to retire to Holland till the storm had passed ; yet this onslaught upon Collins was but symptomatic of the superficial brilliance and the lack of vital faith which characterised the whole Deistic controversy. The central target of Collins's attack was the " vagaries of priests " ; Swift astutely turned the tables not only upon the transparent vanity and shallowness of Collins himself, but upon the follies and foibles of mankind in general : and Swift's attack was incomparably the more devastating. Throughout the whole controversy however, there is apparent an insistent urge to be

---

[1] Matthew Tindal, pp. 22, 58f., 253.
[2] Sir Leslie Stephen, *op. cit.*, I, p. 182ff. ; McGiffert, *op. cit.*, chap. x.
[3] Stephen, I, p. 87.

rational, scintillating, brilliant ; Deist and apologist alike, would exhibit the clarity of his reason and breadth of his mind : but their clarity was the clarity of ice, and their breadth the breadth of shallowness ; it all smacked of undergraduate bombast. " Let that which is written in the New Testament be tried by that which is the touchstone of all religions," wrote Dean Humphrey in 1748. " I mean the religion of nature and reason which God has written in the hearts of every one of us from first Creation : and if it varies from it in any particular, if it prescribes any one thing which may in the minutest circumstances thereof be contrary to its righteousness, I will then acknowledge this to be an argument against us, strong enough to overthrow the whole cause, and make all things else that can be said of it totally ineffectual for its support."[1] Bishop Gibson, in his *Second Pastoral Letter* (1730) said : " It is universally acknowledged that revelation itself is to stand or fall by the test of reason."

Among the " giants " who led the fray against Deism were Clarke, Conybeare, Bentley, Warburton, Berkeley, Law and Butler. The most popular theological apologetic was that of Conybeare, namely that " natural religion is true and good as far as it goes " ; but mankind needs " more light than can be gained from it " ; hence revelation was ordained " to supplement it."[2] Bishop Warburton, trained as a lawyer, not infrequently " justified the Deity " by proving (most rationally) that His conduct was conformable to the provisions of the British Constitution ; while the law of Nature, like that of England, he assumed to embody the perfection of wisdom. For the gymnastic feats of his pious, patriotic logic, he was rewarded with the popular jibe : " There is but one God, and Warburton is His Attorney-General."[3] Law, revolting both against Deism and the current apologetics of his brethren, was in a category by himself. His reverent, mystic spirit was nauseated equally by the crass assumptions of natural religion and the flaunted pride of human reason. More acute than the earlier apologists, he saw and pointed out that natural religion and natural events are themselves beset with difficulties and veiled in mystery quite as impenetrable as direct Revelation, which he believed to be the inspiring source of all true morality, virtue and happiness.[4] The influence too of Law's *Serious Call*

---

[1] Dean Humphrey's, *Letter to Deists.*
[2] See John Conybeare, *Defence of Revealed Religion, etc.* (1732).
[3] Stephen, I, p. 361.
[4] William Law, *Case of Reason or Natural Religion fairly and fully Stated* (1731), pp. 60, 66, 101, 103.

to a Devout and Holy Life (1729) was later to be reflected in the lives of the Wesleys, Dr. Samuel Johnson and other famous men.

But the most celebrated of the apologists was Bishop Butler, whose defence was that of a rationalist Christian influenced conspicuously by the teaching of Law. He accepts the position that " Christianity is a republication of Natural Religion " and asserts that " if in revelation there be found any passage, the seeming meaning of which is contrary to natural religion, we may most certainly conclude such seeming meaning not to be the real one."[1] Butler, however, was chiefly concerned for the defence of revelation, and his persistent method of argument was to throw the burden of proof back upon the Deists themselves. He, with them, accepted the primary postulates of natural religion ; but he demonstrated conclusively that the difficulties in the way of proving those postulates were just as great as in the case of revealed religion. If therefore the difficulties and mysteries of natural religion did not prevent belief in Divine creation and providence, why, he insistently asked, should the difficulties enshrouding revealed religion be permitted to kill faith in revelation ? Butler thus provided a final rejoinder to the *a priori* conclusion of Tindal that natural religion is itself a " complete and perfect whole," to which " nothing can be added by revelation." But his grounds, for the most part, are prudential and negative. Exposing the marked limitations of rational demonstration, he would have men walk " *as if* " the postulates of Christianity were true. Reason, he frankly declares, " the *only* faculty we have wherewith to judge concerning anything, even revelation itself," and repeatedly he returns to the defensive position that the arguments commonly raised against revelation would apply equally to justify the conclusion " that the constitution of Nature is contradictory to wisdom, justice or goodness."[2] Butler's argument therefore was a sword cutting both ways at once. It laid low the assumptions of Deism ; but it did so at the cost of the larger religious issue, by clearing the ground for a sceptical attack on all religion, natural and revealed. As Locke, the Christian philosopher, unwittingly became the forerunner of popular Deism, so Butler, the Christian apologist, unwittingly became the forerunner of open scepticism.

Butler has been compared with Pascal ; both were noble, aspiring souls ; but both had too much doubt and too little

[1] See Pattison, *op. cit.*, p. 295.
[2] Joseph Butler, *Analogy of Religion, Natural and Revealed* (1736), part II, chap. iii ; part I, chap. vii.

faith to be great leaders of men.[1] Professor A. C. McGiffert, writing as an avowed Modernist, concludes his able survey on " Rationalism in England " with the following significant verdict : " That religious faith and devotion still survived and flourished was due, not to the apologists, but to altogether different influences, of which the Great Evangelical Revival was the most important."[2]

(iii) Religion in a Strait-Jacket

With the intellectual swing from Deism and " natural religion " to avowed scepticism we are not here directly concerned. Both the philosophical scepticism of Hume and the historical scepticism of Gibbon had great vogue, wielding immense power in intellectual circles, especially among the ruling cliques. Moreover the encyclopædists and philosophers of France, stimulated first by English Deism, turned increasingly sceptical and exercised a strong reflex impact over all the fashionable set in Britain. But both Deism and the swing towards scepticism were closely related to preceding history. A National Church with vocal organs extracted and with right and left wings so clipped as to fetter the flight of Faith, could only bicker with the Deists and sceptics ; it could give them no vital demonstration of the living and transcendent power of practical, spiritual Christianity. Increasingly, therefore, theology became as deistic as the Deists ; reason, first hailed as a defence for Faith, came finally to be acclaimed as a substitute, while the religious impulse, squeezed officially into a strait-jacket, came to be regarded as a sort of spiritual police—politicians imagining that a religion thus committed to inaction " could retain sufficient power to be useful without being troublesome."[3] Hence a bird born for the open sky was cruelly caged, its spirit was crushed, and its heavenly song was stilled.

Deism, at best, was but a hybrid philosophy and a frigid religion. Starting with a semi-pantheistic conception of the universe, it gradually bowed God to the outer fringes of the stage of life, thus preparing the way for scepticism to push Him off. Fetish words and catch phrases exercised for a time an hypnotic charm, but sophisticated talk about " Reason," " Nature," " Moderation," " Rational Progress " and a perfect,

---

[1] Stephen, I, p. 307.
[2] A. C. McGiffert, *Protestant Thought before Kant*, p. 243.
[3] Stephen, II, p. 415.

unchangeable " Natural Religion " had no sustaining meat for the human soul. The curse of eighteenth century intellectualism was not its common sense, but its lack of anything more dynamic. Its metaphysical deity was too cold, too abstract, to excite real zeal in its worshippers, and the unmistakable tendency of Deism was to plunge its adherents into an inflated " optimism " contradicted by the most obvious facts of life.[1] Deism accordingly merged into rationalism, rationalism into scepticism, and scepticism into cynicism. In all the smart circles and among a large proportion of the " *Intelligentsia*," Mandeville's *Fable of the Bees* (1723) was, for decades, more read than the Bible ; yet Mandeville blatantly affirms that " private vices are public benefits," and that " every species of virtue is at bottom some form of gross selfishness," more or less modified, or masked. True, Mandeville could not properly be classed as a Deist, but his pert, polished paganism was of a piece with the tinsel smartness and underlying cynicism of the Deistic era. Sincerity was at a discount ; superficial brilliance at a premium. Moral expediency ruled the souls of men ; and many a Deist-sceptic like Bolingbroke—whom Lord Morley pronounces " the prince of political charlatans "[2]—recognising the social value of " decorum and respectability," defended organised Christianity as a highly convenient " varnish." A unifying, integrating, inspiring religion was the crying need of the day ; but the mental and spiritual mood of the privileged classes was such that they could not recognise it, even if its power were manifested before their eyes.

The general trend of Deism may be briefly summarised. Religion came to be looked upon chiefly as a matter for intellectual discussion and as such became in large measure the preserve of doctrinaires, with the result that soon in high places it exhibited all the pedanticism so characteristic of that familiar species of art and poetry produced chiefly for critics. Spontaneity, enthusiasm, spiritual experience were chilled and numbed ; prayer, as the lyrical outburst of the soul to its Maker, was dubbed fanaticism, while cold reason was pronounced the all-sufficient guide of life. The reflex of all this upon the bone and marrow of practical religion, became increasingly apparent. The metaphysical Deity was finally resolved into a bundle of barren abstractions ; the Bible, which to the early Reformers and Puritans was the " chart and compass of Life," the Book of Books, came to be regarded simply as *a* book, and

---

[1] Stephen, I, p. 183.
[2] See Dr. R. H. Tawney, *Religion and the Rise of Capitalism*, p. 207.

often a despised book ; while Jesus Christ, far from being acclaimed as the incarnate revelation of God and Saviour of men, was reduced to the level of a mere ethical teacher—and a misleading one. The New Testament, it was conceded, contained a certain nucleus of natural religion ; but this, it was argued, was so obscured by " fanatical " accretions regarding the person of Christ, as to render it practically useless. As for Christian doctrine and the Christian Church, arguments first forged against Rome were now re-shaped and sharpened to apply against Revelation. Orthodox Christianity was pronounced a repository of intolerable superstition, and the Church the nursing-mother of all manner of error ; yet so shallow, so insincere, was all this scepticism, that many a Deist (like Collins and Bolingbroke) desired to retain the Church as a necessary social institution.

With Christian Faith thus undermined, Christian morality was attacked at its roots. The Fatherhood of God being denied, the Brotherhood of Man was robbed of its most fructifying inspiration. Admittedly Addison, Steele, Swift, Fielding, Johnson, Goldsmith, Hogarth, Garrick and others might, in their various spheres, preach certain aspects of Christian morality, but that teaching represented chiefly a " carry-over," either from Puritan or from Catholic sources. The heart of Christian morality had been stabbed.

" Whatever the world thinks," wrote Bishop Berkeley in *Siris* (1744), " he who hath not much meditated upon God, the human mind, and the *summum bonum*, may possibly make a thriving earthworm, but will most indubitably make a sorry patriot and a sorry statesman."[1] Berkeley, as a practical man, was addressing the " thriving earthworms " of his day ; for Hallam's *Constitutional History*, referring to this very period— the thirty years following the Treaty of Utrecht (1713)— pronounces it materially " the most prosperous season that England had ever experienced." " Stomach well alive, soul extinct," is Carlyle's verdict on the era in question, while Mark Pattison says : " The historian of moral and religious progress . . . is under necessity of depicting the same period as one of decay of religion, licentiousness of morals, public corruption, profaneness of language—' a day of rebuke and blasphemy.' "[2] Beneath the polished surface of deistic rationalism, the springs of spiritual life were running dry : and the Church, having no impelling Faith or guiding philosophy of her own, degenerated

[1] George Berkeley, *Siris*, p. 350.
[2] *Essays and Reviews*, p. 279.

not only into a confessed branch of the Civil Service, but into a public sounding-board, which re-echoed the glib phraseology of the new and heady " sciences " of Political Arithmetic and Natural Philosophy.

BLIND GUIDES

" THE Church of England was at its nadir during the reigns of the first two Georges, and during the early years of George III. Convocation remained silenced, and ecclesiastical preferments, invariably made to serve political ends, were regarded by clergy and laity alike as little more than desirable offices. Bishoprics and deaneries were solicited from the Prime Minister of the day with unblushing importunity."

> SIR CHARLES PETRIE, *The Four Georges*,
> p. 235.

" If gold ruste, what shall iren doo ? "

> CHAUCER, " Prologue " to *Canterbury Tales*
> (line 500).

BLIND GUIDES

NOWHERE, perhaps, are the sorry effects of the " Triple Tragedies " and the reign of Deism more unmistakably or more accurately mirrored than in the succession of eighteenth century Archbishops of Canterbury who, as Primates of all England, directed the destiny of the National Church. For during no other century of English history have those commissioned as, and purporting to be, the Apostolic Fathers and Chief Shepherds of the Fold of Christ, represented so materialistic an outlook, or so low a standard of spiritual discernment, as characterised the lives of the eighteenth century Primates. A running review of these ecclesiastical pilots, is essential to an understanding of the wider issues our study involves.

(i) The Eighteenth Century Primates

Thomas Tenison, Primate from 1694 to 1715, who crowned both Anne and George I, was a pronounced political partisan and " a favourite at Court." John Potter (1737-47), Primate at the time of Wesley's " conversion " and during the earliest pioneering period of the great Evangelical Revival, is described by A. W. Rowden, K.C., in his detailed treatise, *Primates of the Four Georges*, as " stilted and starchy." Though the possessor of some scholarship, he failed utterly to understand the needs of his age or to read the signs of the times ; he loathed the new manifestation of " religious enthusiasm " among the " lower orders of society," but true to the current fashion of the " ruling class," into which he (a draper's son) had been lifted, he left behind him £90,000 which he had " saved out of the Church " —a sum equal to at least £200,000 to-day.[1] Potter's successor, Thomas Herring (1747-57), was " less worthy than he." John Moore (1783-1805), Primate when Wesley felt compelled to take the epochal step of ordaining Dr. Coke to superintend the

---

[1] A. W. Rowden, K.C., *op. cit.*, p. 167f.

rapidly growing "Societies" in America, and also during the vital years of the French Revolution, was a confirmed "place-hunter," the most sordid ecclesiastical nepotist of his nepotic century. Frederick Cornwallis (1768–83), Primate during the whole period of the American Revolutionary War, was seventh son of the fourth Lord Cornwallis ; he also was brother to the first Earl Cornwallis and uncle to the first Marquis—the second in command of British troops against the American colonists. On the evidence of Canon Perry, in his *History of the English Church*, Archbishop Cornwallis "appears to have had no Churchmanlike scruples, and was simply of the character of a great nobleman about the Court." Matthew Hutton (1757–58), a constant victim of gout, on attaining the apple of his eye, expresses with characteristic fawning his gratitude to Lord Newcastle, "who brought me into the view of the world and has led me by the hand to what I am now arrived at."[1] Dr. Pyle, a royal chaplain, in a letter written in 1758, says Hutton "died in time for his character ; for he was grown covetous and imperious to excess. He left £50,000 which he had saved out of the Church in twelve years, and not one penny to any good use or public charity."[2]

By the most charitable judgment that can be based on Christian standards, only two eighteenth century Primates were even half-worthy of their sacred office. These were William Wake (1716–37) and Thomas Secker (1758–68). The latter a kindly, scholarly, hard-working prelate awakened sufficiently to the needs of his age to warn his clergy that they were losing much ground by "not preaching in a manner sufficiently Evangelical" ; but he himself was too much victimised by the frigid rationalism dominating "superior" society, to offer any real guidance along the road of deliverance. Wake, whom Mr. Rowden considers the most worthy of eighteenth century Primates (or rather the least unworthy) was a man of some gifts ; but it is significant that, in later life, he spent much time in preparing a treatise on the Antiquity, Honour and Estate of the Name and Family of Wake, wherein he strove to establish for his family a "royal affinity."[3]

Paradoxically, though, by the middle of the century, a mighty movement was stirring in the deeps beneath, though hundreds of humble parsons and thousands of twice-born laymen were now entering into a new realisation of the power of spiritual,

---

[1] Rowden, *op. cit.*, p. 236f.
[2] Edmund Pyle, *Memoirs of a Royal Chaplain*, 1729–1763 (edited by A. Hartshorne), p. 305.
[3] Rowden, p. 1f.

practical Christianity, yet so firm and so stubborn was the grip of political, materialistic and rationalistic influences on the highest offices of the National Church, and so bitter the resentment against the rising tide of " religious enthusiasm," that it was reserved to the latter decades of Wesley's crusade to experience the lowest degradation to which the Primacy fell. Cornwallis and Moore therefore must be recalled as personal witnesses ; and from their own mouths must they be judged. A glimpse at the sinister manner in which Cornwallis mounted to the highest ecclesiastical office, is revealed in parts of his correspondence. On September 26th, 1759, as Bishop of Lichfield and Coventry, he wrote to Lord Newcastle, then Prime Minister, thus :

" Having been informed that the Bishop of Worcester is in such a bad state of health, that in all likelihood he cannot hold out much longer ; I hope your Grace will pardon my troubling you with this, barely to mention, without importuning, that a removal to that see would of all others be most agreeable to me.
" Your Grace's most obliged and most obedient humble servant,
Fred. Lich. and Cov."[1]

In 1765 the Bishopric of Salisbury fell vacant. It was a desirable see and Cornwallis was pulling strings to secure it for himself ; but when in 1766 the King announced appointments, Salisbury was given to another, although Cornwallis was granted the Deanery of St. Paul's. Newcastle wrote congratulations to Cornwallis and the latter, answering, expressed unbridled rancour that the former had not sufficiently pulled political and ecclesiastical ropes in his favour :

" You say you are much rejoiced at my having accepted the Deanery of St. Paul's. For what reason I know not. As for myself, I have no joy in it ; I am not fond of expedients. Had the recommendation to it come from your Grace by way of atonement, I should have rejected the Deanery. After the hard treatment I had met with, I could not with honour have accepted it. It is by no means a preferment either agreeable or suitable to me. It would have been kind of your Grace not to have kept me so long in suspense, with regard to the Bishopric of Salisbury. Had you told me it was a real promise, it would at least have mitigated the severity of the disappointment. You say it is the *only instance* (the manuscript is here underlined) but several years ago you gave Worcester to the Bishop of Gloucester. Surely, my Lord, the disregard then showed to me may be allowed to have given just cause of some dissatisfaction . . . not only to me but to my family and friends. It certainly did. You begged forgiveness ; it was immediately granted, and the hardship forgotten. The late unfortunate circumstance brought it back to my mind . . ."[2]

[1] Newcastle Papers, Addl. MSS., Brit. Mus., 32,896, f. 122.
[2] Newcastle Papers, Addl. MSS., Brit. Mus., 32,976, f. 458ff.

From here the tone of the letter changes and the crouching, fawning spirit, ever angling for future preferments, is exhibited to its close.

Cornwallis married a " great lady," prominent in the " highest social life " ; he made himself a conspicuous character at Court, and, on the first vacancy following the writing of these letters, was appointed Primate of England. Soon, however, Lambeth Palace was the scene of such notorious " routs and feastings " that Lady Huntingdon, after an ineffectual appeal to Cornwallis and his Lady, lodged a protest with the King and Queen. The result was that George III, on investigation, wrote to Cornwallis in no uncertain terms :

" My good Lord Prelate,

" I would not delay giving you notification of the grief and concern with which my breast was affected at receiving authentic information that routs had made their way into your Palace. At the same time I must signify to you my sentiments on the subject, which hold these levities and vain dissipations as utterly inexpedient, if not unlawful, to pass in a residence for many years devoted to divine studies, religious retirement, and the extensive exercise of charity and benevolence ; . . .

" From the dissatisfaction with which you must perceive I behold these improprieties—not to speak in harder terms—and on still more pious principles, I trust you will suppress them immediately, so that I may not have occasion to show any further marks of my displeasure, or to interpose in a different manner.

" May God take your Grace into His Almighty protection.

" I remain, my Lord Primate,

" Your gracious friend,

" G. R."[1]

Archbishop Moore, if possible, was even more crassly self-seeking than Cornwallis. Having married, as his second wife, a sister of Lord Auckland, and now commanding influence in high places, he begins to reckon on the material advantages of a bishopric, as compared with certain preferments already in his grasp, some of which might have to be dropped. " How much already in possession must be given up ? " he asks : " There are bishoprics and bishoprics—small, middling and pretty good—what is the net gain on such a change ? "[2] Writing to his influential brother-in-law in 1772, when climbing rapidly the social ladder, he says : " Lord North must understand I will *not* be a bishop, unless he contrives that I live with some degree of comfort, I mean with such an income as may

[1] See W. C. Sydney, *England and the English in the Eighteenth Century*, Vol. II, p. 337 ; Dr. A. D. Belden, *George Whitefield, the Awakener*, pp. 55–56 (this book has misprinted George II for George III) ; and Ryle's *Life and Times of Lady Huntingdon*. The " routs and balls " complained of were held even on Sundays.

[2] Rowden, p. 350.

THE FAT PLURALIST AND HIS LEAN CURATES (From Gentleman's Magazine, 1772 —by courtesy of British Museum). Note two Churches tucked under left arm; fatted pigs and poultry (tithes); wheel running over Thirty-Nine Articles; rents in curates' gowns

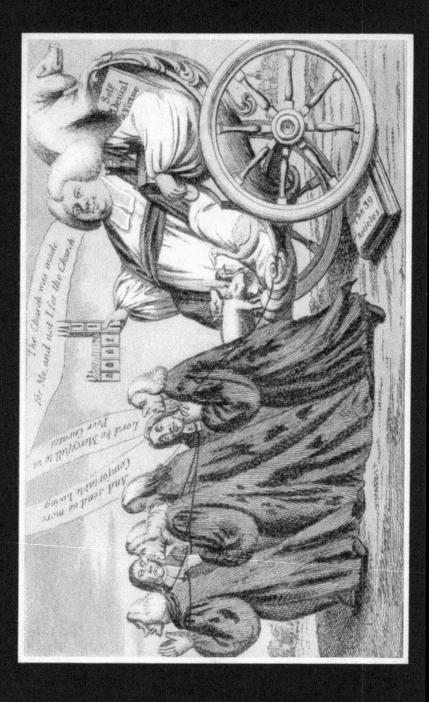

enable me to support my station."[1] Again, in 1775, he writes to Lord Auckland in words which recall Cornwallis's correspondence with Newcastle : " It is thought the Bishop of Rochester can last but a very short time ; if the Duke of Marlborough will move on this occasion, it will at least bring me forward."[2] On another occasion, with unconscious irony, he writes : " The more I know of the world, the less I expect of personal satisfaction in entering into the bustle of it."[3]

On April 26th, 1783, the very day of his appointment as Primate, and fourteen days before he was enthroned at Canterbury, we find Moore corresponding regarding high preferment for his brother-in-law, and on April 28th, twelve days before he was actually installed as Head of the Church, he writes : " In the meantime should Dr. Stinton drop, his preferment, in the gift of the Archbishop, will I fear be in hazard . . . what interests my feelings is that the preferment would at once reach the utmost wishes of my sister's husband, J. Cantaur."[4]

Having shown such solicitude for his sister's husband, it is not surprising that Moore used his authority as Primate to secure well-feathered nests for his five sons, three of whom he made Joint Registrars of the Prerogative Court of Canterbury, and the other two Joint Registrars of the Vicar-General's Office.[5] One of these sons, for more than fifty years, was the recipient of an average annual income from the Church of " not less than £12,000."[6] Moore's own Archiepiscopal revenue averaged £11,000 a year, the equivalent of some £25,000 to-day. It surely is a sorry commentary on the Church's government, that each of these preferment-hunters received from the ecclesiastical treasury more than a thousand times the customary stipend of the self-sacrificing missionary teacher, who, taking his life in his hands, went as a servant of Christ to minister to the Indians in the wilds of North America.[7]

---

[1] Auckland Correspondence, Addl. MSS, Brit. Mus., 34,412, f. 281.

[2] *Ibid.*, 34,412, f. 292. Moore had once been a tutor to the Marlborough family.

[3] *Ibid.*, 34,412, f. 298.

[4] Addl. MSS., Brit. Mus., 34,419, f. 185.

[5] Rowden, p. 378.

[6] *Ibid.*, p. 378.

[7] See eighteenth century reports of the Society for the Propagation of the Gospel in Foreign Parts. They show that many of these missionaries were paid only £10 a year, and few as high as £30. The author examined these Reports in Lambeth Palace Library (i.e. the Archbishop of Canterbury's Library).

D

(ii) *Lesser Prelates and Their Outlook*

" Archbishops of the eighteenth century," says Rowden, " were great potentates, if not princes. A coach and six horses, a private state barge on the Thames, with its liveried crew, properly belonged to such a dignitary."[1] Primates, however, had no monopoly of this carnal, pompous spirit ; in one way or another the wealthier bishops and deans succeeded in keeping the pace set by their Spiritual Heads. Even Overton points out that Bishop Hurd, nicknamed the " Beauty of Holiness," a prelate who not unnaturally could see nothing but " folly and fanatical madness " in the Evangelical Revival, always travelled from his palace to his cathedral, a bare quarter-mile, " in his episcopal coach with his servants in full dress liveries ; and when he used to go from Worcester to Bristol Hot Wells, he never moved without a train of twelve servants."[2] Following the current fashion, too, he left behind him an account of his " Life," nearly a quarter of which is given to describing a visit of the King (George III) to his palace. Jonathan Trelawny, Bishop of Winchester, who died in 1721, used to " excuse himself for his much swearing by saying he swore as a baronet, and not as a bishop."[3] Thackeray recalls that in the reign of George II Lady Yarmouth, a Court favourite, was instrumental in having a certain clergyman made a bishop because he bet her £5,000 he would not be one ; and the lady collected the debt.[4] Bishop Watson, himself playing the rôle of gentleman farmer, declares that bishoprics " are often given to the flattering dependents and unlearned younger branches of noble families," and adds : " I saw the generality of bishops bartering their independence and the dignity of their order for the chance of a translation, and polluting Gospel humility by the pride of prelacy."[5] Bishop Newton's *Autobiography* is a mirror of self-seeking ; and Dr. Johnson, who in his *Dictionary* had defined a pension as " pay given to a street hireling for treason to his country," though meanwhile a pensioner himself, admitted frankly that " no man can now be a bishop for his learning and piety." " His only chance of promotion," said

---

[1] *Op. cit.*, p. 378.
[2] Abbey and Overton : *English Church in the Eighteenth Century*, Vol. II, p. 30.
[3] Rowden, p. 75.
[4] W. M. Thackeray, *The Four Georges* ; see *Works of Thackeray* (1882) Vol. X, p. 315f.
[5] *Anecdotes of the Life of Richard Watson*, by himself, I, p. 116.

Johnson, " is being connected with someone who has parliamentary interest." Yet, perversely, Johnson justified this condition. The Government " in these days," having " too little power," he argued, must make all appointments in its own support ; " it cannot reward merit "[1]

Nor could it neglect proud family influence. Certain correspondence between Bishop Cornwallis, nephew of our lordly Primate, and the Younger Pitt, as Prime Minister, is here illuminating. In June, 1791, Cornwallis wrote :

" After the various instances of neglect and contempt, which Lord Cornwallis and I have experienced, not only in violation of repeated assurances, but of the strongest ties, it is impossible that I should not feel the late disappointment very deeply.

" With respect to the proposal concerning Salisbury, I have no hesitation in saying that the see of Salisbury cannot be in any respect an object to me. The only agreement which promises an accommodation in my favour is the promotion of the Bishop of Lincoln to Salisbury, which would enable you to confer the Deanery of St. Paul's upon me.

" I have the honour to be, &c.,
" J. Lichfield & Coventry."[2]

Like his uncle, this " high born " Bishop would " persuade " the Prime Minister to juggle other bishops about that he might gain his coveted preferments. It is passing humorous, too, that this peevish prelate is here spurning the see of Salisbury, which his uncle, the Primate, had coveted, and is coveting the Deanery of St. Paul's, which the uncle had spurned. Were these blue-blooded prelates being whimsical to exhibit their breeding ? Pitt's reply, in any case, is refreshing. Writing from Downing Street the following day, he was both tense and terse :

" My Lord :
" On my return to town this afternoon I found your Lordship's letter. I am willing to hope that on further consideration, and on recalling all the circumstances, there are parts of that letter which you would yourself wish never to have written.

" My respect for your Lordship's situation and my regard for Lord Cornwallis, prevent my saying more than that until that letter is recalled your Lordship makes any further intercourse between you and me impossible.

" I have the honour to be, &c.,
" W. Pitt."[3]

On receipt of Pitt's reply, Cornwallis revealed a diplomatic

---

[1] Boswell's *Life of Johnson*, Vol. V, p. 298f.
[2] Earl Stanhope, *Life of Pitt*, Vol. II, p. 128.
[3] *Ibid*

capacity for " repentance." That same day, June 11th, he
wrote :

" Under the very great disappointment which I have felt upon the last
occasion, I am much concerned that I was induced to make use of expressions in my letter to you of which I have since repented, and which upon
consideration, I beg leave to retract, and I hope they will make no un-
favourable impression upon your mind.

" Whatever may be your thoughts regarding the subject matter of the
letter, I trust you will have the candour to pardon those parts of it which
may appear to be wanting in due and proper respect to you, and believe
me to have the honour to be, &c.,
                                        " J. Lichfield & Coventry."[1]

Pitt answered expressing " great satisfaction in being able
to dismiss from mind any impression occasioned by a paragraph in the former letter."[2]   But the Cornwallis connection
was too influential to be ignored, even by Pitt ; so two months
later Bishop Cornwallis was named Dean of Windsor, and in
February, 1794, was given the rich deanery of Durham.

(iii) " *How to Organise a Chaos !* "

With men of this ilk occupying key posts in the National
Church it is not surprising that much of the " Persecuting Code "
remained on the Statute Books to the end of the eighteenth
century, and after.   By the *Uniformity* and *Test* Acts all persons
holding state office, civil or military, had to " receive the
Sacrament according to the rites of the Church of England."
Hence, Dr. Price's taunt that the Holy Communion was made
" a qualification of rakes and atheists for civil office,"[3] and
Cowper's scathing couplet :

> " To make the symbols of atoning grace,
> An office-key, a pick-lock to a place."[4]

In 1772 both Houses of Parliament witnessed historic debates
on the attempted repeal of these enactments.   A bishop had
just depicted Dissenting ministers as " men of close ambition,"
when Lord Chatham (the Elder Pitt) entered the lists :

" The Dissenting ministers are represented as 'men of close ambition.'
So they are, my Lords ; and their ambition is to keep close to the college

---

[1] Earl Stanhope, *op. cit.*, Vol. II, p. 130.
[2] *Ibid.*, p. 130.
[3] Richard Price, *Love of Country*, p. 36.
[4] See *Social England*, Vol. V, p. 230ff.

of fishermen, not of cardinals ; and to the doctrine of inspired apostles, not to the decrees of interested and aspiring bishops. They contend for a Scriptural creed and a Scriptural worship. We have a Calvinistic creed, a Popish liturgy and an Arminian clergy. The Reformation has opened the Scriptures to all. So let not the bishops shut them again. Laws in support of ecclesiastical power are pleaded for, which it would shock humanity to execute. It is said that religious sects have done great mischief when they are not kept under restraint ; but history affords no proof that sects have ever been mischievous, when they were not oppressed and persecuted by the ruling Church."[1]

That year (1772) a Repeal Bill was passed by the Commons, but owing to fierce opposition by the Episcopal Bench, it was thrown out by the Lords.

Britain, in the eighteenth century, was ruled by a landed gentry, which, as Disraeli pointed out, was almost as exclusive as the infamous " Venetian oligarchy." " A few family clans," writes C. H. K. Marten, " composed the governing classes of the period. . . . In one Cabinet half the members were Dukes, and in another there was only one commoner. This land-owning oligarchy ' encircled and enchained the throne,' dominated the House of Lords, and possessed enormous influence in the House of Commons."[2] " To this régime," affirms Rowden, " the Church, alas ! was no exception. If a scion of a great family had no taste for war or diplomacy, the Church should provide for him. It was avowedly a department of State. Any idea of an organisation of spiritual forces, and of its officers as those who should develop, promote and guide those forces, was wholly wanting, alike in the givers and recipients of Church patronage. Learning in a bishop had been known to give trouble ; zeal was highly dangerous."[3]

This decadence of Church leadership was, however, by no means absolute. Butler, Berkeley, Atterbury, Sherlock and Warburton were high-minded bishops of initiative and ability. But the cumulative effects of the Puritan and Nonjuring expulsions, of the suppression of Convocation, of the political domination of the Church, and of the ascendency of Deistic rationalism, were such as to make the prelates of the latter half of the century even less vital and less worthy than those of the former half. Thus seeds sown in the later part of the seventeenth century, bore certain of their bitterest fruits in the later part of the

[1] See Dr. Richard Price, *Discourse on Love of Country*, pp. 67–68, for a discussion of this matter. The increasing safeguard of Nonconformists and Catholics alike, was that some enlightened statesmen, such as Chatham, far from enforcing the *Uniformity* and *Test* Acts did all they could to make them inoperative and ridiculous.

[2] Warner and Marten, *Groundwork of English History*, Vol. II, pp. 479–80.

[3] *Op. cit.*, p. 311.

eighteenth century. Few prelates of this latter period are even remembered to-day. Perhaps the best known of its ecclesiastics, inside the hierarchical succession of preferment, are Paley and Malthus, two men who admittedly have often been cruelly caricatured. Yet Shelley epitomised the reaction of thousands when he declared that he would " rather be damned with Plato and Lord Bacon than go to heaven with Paley and Malthus."[1]

Among the élite coterie of Church rulers prophetic, regenerative teaching was practically dead. Far from preparing the way for the advent of Democracy, which already was knocking at the door, the hierarchical dignitaries were content to chant platitudes and to write pamphlets instructing " the poor " (the whole labouring populace) that it was their high privilege " cheerfully to perform their various duties " in " those stations of life in which it had pleased God to place them."[2]   As for the Industrial Revolution, which was already changing catastrophically the face of England, these " blind guides " were as insensitive to its challenge as though it were taking place on the soil of an unknown hemisphere ; while the Evangelical Revival, now bearing to the outcast multitude the Christian message of hope, fellowship, sobriety and salvation, they lashed and lampooned with venomous spleen. Rarely, in modern times, has an assuming, usurping ecclesiastical caste merited more completly the indictment of Jesus Christ : " Woe unto you, scribes and pharisees, hypocrites ! for ye shut up the kingdom of heaven against men : for ye neither go in yourselves, neither suffer ye them that are entering to go in."[3]

Oxford University, the chief training centre for those in line of ecclesiastical preferment, sank during this century of " moderation and reason," to its lowest ebb of scholarship. During the earlier half of the century it was the chief seed bed of Jacobite plotting ; after the accession of George III (1760) it was the primary nursery of the bluest Toryism. Southey, who went to Oxford " with a view to Orders," learned there " two things, to row and to swim." So " to save his soul " he left " the place." Gibbon, referring to his Oxford days as " fourteen idle and unprofitable months," says his tutor " remembered he had a salary to draw, but forgot he had duties to perform." And Cambridge, apparently, was little, if any, better than Oxford.

Professor D. A. Winstanley, Vice-Master of Trinity College,

---

[1] *Prometheus Unbound*, Preface, p. 15.
[2] As Professor Tawney points out, " almost all below the nobility, gentry and freeholders," by the curious current phraseology, were designated " *the poor.*" See his *Religion and the Rise of Capitalism*, p. 189.
[3] St. Matthew xxiii, 13.

Cambridge, in his recent book, *Unreformed Cambridge*, says : " The University of Cambridge in the eighteenth century has been convicted of violating its Statutes, misusing its endowments, and neglecting its obligations. It is impossible to dispute the substantial justice of this verdict." Professor G. M. Trevelyan, too, commenting on the academic life of the times points out that : " Universities could sell degrees without holding examinations or giving instruction." " Whatever is, is right—if it can show a charter," was the practical creed of the whole prevailing hierarchy of vested interests.[1] And few vested interests were more assumingly complacent than the ancient and Church-dominated Universities, which mistook the formal dissection of " political and philosophical corpses " for scholarship.

The most obvious marks of the hierarchical degradation manifested themselves mainly in the sphere of patronage, sinecures and pluralities. What " rotten " and " pocket " boroughs were to the Parliamentary government of the time, that and more were patronage, sinecures and pluralities, with their accompanying non-residence, to the Ecclesiastical government ; but with this difference : whereas Parliamentary corruption could at least be debated in the House of Commons and exposed by the Opposition, ecclesiastical corruption battened under cover ; for Convocation, where those evils should have been debated and exposed, being suppressed, the coterie of prelates who ruled the National Church became themselves the worst culprits. Many parishes accordingly had no shepherd of souls ; and whereas Primates and prelates lived much like princes, and many a hard-drinking, fox-hunting parson with family and political influence " swallowed more livings than he could chew," the vast majority of the humbler clergy were half-starving on from £20 to £60 a year. Fielding, in his famous creation, Parson Adams (1742), depicts a pious, capable clergyman, who at the age of fifty, with a wife and six children, was " provided with the handsome income of £23 a year."[2] Goldsmith's father was one of many eighteenth century parsons " passing rich on £40 a year " ; and Samuel Wesley, the father of John and Charles, a capable, thrifty, hard-working priest, was for months detained in gaol for debts contracted in purchasing the barest necessities of life. Richard Bentley, answering Collins's complaint as to the national expense of the clergy, pointed out that Parliamentary accounts proved that 6,000

[1] Trevelyan's *History of England* (fifth imp. 1927), p. 506.
[2] Henry Fielding, *Joseph Andrews*, p. 25.

clergymen had an average annual income of less than £50 a year, and later Sydney Smith says : " Six thousand of your clergy—the greater part of your whole number—had, at a middle rate, one with another, not £50 a year."[1] The average income, therefore, of the century's Primates, to say nothing of certain arch-pluralists, was more than two hundred times that of the average income of the humbler half of all the national clergy.

Little wonder that Jeremy Bentham, in his *Church of Englandism*, has a chapter on " How to Organise a Chaos ! " Neither, in the light of stubborn facts, can one doubt the essential accuracy of Dean Swift's satire on those scaling the dizzy heights of ecclesiastical preferment. Portraying one prelate " mounting fast toward the top of the ecclesiastical ladder, without the merit of a single virtue," Swift says : " He treated all his inferiors in the clergy with a sanctified pride ; he had neither eyes nor ears for the faults of the rich ; . . . he was never sensible of the least corruption in courts, parliaments or ministers, but made the most favourable construction of all possible proceedings ; and power, in whatever hands or whatever party, was always sure of his most charitable opinion."[2]

This good cleric, too, " could be soberly drunk, at the expense of others, with college ale, and at such times he was always most devout " ; he was in the habit of " dropping in his own half-crown among the collection and taking it out when he disposed of the money " ; he " paid his curates punctually at the lowest salary and partly out of the communion money, but he gave them good advice in abundance."[3]

Archdeacon Blackburne, in 1754, describes the English clergy as " with few exceptions," men " whose lives and ordinary occupations are most foreign to their profession " ; he also speaks of his countrymen as " the most ignorant common people that are to be found in any Protestant, if not in any Christian, country." [4] And Thackeray, portraying the Court life of George II, says :

" No wonder the clergy were corrupt and indifferent amidst this in-difference and corruption. No wonder that the sceptics multiplied and morals degenerated so far as they depended on the influence of such a

[1] Sydney Smith, *Remarks* etc., Part II (40). Smith, for twenty years, served a Yorkshire parish which, prior to his coming, for more than a century, had no resident clergyman.
[2] Jonathan Swift, *Writings on Religion and the Church*, Vol. I, p. 296 (Temple Scott edition).
[3] *Ibid.*, pp. 295–96.
[4] Rowden, *op. cit.*, p. 247 ; C. J. Abbey, *The English Church and its Bishops*, 1700–1800 (two vols.) throws much light on the subject of this chapter.

King. No wonder that Whitefield cried out in the wilderness, that Wesley quitted the insulted temple to pray on the hillside. I look with reverence on those men at that time. Which is the sublimer spectacle—the good John Wesley surrounded by his congregation of miners at the pit's mouth, or the Queen's chaplains, mumbling through their morning office in the ante-room, under the picture of the great Venus, with the door opened into the adjoining chamber, where the Queen is dressing, talking scandal . . . or uttering sneers . . .? I say I am scared as I look around at this society—at this King, at these courtiers, at these politicians, at these bishops—at this flaunting vice and levity. Whereabouts in this court is the honest man? Where is the pure person one may like? The air stifles one with its sickly perfumes."[1]

(iv) *Pride Precludes Fellowship*

Nevertheless, before the death of George II (1760), indeed by the middle of the century, new influences were astir yet destined to baptise with spiritual power this pagan and unregenerate century. Even prior to 1750 such Evangelical clergymen as Grimshaw, Hervey, Walker, Adam and Romaine had caught the Revival fire and already were radiating its light, its warmth, its fellowship and its inspiration. Before the close of the eighteenth century, the Evangelical zealots within the National Church included a truly historic band of veterans of the Cross, among whom were such varied and remarkable characters as the Venns, Berridge, Fletcher, Newton, the Milner brothers, Robinson, Wilson, Cecil, Scott, Biddulph and Simeon. And the character of the service they rendered is typified in the life of the almost forgotten Thomas Jones. Driven at first from parish to parish because of his hated " enthusiasm," at length, under Simeon's influence, he was given the curacy of the village of Creaton, Northamptonshire, at £25 a year. In that unpromising hamlet of forty-six houses Jones laboured without any preferment for forty-three years, and never was he promoted beyond the rectorship of the said parish. Yet from that humble base this despised zealot transformed the surrounding community, and threw out influences which affected the nation ; he was a founder of Sunday Schools, " Dame-Schools," Sick Clubs, and Clothing Clubs ; with the profits from his devotional books, published both in English and Welsh, he built six almshouses for aged widows ; through the efforts of the Creaton Clerical Education Society, which he founded, he enabled fifty Evangelical laymen to enter the Ministry ; and during the first eighteen years of its work,

[1] W. M. Thackeray, *The Four Georges* (lecture on George II) ; see *Works*, Vol. X, pp. 315–16.

the Society for Poor Pious Clergymen, which also he created, distributed more than £35,000 ; while besides all this, he established a post-Easter spiritual Retreat to which for prayer, Bible-study, fellowship and consultation earnest clergymen from several surrounding counties annually repaired.[1]

As for " Church " *laymen*, who before the end of the century were torch-bearers in the Evangelical ranks, they include characters who will be remembered as long as English, or indeed humanitarian, history endures. Among them were William Wilberforce, the Parliamentary and national leader of the mighty Crusade against the slave trade, and Zachary Macaulay, the Governor of the famous colony of emancipated slaves at Sierra Leone. Among them, too, were Lord Teignmouth, who for five years was Governor-General of India, John and Henry Thornton, the philanthropic bankers, William Cowper, the leading poet of his age, Robert Raikes, of Sunday School fame, Charles Grant, Chairman of the East India Company, and not least Lord Dartmouth, Colonial Secretary, whose conversion was commemorated by Cowper in the memorable lines :

> " We boast some rich ones whom the Gospel sways,
> And *one* who wears a coronet and prays."

Among *women* who already had risen to high influence and rendered mighty service was that amazing and much maligned leader, Selina, Countess of Huntingdon, who without stint consecrated her time, fortune and genius to the Revival's work ; whilst Hannah More, the most widely read literary woman of her century, both by her writings and her philanthropic achieve-ments, was now exercising an influence accurately described as " nation-wide." Nor should it be forgotten that Hannah Ball's unobtrusive Sunday School labours preceded those of Raikes by eleven years.

Before the close of the century, too, certain remarkable fruits of the Revival were unmistakable. Nonconformity, turning from a frigid Unitarianism, was gradually assimilating power by contact with the Movement it first had reviled ; everywhere it was manifesting new faith, vision and vigour.[2] Groups of Anglicans, moreover, both clergymen and laymen, for the first time since 1662, were working harmoniously in a score of " common causes " with Dissenters, as " their brethren in Christ."

---

[1] G. R. Balleine, *A History of the Evangelical Party in the Church of England*, pp. 122–23.

[2] See Dr. R. W. Dale's *History of Congregationalism* for a poignant study of this subject.

Already the pioneer Missionary Societies of Protestantism had sprung up and Evangelical zealots were sacrificing to send their bearers of " glad tidings " to all quarters of the globe. Evangelical " outriders " were now scouring the wilds of North America, bringing deep meaning and significance to the pioneer's task, and organising scattered, lonely settlers into religious communities. Howard and other Christian zealots had modified the barbarities of the prison system and challenged the vicious penal code. The Sunday School movement, the Lancastrian School Society and the Religious Tract Society were laying the rude foundations of popular education. Still more significant, the crusade destined to achieve " the noblest triumph of modern history " was now probing the soul of England as never had a moral or social issue probed it before ; and both the inspiration and the leadership of that crusade were born of the Evangelical Revival. The famous historian, Dr. J. H. Overton, a High Churchman, writes : " It was not only Evangelicals, but Evangelicalism that abolished the slave trade."[1] The same was true of the later phase of this struggle, for finally the Revival's influence killed the *institution* of slavery throughout the British Empire and emancipated all British slaves. Yet, incredible as is the fact, to the end of the eighteenth century, and for more than a decade into the nineteenth, the Religious Awakening that saved the soul of England had not a single representative on the Episcopal Bench.

Among all the fallacies of popular belief none is more rampant than the universal delusion, circulated even by scholars and historians, that the dawning years of the nineteenth century saw the National Church in the control of Evangelicals.[2] The reason for this delusion is too obvious for argument ; Evangelicalism, by common consent, within and without the National Church, represented the only virile, creative religion of the period ; but a delusion it remains, for until the second decade of the nineteenth century Evangelicals, as such, were all but unrepresented in the higher Councils of the Church. And when, in the belated year of Waterloo (1815), they were represented by their *first* bishop, Dr. Ryder of Gloucester, he was the brother of a Cabinet Minister.[3] Nevertheless, despite Ryder's ability, high character and family influence, Archbishop Sutton, the blue-blooded Primate who succeeded Moore, and

[1] J. H. Overton, *The English Church of the Nineteenth Century*, p. 77.
[2] Lecky, Macaulay, Ranke, Green, Overton, Abbey and Hammond, as well as most Anglo-Catholic historians, have tended to propagate this plausible delusion.
[3] Dr. W. L. Mathieson *English Church Reform*, 1815–1840, pp. 3–15.

like Moore " died rich," flew into an uproar on the appointment and tried to prevent Ryder's installation ; while the Dean and Chapter of Gloucester strove to exclude him from the Cathedral pulpit, and crowds flocked " to see this great curiosity, a religious bishop."[1]

The expulsion of six Evangelical students from St. Edmund Hall, Oxford, in 1768, for their religious zeal, was but indicative of the attitude of the higher Church officials to the Revival. St. Mary Magdalene Church, the only Evangelical centre at Oxford, was " put out of bounds " for all undergraduates ; Trinity, Simeon's Church at Cambridge, was long the scene of the most incredible persecutions,[2] and until 1788, when Isaac Milner, a brilliant mathematician, was made President of Queens' College, Cambridge, Evangelicals experienced the greatest difficulty in finding either Oxford or Cambridge Colleges which would so much as admit their candidates for Holy Orders. Even at the close of the century, Evangelicals in Greater London were " excluded from all but three of the livings."[3] And were it not for the numerous " proprietary Chapels " built by consecrated laymen ; for the many Lectureships to which, despite the bishops, parishioners could *elect* clergymen ; and for various Evangelical trust-funds raised to " purchase spheres of work,"[4] while ecclesiastical dignitaries continued to pile up pluralities, the professional " Judaisers " might indeed have succeeded in freezing the Revival heralds completely outside the National Church.

For seventeen years, in the teeth of the bitterest official opposition, was the benign, scholarly William Romaine, by his lectureship in St. Dunstan's, Fleet Street, stirring the soul of London, before he was granted any other permanent appointment ; and when at last he was made the rector of a Blackfriars parish, it was because the parishioners there enjoyed the right of electing their own clergy. Even " as late as 1824," the saintly Charles Simeon, " was blackballed when he was proposed as a member of the Society for Promoting Christian Knowledge."[5] Yet Lord Macaulay, who graduated from Cambridge in 1822, in a letter years afterwards to his sister, wrote : " If you knew what Simeon's authority and influence were, and how they

---

[1] G. R. Balleine, *op. cit.*, pp. 192–3.   Professor N. Sykes, *Church and State in England in the Eighteenth Century* (1935) makes clear that the prevailing conception of a bishop was that of a high State official.

[4] *Ibid.*, pp. 124–5, 129–31.

[3] *Ibid.*, p. 63.

[4] Simeon said, of his Trust : " Others purchase income, I purchase spheres of work."

[5] Balleine, *op. cit.*, p. 181.

extended from Cambridge to the most remote corners of England, you would allow that his real sway in the Church was far greater than that of any Primate."[1] That "sway" however was entirely among despised "enthusiasts." Dr. W. L. Mathieson in his close study, *English Church Reform 1815-1840*, points out that, even as late as 1810, Evangelical clergymen, dubbed "Church-Methodists," were officially considered a "pestilence."[2] Old fashioned High Churchmen (i.e., ultra-National Churchmen) commonly designated Dissenting Chapels, "Synagogues of Satan"[3]; yet Evangelicals *within* "the Church" they considered "far more obnoxious than Nonconformists," and during the opening years of the nineteenth century it was a real "test of courage" for any clergyman to join the Church Missionary Society, lest he lose ecclesiastical caste.[4] Low Churchmen (Latitudinarians) were just as intolerant of the Revival influence, as were Highchurchmen. What the early Christian evangelists were to the scribes and pharisees of Judaism, that were the apostles of Evangelicalism to both the "High and Dry" and "Low and Slow" officials of the National Church. As "old and recognised" factions they might continue to squabble with each other, but they united to exorcise the loathsome spectre of "Methodism."

Again, it is continuously asserted, or assumed, that, (1) ere the dawn of the Oxford Movement (1833), when Keble launched his famous attack on all Liberalism, ecclesiastical and political,[5] Evangelicalism already had experienced a period of domination in the Courts of the National Church, and that, (2) it now was decadent or dead. The latter assumption is refuted from the mouth of Keble himself, who, in 1828, deplored "the *amazing rate* at which 'Puritanism' seems to be getting all over the Kingdom";[6] the former assumption is at variance with the stubborn fact that up to the beginning of the Tractarian Movement, the total number of Evangelical bishops yet appointed numbered only three.[7] Eleven years after Ryder was made a bishop, Charles Sumner was appointed to the see of Llandaff, in Wales, and the following year translated to Winchester; while in 1828 John Bird Sumner, his elder brother, was made bishop of Chester, and in 1848 was elevated to the Archbishopric

[1] See Sir G. O. Trevelyan, *Life and Letters of Lord Macaulay*, chap. I.
[2] *Op. cit.*, p. 6.
[3] Mathieson, *op. cit.*, p. 11.
[4] *Ibid.*, pp. 12-14.
[5] See John Keble's Oxford Sermon, *National Apostasy*.
[6] Mathieson, pp. 15-16.
[7] Balleine, p. 209.

of Canterbury, in which office he forsook the whole tradition
of the Primate's pomp and state. Criticised for walking to
the House of Lords and thus abandoning the gorgeous official
coach with its " outriders and attendants with drawn swords,"
Archbishop Sumner replied : " I cannot imagine that a greater
reproach could be cast on the Church than to suppose that it
allowed its dignity to interfere with its usefulness."[1] As for
the *numerical following* of the Evangelicals within the State Church
during the early years of the Oxford Movement, it is suggested
by the most characteristic representative of the old Low Church
school. Sydney Smith, of *Edinburgh Review* fame, always smart,
often shallow, and sometimes stupid, speaks of turning aside
from attacking " the nasty and *numerous* vermin of Methodism "
to exterminate the " pragmatical, perpendicular, Puseyite
prigs." As for Episcopal representation of Evangelicalism,
Ryder and the Sumner brothers as yet continued alone. Indeed
the fact is that until Lord Shaftesbury, from 1856 till 1865,
appointed the much maligned " Palmerston Bishops,"[2] Evangelicalism had less than a tithe of its proportionate representation
on the Episcopal Bench : nevertheless because a bare half of
Shaftesbury's numerous nominations went to avowed Evangelicals, " The Good Earl " was violently attacked as a rabid
partisan making " wicked appointments."[3]

*   *   *   *   *

With withering sarcasm, D'Alembert, the famous mathematician and one of Diderot's foremost editors of the *Encyclopédie*,
depicting the pre-Revolution France of his day, wrote : " The
highest offices in the Church and State resemble a pyramid,
whose top is accessible to only two sorts of animals, eagles and
reptiles." [4] This aphorism, coined to describe Catholic France,[5]
was thought by many on the British side of the Channel equally

[1] Balleine, p. 196.
[2] " I am a very lucky man," wrote Palmerston, " luckier than most
Ministers. I have no sons, grandsons or nephews to stuff into the Church ;
. . . I can do what I think right." He left appointments entirely to
Shaftesbury, who accordingly was dubbed " the Bishop-maker." See
E. Hodder's *Life of Shaftesbury*, pp. 197–99, also Bready's *Lord Shaftesbury
and Social-Industrial Progress*, p. 44.
[3] *Life of Bishop Wilberforce*, by his son, Vol. III, p. 84. G. R. Balleine,
op. cit., pp. 265–68, gives an illuminating analysis of the " Shaftesbury
appointments."
[4] Abbey and Overton, *op. cit.*, Vol. II, p. 23.
[5] Prior to the French Revolution the Archbishop of Narbonne, conspicuous in a society remarkable for " high living and loose thinking,"
had an ecclesiastical income of £40,000 a year ; 116 French Prelates had
stipends between £7,000 and £10,000 a year, " often increased by pluralities
and sinecures." Yet some French *curés* had but £10 a year. See J.
Holland Rose, D.Litt., *Christianity and the French Revolution* (published
in *Christ and Civilisation*), p. 418ff.

applicable to Protestant England, where it was quoted even by a bishop. Certainly it contained enough truth to bite. John Wesley by blood was partly Irish ; by instinct, temperament and outlook he was singularly English ; nevertheless clannish Presbyterian Scotland, as later will appear, first recognised his world greatness by beginning as early as 1772 to bestow upon him the freedom of certain of her cities and corporations, while still earlier she had begun inviting him to preach in College, and other prominent, Kirks. In England the " Blind Guides " showed a different front. Though Wesley, as an Anglican priest, did everything reasonably possible to keep his rapidly increasing Societies within the National Church, and though during the last two or three decades of his long life he was recognised by the common people as a national character —even indeed as a national " institution "—yet never was he invited to preach in any English cathedral, much less in Canterbury, Westminster Abbey or St. Paul's.

The English episcopate of the eighteenth century, though still purporting to be the exclusive mediators of Apostolic Grace, by the pride, arrogance and venality of their lives, and by compromising Christianity to the idolatry of wealth, class, " reason " and Constitution, caused the light that was in them to turn to darkness : and how great was that darkness is nowhere more clearly revealed than in the fact that these solemnly ordained ecclesiastical " guides " failed utterly to recognise either the importance or the majesty of the most selfless, most heroic, and most truly amazing life's work ever spent for the salvation of England or, through England, of the world. The episcopal bench of Wesley's day, with but few and notable exceptions, was spiritually unbaptised.

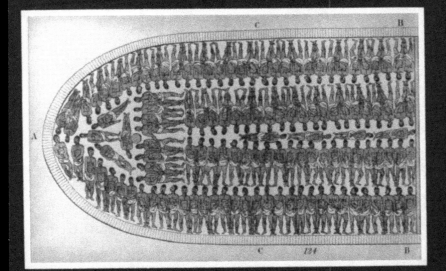

SLAVE-TRADING ON AFRICAN COAST, AND
SECTION OF SLAVE SHIP (By courtesy of Anti-
Slavery Society)

1. Note sale and branding of Negroes; and whipping them into boat; also slave-ship in background (top)

2. Africans packed on ship, "like books on a shelf"
Chained together at wrists and ankles (bottom)

PULPITS PROFANED

" Kings are gods but once removed. It hence appears
No court but Heaven's can trie them by their peers,
So that for Charles the Good to have been tryed
And cast by mortal votes was Deicide."

See *Monumentum Regale* (Select Epitaphs and Poems on Charles I, 1649) and *Vaticinium Votivum.*

" OF all birds the eagle alone has seemed to wise men the type of royalty (i.e. nationalism)—not beautiful, not musical, not fit for food, but carnivorous, greedy, hateful to all, the curse of all ; and, with its great powers of doing harm, surpassing them in its desire of doing it."

ERASMUS, *Adagia* (1515).

E

PULPITS PROFANED

JOSEPH ADDISON, in the early years of the eighteenth century, drew an amusing sketch of a certain innkeeper who, " lacking time to go to Church himself," had nonetheless " swelled his body to a prodigious size and worked up his complexion to a standing crimson by his zeal for the prosperity of the Church." This pious publican, too, had given tangible proof of his devotion to the Establishment by " heading a mob at the pulling down of two or three meeting-houses " ; but as to the content of his Faith, Addison vows : " He had learned a great deal of politics, but not one word of religion from the parson of the parish ; and had scarce any other notion of religion but that it consisted in hating Presbyterians."[1] Thackeray, in the perspective of a century's distance, examined the sermons of the humorous and popular Laurence Sterne and declared that they contained " not a single Christian sentiment."[2] These judgments seem harsh ; but a perusal of hundreds of eighteenth-century sermons preached by ecclesiastics in the recognised " succession of preferment," especially up to the sixth and even seventh decades, will dispel all doubt that they are rooted in truth.

From the Restoration (1660) till the year 1795 special " Martyrdom " and " Restoration " sermons were preached annually both before the House of Lords and the House of Commons, and also in parish Churches throughout the country. The former, delivered each year on January 30th, were designed to call the nation " in fasting and mourning " to commemorate

---

[1] *Freeholder*, No. 22, March 5th (1716–17).

[2] See *Sermons of the Rev. Mr. Yorick* (1760) ; also Sterne's *Sermons* (1765). In his essay, *Sterne and Goldsmith*, Thackeray says : " There is not a page in Sterne's writing but has something that were better away, a latent corruption—a hint, as of an impure presence." (Thackeray's *Works*, Vol. X, p. 569.) Coleridge says : " Sterne cannot be too severely censured for . . . using the best dispositions of our nature as the panders and condiments for the basest." (*Literary Remains*, Vol. I, p. 142).

the " Sacrifice of the Blessed Martyr, Charles I " ; the latter (May 29th) were to lead the people in " Thanksgiving for the Restoration of the King and the Royal Family." Occasionally these January 30th and May 29th homilies were unitedly referred to as " Commemoration Sermons " ; and generally both were of the nature of Cavalier " patriotic effusions," foreign alike to charity and grace.

(i) Martyrdom and Restoration Sermons

Samuel Asplin, M.A., preaching on May 29th, 1715, in the parish Church of St. Mary, Woolwich, said : " With the Restoration the true religion, our Redeemer, is raised from the grave, almost by the same miracle, when it was dead and buried in anarchy, hypocrisy and enthusiasm." This reverend gentleman was following a genteel fashion in comparing the restoration of the profligate Charles II, with the resurrection of Jesus Christ ;[1] but by way of excuse for the well-known sensuality of Charles and his Court the preacher proceeds : " As often as I read over the miserable scene of things in those days of Cromwellism, villainy and ravage ; when hell itself had broken loose and confusion had so long time obtained dominion over us . . . I say when I reflect upon this dismal state of things, I cannot but wonder at the temper of the good old Royalists, when God, by a miraculous turn of Providence, restored them to peace and Kingly Government, that instead of committing less extravagances, they had not (like nature out of a starved condition feeding upon plenty) even surfeited themselves in an excess of joy."[2] Further on, Asplin continues thus : " I believe there is something so sacred in the Divine Right of Kings and in their legal accession to their respective thrones (by the legality of their succession, I mean by God and their birthright) that there are some invisible irradiations and streams flowing from their persons that strike both the upper and lower part of mankind with a religious obedience to them and a more than common veneration."[3]

As for this divine's description of Oliver Cromwell, it reveals

---

[1] The death of Charles I, too, was repeatedly connected with the crucifixion of Christ. " The University of Oxford caused two similar pictures to be painted, the one representing the death of Christ, the other the death of Charles. An account of the sufferings of each was placed below, and they were hung in corresponding places in the Bodleian Library.' (W. E. H. Lecky, *History of England in the Eighteenth Century*, Vol. I, p. 67.)

[2] Rev. Samuel Asplin, M.A., *Restoration Sermon*, May 29th, 1715, p. 4.)

[3] *Ibid.*, p. 13.

the type of preaching then approved and rewarded. He speaks of " that execrable monster Cromwell " rearing " his Babel scheme of Government and tyrannising over everything that looked like loyalty and conscience, and conformity to the best Church and King in the world." " To the Royalist Martyr," declares our Cavalier oracle, " a King not to be matched for excellencies . . . there succeeded a wild kind of Atheism, under the veil of purity, reformation and fanatic rage ; while tinkers, cobblers and draymen became lords over God's inheritance."[1] Asplin would have argued himself blue in the face to prove his Apostolic Succession, through the fishermen of Galilee, to the Carpenter of Nazareth ; but the mere suggestion that tinkers, cobblers and draymen could be soulful, responsible men, drove him mad. By this King-worshipping sycophant, Cromwell and all his colleagues are dismissed as " that hypocritical brood of infernal vipers."[2] " Upon my soul," concludes this harangue, " I believe . . . it was only for the sake of the old persecuted Royalists, who had suffered a great sight of afflictions, that God delivered these sinful nations from a twenty years tyranny and rebellion."[3]

On January 31st, 1703, Dr. White Kennett (later Bishop of Peterborough) preached in the Church of St. Botolph, Aldgate, on the subject *A Compassionate Inquiry into the Causes of the Civil War*. His sermon opens : " The evil of this day, which we now deplore in Fasting and Mourning, was an unnatural Civil War, that overturned the best Constitution in the world, that made our whole Island an Aceldama, a Field of Blood, and through heaps of rapine and slaughter, proceeded to the deplorable death of the Martyr of this day, one of the most virtuous and most religious of our English Princes." Following the correct style, he extols " our Happy Constitution," denounces the " hypocrisy and fanaticism " of the Puritans, and castigates the Commonwealth leaders as " Men of Craft "—" dreadful dissemblers with God and Heaven."[4] On January 30th, 1705, in the Church of St. Margaret, Westminster, Kennett preached the Martyrdom Sermon before the House of Commons. The Commonwealth era he depicts as striving to " turn the world upside down " ; Queen Anne he describes as " Our Sovereign Lady . . . the manifester of God to us for Good " ; while concerning the Majesty and glory of the " Royal Martyr," he concludes : " But should I attempt to enumerate his virtues

[1] Rev. Samuel Asplin, M.A., *Restoration Sermon*, May 29th, 1715, p. 16.
[2] Asplin, *op. cit.*, p. 15.
[3] *Ibid.*, p. 18.
[4] Bishop White Kennett, *op. cit.* (dated " 170¾ "), pp. 1, 24, 27.

and recommend his example, the time would fail . . . 'He was the worthiest Gentleman, the best Master, the best Friend, the best Husband, the best Father, the best Christian, that the age in which he lived produced.' "[1] There being however depths below depths, this good Doctor was vehemently criticised as not sufficiently appreciative of "the glorious Martyr, Charles I."[2]

On May 29th, 1717, Dr. Andrew Snape, preaching before the House of Commons, used language characteristic of scores of the printed "Restoration Sermons." The trial and execution of Charles I he pronounced the "murder of the best of Kings" and the "overturning of the best of Constitutions"; while as for any semblance of Democracy, political or social, his loathing is complete. "Surely there is no bondage so irksome," he exclaims, "no chains that feel so weighty, or gall so sorely, as those which are imposed by one's equals or inferiors; which was the case in those rebellious times, when the vilest of people had thrust themselves into the highest stations and, with a full swing of violence and oppression, lorded it over their superiors."[3] The Bishop of Chester, preaching before the House of Lords, in 1714, concludes his sermon by pointing the moral: "It is likewise our duty, as good subjects, to put a favourable construction upon the actions of our Prince, and never to give way to suspicions, contrary to a settled character and solemn declarations."[4] The famous Bishop Atterbury, preaching before Queen Anne, refers to the Restoration of Charles II as "reducing us from confusion and rage to order and friendliness, and making us a nation at unity in itself; lovely at home and terrible abroad."[5] Dr. Thomas Rymer, preaching before the House of Commons (1733) concludes his address by striking a note appallingly common to the preaching of the ruling ecclesiastics of the time: "It is to be hoped that we shall endeavour to preserve the blessings we enjoy, by submitting in our several stations, to the Powers under which we live."[6] It was this emphasis on submission "in our several stations," to "God-appointed superiors" that retained for the National Church the support of many who, caring nothing for Christianity, desired nevertheless the maximum protection of all vested

---

[1] Kennett, Martyrdom Sermon before House of Commons (dated " 170⅝ "), p. 26.
[2] See *White against Kennett . . . with a letter to the Doctor on his last Jan. 30 Sermon* (Anonymous), 1704.
[3] Andrew Snape, *Restoration Sermon*, 1717, p. 4.
[4] Francis Gastrel *Restoration Sermon*, 1714.
[5] Printed in a volume of selected *Restoration Sermons* (1661–1758).
[6] *Ibid.* (Thomas Rymer, p. 16).

interests, and who looked upon the clergy as faithful watchdogs and dependable police corps ; but it was this emphasis, too, that finally alienated so completely from " *the* Church " the respect and allegiance of the working multitude.

Bishop Lavington, the sworn foe of " Methodism " and " enthusiasm," preaching on May 29th, 1747, in Westminster Abbey, before the House of Lords, propounded the thesis that " God is a despotic, arbitrary King," and in the process of his sermon attacked the " King-Killing doctrine of dominion founded in grace," all the while inferring that King-Killing and God-Killing are synonymous terms.[1] Cromwell, he pronounces, the " mock-protector," who gaining power by " a daring spirit and profound hypocrisy, waded through the blackest crimes of perjury, oppression and treason . . . through rivers of blood and blood royal."[2] Then " interpreting " history in a manner no doubt pleasing to most of the Lords, Lavington proceeds : " Consider if you can without abhorrence and indignation, the Lord's anointed barbarously murdered, yourselves turned off as useless and dangerous ; and supreme authority usurped by a scant remnant of the Commons, supported by the guards of hypocrisy and enthusiasm." While turning anon to another well-beaten trail, the good bishop, after panegyrising " the best Constitution under heaven," concludes by assuring his lordly hearers that it is the duty of all good subjects " to make the King's sacred life and reign as easy and comfortable as they can."[3] Continually the same note is struck ; " the King's sacred life " becomes a monotonous chant in nearly all Commemoration sermons : the axiomatic Christian principle of " the sacredness of *all* human life " is completely forgotten. The Common People apparently were to rejoice that their Prince vicariously, and by " Divine appointment," enjoyed " ease and comfort " on their behalf, while they sweated for meagre subsistence.

Even Bishop Warburton, who, despite his egotism and Constitution-worship, was a man of independence and courage, joins the general chorus. In his Martyrdom Sermon before the Lords (1760) he dismisses the Commonwealth period as " that disgraceful epoch in our story " when the subjects

[1] A popular poem ran :
  " Kings are gods but once removed . . .
  So that for Charles the Good to have been tryed
  And cast by mortal votes was Deicide."
                              (See Lecky, I, p. 65.)
[2] George Lavington (Bishop of Exeter), *A Restoration Sermon* (1747), p. 13.
[3] *Ibid.*, p. 26.

" renounced the protection of their common Sovereign and invaded and insulted his imperial crown."[1] Swift rehashes the same perennial jingo. In a typical January 30th sermon, he does obeisance before " that excellent King and blessed martyr, Charles I,[2] who rather *chose* to die on the scaffold, than betray the liberties of his people, wherewith God and the laws had entrusted him."[3] Dr. Barnardiston, preaching to the Commons in 1766, says : " We are governed by a Prince, who in imitation of his royal Ancestors is a nursing Father to his people."[4] Dr. George Stinson, two years later, addressing the same venerable body, calls the Commonwealth era " a fit of frenzy," and urges " dutiful submission to authority." Dr. Lowth, Bishop of Oxford, preaching the Martyrdom Sermon in Westminster Abbey before the Lords (1767) used a much worn text ; " My son fear thou the Lord and the King ; and meddle not with them that are given to change." The occasion afforded him opportunity for a veiled stab at the Evangelical Revival, " the dotage and frenzy of false religion." " It is no uncommon thing with modern enthusiasts," asserted Bishop Lowth, " to ascribe the works of Beelzebub to the operation of the Holy Spirit of God."[5] Advancing to matters of State, Lowth lauded the " firmness and stability " the " beauty and perfection " to which the Constitution had now attained and called upon the Legislature " to *repress* the spirit of licentiousness and outrage which so much prevails among the people." The chords again are familiar ; it was common for the highest ecclesiastics to appeal in one breath for the suppression of all opposition to oligarchic Government in Church and State, as " licentiousness and outrage," while, in the next, they besought the people to fall down in obeisance before " our excellent Constitution, both civil and religious."

In Westminster Abbey, on January 30th, 1764, Bishop Newton of Bristol, preaching the Martyrdom Sermon before the House of Lords, took as his text : " Let your moderation be known to all men " ; and assuring his hearers that " the Lord will judge and punish for nothing more surely than the want of moderation," he proceeded to instruct their lordships that " Moderation

---

[1] William Warburton, *Martyrdom Sermon* (1760), p. 2.

[2] Lecky quotes a writer at the time of the Sacheverell agitation who says : " I may be positive at Westminster Abbey where I heard one sermon of repentance, faith and renewing of the Holy Ghost, I heard three of the other, and it is hard to say whether Jesus Christ or King Charles were oftenest mentioned and magnified." (*Op. cit.*, Vol. I, p. 67.)

[3] Jonathan Swift, *Writings on Religion and the Church*, Vol. II, p. 190.

[4] *A Martyrdom Sermon*, pp. 23–24.

[5] Robert Lowth, *Martyrdom Sermon* (1767), pp. 9–10.

is not even righteous overmuch."[1] Of this same genial bishop
Sir Leslie Stephen says that his " intimacies with great men "
enabled him " to worm himself into the high places of the
Church."[2] Certainly Newton's *Autobiography* proves that on
questions of preferment and pluralities he was by no means so
squeamish about observing the necessity for " moderation "
as on questions of " righteousness." To Bishop Newton moderation in righteousness was a cardinal article in the correct
code of religious manners, and " enthusiasm " the unpardonable
sin ; but in the sphere of self-seeking preferment, Newton
conveniently forgot all about moderation. This tolerant,
" moderate " prelate suppressed the attempt to build a Catholic
" Mass-House " in Bristol ; and " Methodism " which dared
to approach the denizens of the unwashed underworld and
teach them they had souls, he lampooned as " a bastard kind
of popery." Newton, like most of the hierarchy of his day,
prided himself that he lived in a classical, royalist society, far
above the foolish enthusiasms and loathsome " immoderations "
of the vulgar menial herd.[3]

(ii) *Influence of the Revolution of* 1688

But cringing, assuming and insincere as is the tenor of most
eighteenth century Commemoration Sermons, those preached
prior to the Revolution of 1688 (the prelude to eighteenth
century history) are worse ; indeed in pre-Revolution discourses the " creeping sycophant " appears *par excellence.* The
reason is that large numbers of Jacobite clergy regarded William
of Orange only as regent, not King ; hence, though by no means
converted from their idolatry of King-worship, they were
dissatisfied with their new idol. The result was that whereas
the " Divine Right of Kings " doctrine lost considerable of its
former glamour, a pronounced deification of the Constitution
made it a formidable rival in the Temple of State. The subservience of the hierarchy to the " power of State " accordingly
was little, if any, abated by the Revolution and the ensuing
Bill of Rights, but the unpopularity of William III among
large numbers of influential clergy, caused a marked change

---

[1] This sermon is bound with others in a volume of *Martyrdom Sermons*
(1757–1770). See Bishop Thomas Newton's *Sermon*, p. 9.
[2] *English Thought in the Eighteenth Century*, Vol. I, p. 227.
[3] *Autobiography of Dr. Thomas Newton, Bishop of Bristol*, throws much
light on the ruling ecclesiastics of the time. See also Abbey and Overton,
op. cit., Vol. II, p. 11.

in the interpretation of the power of State.   To many clergymen
who previously had been flaming exponents of the "Divine
Right of Kings," the regal Divinity was now shared by, and in
some cases wholly transferred to, the Constitution.   The
Revolution of 1688, then, meant that the Constitution was
admitted into the very "Holy of Holies," alongside the King.
Both now were primary idols, contending for supremacy in the
Temple of State.   The Revolution therefore by no means dispelled the subservience ecclesiastical dignitaries were ever
ready to pay the State, which then represented a government
of the people, *for* the privileged, *by* the ruling class ; it did
however considerably curtail their *King-worshipping* idolatry.

On May 29th, 1685, Dr. William Sherlock, "Master of the
Temple and Chaplain in ordinary to his Majesty," preaching
the Restoration sermon in St. Margaret's, Westminster, "before
the Honourable House of Commons," used the text "Blessed
art thou, O land, when thy King is a son of nobles."[1]   And
forthwith he proceeded to elaborate three points : (1) that
Kingship is the government most in harmony with the Will of
God, (2) that a king should be a son of nobles, (3) that kingship
should be hereditary.   "With what surprising joy," Sherlock
breaks out, "we beheld our banished Prince return again to
his throne ; who brought back with him our laws, our liberties
and our religion ; that is brought England into England again,
which was banished with its Prince, without changing its place
and climate."[2]   To this royal Chaplain, the Prince apparently
was England.   Panegyrising Charles II as "that beloved and
admired Prince who gave the first lustre and glory to his day,"
he reminds the House of Commons that the Gay Monarch has
"left the memory of his Princely virtues to adorn the records
of time" ; while again he describes this royal debauchee,
whose rule responsible historians have pronounced "the worst
reign in English history,"[3] as "the Great Charles."

Of Charles I Dr. Sherlock says : "I know of no Prince, in
any age, under whom an obedient and governable people
might have lived more happily than under our late martyred
sovereign."[4]   But the climax of cringing subservience is reached
in the conclusion of this royal Chaplain's oration, where tacitly
he admits that the National Church is the bond-slave of the
King.   "For Princes must value obedience and subjection,"
cries Sherlock, "as they do their Crowns.   To this we owe our

---

[1] Dr. W. Sherlock, *Restoration Sermon*, (1685), p. 1.
[2] *Ibid.*, p. 2.
[3] See article on Charles II in *Chambers's Biographical Dictionary*.
[4] Sherlock, *op. cit.*, p. 29.

present security and protection of the Church of *ENGLAND* ; for if there were nothing else to be liked in it, yet the generous Prince could not but like and reward its Loyalty ; and it would seem very harsh for any Prince to desire that Religion should be turned out of the Church, which secures him in the quiet possession of his Throne[1] . . . It is a Church of *ENGLAND*-loyalty I persuade you to ; this our King approves, commends, relies on . . . a loyalty without reserve. . . . There is no such lasting and immovable loyalty as that of the Church of *ENGLAND*."[2]

Dr. Sherlock, however, was one of many Commemoration preachers who not only accepted, but frankly advocated, the policy that the National Church was a Government instrument, designed to propagate subservience to the Crown and unquestioning submission to State authority. In view of the discourses already reviewed, it is hardly surprising to discover that the vast majority of Martyrdom and Restoration Sermons were preached from Old Testament texts. One volume of " Restoration Sermons," for instance, continuing down to 1758, contains twenty-two sermons ; and only two were from New Testament texts. The reason is apparent ; most of these harangues could never have been preached from New Testament texts. Indeed one may spend months in perusing these Commemoration sermons, especially those of the earlier period, and find never a glimmer of the courage of a Nathan or an Amos, or the faith of a St. Peter or St. Paul. Even Abbey and Overton point out that : " Notably on such days as January 30th, and May 29th, the High Church Clergy were eager to improve the occasion by venting the most violent abuse upon their political adversaries."[3] Nor, in this regard, were High Churchmen a peculiar people.

(iii) *History à la Mode*

Upon the contortion of History by these memorial sermons we need not dwell. That " Spotless Saint " and " Blessed Martyr," Charles I, continually idolised in these sentimental raptures as " the worthiest gentleman," " the best friend " and

---

[1] These words suggest that Sherlock knew well that James II, who had just succeeded to the throne, was an aggressive Roman Catholic, though " Head " of the National Church.

[2] *Ibid.*, pp. 30–31. Little wonder that Bentham wrote of " The Church of Englandism."

[3] *English Church in the Eighteenth Century*, Vol. II, p. 43.

" the best Christian " his age produced,[1] has left many self-portraits of his perfidy. " I am not without hope," he wrote coolly, " that I shall be able to draw either the Presbyterians or the Independents to side with me for extirpating one another, so that I shall really be King again."[2]　No mention is made in these discourses of Charles's guilt in violating the " Sacred Constitution " ; neither is any pity expressed for the thousands of courageous citizens who perished in the Civil War which he, not Parliament, began.　Charles I undoubtedly was possessed of certain chivalrous, romantic virtues : but are Gardiner, Ranke, Hallam, Macaulay, Carlyle and many other historians all mistaken in concluding that the " grand trouble " with the First Charles Stuart was that he " would not keep faith with any man or institution on earth."[3]

As for " that execrable monster, Cromwell," his famous despatch from Dunbar to Parliament contains, surely, more practical religion than scores of Commemoration Sermons rolled together.　" Relieve the oppressed," urged Cromwell, " hear the groans of poor prisoners.　Be pleased to reform the abuses of all professions ; and if there be any that make many poor to make a few rich, that suits not the Commonwealth."[4] Concerning the " tinkers, cobblers and draymen " of Commonwealth days—" that hypocritical brood of infernal vipers," those " dreadful dissemblers with God and Heaven "— J. R. Green, an historian still to be reckoned with, says : " For the last two hundred years England has been doing little more than carrying out in a slow and tentative way the scheme of political and religious reform which the Army proposed at the close of the Civil War " ; while also he concludes : " The whole history of English progress since the Restoration, on its moral and spiritual sides, has been the history of Puritanism."[5]

---

[1] In a sermon preached before Charles II at Breda (1649), the preacher declared that, " Among all the martyrs that followed Christ into heaven bearing his cross never was there one who expressed so great conformity with our Saviour in His sufferings " as Charles I.　In 1702, Dr. Binckes, preaching before the Lower House of Convocation, went so far as to argue that the execution of Charles I, at several points, " transcended in enormity the murder of Christ." (Lecky, Vol. I, pp. 64–67.)　The New Testament Scripture Lesson accompanying Martyrdom Sermons, was commonly the narrative of the sufferings of Christ.

[2] See J. R. Green, *Short History of the English People*, p. 564.

[3] G. M. Trevelyan, too, says that Charles I " was by temperament incapable of coming to an honest agreement and abiding by it." (*History of England*, p. 419.)

[4] See *Property : Its Duties and Its Rights* (composite authorship), pp. 143–46 ; also see Green, *op. cit.*, p. 577.

[5] Green, *op. cit.*, pp. 565, 604.

The fact, too, that the shameless Charles II could be lauded from the most historic pulpits in the land as " The Great Charles " and as " that beloved and admired Prince," who had " left the memory of his Princely virtues to adorn the records of time," suggests the degree to which the dead hand of Restoration debauchery loomed as a sinister shadow over later decades. The deification of the Restoration and of Charles the Second's Kingship tended directly to idealise the fickle, dashing, voluptuous and godless mode of life " the Gay Monarch " flaunted before the nation. That sovereign's libertinism in fact established, or confirmed, the fashionable social criteria of the young " squirearchy " ; while a studied, persistent, revengeful abhorrence of " the Saints " and all their " puritan hypocrisy," tended to put virtue and sobriety, faith and reform, to rout. The National Church, moreover, being an arm of Government, and being officered almost exclusively by scions of privileged, autocratic families, lent itself all too freely to this general stream of Restoration influence, and, for more than a century, the annual Martyrdom and Restoration sermons afforded unique vehicles for its expression.

THE BETTER TEACHING

" WHAT is it that so greatly discredits the dispensations
of Providence, but that state of misery to which the bulk
of mankind is condemned in order to support the few
in the full tide of wantonness and riot ? "

BISHOP WARBURTON, *Sermons on Principles of Natural
and Revealed Religion.* (1753) Vol. 1, p. 104.

" THOUGH it may be a wise or virtuous poor man hath
more right to our esteem than a fortunate knave or fool ;
yet, for as much as in outward rank or condition God
hath preferred the latter, he hath the right of precedence and of outward respect and observance. This
is a duty so incumbent upon all, that our Church hath
thought proper to teach it in her first rudiments of
Christianity ; when the children are taught *to order
themselves lowly and reverently to all their betters.*"

The Whole Duty of Man (Anonymous) p. 293 : first
published in 1658, and long used as a religious handbook alongside the Prayer Book.

THE BETTER TEACHING

For folly and flattery, for vindictiveness and idolatry, the Martyrdom and Restoration sermons are in a class by themselves. Their very origin committed them to violently partisan, if not ludicrous, panegyrics and anathemas. It therefore would be erroneous to infer that these " Commemoration " sermons, preached annually before Royalty and the Houses of Lords and Commons, as well as throughout the nation, illustrate the only type of eighteenth century sermon within the Established Church. It would, moreover, be unfair to conclude that they are representative of " the Church " as a whole. Their historical value lies rather in the fact that they show both the kind of doctrine the overshadowing oligarchy expected the National clergy to preach and the servile way in which highly placed ecclesiastics fulfilled that expectation ; while also they reveal the paralysing influence of the Restoration spirit of revenge upon " the Age of Enlightenment." It is with some relief therefore that we turn to survey the better pulpit teachings of the same period. If the Martyrdom and Restoration sermons represent the most servile and most pagan of the Church's eighteenth century preaching, the benevolent and philanthropic sermons, including those in support of the Society for Promoting Christian Knowledge, the Society for the Propagation of the Gospel in Foreign Parts, the Charity Schools, the Hospitals and later the Sunday School movement, represent perhaps the most courageous and most Christian.

(i) *The Higher Strains*

Bishop Hough, preaching a Charity Sermon in 1712, spoke poignantly on some of the social evils of his day. " Riches," he cried, " can put evil for good and good for evil." Again, he averred that in so far as men " take from the rich the fashion of their lives and manners as much as their clothes, and deportment," the rich must " stand accountable to God not only for their own faults, but for as many as have sinned by their example."[1] In conclusion, Hough, far from exhorting his

[1] John Hough (*Charity Sermons*, 1712–1715), pp. 11–14.

congregation to an acceptance of the " Divine Right of Kings,"
the sanctity of the Constitution and the religious duty of submission to authority, urged upon them their duty to " feed
the hungry, clothe the naked, relieve the distressed, support the
feeble, enlarge the prisoner, instruct the ignorant and educate
the helpless orphan."[1] Incidentally also he pointed out that
during the year 1711 the old hospitals of St. Bartholomew and
St. Thomas had rendered curative care to over 5,000 " wounded,
sick and maimed soldiers and seamen."[2]   Bishop Atterbury,
delivering a Charity Sermon in 1723 was refreshingly direct.
" Our Saviour," he reminded his hearers, " is represented everywhere in Scripture as the special patron of the poor and afflicted,
and as laying their interests to heart, as it were more nearly
than others of his members." Atterbury's application too, was
fearless and uncompromising : " Hear and tremble all ye who
have this world's goods, and see your brother have need and
shut up your bowels of compassion from him." Then he
pressed home the duty, " to relieve the helpless poor, to make
sturdy vagrants relieve themselves ; to hinder idle hands from
becoming mischievous to the commonwealth ; nay, to employ
them so that they may be of public service ; to restore limbs to
the wounded ; health to the sick, and reason to the distracted ;
to educate children in an honest, pious and laborious manner,
and by that means to sow the good seed of which perhaps
another age and another race of men may bear the benefit."[3]
   In 1740 Dean Swift, preaching on " Mutual Subjection,"
said : " No man ought to look upon the advantages of life,
such as riches, honour, power and the like as his property, but
merely as a trust which God hath deposited with him, to be
employed for the use of his brethren ; and God will certainly
punish the breach of that trust, although the laws of man will
not, or indeed cannot."[4] " You cannot," declared Swift,
" envy your neighbour's strength, if he maketh use of it to
defend your life or carry your burden ; you cannot envy his
wisdom if he gives you good counsel ; nor his riches if he
supplies your wants ; nor his greatness if he employs it to your
protection." Furthermore, he reminded " those whose riches
serve them only as a spur to avarice, or an instrument to their
lust," that " God seeth all and will treat them as stewards."[5]

[1] John Hough (*Charity Sermons*, 1712–1715), p. 18.
[2] These were victims of the War of the Spanish Succession concluded
by the Treaty of Utrecht in 1713.
[3] Bishop Francis Atterbury, *Sermons*, p. 176ff.
[4] Jonathan Swift, *Writings on Religion and the Church*, Vol. II, p. 116.
[5] *Ibid.*, p. 117.

Bishop Warburton, preaching a Fast Sermon in 1745, when the Pretender's army was in England, expostulated : " The epidemic evils of every powerful community, in its decline, are luxury and avarice ; which by an unnatural mixture are incessantly begetting one another even in the same breast. By these means the national wealth becomes in part exhausted ; and which is almost as bad, in part unequally distributed ; and the personal vigour of the people is either enervated by opulence, misemployed, or debased by sordid and inactive poverty. . . . These are the epidemic evils which fill private families with unnatural quarrels, infest courts of justice with chicane ; and distract the councils of Government with faction —faction which scruples no shape however venerable, no name, however sacred, to draw the deluded people to second her private and corrupt purposes, *masked over with pious zeal for religion and disinterested love of country.*"[1]   Again, in 1753, Warburton asks : " What is it that so greatly discredits the dispensations of Providence, but that state of misery to which the bulk of man-kind is condemned in order to support the few in the full tide of wantonness and riot ? "[2]   Nor would he countenance any divorce between charity and piety. " Many " he protested, " assume to themselves great merit in loving God, while they treat their brothers with contempt and cruelty. But what says the Apostle in my text ? Provoked at their hypocrisy, he strips off the mask and brands them with the odious name of liars." Whatever were Warburton's sins—and he was far from a saint—he was no puppet of party or class. The soulless plutocrat he could not abide. " So much excess of corruption," he warned, " hath unblessed riches brought their possessors, that some can make that very sordidness itself, that miserable clothing of poverty, a subject for their scorn and ridicule. So that whether it be for want of those advantages of mind and person, which their poverty disabled them from possessing, or whether it be from that poverty itself, they are sure never to escape the inhumanity of unfeeling wealth."[3]   William Law, too, boldly taught that, " the honours which a King can give are literally no more than the toys with which a nurse amuses a child."[4]

Or if we proceed toward the latter end of the century and examine the sermons of Robert Lucas, a Church pioneer of the

---

[1] William Warburton, *Fast Sermon* (1745).
[2] Warburton, *Sermons on Principles of Natural and Revealed Religion,* Vol. I, p. 104.
[3] *Ibid.,* pp. 83, 95.
[4] See Stephen, *op. cit.,* Vol. II, p. 397.

Sunday School movement, we catch some glimpse of the new passion for the education of the poor. When powerful vested interests opposed the Sunday School crusade as " educating children above their station " and " unfitting them for their God-appointed tasks," he nobly championed its aims. " Away with those selfish notions," admonished Lucas, " which would repress the generous struggle of the poor man's mind after information and instruction, which would bar the gates of knowledge to him nor suffer one ray to enliven the gloom that surrounds him." " The general mass of the people," he complained, " still remain overwhelmed in a sort of hereditary ignorance and sloth. . . . The lamp of reason is scarcely alive in them."[1] " While the sun," he expatiated, " sheds its benign influence with equal kindness upon the cottages of the poor and the mansions of the affluent, the latter uncharitably would deny the former any part in that better radiance by which their own lives are illumined."[2] But to the student of social and religious problems the most revealing aspect of Lucas's *Sermons on Sunday Schools* is their reiterated references to the fears and stock-arguments of his opponents. " In ignorance the poor were born, and in ignorance let them remain," was a rejoinder confronting him at every turn. " It is impolitic," continually argued his detractors, " to give these children knowledge ; it will but unfit them for their respective stations, make them bad labourers and mechanics, and raise them above their order in the community."[3]

(ii) *Discordant Notes*

But although these sermons are typical of the most courageous and most Christian preaching within the National Church of the eighteenth century, almost invariably they contain notes which cancel the bolder aspects of their own teaching. Despite Dean Swift's refreshing emphasis on stewardship—a rare note in the National Church of his day—he concludes the said sermon by resorting to the pious delusions of his age. " The practice of this duty of being subject one to another," he contends, " would make us rest contented in the several stations of life, wherein God hath thought fit to place us."[4] Again, in his sermon, *The Poor Man's Contentment*, we have an admirable

[1] Robert Lucas, B.D., *Three Sermons on Sunday Schools* (in Lambeth Palace Library), pp. 15–18.
[2] *Ibid.*, p. 78.
[3] *Ibid.*, p. 79.
[4] Swift, *op. cit.*, Vol. II, p. 117.

illustration of the abrupt terseness and dictatorial manner of most of Swift's preaching. "I shall therefore show," he says, "first that the poor do enjoy many temporal blessings not common to the rich and great, and likewise that the rich and great are subject to many temporal evils not common to the poor."[1] Sir Walter Scott described the Dean's preaching with high charity when he said : "Swift tears the bandages from the wounds like a hasty surgeon in a crowded hospital, and applies the incision knife and caustic with salutary but rough and untamed severity." Bishop Warburton too, for all his forcefulness and audacity, gives characteristic expression to the most patent enigma of his time. After his broadside upon the heartless avarice and luxury at the top of society and the sordid, degrading poverty at the bottom, he begs the whole question by resorting to the Christless conscience-soother that the yawning gulfs between the social classes are divinely ordained. "These different stations in society were marked out and disposed of," he avers, "by the peculiar ordinance of Providence " ; while again, he refers to the poor as " those whom Providence has thrown beneath us, on the distressful stage of human life."[2]

Even the great and good Bishop Berkeley, in his powerful sermon before magistrates, takes for granted the Providential origin of a caste-privileged society and accepts for the National Church the police rôle of being its guardian and protector. "And if religion," pleads Berkeley, "in all Governments be necessary, yet it seemeth to be more especially so in monarchies ; for as much as the frugal manners and more equal fortunes of republics do not so much inflame men's appetites, or afford such power or temptation to mischief, as the high estates and great wealth of nobles under a King."[3] To find Berkeley appealing to magistrates to support religion as a bulwark to those class divisions which he himself maintained, " inflame men's appetites " and " afford such power or temptation to mischief," is a trenchant commentary on the social assumptions of his era.[4]

---

[1] Swift, *op. cit.*, Vol. II, p. 204.
[2] Warburton, *op. cit.*, Vol. I, pp. 96, 91.
[3] George Berkeley, *Address to Magistrates, etc.*, p. 24.
[4] In the eighteenth century, says Dr. R. H. Tawney, " it is almost superfluous to examine the teaching of the Church of England as to social ethics . . . except by a few eccentrics, the very conception of the Church as an independent moral authority, whose standards may be in sharp antithesis to social conventions, has been abandoned. (*Religion and the Rise of Capitalism*, pp. 188–9.) In the latter part of the century, however, this stagnation was being sternly challenged.

Lucas, too, despite his passion for the education of the poor, reverts repeatedly to the inevitable strain that an all-wise Deity had ordained the prevailing social order. "Because Providence," he pleads, "has thought good to place some in a helpless and forlorn situation, shall we deny them the consolation of knowing from the operation of their own minds, that they are reasonable creatures?" Or again: "But truly it is a strange idea (adopted however by some) which supposes that knowledge, arising out of a decent and Christian-like education, indisposes the poor for their respective callings."[1] The mesmerism cast by the Feudalistic exclusiveness of a class-divided society held even Lucas in its toils. "The acquisition of knowledge," he argues, "cannot injure or change the texture of that society; its principal effect will be to stimulate the other classes to increase theirs in due proportion." But he meets his critics still further: "The objectors need be under no fears lest, by the operation of these schools, there should be no dregs in the community, no bottom class to do the labour and drudgery of the public."[2] He even refers to "such employments as Providence has *unalterably allotted* to the lowest orders of the state," and hints that the privileged classes should support the Church's Sunday Schools as a sort of social insurance. "Their force is employed," he points out, "to correct and control those parts of the community, which have been accustomed most to disturb its peace and tranquillity."[3]

The reasons for this perennial class emphasis, which degraded Providence into a Chief of Police utilising the National clergy as His special constabulary to keep the populace in their "appointed stations," is not difficult to trace. With the "Puritan Rebellion" the National Church, as an hierarchical institution, had suffered something approaching the same fate as befell Royalty and the Nobility; consequently the whole Cavalier party, in Church and State, were determined above all else that if again they achieved power, from henceforth and forevermore "tinkers, cobblers and draymen" should be taught their proper places and kept in them. . . . Restoration legislation, with its "Anti-Puritan Code," was therefore but one means of achieving this end, and that the crudest.[4] The subtler means was religious propaganda and dogma; and this began to appear during Commonwealth days. Various hand-

[1] Robert Lucas, *Three Sermons on Sunday Schools*, pp. 15, 17.
[2] *Ibid.*, p. 80.
[3] *Ibid.*, p. 72f.
[4] See Chapter I (i).

books from time to time were published, purporting to interpret their religious duties to the different classes of society ; but in the year of Cromwell's death (1658) there appeared a manual which, quickly superseding all others, held for nearly a century an undisputed place alongside the Prayer Book as a practical Church guide to social conduct and duty.

This anonymous volume, based largely on Mediaeval precedent and tradition, and for generations preached on and quoted from National pulpits all over the realm, was entitled *The Whole Duty of Man*. Admittedly it contained many excellent Christian precepts and much skilful ethical casuistry. " He that is unjust," it taught, " for greediness of gain is like to multiply more acts of this sin (covetousness) than he that is so by malice. . . . The covetous man hath as many objects of his vice as there be things in the world he counts valuable."[1] Or again : " The very necessities of the oppressed," it emphasised, " are the means of his oppression ; thus it is in the case of extortion and griping usury : a man is in extreme want of money, and this gives opportunity to the extortioner to wrest unconscionably from him ; to which the poor man is forced to yield to supply his present wants. And thus it is also with exacting landlords, who, when their poor tenants know not how to provide them-selves elsewhere, rack and screw them beyond the worth of the thing."[2] The book also taught squarely that in all cases of oppression " the sin is greater in proportion to the helplessness of the victim," so that " the oppression of widows and the fatherless is the worst."

But despite this and much other pungent teaching to the same end, *The Whole Duty of Man* reverts ever and anon to its underlying theme that rigid class divisions were divinely ordained, and that all good subjects must faithfully perform their duties in those particular stations of life wherein it has pleased God to place them. Thus, for instance, after laying down the chief duties of servants as " obedience, faithfulness, silence and diligence,"[3] it smugly depicts the rights of wealth and birth as follows : " Therefore, as titular dignities entitle men to outward respect and observance, so also does wealth and large possessions ; for when God bestows on one man a larger fortune and possession than on another, he does thereby prefer and advance him to a higher sphere and condition : and when God hath set him above us, it is just and fit that we

---

[1] *Whole Duty of Man, laid down in a plain and familiar way for the use of all*, p. 240. (Anon.)

[2] *Ibid.*, p. 241.

[3] *Ibid.*, p. 216.

should rise and give that place to him which is God's appointment." " Though it may be," continues the Text, " a wise or
virtuous poor man hath more right to our esteem than a fortunate knave or fool ; yet, forasmuch as in outward rank or
condition God hath preferred the latter, he hath the right of
precedence and of outward respect and observance. This is a
duty so incumbent upon all, that our Church hath thought
proper to teach it in her first rudiments of Christianity ; when
the children are taught *to order themselves lowly and reverently
to all their betters.*"[1]

Prior to his " conversion," in the days of his sacerdotal
rigidity, Wesley had held this religious manual in the highest
esteem as an invaluable guide in all matters of conscience and
duty. But is it surprising that after his " spiritual emancipation," when the pure light of God had flooded his soul, when
the tattered robes of legalism had fallen from him and he had
experienced the ecstasy of being " clothed upon " by the
wondrous mantle of the spirit, when, too, his Faith no longer
being that of a servant but that of a son, he knew himself commissioned by the Father of Truth to proclaim Liberty through
Christ to *all* the children of men—is it surprising that after his
" New Birth " he cast aside *The Whole Duty of Man* as a pedantic,
if not hypocritical, heap of scribal and legalistic verbiage,
which, precluding the centrality of Gospel Grace, obscured
and even nullified the Brotherhood of Man ? Is it surprising
either that Whitefield revolted equally against its teaching,[2]
or that William Cowper, the chief literary spokesman of the
Evangelical Revival, characterised this text of religious etiquette
as " a repository of self-righteousness and pharisaical lumber " ?
The National Church, nevertheless, till *late* in the eighteenth
century, continued to hold it dear ; and like the annual pulpit
effusions on Martyrdom and Restoration days, it helps to explain the rigid class consciousness which, overleaping even the
bitterest internal factions, so peculiarly characterised the
privileged and assuming oligarchies in Church and State.

(iii) *Dr. Price's Famous Discourse*

With the Nonconformist preaching of the century we are not
here especially concerned. A passing exception, however,
must be made in the case of Dr. Richard Price's sermon on

---

[1] *Whole Duty of Man*, p. 293.
[2] Whitefield said of the author of this manual that he " knew no more
about Christianity than Mohammed." (See Balleine, pp. 74–75.)

Love of Country, in 1789, which drew forth Burke's *Reflections on the French Revolution* ; for Price's sermon illustrates in marked degree both the explosive spirit of " Nonconformity," with its passion for independence, and the rapidly spreading Evangelical " enthusiasm," which by that date was mightily influencing many leading minds, even in quarters which would have indignantly repudiated the debt. The ostensible purpose of Price's sermon was the celebration of England's " bloodless Revolution of 1688 " ; its real purpose was the celebration of the storming of the Bastille and the application of France's " March for Liberty " to English affairs. " Why," asked Price, " are the nations of the world so patient under despotism ? Why do they crouch to tyrants and submit to be treated as though they were a herd of cattle ? Is it not because they are kept in darkness and want knowledge ? Enlighten them and you will elevate them. Show them they *are* men, and they will *act like* men." Price's eyes were but half focused on the old tyranny in France when he cried : " Most Governments in the world to-day are contrivances for enabling the few to oppress the many " ;[1] one eye was slyly casting toward " *the* Happy Constitution in Church and State."

" Ignorance," stormed Price, " is the parent of bigotry, intolerance, persecution and slavery. . . . It has oftener happened that men have been too passive than too unruly, and the rebellion of Kings against their people has been more common, and done more mischief, than the rebellion of people against their Kings." Then, recalling the recent Public Address to George III, on his recovery from a severe illness and temporary insanity, Price continued : " We have appeared more like a herd crawling at the feet of a master than like enlightened and manly citizens, rejoicing with a beloved sovereign, but at the same time conscious that he derives all his consequence from themselves." " A King," contended this Nonconformist Divine, " is no more than the first servant of the public, created by it, maintained by it, and responsible to it. . . . The majesty applied to him is by no means his own majesty but the majesty of the people," and " forgetting this is to be like ancient heathens, who after fabricating blocks of wood and stone fell down and worshipped them."[2] Price furthermore laid down what he believed to be three basic rights of all free peoples : (1) " Liberty of conscience," (2) " The right to resist power when abused," (3) " The right to choose our governors ; to

---

[1] Richard Price, D.D., L.L.D., F.R.S., *Discourse on Love of Country*, p. 12.
[2] *Ibid.*, pp. 22-24.

cashier them for misconduct ; and to frame a Government for
ourselves." He implored his hearers to " detest " the " odious
doctrines of passive obedience, non-resistance and divine right
of Kings," protesting that these doctrines had left them
" wretched slaves "[1] : then, after an adroit attack upon the
Corporation and Test Acts as suppressers of liberty, and a
rapier thrust at " that separation of private from public virtue,
which some think to be possible,"[2] he lashed the prevailing
accumulation of " luxury, avarice, vice and venality " which
could merit " only God's displeasure."[3]

Price's conclusion reflects that first great flare of liberty with
which the French Revolution, in its initial, idealistic stages,
inspired liberal English thought.[4] " I have lived," cried the
preacher, " to see the rights of men better understood than
ever ; and nations panting for liberty, which seemed to have
lost the idea of it." He rejoiced " to see an arbitrary King
surrendering to his subjects . . . the Dominion of Kings
changed for the Dominion of laws, and the Dominion of priests
giving way to the Dominion of reason and conscience." Then,
in peroration, he burst into unrestrained exultation : " Behold
kingdoms starting from sleep, breaking their fetters and claiming
justice from their oppressors ! . . . Behold the light you have
struck out after setting America free, reflected in France, and
there kindled into a blaze that lays despotism in ashes and
warms and illumines Europe ! . . . Take warning, all ye
supporters of slavish governments and slavish hierarchies !
Call no more reformation, innovation."[5]

(iv) *Contemporary and Succeeding Verdicts*

Having now striven, by the examination of *primary* sources,
to illustrate in some measure both the most craven and the most
courageous preaching of the century, as well as to recapture
certain ever-recurrent emphases, it only remains to examine
representative *secondary* sources and present briefly the verdicts
of typical contemporaries and reputable later authorities.
Very early in the reign of George III, Sir William Blackstone,
the eminent jurist and author of the celebrated *Commentaries on
the Laws of England*, had the curiosity to go from Church to

---

[1] Richard Price, *Discourse on Love of Country*, pp. 34–35.
[2] *Ibid.*, p. 43.
[3] Price, *op. cit.*, pp. 46–47.
[4] See P. A. Brown, *French Revolution in English History*, Chapters I–III.
[5] Price, *op. cit.*, pp. 49–50.

Church and hear every clergyman *of note* in London. His reaction to all these sermons was that he " did not hear a single discourse which had more Christianity in it than the writings of Cicero," and that " it would have been impossible for him to discover from what he heard whether its preacher were a follower of Confucius, of Mohammed, or of Christ."[1] Blackstone's judgment may appear caustic ; for certainly by the accession of George III the moral and spiritual life of England was already improving. But if his " clergymen of note " meant those most popular in the exclusive social circles wherein he himself moved, his verdict was not inaccurate, for the cleansing came not through the upper, but through the lower and middle classes ; and for long it was bitterly opposed by the ruling hierarchy.

As early as 1709 Bishop Horsley, in his *Charge to the Diocese of St. David's,* complained : " We make no other use of the high commission we bear than to come abroad one day in seven, dressed in solemn looks and the external garbs of holiness, to be the apes of Epictetus." Even the free-thinking, free-living and arch-scheming Bolingbroke had sufficient appreciation of the gulf between real Christianity and its current official expression, to provoke him once to cry sneeringly to a group of clergymen : " Let me seriously tell you that the greatest miracle in the world is the subsistence of Christianity and its continued preservation as a religion, when the preaching of it is committed to the care of such un-Christian men as you."[2] Again, as even icebergs may thaw, we find the bloodless, metaphysical Paley admitting that the Church " was setting up a kind of philosophical morality, detached from religion and independent of its influence, which may be cultivated, it is said, without Christianity as well as with it, and which, if cultivated, renders religion and religious institutions superfluous."[3] But even when the ice in Paley's frog-like veins was half-thawed, his Providence remained a giant Magistrate, who, having allocated the various " social stations," guarded jealously the *rights* of the privileged and interpreted austerely the *duties* of the dispossessed. Paley was peculiarly typical of his class when he asked : " What does the labouring man's child require but innocence and industry ? "[4] Moreover he was greatly perturbed that the poor did not " rest

---

[1] Abbey and Overton, *English Church in the Eighteenth Century*, Vol. II, p. 37.
[2] See A. D. Belden, *George Whitefield*, p. 56.
[3] W. Paley, *Works*, Vol. VII. (Charge 7.)
[4] See Paley's *Reasons for Contentment addressed to the Labouring Part of the British Public.*

contentedly " in, and continually give thanks for, the winsome simplicity of their lot of " innocence and industry "—which, being interpreted, meant generally a life of abysmal ignorance and ceaseless toil.[1]

An anonymous " Church " convert to " Methodism," writing in 1753, a sort of *apologia*, declared that " many of the Church sermons of the day were in an unknown tongue to the common man."[2]   Most preachers, he protested, seemed to care very little what effect their preaching had on their audiences.   Rules, not convictions, were their great guides."[3]   This same sober-minded contemporary deplored the " uniform tone and unmeaning countenance which are the fashionable distinctions of our most applauded preachers " ; he objected that " sinners are not to be convicted by philosophical dissertations," and asked :   " Are such feeble attacks upon the strongholds of Satan ever like to dispossess him of his dominion, confirmed perhaps by a reign of half a century ? . . . That Leviathan laughs even at the shaking of the Gospel spear in the hands of those who know so little how to use it.   Much less will he be terrified by Heathen moralists, or quaint maxims extracted from Seneca or Epictetus."[4]   This critic here put his finger on a pregnant truth.   The ruling class of 1753, both political and religious, lived its life in an atmosphere of pagan culture, with Pericles and Plato as their guides : but under the influence of the Christian Revival, started by Wesley and Whitefield, the lower and middle classes were soon to live their lives in an atmosphere of religious aspiration with St. Paul and St. John as their guides, and the Bible as their Charter of Liberty.

Defoe, early in the century, complained that " the pulpit is daily profaned with invectives instead of sermons."[5]   White-field was scarcely started on his life-crusade when everywhere he was attacked by Church officials because he preached the incompleteness of the formal rite of Baptism as a regenerative power, and insisted upon " new birth."[6]   This Scriptural emphasis indeed was so obnoxious to Officialdom that soon Whitefield was precluded from preaching even in prisons, and the Bishop of Gloucester gave characteristic expression to

---

[1] Dr. George's researches (*op. cit.*, Chap. IV. and Appendix VI) show that in the eighteenth century the wives of the working classes were commonly " expected to contribute to family earnings."
[2] *Tracts Relating to Methodists*, p. 14.
[3] *Ibid.*, p. 25.
[4] *Ibid.*, p. 35.
[5] Daniel Defoe, *Review*, ii, p. 194.
[6] J. S. Simon, *Revival of Religion in Eighteenth Century England*, p. 156f.

prevalent ecclesiastical repugnance when he sneered : "But is it not mere enthusiasm or fanaticism to speak of new birth ! "[1] And the Bishop of Gloucester was not the only prelate of his day whose ministry had never brought him into contact with a "changed" life. Memorable, too, is Wesley's caustic jibe : "So we are forbidden to go to Newgate, for fear of making them (the inmates) wicked ; and to Bedlam for fear of driving them mad."[2] Dr. Johnson, as Boswell abundantly shows, was a vehement supporter of the Established Order in Church and State, yet, complaining of the frigid ineffectiveness of much Church preaching in his day, he declared : "We have no sermons addressed to the passions (emotions) that are good for anything " ;[3] and despite the much pulpit haranguing on "patriotism," Johnson once cried : "Patriotism, Sir, is the last refuge of the scoundrel ! "

Sir Leslie Stephen, rather too sweepingly, classifies the general run of eighteenth century sermons as "dull, duller and dullest."[4] Mark Pattison, with more charity, reserves his censure for the hard-drinking, fox-hunting and pluralist parsons, who, "careless of dispensing the bread of life to their flocks," and "trafficking in the souls of men by receiving money for discharging the pastoral offices in parishes where they do not so much as look on the faces of the people more than once a year," preached only a "carnal and soul-benumbing morality."[5] Dr. J. H. Overton, the standard authority on Anglican Church History in the eighteenth century, surveying the moral and spiritual life of the nation, is emphatic in his belief that "a gradual but distinct alteration for the better may be traced in the latter part of the century."[6] This gradual improvement is certainly not so apparent in the characteristic preaching of the National Church as in certain other directions ; but here, too, it is traceable. Even the Martyrdom and Restoration sermons, in the closing decades of the century, grew less objectionable ; the violent, irresponsible ranting against Cromwell and Puritanism, and the white-washing of Charles II, were no longer quite palatable : and finally some Commemoration preachers, even before the Commons and the Lords, half-apologised for

[1] *Tracts Relating to Methodists*, p. 14.
[2] *Journal*, February 22nd, 1750. See, too, Augustine Birrell's *Appreciation of Wesley's Journal*, prefaced to Parker's abridged edition, pp. xxiii and xxiv. (Birrell's quotation is obviously from memory and is scarcely accurate.)
[3] See Abbey and Overton, *op. cit.*, Vol. II, p. 38f.
[4] *English Thought in the Eighteenth Century*, Vol. II, p. 337.
[5] See *Essays and Reviews*, p. 349.
[6] Abbey and Overton, II, p. 55ff.

the brand of " patriotism " the Martyrdom and Restoration Days were designed to propagate.

(v) *Art without Soul*

But however great was the improvement as the century wore towards its close, it may confidently be said that, for at least five or six decades, paltroons and pedants, time-servers and sycophants, pluralists and place-hunters revelled almost unrestrained in the heyday of their theological and ecclesiastical opportunism ; while faithful, consecrated parsons—and there were still many who had not bowed the knee to Baal—were left crying in the wilderness. Place and preferment were not for them : they were outside the pale of the fashionable and family cliques representing the Apostolical Succession of the period. Deism, with its naturalistic fatalism ; the new " science " of " Political Arithmetic," with its " enlightened self-interest "[1] ; and Pagan Culture, with its background of slavery ; along with King and Constitution worship, were all strangely wrapped together in the correct preaching of the National Church : and Providence, a personification of " the Natural Order," was called in to ordain and bless this frigid, half-baked and non-digestible conglomeration, which the Age of Reason had so brilliantly devised. The orthodox preacher of the middle Hanoverian period protested vehemently against the " superstition " of Romanists on the one hand and the " fanaticism " of Nonconformists and Evangelicals on the other : then the " moderation of our Happy Establishment," with great assurance, he lauded to the skies.[2]

Yet despite the stilted artificiality which passed for " moderation and reason," many of these approved sermons were, in a manner, " works of art." Theory and speculation, dogma and adage, metaphor and rhetoric, technique and polish all contributed to the élite preacher's stock-in-trade. Not a few of the applauded sermons indeed were " artful " to a degree. But therein lay their damnation ; if as smooth and polished as marble, they at heart were as cold and dead as marble : they were too artful to convey life and warmth to the souls of men.

---

[1] Professor R. H. Tawney's *Religion and the Rise of Capitalism*, proves conclusively that the new " Political Arithmetic," with its gospel of " enlightened self-interest," had come to maturity before the close of the seventeenth century. See Chaps. III and IV. Adam Smith finally gave it classic expression in 1776.

[2] Abbey and Overton, I, p. 38.

Little of the approved preaching of the eighteenth century ever passed through the crucible of personal experience. A large percentage of the acclaimed sermons are best described as metaphysical essays or moralising dissertations. Preachers, lacking the authority of any consuming conviction, and devoid of living communion with the glorified Christ, fell back on theories, dogmas, formalities, rules and precepts, with the result that finally they were little more than the washed-out retailers of threadbare platitudes. Their sermons offered no redemption from inward sin, no deliverance from outward wretchedness—no dynamic for social reform. The Faith, vision, sincerity and sacrifice which alone can lead great causes and inspire great crusades was gone; gone, too, was the sense of the imminence of God and the stewardship of man. Gone, in fact, was every unifying harmony, every comprehensive synthesis, which enriches and sustains the soul[1] : and all that was left in high places was a religion of manners, of patriotism, of moderation, of Nature-prattle and of Class-duty. From the days of Walpole the practical Whig doctrine was : " Let parsons quarrel about the creeds, so long as they support the police."[2] But most parsons, whether Whigs or Tories, went further and assumed the functions of an order of spiritual police, hundreds of them becoming local magistrates as well.

Little wonder that with Potters and Herrings, Cornwallises and Moores as Primates, the complaint was noised abroad that the State Church was apostate, and that its guides revered the bag of Judas more than the Cross of Christ. Little wonder either with Asplins and Kennetts, Lavingtons and Paleys profaning the sacred pulpit by the basest of flattery for royalty, and the smuggest lectures on manners and contentment for the poor, that the toiling multitude came to regard the National Church as paralytic, if not parasitic. Little wonder, too, that the rapidly increasing industrial population came to account the parish clergy among the most merciless of all the forces of reaction and subjugation. If the working man attended the Established Church, his recognised place was the rough, rude bench in the gloomiest corners of the edifice, and his prescribed spiritual diet, instruction on how to order himself " lowly and reverently " before his " betters,"

---

[1] See chap. X (" The Principle of Coherence in Philosophy and Religion ") of Professor F. Tracy's *Broken Lights* (1935.). Dr. Tracy's conclusion is that religion should afford " the supreme synthesis in which all lesser syntheses are bound together into a coherent whole."

[2] Stephen, II, p. 151.

"worshipping," amidst sumptuous cushions and carpets, in locked pews.[1]

Of what inspiration then was this religious pedantry to the miner in the bowels of the earth, to the mechanic amidst the grime and sweat of the workshop, or to the foundryman daily facing an inferno of flame? Did it bring to his life meaning, power, purpose or poise? Labourers who revolted dumbly against their "seeming heritage" of hoarded weariness and poverty, resented a religion that invoked them, in the name of Nature or Providence, to do obeisance before those whose "obvious heritage" was hoarded privilege and wealth. Fire from Heaven was needed to melt these icebergs of human pride and transform them into refreshing streams, meet to revive a parched land. Such fire, moreover, in the form of a mighty spiritual Baptism, already was at hand; but that Baptism of Fire the "Age of Reason" loathed.

---

[1] During a Church service Bishop J. B. Sumner once sent for a blacksmith "to take off the locks" from certain pews. He asked the congregation to "sing a hymn" while the blacksmith performed his task. (Balleine, *op. cit.*, pp. 195–96.)

CHAPTER VI

SLAVE-TRADING AND BUBBLE FINANCE

" To be sold at the Exchange Coffee House, in Water Street, this day, the 12th instant, September, at 1 o'clock precisely, eleven negroes imported by the *Angola*."

Liverpool Advertiser, September 12th, 1766.

" 'Change Alley became a roaring Hell-porch of insane and dishonest speculators." (1720.)

Sir C. Grant Robertson,
England under the Hanoverians, p. 39.

G

SLAVE-TRADING AND BUBBLE FINANCE

NOWHERE, perhaps, is the *Zeitgeist* of the earlier half of eighteenth century Britain more clearly reflected than in the popular acclaim which greeted the Asiento clauses of the Treaty of Utrecht (1713), by which England wrung from Spain and France the virtual monopoly of the slave trade, at the same time contracting to supply to the Spanish West Indies alone 144,000 negroes within thirty years.[1] Nowhere, on the other hand, is the marked change of *Zeitgeist*, which within a century had swept silently over England, more unmistakably registered than in the clauses of the Treaties of Vienna and of Paris (1814–15), which anathematised the whole slave traffic and committed British policy and British diplomacy to nothing short of its world-overthrow.[2]

That amazing reversal of outlook, moreover, was much more immediately connected with the things of the heart and the spirit than the modern vogue for economic, materialistic, political and " scientific " interpretations—which commonly calls itself Social history—would have us believe. It was the outward manifestation of an inward experience ; and that inward experience, in turn, was the product of a quickened conscience, a moralised will and a humanised heart, which an intervening spiritual awakening had wrought. The soul of England, despite her many grievous and lingering sins, had now been transfigured. But meanwhile facts compel us to dwell on less pleasant themes.

(i) *Nature and Proportions of Slave Traffic*

The demoralising impact of the slave trade on the economic and social life of eighteenth century England, is a subject which has strangely escaped the investigations of most recent historians. Upon the origin of this modern traffic in human blood, following

[1] Sir John Harris, *A Century of Emancipation* (1933), p. 6.
[2] Dr. W. J. Warner, *The Wesleyan Movement in the Industrial Revolution*, p. 239 ; Professor Elie Halévy, *History of the English People in 1815*, pp. 400–401.

the development of the New World and the exploration of the West Coast of Africa, we need not pause. Portugal and Spain were the initial offenders in reviving this nefarious commerce ; but the " sea-dogs " of Elizabethan England could not long resist the lure of its proffered gold. Nor indeed could Elizabeth herself. For, though expressing a formal, flimsy concern that " the negroes should not be taken away to labour against their will," she lent Admiral Sir John Hawkins her own ship, *Jesus*, of Lübeck, for his second slave voyage and, on his return from that highly lucrative expedition, received him at Court.[1]

Stuart policy, after the Restoration, made the slave traffic a recognised and regular avenue of England's high seas commerce, and members of the Royal Household scrupled not to share in its sordid gains. But it was not till the " winning " of the Asiento concessions, in 1713, that Britain assumed the dominant rôle in the slave trading " business." From that business she extracted fabulous wealth ; but for such wealth she paid a ghastly price. It is doubtful indeed if any single Treaty agreement in modern history—*Versailles* possibly excepted —injected more economic and social poison into the British body politic than did those stipulations of Utrecht which acquired for England the lion's share of this inhuman traffic. Lecky speaks of " the immense accession of guilty wealth acquired through the Asiento treaty " ;[2] and that this accession carried within itself its own Nemesis is indisputable. The spirit of cupidity which it bred and fed, the cheapening of all human life which it engendered and the vulgarisation of all labour which it implied, branded and cursed the economic and the political life of the century. The all-embracing character of the tentacles which the slave trade coiled about the nation may be imagined when it is recalled that " no less a statesman than the elder Pitt made its development a main object of his policy."[3]

In our industrial age it has quite become the fashion to speak of " white-slavery," " child-slavery," " industrial-slavery," " wage-slavery " and the like, and to suggest that the evils of the factory system and the industrial era were quite as bad as, if not worse than, those associated with negro-slavery. J. L. and Barbara Hammond, for instance, especially in their *Town Labourer*, have repeatedly thrown out this suggestion, while William Cobbett and other of his radical contemporaries were merciless in their attacks upon Wilberforce on the same score. But such deductions lose the perspective of historical truth.

---

[1] Harris, *op. cit.*, p. 6.   [2] Lecky, Vol. I, p. 122.   [3] *Ibid.*, Vol. I, p. 504.

The slave trade, with its concomitant evils, was the root cause and nursing mother of the worst industrial and commercial evils that grew up both around it and beside it.[1] To procure crews for slave-ships the wiles of crimps, decoys and sharks were widely employed. Here a tenant or a lodger was lured into debt and finally was offered the alternative of prison or service on a slave-ship ; there a sturdy youth was induced to run up a drink bill in a gin shop, and soon was presented with the same option. The diabolical ingenuity of slave-ship crimps, who contracted with " slaving " captains for a supply of seamen, forms a sordid chapter in base cunning.[2] And as for the procuring of slaves on the African coast, intoxication, tribal warfare, arson, rapine and plunder were all part of the traffic's stock-in-trade. Annually scores of African villages were razed to the ground and, as Wilberforce pointed out in Parliament, cases were proved where British ships bombarded " West Coast " towns for no other purpose than to force them " to lower the price of slaves."[3]

The barbarities practised on many slave ships were enough to chill one's blood. The *Annual Register*, in 1762, carries this first hand report : " On Friday the men slaves being very sullen and unruly, having had no sustenance of any kind for forty-eight hours except a dram, we put one half of the strongest of them in irons. On Saturday and Sunday all hands, night and day could scarce keep the ship clear, and were constantly under arms. On Monday morning many of the slaves had got out of irons, and were attempting to break up the gratings ; and the seamen not daring to go down the hold to clear our pumps, we were obliged, for the preservation of our lives, to kill fifty of the ringleaders and stoutest of them. It is impossible to describe the misery the poor slaves underwent, having had no fresh water for five days. Their dismal cries and shrieks, and most frightful looks, added a great deal to our misfortune ; four of them were found dead, and one drowned herself in the hold."[4]

[1] Dr. R. H. Tawney (*op. cit.*, p. 269) says of the " economics of employment " and the accompanying harsh exploitation of workmen in the century immediately *preceding* the " industrial revolution " and the factory system, that they have " no modern parallel except in the behaviour of the less reputable of white colonists towards coloured labour."

[2] Thos. Clarkson, *History of the Abolition of the Slave Trade*, Vol. I, p. 294. See, too, Dr. M. D. George, *London Life in the Eighteenth Century*, p. 312, and W. C. Sydney, *England and the English in the Eighteenth Century*, Vol. I, p. 349.

[3] See Professor Coupland's *William Wilberforce*, p. 163. Wilberforce gave the names in Parliament of six ships so used.

[4] *Ann. Reg.*, 1762, p. 118.

Clarkson's diagram of a slave-ship shows that the male negroes
" in chains " were packed almost as close together as " rows
of books on shelves." And, incredible as it seems, a case was
discovered as late as 1788 in which thirty-four female slaves
were crammed for sleeping quarters into a hole in a ship
" measuring only 9 feet 4 inches in length, 4 feet 8 inches main
breadth, and 2 feet 7 inches in height."[1]   Slave-ship captains
indeed reckoned on an average death toll in " middle-passage "
of at least ten per cent. The *Memoirs* of Gilbert Wakefield record
the case of a slave-ship reduced to great scarcity of water.
The captain " caused the hand-cuffed blacks to be brought
one by one out of the dungeon on to the deck," whence they
were " pitched overboard to the number of 130."[2]   Wakefield
also recounts the conduct of a Liverpool captain, who finding
a negro mother fretting over her ailing infant, " snatched the
child from her arms, knocked its head against the side of the
ship, and threw it into the sea."[3]

As for the numbers of negroes transported from Africa during
the eighteenth century, it is extremely difficult to acquire
accurate information ; but it is certain that the total runs into
millions,[4] while the processes of tribal warfare, capture, transportation, suicide, acclimatisation and early " discipline "
account for the death of perhaps equal numbers.   Horace
Walpole, writing to Sir Horace Mann, on February 25th, 1750,
says : " We, the British Senate, that temple of liberty and
bulwark of Protestant Christianity, have this fortnight been
pondering methods to make more effectual that horrid traffic
of selling negroes.   It has appeared to us that *six and forty
thousand of these wretches are sold every year to our plantations
alone*[5] . . ."[5]   During the first quarter of the year preceding
the outbreak of the American Revolutionary War, 136 Liverpool
ships were engaged exclusively in the African slave trade, and
Baines, the historian of Liverpool, places their tonnage as
" about a twelfth part of that which entered the port " ; while

---

[1] See Sir Walter Besant, *London in the Eighteenth Century*, p. 61 (quoted
from *Ann. Reg.*, 1788).
[2] Sydney, Vol. I, p. 352.
[3] See Roberts's *Memoirs of Hannah More*, Vol. I, p. 25.
[4] Bancroft's *History of the United States* (1885 ed.) claims that *by* 1776
the British had supplied to the French, Spanish and English colonies of
the New World no less than three million African slaves.   Vol. III, pp.
411-12.   See, too, Dr. J. B. Botsford, *English Society in the Eighteenth
Century*, p. 332.   About one-tenth of these were supplied between 1680
and 1700.
[5] Horace Walpole's *Letters* (Cunningham ed.), Vol. II, p. 197.   David
Macpherson's *Annals of Commerce*, Vol. III, p. 403, gives the same number.

many other ships, not ranked as " slavers," conducted a partial business in human chattels. Indeed, so titanic became the proportions of this " business " that, during the thirteen years beginning with 1783, it has been estimated that some 814,000 slaves were conveyed from Africa to the New World plantations, and the vast majority were transported in British ships.[1]

Before the days of *Uncle Tom's Cabin*, Britain, inspired by a mighty moral and spiritual crusade, already had purged her slavery scroll throughout the Empire, and even United States slavery meantime was being subjected to poignant and humanising criticism from many quarters throughout America ; but during the first half of the eighteenth century both the slave trade and the " Institution " of slavery prosecuted their foul work with comparative impunity—traders, captains and planters having practically the power of life and death over their human " possessions." When the modern slave trade was started it was actually urged that slaves would soon better their lot by being brought into contact with Christian teaching and influence, but this was the sheerest hypocrisy. Most slaves received no religious instruction whatever ; few were baptised, and almost none were permitted the privilege of marriage. Even as late, indeed, as Fowell Buxton's crusade, chains and manacles were not uncommon. A certain gentleman from Mauritius, for instance, once assured Buxton that, " the blacks were the happiest people in the whole world," and appealing to his wife, said : " Now, my dear, you saw Mr. T.'s slaves. Do tell Mr. Buxton how happy they looked." " Well, yes," replied the good spouse, " they were very happy, I'm sure, only I used to think it so odd to see the black cooks chained to the fireplace."[2]

(ii) *Actual Slavery on English Soil*

As early as the first quarter of the eighteenth century some of the reflexes of the slave traffic were leaving a marked impression on English life. Numerous planters, having made fortunes out of " the Institution "—then complacently described as " the great pillar and support of the British plantation trade in North America "—returned to England, bought large estates,

---

[1] Baines's *History of Liverpool*, p. 719. See, too, J. R. B. Muir, *History of Liverpool*, p. 193f. The figure here quoted may be too high. Wilberforce, who always accepted a conservative figure, in his famous *Twelve Propositions* (1789) says : " The number of slaves annually carried from the coast of Africa in *British* vessels is about thirty-eight thousand."

[2] Sir John Harris, *A Century of Emancipation*, p. 5.

and brought over negro slaves as their servants and menials. But more : being covetous of social and political power, and prepared to pay handsomely for both, they soon entered the market as bidders for " pocket " and " rotten " borough seats in Parliament, with the result that finally the price of marketable constituencies rose from around £1,000 to even £5,000.[1] Meanwhile, however, a new and highly paradoxical problem confronted them, and only temporarily could their political and financial power solve it in their favour.

Slaves being human, they were not long on English soil till they sensed the normal Englishman's passion for liberty ; and having but tasted of that exhilarating cup, desertions began to ensue. These, moreover, were encouraged by the rumour spread among them that if only they could be baptised they would be legally free ; and sympathetic clergymen could generally be found who secretly would perform that office. So great therefore became the problem of absconding slaves that in 1729 gentlemen planters, retired in England, petitioned both the Attorney-General and the Solicitor-General of the day (Yorke and Talbot) for an opinion upon the legal status of slaves on English soil. The judgment was to the effect " *that no slave coming into the British Isles from the West Indies became free, and that baptism had no power whatever to absolve them of their condition.*"[2]

This judgment so emboldened the English slave owners that forthwith they began publicly to advertise for run-away slaves, offering handsome rewards for their apprehension, and threatening in the name of the Laws of England any who sheltered them. The net result was that slavery on English soil substantially increased, as also did the wily schemes of the slave owners' crimps and touts, who always were on the trail for " easy gain." Indeed, in 1765 we find Blackstone, though striving simultaneously to ride both the horses of liberty and slavery, pronouncing in his *Commentaries* the owner's property right to the life labours of his negro-slaves, *in England.* " And now it is laid down," says Blackstone, " that a slave or negro, the instant he lands in England, becomes a free man, that is, the law will protect him in the enjoyment of his person and his property. Yet with respect to any right the master may have

[1] See Lord Chesterfield's letter to his son (Dec., 1767), in which he says the " borough jobber " to whom he offered £2,500 for a seat, " laughed at " his bid, and said the East and West Indian planters " had secured them all " at from £3,000 to £5,000. (The letter is quoted in J. W. Jeudwine's *Religion, Commerce, Liberty*, p. 219.)

[2] Sydney, I., p. 351. See, too, Dr. George, *op. cit.*, p. 361 (note 76).

lawfully acquired to the *perpetual* service of John or Thomas, *this will remain exactly in the same state of subjection for life,* which every apprentice submits to for a space of seven years and some-times for a longer term . . . and whatever service the heathen negro owed of right to his American master . . . the same (whatever it is) he is bound to render when brought to England and made a Christian."[1] Blackstone, moreover, explicitly told Granville Sharp, when fighting for the liberty of the maltreated slave, Jonathan Strong, that the " legal rights of the slave owner " over his human property existed " in England."[2]   And so the legal interpretation stood until in 1772 Lord Chief Justice Mansfield, in the famous Somersett case, having failed to effect a compromise,[3] reluctantly ruled that " slavery is not tenable in England," and that " as soon as any slave sets foot upon English soil he becomes free."

This verdict, supported in 1778 by a large majority of the Lords of Session, put a peremptory stop to the bringing of slaves to England ; but meanwhile, on Lord Mansfield's own admission, there were already between 14,000 and 15,000 slaves in the country,[4] and open slave sales had actually taken place in England. The *Liverpool Advertiser* (September 12th, 1766), for instance, carries this notice : " To be sold at the Exchange Coffee House, in Water Street, this day, the 12th instant, Septem-ber, at 1 o'clock precisely, eleven negroes imported by the *Angola.*" Hence, contrary to popular belief, it is no fable to say that modern slavery was not unknown on English soil.[5]

(iii) *Kidnapping, " Bound Labour " and Transportation*

The concomitant and subsidiary evils of slavery, however, were perhaps even more devastating to the social and economic life of eighteenth century Britain than the accursed " Institu-tion " itself. The name of these associated evils is Legion, and their exhaustive examination would itself fill a volume ; certain of them, nevertheless, dare not wholly be overlooked. Kid-napping in its various forms, for instance, reached the proportion of a very considerable business ; and for many decades it was

[1] Sir Wm. Blackstone, *Commentaries on the Laws of England* (1765–69) Vol. I, p. 423.
[2] See Professor Coupland's *William Wilberforce,* p. 81f.
[3] Sir C. Grant Robertson, *England under the Hanoverians,* p. 351.
[4] Dr. George, *op. cit.,* p. 134.
[5] See Granville Sharp's *The Injustice and Dangerous Tendency of Tolerating Slavery in England.*

winked at, if not encouraged, in high places. The East India Company got a large percentage of its sailors through the guile or treachery of the same sort of crimps, decoys and kidnappers as supplied crews for slave ships. In London these nefarious agents, working in bands, seduced lusty youths into questionable quarters, and there entrapping them, spirited them off to " lock-up " houses and other secret detention dens " until they could be *sold* into the hands of Bengal ship captains."[1]   The appalling death rate, moreover, among these East India crews often exceeded the death rate prevailing among " slaver " crews.

But far wider flung was the kidnappers' net for white workers to sell through " contractors " to planters in America.   Early in the Restoration period the kidnapper, or " spiriter " of children and young persons to sell as workers (virtual slaves) on American plantations, was becoming a social pestilence.   In 1671 an affidavit was sworn against a certain William Thiene, " who in one year spirited away 840 " ; while three years earlier there were simultaneously three ships in the Thames on which " spirited " children had been embarked, and " though the parents see their children in the ships, without money they will not let them have them."[2]   But in the eighteenth century with the further growth of the slave trade came a corresponding revival in the whole kidnapping, or spiriting, trade.   Its victims were chiefly young persons and children of working age, and in plying its wiles it was no respecter of sex. " It is clear," says Dr. M. Dorothy George in this connection, " that all sorts of villainies were practised.   For instance, the captain of a ship trading to Jamaica would visit the Clerkenwell House of Correction, ply with drink the girls who had been imprisoned as disorderly and *invite* them to go to the West Indies."[3]   Then, in their intoxicated condition, he would have the " volunteers " spirited off to be sold into perhaps seven or ten years of plantation labour without pay.   Generally, however, the means of appropriation were more direct.   The kidnapping of Elizabeth Brickleband in 1775 is a case in point.   This girl of seventeen was decoyed from her mother's house to an " office," and thence spirited on board the brig *Nancy* and sold at Baltimore. Her mother, by sheer persistence, had the " office-keepers "

---

[1] Sydney, I, p. 353.
[2] *Cal. of State Papers, Colonial, Addenda*, 1574–1674, p. 521. *Ibid.*, 1661–68, p. 555.   Dr. George, *op. cit.*, p. 142 and p. 363 (note 98).   Stuart social policy at this time was to discourage the growth of London by encouraging the vilest cellar and attic dwellings for the poor.   Hence, not being wanted in London, the poor had very little legal protection either for themselves or their children.
[3] *Op. cit.*, p. 143 and p. 363 (note 101).

(a man and wife) brought to trial, and in the evidence it was revealed that the " sponging-house " run by these infamous characters was a drag-net by means of which " near a hundred " similar victims had been caught.[1]

J. W. Jeudwine, in his book, *Religion, Commerce, Liberty, 1683–1793*, speaks of " the *immense numbers* exported by the kidnapping trade both on the coast of Scotland and Ireland for the ' indented ' labour of the planters."[2] This is an aspect of eighteenth century social history which has been much neglected ; but beyond doubt the " kidnapping trade " threw out multifarious tentacles along the coast of Scotland and Ireland, whence it commanded an even more voluminous commerce than from England and Wales. Dr. George refers to " the days when the kidnapping of children for the plantations was general " ;[3] but being commonly regarded as the most daring branch of the gigantic smuggling business of the time, its movements were necessarily kept secret, thus making accurate contemporary evidence very hard to come by. Certain it is that the whole " spiriting " trade was a closely related and secret auxiliary to the slave traffic, but as the negro slave trade was legal and the kidnapping trade illegal, the latter resorted to every possible artifice to cover its tracks : and the fact that its victims belonged chiefly to the ignorant, poverty-stricken and often rum-sodden classes, who could afford no litigation, makes the veil of mystery surrounding this " spiriting " traffic the more inscrutable.[4] Nor was the government in this matter inclined to be over-inquisitive. Its own Press Gangs were birds of a feather. It was resorting to similar devices to rid itself of many prisoners and of such felons as had escaped the gallows ; and directly or indirectly, it was dependent upon the same ruthless set of contractors, touts and crimps for the execution of its own " Transportation " schemes. In the last analysis, too, many of the " retired " planters from the West and East Indies were almost as immediately implicated in the kidnapping traffic as in the slave traffic ; yet these " gentlemen," as we have seen, outbidding all comers in the purchase of rotten-borough seats in Parliament, had acquired substantial influence in Government circles.

Of the " bound servants," who during the eighteenth century

---

[1] George, p. 146.
[2] Jeudwine, *op. cit.*, p. 206.
[3] M. D. George, *London Life in the Eighteenth Century*, p. 230.
[4] Kidnapping was also resorted to as a means of disposing of persons who " knew too much " regarding certain crimes, or who blocked the avenues of avarice among the unscrupulous.

were sent to the American plantations—chiefly Maryland and Virginia—there were three clearly distinguishable kinds, (1) " indented " workers, (2) " redemptioners " or " free-willers," (3) convicts. The indented workers entered into a written contract with the master of their ship to serve for a fixed terms of years—generally four, though varying from two to seven—in return for their passage.[1] Redemptioners were *promised* a stated length of time after landing wherein to find masters willing to advance their passage money and so " redeem them," it being agreed that if they failed in this the captain reserved the right to dispose of them after the manner of indentured servants. But the truth is that they were lured to the tobacco and cotton plantations under false pretences. Despite alluring assurances, it was next to impossible for them to find masters willing at once to advance " redemption money," and the ship captains, well knowing this, rarely let them land until conditions of semi-slavery were saddled upon them.[2]

W. Eddis, the surveyor of customs at Annapolis, describing in 1770 the condition of these redemptioners, said : " The situation of the ' free willer ' is, in almost every instance, more to be lamented than either that of the convict of the indented servant ; being attended with circumstances of greater deception and cruelty." The negro, contended Eddis, " being a property for life," was often better treated than " the miserable European, over whom the inflexible planter exercises an inflexible severity." Exceptions he was prepared to admit ; but especially of the Maryland " indented servant " and " redemptioner," Eddis affirmed that " they groan beneath a worse than Egyptian bondage."[3]

As for the transportation and sale of convicts, this procedure was regularised by an Act passed within five years of Britain's acquiring the lion's share of the slave trade ; and from then (1718) till the outbreak of the American Revolution (1776), when Franklin and other Colonials protested vehemently against " the dumping upon the New World of the outcasts of the Old," it continued in close relation with the slave trading and kidnapping traffics. The Act in question[4] legalised and encouraged a system whereby contractors, assuming responsibility for convicted prisoners, at their own expense shipped them to the

[1] George, *op. cit.*, p. 146. Passage at this time often took two or three months. Hence the excuse for extortionate charges.
[2] Captains, of course, knew from experience that if " redemptioners " were allowed to land, some would run away, and thus avoid any payment for passage.
[3] W. Eddis, *Letters from America*, pp. 67–8.
[4] 4 George I, c. 11.

American plantations, where " by selling them, usually at auction, to the tobacco planters, for the term of their sentences,"[1] they acquired handsome profits. The voyage death-rate among these convicts, owing largely to prison-contracted diseases, seems to have equalled, if not surpassed, that of negro slave ships. " The mortality we met with in our last ship," reported one contractor, " if repeated in this, will so surfeit us, that we shall never take another." A different contractor estimated that over " an average of seven years he lost a seventh of his cargo." And the lists of three convict ships " belonging to 1740 or 1741," show that one carried 153 convicts, 61 of whom died on the voyage ; the second had 108, of whom 37 died at sea ; the third carried only 50, and of these 15 died on the voyage.[2]

Figures concerning the proportions of the traffic in " bound labour," though incomplete, are suggestive. In 1774 the numbers of " indented servants and redemptioners," registered as sailing *from London alone*, are 1,124 for Maryland, 548 for Virginia, 456 for Philadelphia and 66 for Georgia, Carolina and Jamaica.[3] Statistics concerning transported convicts are, for obvious reasons, more complete and more easily ascertained. " From 1769 to 1776 the yearly number of felons transported averaged 960," of whom exactly a quarter were women ;[4] and the sentences of most convicts ranged between seven and fourteen years, while a few were " for life."

To realise how very thin was the partition which separated all this " bound " and convict labour from the actual " Institution " of slavery, certain incontrovertible facts must be constantly in mind. The indentured labourer was sent chiefly to slave areas ; on arrival he was advertised for sale for the period of his indenture ;[5] frequently he worked alongside, and partook of the same lash and the same food, as the negro slave ; at many points his legal protection was no whit better than that of the black chattel ; during the period of his subjection he could be bought, sold or trucked about at the master's will ; and nearly always he laboured under the bitter handicap that the planter assumed he was " white trash," deserving the roughest handling and fit only for exploitation. The master, too, having only a temporary property in his labour, had less economic interest in protecting his health and well-being than

---

[1] J. L. and B. Hammond, " Poverty, Crime, Philanthropy " (*Johnson's England*, I, p. 322).
[2] Sir Walter Besant, *London in the Eighteenth Century*, p. 557.
[3] George, *op. cit.*, p. 145.
[4] Hammond, *op. cit.*, p. 322.
[5] J. Boucher, *A View of the Causes . . . of the American Revolution*, p. 183.

if he were a lifelong slave, of substantial capital value. And as for transported women, their lot frequently was more pitiable than that of men.

Both numerous and malignant were the economic and political corruptions which, during most of the eighteenth century, attacked the social life of Britain and her expanding Empire ; but most devastating of them all, by far, was the slave traffic, with its odious retinue of derivative and attendant evils. That traffic bequeathed to America the social perversions later to issue in a ghastly Civil War ; it bequeathed to England—the chief financial and political source of its expansion—a regiment of social and economic ills, which soon, on a vast stage, were to manifest themselves in the cruel exploitations of the Industrial Revolution. Indeed upon whatever it touched the slave traffic left the marks of the beast ; and the fact that those marks were often concealed, and not infrequently unsuspected, made them none the less real and none the less vicious in their effects.

(iv) *South Sea Company and Lesser Bubbles*

On the surface it might seem that the slave trade had no peculiar relation to that mad financial hoax historically remembered as the " South Sea Bubble " ; yet both undoubtedly were children of the same " *Zeitgeist*," for the unrestrained cupidity of the elder brother, the slave trader, influenced perniciously the wild blood of the younger brother, the stock-jobbing gambler.

In 1711, in an atmosphere thick with mystery and intrigue, there had been established by Robert Harley, as Chancellor of the Exchequer, a chartered trading corporation, half-commercial, half-political, known as the South Sea Company. In return for certain semi-chimerical commercial concessions in the South American slave-trading and slave-labour areas, this concern was to relieve the Government of some £10,000,000 of specified public debts, chiefly Naval, which had been funded for the purpose. The trading concessions of the Treaty of Utrecht (1713) increased interest in the scheme. By 1720 the Company's stock was selling at a substantial premium ; so, influenced by the temporary magic of that swashbuckling Scottish adventurer, John Law, who through the " high finance " of his Mississippi Company was now deluding the sovereign and robbing the people of France, the English Ministry entered into a shady agreement with the South Sea Company for a vast extension of its joint-stock business.[1]

Nor was the project difficult to foist upon the public. Seven years of comparative monopoly in the South Seas slave trade had already brought the country huge accessions of guilty gain. Wildly exaggerated stories, too, of the fabulous wealth brought to England in Elizabeth's reign by the expeditions of Drake and Hawkins, were noised everywhere and avidly consumed. A spirit of reckless gambling pervaded the air. Meanwhile also the black arts of Law's " paper finance " had caused the stock of France's Mississippi Company to rise to 1,200 per cent. ; and why should British finance be less " modern " or less astute than that of France ? Nevertheless, before the scheme could be hatched, " fictitious stock of £574,000 " had to be distributed to itching palms ; the recipients of these gratuities including " the Earl of Sunderland, Mr. Secretary Craggs, Mr. Aislabie, the Chancellor of the Exchequer, the King's German mistresses," and certain influential Members of Parliament.[2]

In February, 1720, a grandiose plan, " too complicated to be generally understood,"[3] was brought forward in Parliament. By its provisions, the South Sea Company was to be wholly re-organised and its privileges immensely enhanced ; while, in return for extended scope, it was not only to free the Government of tens of millions of funded National Debt, but also to pay it the equivalent of £7,500,000 by way of appreciation of the monopoly " bargain " conferred upon it. Despite the repeated warnings of Walpole, whose saving grace was his business sense, this wild Bill passed unimpeded through Parliament, and on April 7th received the Royal Assent. So forthwith was begun the gentle art of " bubbling the nation."[4] And as bubbles are short-lived, the Company's business required haste.

Romantic tales, studiously and stealthily circulated, caused the South Sea Stock immediately to rise, but scarcely fast enough to suit the Company's ends. Hence Sir John Blunt, a director, let loose a rumour to the effect that Gibraltar and Port Mahon were to be exchanged for rich gold mines in Peru, and that British trade in the South Seas was to be " protected and

---

[1] Law's chequered continental career began in 1694, when, having killed " Beau " Wilson in a duel, he thought fit to flee from London. Before initiating his famous " Mississippi Scheme," he had " won and lost vast sums in gambling and speculation."

[2] J. W. Jeudwine, *op. cit.*, pp. 89–90.

[3] Lecky, I, p. 323.

[4] T. Wright, *Caricature History of the Four Georges*, (1898), p. 42.

enlarged."[1] The desired effect was produced. At once the
directors opened to the public a subscription " for two millions
at £300 for the £100." It was heavily over-subscribed and
immediately began to sell at a premium. The accumulating
snowball had now started rolling and deep clouds of delusion
were long to obscure the burning light of truth, which alone
could melt it away. On April 30th the Company offered a
second subscription for " a million at £400." It, too, was
immediately snapped up ; and the multitude of subscribers,
representing all classes, became boosters of the wondrous
Company which " could turn stones to gold." A mania had
now possessed the nation : thousands sold property or pawned
heirlooms to gamble in the Company's stock ; 'Change Alley,
literally " blocked with desks and clerks," became " a roaring
Hell-porch of insane and dishonest speculators."[2]

> " While some build castles in the air,
>   Directors build them in the seas ;
> Subscribers plainly see them there,
>   For fools will see as wise men please."[3]

By the end of May, £100 stock stood at £890 ; and the Company, by a premature dividend, by circulating the " news "
that the next *half-yearly* dividend would be 30 per cent., and
that for many years it *could not* be less than 50 per cent. per
annum, floated third and fourth issues at £1,000 for £100 shares.
Nevertheless, even the fourth issue was oversubscribed ; and
when, in midsummer, prices in 'Change Alley and Thread-
needle Street reached their peak, South Sea stock sold at £1,060.
Meanwhile, however, the gambling frenzy was not confining
itself to South Sea stock, and Exchange Alley had many a
competing " Hell-porch." The *Political State of Great Britain*
gives a list of one hundred and four mushroom companies which,
basking in the glory of the Great Bubble, were, during July,
offering their alluring stocks to the gullible public. The nature
of some of these companies is both amusing and revealing.
Among them are concerns for "a wheel of perpetual motion,"
" the assurance of seamen's wages,"[4] " insuring and increasing
children's fortunes," " improving malt liquors," " the extraction
of silver from lead," " the importation of great jackasses from

---

[1] Jeudwine, *op. cit.*, p. 87 ; Lecky, I, 323.
[2] Sir C. Grant Robertson, *England Under the Hanoverians*, p. 39.
[3] Swift, *The South Sea Project*.
[4] The Royal Navy, at this period, made it a regular policy to keep sailors
pay nearly a year in arrears. Hence if they deserted they lost the wages
due to them.

ON THE ROAD TO TYBURN (Hogarth)
Note spectators' gallery on right; the gallows; sale
of gin below gallery; child trampled down; woman
selling "Death Speeches"; and Methodist preacher
in Death Cart with victim and coffin

Spain," " the breeding of silkworms in Chelsea Park," and " trading in human hair." A clergyman proposed a company to " discover the land of Ophir and monopolise its gold and silver." One projector, claiming to have control of a marvellous invention, " later to be disclosed," offered £100 shares for two guineas. In a single day his bag was full of gold ; and by nightfall he was on the Continent, never to be heard of again.[1] His marvellous invention had indeed worked !

The ever-growing array of lesser swindles aroused the jealousy and wrath of " the great Company " ; so, on August 18th, the South Sea directors " sued out writs of *scire facias* " against certain of the minor frauds.[2] This action precipitated their own destruction. The explosion of the smaller bubbles, instead of diverting suspicion, reflected all too clearly the substance of the greater swindle. Pressure rapidly was becoming tense : to seeing eyes it already was clear that the Great Bubble must soon burst. Shortly prior to the legal actions of the South Sea Company, the " paper value " of the various bubble stocks was estimated at " about £500,000,000 "—more than twice the value of all the houses and lands in Great Britain. Before the year closed, it seemed that their only remaining substance was the taste of dust and ashes in the mouth of a disillusioned but unchastened people.

In September appeared the famous " *South Sea Ballad*," soon to be sung up and down the streets of London. With humorous satire it jeered the " airy millions " and " scraps of paper " wherein the nation was trusting, at the same time mocking the Company which, " like the gods, turns nothing into all things," and predicting, at the end of the mad carnival, much " hanging " and " drowning."

> " Our South Sea ships have golden shrouds,
>   They bring us wealth, 'tis granted ;
> But lodge their treasure in the clouds,
>   To hide it till it's wanted."[3]

In November came tidings from Paris that Law, deserted by the Regent, had fled the country with vast stores of loot. In December, on the assembling of Parliament, the South Sea directors were ordered to produce all their accounts. Pandemonium ensued. Knight, treasurer of the Company, escaped to the Continent with most of the incriminating documents,

---

[1] For the record of these wild schemes, see *The South Sea Bubble*, Anonymous (second edition, 1825).

[2] T. Wright, *op. cit.*, p. 48 ; Jeudwine, *op. cit.*, p. 88.

[3] For the whole of this ballad see Wright, *op. cit.*, pp. 49–51.

H

and the Government seemed impotent to effect his return. Craggs, Secretary of State, committed suicide. The preliminary bribes of £574,000 were soon discovered, and the Prime Minister and Chancellor of the Exchequer forced to resign. The great, glittering bubble had burst.

> " There is a gulf where thousands fell,
>   Here all the bold adventurers came ;
> A narrow sound, though deep in hell ;
>   ' Change Alley ' is the dreadful name."

Many who had developed habits of profligate luxury now found themselves beggars, in an age when friendships were frail and sentiments cold.

> " Behold a poor, dejected wretch,
>   Who kept a South Sea coach of late,
> And now is glad to humbly catch
>   A penny at the prison gate."

So furious was the cry for vengeance that it was " seriously proposed " by Lord Molesworth in Parliament, " to tie the directors up in sacks and throw them into the Thames."[1]

Professor R. H. Tawney has left a memorable account of certain of the sixteenth century infamies of the famous Fugger bankers, whom, despite their pious trappings of orthodox Catholicism, he depicts as the economic counterpart of the political morality typified by Machiavelli's Prince.[2] Yet, " compared with the men who engineered the South Sea Bubble," says Dr. Tawney, " the Fuggers had been innocents."[3]

* * * * *

The year 1720 is still remembered as that of the most colossal and dramatic financial swindle in British history. As its last days ebbed away it seemed that South Sea stock, which a few months before had sold at 1060 per cent., was utterly worthless. Nor of the multitudes once in opulence, who now faced the new year in destitution, were all guilty of stock-gambling. The collapse of this financial Tower of Babel buried many of the innocent along with the guilty ; for hundreds of honest businesses were ruined through the bankruptcy of their stock-plunging debtors. With the fall of the great Company, however, Walpole's hour of opportunity had struck. Very fortunately for him, he had quarrelled with his Whig colleagues in 1717, and being out of office, had criticised mercilessly the

[1] Warner and Marten, *Groundwork of Brit. Hist.*, Part II, p. 489.
[2] *Religion and the Rise of Capitalism*, pp. 78–9.
[3] *Ibid.*, p. 191.

South Sea schemes. This did not prevent him from gambling privately in the stocks and, by selling at an opportune time, making " a good thing " for himself; but that was reckoned his own affair. Now, by general acclaim, he was summoned to the helm of State ; and nowhere was the rough genius of this coarse, cynical, drunken, but good-natured and capable man—whose education at Eton and Cambridge had been designed to fit him "for the Church "[1]—more aptly displayed, than in his handling of the South Sea Débâcle.

Realising that, in such circumstances, a statesman's primal duty was to restore public confidence, he opposed resolutely the cry for blind vengeance ; and knowing that the State was as deeply involved as the Company, he set himself with despatch to salvage whatever of the tangled wreckage remained. Immediate confiscation of the Company's property would, he knew, not only have defeated the victims' interests, but also have involved the Government in another panic. Most of the directors' private property, however, he did confiscate, and this realised £2,000,000.[2] Wisely, too, he released the Company from the £7,500,000 they had agreed to pay the State ; and when finally all salvaged assets were pooled, he was able to pay thirty-three per cent. of its face value to all holders of South Sea stock.[3]

This was far more than sufferers in the hour of their blank despair had dared to hope for ; hence Walpole began his domination of twenty-one years hailed as a financial wizard, if not a national deliverer. But when the great Sir Robert revealed himself (and that was soon) it was obvious that his own financial principles were scarcely higher than those of the South Sea hoaxers, whom he had so scathingly condemned. For all his sagacity, his tolerance and his love of peace, Walpole, perhaps as much as either the slave traffic or the South Sea Bubble, was an expression of the spirit of his time. In a great age, with a great Faith, he might have been a great man : in the England of 1721 to 1742 he came perilously close to being a great charlatan.

---

[1] Lecky, I, p. 324.

[2] Gibbon's grandfather was one of the directors. " Out of an estate worth no more than £60,000," he had to disgorge £50,000. (Sir W. Besant, op. cit., p. 8.)

[3] Robertson, op. cit., p. 40f ; Lecky, I, p. 324ff.

POLITICS, PENAL CODE AND PRISONS

" As each faction supplanted the other, they arranged the shift by providing the retiring official with a pension or a title or both. Their use of the revenues of the country to fill their own pockets is too large a subject for any one volume."

J. W. JEUDWINE,

Religion, Commerce, Liberty, 1683–1795, p. 185.

" The Criminals pass through the streets in carts, dressed in their best clothes, with white gloves and nosegays, if it be the season. Those that die merrily, or that don't at least show any great fear of death, are said to die like gentlemen ; and to merit this encomium most of them die like beasts, without any concern, or like fools, having no other view than to divert the crowd."

MURALT's *Letters on the English Nation*

(about 1730), p. 42.

" I visited one in Marshalsea prison, a nursery of all manner of wickedness. O shame to man, that there should be such a place, such a picture of hell upon earth ! . . ."

JOHN WESLEY's *Journal* (February 3rd, 1753).

POLITICS, PENAL CODE AND PRISONS

OFTEN it is assumed that the period of notorious " political bribery and corruption " began with Walpole. Lecky, however, points out that the " systematic corruption of Members of Parliament " had begun " under Charles II, in whose reign it was practised to the largest extent."[1] It continued both under James II and after the Revolution of 1688 ; and by the Septennial Act of the first Parliament of George I, which more than doubled the life of Governments, its powers of mischief were vastly enhanced. To Walpole, none the less, was left the shameful distinction of making bribery and corruption a persistent and consistent policy of State. The first real " Prime Minister " of Britain, he vied with any Stuart sovereign in the misuse of Government funds and places for the maintenance and augmentation of personal power. Once, on scanning a gathering of Members of Parliament, he observed : " All these men have their price." That conjecture, unfortunately, was far too true, and on it he moulded his policy.

(i) *Walpole and the Whig Oligarchy*

Government, Walpole believed, must be sustained either by corruption or force, and the former he chose as the " basis of his rule." " Sleeping dogs " persistently he " let lie " ; but if they awoke barking, and angrily showed their teeth, he was always ready with a meaty bribe. " He bribed George II by obtaining for him a civil list exceeding by more than £100,000 a year that of his father. He bribed the Queen by securing for her a jointure of £100,000 a year, when his rival, Sir Spencer Compton, could only venture to promise £60,000."[2] His immense expenditure of " secret service money " went chiefly to the buying of " rotten " and " pocket " boroughs and to the

---

[1] W. E. H. Lecky, *History of England in the Eighteenth Century*, Vol. I, p. 366.
[2] *Ibid.*, p. 365.

upkeep of a retinue of political jobbers and henchmen.   During his long administration a large percentage of the Members of Parliament were *secret* pensioners or placemen, while variegated bribes were also resorted to in the House of Lords, where means were found of keeping even the bishops within his control. Indeed, in 1733, in " two critical divisions " of the Upper House, Walpole actually was " saved from defeat " by the fact that " out of twenty-six bishops, twenty-five were present, or voted by proxy, of which twenty-four were for the court."[1]

Again, on February 20th, 1739, Walpole carried a critical division of the House of Commons by 262 votes against 235. " Among those who voted for the Government," it has been discovered, " were 234 placemen, whose employment was worth £212,956 13s. 4d."[2]   In one revealing sentence Lecky depicts the crassness of Walpole's political strategy and its danger to the liberties of any free people :—" It was his settled policy to maintain his Parliamentary majority, not by attracting to his ministry great orators, great writers, great financiers or great statesmen, not by effecting any combination or coalition of parties, by identifying himself with any great object of popular desire, or by winning to his side young men in whose character and ability he could trace the promise of future eminence, but simply by engrossing borough influence and extending the patronage of the Crown."[3]

Walpole was the arch-political expression of his Deistic, slave-trading age.   As he said of himself, he was " no saint, no reformer, no Spartan."   He might have said much more. In his person and policy the prevailing " Natural philosophy " bore its natural fruit.   The pursuit of self-interest was to him the " law of Nature," though he left it to ambitious State prelates and assuming economists to adorn it and call it the " law of God."   " Nature " to Walpole connoted, not divine ordinance, but human appetites ;   and " natural rights " to him spelled self-aggrandisement, unabashed.   Ruthless materialism and *laissez faire* economics therefore were the habitual moulds of his thought and expression, which withal were metallic and vulgar.   Wittingly or unwittingly, Walpole mentally was a child of Machiavelli and of Mandeville.   His personal habits, too, were as gross and sensual as his mind and spirit were cunning and coarse.   He was given to drunkenness and gluttony ; he lived in open adultery ; and having a positive taste for obscenity,

---

[1] See Professor N. Sykes, " The Church " (*Johnson's England*, I, p. 17)
[2] See Sir Walter Besant, *London in the Eighteenth Century* (Appendices p. 643).
[3] *Op. cit.*, I, 369.

" the gross sensuality of his conversation was conspicuous in one of the coarsest periods of English history."[1]   This lewdness, moreover, he carried not only into public life but also to Court, where he jested drolly with the capable, disillusioned and cynical Queen Caroline, even upon the infidelity of her husband, the King.

Under Walpole England was waxing fat ; but this obesity betokened moral and spiritual disease. True, during his long administration, all absolutism on the part of the sovereign was broken, and Parliamentary government by a Prime Minister and Cabinet, responsible to the Legislature, was being evolved :[2] but it is equally true that systematic and organised corruption was rapidly making the House of Commons a non-representative body and that the arrogant, acquisitive, quarrelsome Whig oligarchy which for half a century dominated English politics was, at the termination of Walpole's rule, already putrid to the bone. Besides certain titles and honours, Walpole, during his tenure of power, bestowed upon his own sons " permanent offices, chiefly sinecures," totalling " about £15,000 a year " ;[3] and foreseeing his own downfall, he procured for himself not only the title, Earl of Orford, but also a pension of £4,000 a year—the equivalent of some £10,000 to-day. The great Whig families who supported him, accordingly, expected and got proportionate " rewards " ; while meantime there was growing up that nauseating brood of political-jobbing attorneys who " rode the country and bought and sold seats openly," thus anticipating, if not actually heralding, the day when venal boroughs were " publicly advertised for sale in the newspapers," and when the scandals of a great county election made it cost as much as £100,000.

With a lawyer's characteristic love of a " case," Mr. J. W. Jeudwine, the barrister-historian, holding a brief for George III as a great Constitutional monarch, tries to establish the double thesis, (1) that George and his " only strong ministers " were " non-party men " who sought unswervingly the common good, and (2) that the Whig oligarchy, or confederation of family clans, which with difficulty they dislodged, had not only " gorged itself with political spoil,"[4] but literally was rancid with internal corruption. That he fails to establish the first part of this thesis

---

[1] Lecky, I, 365.
[2] This was due largely to the fact that George I knew no English and that even George II, who also spent much of his time in Hanover, was not sufficiently conversant with English institutions to preside at Cabinet meetings.
[3] W. Coxe, *Memoirs of Sir Robert Walpole* (1798), I, p. 730f.
[4] See *Religion, Commerce, Liberty*, p. 182.

is not surprising. To argue that George III, Bute, North and the younger Pitt were not Tories but were all "non-party men," seeking disinterestedly the Nation's good, is to fly in the face of a vast volume of established and irrefutable evidence : it savours too much of case pleading and legal casuistry to carry conviction, even though admittedly some of these men have been unjustly maligned by "Whig historians." Certainly it is well to remember that in 1768 Benjamin Franklin, then a resident in England, writing from London when the excitement and turmoil of the Wilkes riots were at their height, said : "What the event will be, God only knows. But some punishment seems preparing for a People who are ungratefully abusing the best Constitution and the best King any nation was ever blessed with."[1] Certainly, too, it is wise always to bear in mind that the turn of events associated with the American Revolutionary War has caused most popular historians to paint the characters of Bute, North and George III in colours unreasonably sombre and dark.

Such facts, nevertheless, do not establish the contention that George III and his " strong ministers " were non-party men, actuated only by the highest National ideals : they all were Tories, and for the realisation of their schemes they played Tory politics and depended on Tory support. They laboured, however, in an atmosphere which gradually was being impregnated with new moral and spiritual life, and wherein higher ideals of public service were slowly being evolved. But if Mr. Jeudwine fails to establish the first part of his thesis, the second he proves to the hilt : for the solid historical evidence establishing the " rottenness " of the " Whig clans," which for two generations manipulated and corrupted English politics, is overwhelming. Even Horace Walpole, that vain, polished, gossiping man of affairs, who lived smugly on sinecures left him by his father, complains, despite his Whig prejudices, of " the growing danger from aristocracy and from those confederacies of great lords." In 1770, for instance, he writes of the Whigs : " The various factions hated each other more than they did their common enemies, and most of the leaders of the opposition had in their time contributed to the grievances of which they complained." Again, of the " proud aristocracy of Whig lords," he says : they " thought of nothing but establishing their own power " and " as it suited their occasional purposes, now depressed and insulted the Crown and the royal family, and now raised the prerogative."[2]

[1] Grahame's *History of the United States*, Vol. IV, p. 453.
[2] Jeudwine, *op. cit.*, pp. 83–4.

When Dr. Johnson, in his *Dictionary*, defined " Whig " as " the name of a faction," and declared " patriotism " the " last refuge of the scoundrel," he was turning a realist eye on the politics of much of his lifetime. " Popular representation " was so corrupted as to be " almost a dead letter " ; " election petitions were heard and decided solely by favour or party in the House of Commons," while designing politicians were, in Burke's phrase, " pigging together " in the same truckle trough —the better to feed upon the State. Of this plutocracy of nobles, Jeudwine says : " They were supported by great wealth and enormous borough interest ; the secret service money was at their disposal ; the whole official world, owing to their long tenure of office, was filled with their partisans, including the bishops."[1] And again : " As each faction supplanted the other, they arranged the shift by providing the retiring official with a pension or a title or both. Their use of the revenues of the country to fill their own pockets is too large a subject for any one volume."[2]

One need not, however, as Johnson observed, eat a whole ox to tell " if the meat be tough " : and of the rare toughness of the English political carcass during at least the first six decades of the eighteenth century there can be no doubt ; it has tried both the temper and the digestion of many a hardy historian. Pulteney once said that political " parties, like snakes, are moved by their tails " ;[3] and he knew whereof he spoke : for certainly at this time the slimy, murky end of politics was its propelling force. Bribery and corruption, duplicity and deceit were the very cogs and levers of the political machine. Lecky says of the " assembly " behind Walpole's Government that it was " saturated in corruption " ; and if it inherited much of this corruption, it propagated more. Well into the second half of the century Members of Parliament enjoyed immunity from all actions of law and suits of equity, thus being able to defy their creditors, while to their servants was extended the same immunity.[4] Not till the early years of the reign of George III, moreover, were Press reports of Parliamentary debates permitted to the public ; hence the secrecy originally conceived as a protection against the absolutism of the King was perverted into a " shelter from the supervision of the constituencies."[5] Parliamentary representation therefore at many points was

---

[1] Jeudwine, *op. cit.*, p. 181.
[2] *Ibid.*, p. 185 and pp. 178–193.
[3] Lecky, I, p. 316.
[4] See Burgh's *Political Disquisitions* (1774), I, p. 205ff.
[5] Lecky, I, 442–3.

a farce. Some venal boroughs, like Old Sarum, " without house or inhabitants," sent two Members to Parliament, while large centres of the growing industrial population, such as Manchester, had no Member at all.

Eighteenth-century politicians long preceded the formulation and elaboration of the doctrine of " the survival of the fittest " ; but their pert, glib, soulless Deism, with its " religion of Nature " and its paganistic morality, made them strangely familiar with the sharp claw, the bloody tooth and the mailed fist. The spirit of the century was one of ruthless individualism, and nowhere was it more ruthlessly expressed than in politics. If indeed one were " cousin to a lord, or had a vote in a rotten borough," then " the lord would provide,"[1] such provision generally taking the form of a sinecure post—possibly that of a paid commission in the army to a young lady or a child.[2] But the political life of the average subject consisted in obeying the laws devised, " under the Happy Constitution " by his " betters " ; in paying cheerfully the taxes, tithes, tolls and duties imposed upon him by the ruling oligarchy ; and in praying fervently that he escape the press gang, the highwayman, the stocks, the debtors' prison or the gallows, all of which were highly characteristic institutions of the " Land of Liberty " in the " Age of Reason."

*   *   *   *   *

Court life under the first two Georges (1714–1760) was no more chaste than that of Parliament and general politics. Overton and Relton, authoritative historians of the National Church of this period, describe the Court of these sovereigns as " little less immoral than that of Charles II, and infinitely more gross."[3]   Adam Smith's *Theory of Moral Sentiments* (1759) bristles with scathing references to the jealousy, pettiness, artificiality and indecency which long had pervaded Court society. " Are you in earnest resolved," asks Smith, " never to barter your liberty for the *lordly servitude* of a Court, but to live free, fearless and independent ? " If so, he advises one " never to enter " the place whence " so few return unspoiled."[4] He claims, too, that society is " dishonoured and degraded " by the " vices and follies " of the titled and the élite, and that " the great never look upon their inferiors as their fellow creatures."[5]

[1] G. M. Trevelyan, " The Age of Johnson " (*Johnson's England*, Vol. I, p. 1).
[2] W. C. Sydney, *England and the English in the Eighteenth Century*, I., pp. 347–8 ; also an historical paper by Sir Walter Scott in *Edinburgh Weekly Journal*, January 10th, 1827.
[3] *History of the English Church from George I to the end of the Century*, p. 7.
[4] A. Smith, *op. cit.*, p. 95.
[5] *Ibid.*, p. 93. See, too, pp. 87–101.

It is possible, however, to portray the ruling castes of eighteenth-century England in aspects too harsh and bleak. The well-known panegyrics of Voltaire and Montesquieu are a constant reminder of the enthusiasm which brilliant Frenchmen could generate for the English Constitution and for the practical working of the English political system. But even so, such panegyrics need not be taken too seriously. Voltaire, with his annual income of perhaps £7,000,[1] during his three years in England (1726-29), was received with open arms into the society of all the smart set, including Bolingbroke, Pope, Chesterfield, Gay and the Duchess of Marlborough : and his joyous discovery that the English nobility were as interested in all affairs of " money-making " as he himself, together with the pleasurable flattery he here received and his free participation in the free-thinking and free-living of the most exclusive Deistic society, caused him to acclaim England—" The land of Liberty." But pronounced as were Voltaire's courage and sagacity, his vanity, spleen and personal ambition were more pronounced ; and among the English oligarchy they were well fed. Of the *masses* of Englishmen, there is no evidence that Voltaire knew anything at all, or indeed that he cared to know anything. Montesquieu, who spent the years 1729 to 1731 in England, was received by the same circles as had fêted Voltaire ; but, as has often been observed, he never really understood the working of the " happy English Constitution " which in his *De l'Esprit des Lois* he so loudly extolled. Voltaire and Montesquieu, in brief, were spokesmen of those social classes (largely commercial) which already were wielding political power in England, but as yet only lusted for it in France. They therefore saw England through rose-coloured spectacles.

The glowing eulogies, too, of our " glorious " and " inimitable " Constitution by Blackstone and Burke require much toning down. Ere the advent of Blackstone's fame the public life of England was admittedly much improved, while certainly in the days of Burke's triumph that improvement was yet more pronounced. But both Burke and Blackstone were case pleaders : and is it not significant that whereas the Puritan Milton had received but £5 for his *Paradise Lost*, Blackstone, the Tory professor of English Law at Oxford, received £14,000 from his *Commentaries* ? Blackstone's laudation, therefore, of " English liberty "—which he himself denied to the negro slaves *in England* —was to the ruling oligarchy a highly appetising, if expensive, diet. Burke's deification of the English Constitution represented,

Voltaire " ultimately derived what would now be £20,000 a year." See *Chambers's Biog. Dict.*)

of course, the patriotic reactions of the decent and law-abiding Briton to the barbarities and atrocities of the French Revolution, which, for a generation, were to impede all English reform.[1] But when Burke's patriotism overflowed into economics and he formulated the neat but diabolical slogan, " the laws of commerce are the laws of nature and therefore the laws of God,"[2] he not only showed himself a slave to the " philosophy " of his age, but invited the venom of Marx who later retorted : " No wonder, then, that, true to the laws of God and nature, Burke always sold himself in the best market."[3]

On the accession of George III, Court life was sternly purged ; for whatever the failings of this enigmatic sovereign, the moral standards of his home and Court were unimpeachable. This fact largely explains both the admiration of practical moralists, like Wesley, and the smouldering fury of " free-living" aristocrats, like Fox, who resented the introduction of what they styled a " puritanical Court."[4] Then, too, it must be admitted that the Constitution, as interpreted after the " Revolution Settlement " of 1689, despite its many perversions, at least guaranteed to Parliament the right of reasoned criticism and debate, so that, as Walpole found in the case of his Excise Bill, and on other occasions, even a supreme oligarchy could not completely defy public opinion. Moreover the ruling class of England, different from the lordling satellites who surrounded the French and certain other Continental Courts, were firmly attached to the country-side, and thus knew something of the Nation's life ; while also, by heredity, tradition and experience, they were possessed of " political capacity "[5] in no mean degree. But all this admitted, the political and economic corruption of most of the century is undeniable ; and the more exhaustively it is probed, the more irresistibly does it point to a moral and spiritual source ; the bitter fruit sprang from a poisoned root.

(ii) *Criminal Laws and Their Administration*

The penal code, together with its legal administration and the prison system, even more than the corruption of politics, reveals the thinness of the cultural veneer disguising the deep savagery

[1] See P. A. Brown, *The French Revolution in English History* (1918) ; Edmund Burke's *Reflections* and *Thoughts on French Affairs*.
[2] Edmund Burke, *Thoughts and Details on Scarcity* (1800), p. 31.
[3] Karl Marx, *Capital* (Everyman ed., 1932), Vol. II, p. 843. The German original, *Das Kapital* (Vol. I), appeared in 1867.
[4] Jeudwine, *op. cit.*, p. 192.
[5] Lecky, I, p. 451.

of much of the eighteenth century. Even when Blackstone was elaborating the glories of our "unmatched Constitution," not only adults but children of both sexes, enjoyed the liberty of being hanged for no less than 160 different violations of the law.[1] To pick a pocket for more than one shilling, to grab goods from any one's hand and run away with them, to shop-lift to the value of five shillings, to steal a horse or a sheep, to cut a hop-bind, to break a young tree, to snatch gathered fruit and make off with it, to snare a rabbit on a gentleman's estate, or even to appear on the high road with a blackened face : these are typical offences for which a free Briton could be hanged. Charles Wesley's *Journal* records the fact that he preached in one jail to fifty-two felons waiting to be hanged, among them a child of ten.

In 1732 seventy persons received sentence of death in the Old Bailey alone,[2] while, throughout most of the century, at important quarters in cities and on highways, were to be seen gallows, often with their last corpses " left rotting in chains " —a gruesome warning to the populace. Lecky describes this penal code as " a mere sanguinary chaos," and Professor Rogers, in his *Six Centuries of Work and Wages*, depicts it as, " more sanguinary and brutal than any which a civilised nation had hitherto devised, or a high spirited one submitted to."[3] Moral and spiritual standards had largely broken down ; crime was mounting at an alarming pace, and the police system, as Fielding and others have shown, was little more than a farce. So the ruling castes turned to a ferocious penal code as a defence of their " property rights " ; and the fact that juries often would perjure themselves rather than convict for minor offences, was about the only check upon the ferocity of the Law.

Not infrequently seven, ten or fifteen culprits were executed at the same time and place, and these occasions came popularly to be styled " Hanging Shows." The executions at Tyburn, West London, for instance, which recurred every six weeks, drew such crowds that spectators paid for grand stand seats, and other " points of vantage " around the gallows, to see the " show " ; while multitudes packed the streets for the processions in which the " guests of honour " were the cart-loads of brandy-benumbed victims on their way to the Slaughter. Many are the contemporary impressions of these gallows

---

[1] See Sir Samuel Romilly, *Observations on the Criminal Code* (1810), also his *Observations on the Late Publication entitled " Thoughts on Executive Justice,"* p. 6.

[2] Andrews's *Eighteenth Century*, p. 271.

[3] J. E. T. Rogers, *op. cit.*, Vol. II, p. 490.

processions and hanging shows. But always there is depicted a roaring sale of " sots' comfort " (gin) from street barrows ; always a drunken brawl ; always a number of women with infants trampled down by the ruffian throng ; always a troop of hawkers, pickpockets, fakirs and prostitutes ; always a rabble of leary-eyed and tattered urchins, looking for pelf ; always a bevy bawling out the sale of " Dying Speeches " : and always these " speech-vendors " used the " same words, and the same tone " in *chanting* them. " Here's all the right and true last dying speech and confession," they droned, " birth, parentage, education, life, character and behaviour " . . . of the three, six, ten or fifteen " unfortunate malefactors " about to be executed.[1] The march from Newgate to Tyburn took about three-quarters of an hour. For a " good show " all the route partook of an extended carnival or fair. Hats, sticks, clubs, cloaks and kerchiefs were waved high in air ; dogs barked and yelped ; the half-inebriated roared and sang ; swaggering men and women pushed around the death-carts to grasp the culprits' hands and commend their high spirits. Sometimes the victims themselves actually fought with one another concerning their " order of precedence " in the carts. And always there were present—lurking, sinister characters " in mourning "—the " resurrection women," paid by surgeons to procure bodies for dissection ; for " gallows birds " were easy and coveted prey.

One contemporary, concluding a long description, says : " It is incredible what a scene of confusion all this makes, which yet grows worse near the gallows ; . . . the terrible blows that are struck, the heads that are broke, the pieces of swinging sticks and blood that fly about, the men that are knocked down and trampled upon, are beyond imagination."[2]

Muralt, too, a Swiss traveller in England, in the third decade of the century, has left an illuminating impression. " The criminals pass through the streets in carts," he says, " dressed in their best clothes, with white gloves and nosegays, if it be the season. Those that die merrily, or that don't at least show any great fear of death, are said to die like gentlemen ; and to merit this encomium most of them die like beasts, without any concern, or like fools, having no other view than to divert the crowd." Such, too, were the applauses of spectators and the general levity of these occasions, that Muralt confesses : " A man cannot well forbear laughing to see these rogues set themselves off as heroes, by an affectation of despising death."[3]

---

[1] See Sir Walter Besant, *op. cit.*, p. 548.
[2] *A Trip Through the Town*, pp. 26–31. Quoted by Besant, pp. 550–52.
[3] Muralt's *Letters on the English Nation*, p. 42f.

EIGHTEENTH CENTURY "SPORT"
(From old prints by courtesy of the R.S.P.C.A.)
1. Bull-baiting (top)   2. Bear-baiting (bottom)

Henry Fielding, the novelist, who in 1749 became chief magistrate of Westminster, speaks of these wretches as being " attended with the compassion of the meek and tender-hearted, and with the applause, admiration and envy of all the bold and hardened."[1] He also says of the hanging spectacles : " We sacrifice the lives of men, not for the reformation but for the diversion of the populace."[2] Yet Dr. Johnson, who, on the whole, was more compassionate towards criminals than Fielding,[3] was thoroughly upset when finally, in 1783, *public* executions were suppressed. Boswell faithfully records the Doctor's wrath : " The age is running mad after innovations . . . Tyburn itself is not safe from innovation. . . . Sir, executions are intended to draw spectators. If they don't draw spectators, they don't answer their purpose. The old method was satisfactory to all parties ; the public was gratified by a procession ; the criminal was supported by it ; why is all this swept away ? "

The hanging shows, however, were but symbolic of the spirit behind the penal code. After the Rebellion of 1745, Temple Bar, London, was long decorated with a row of heads betokening the fate of the Pretender's captured leaders ; and Horace Walpole points out that a flourishing business was there being conducted in renting spy glasses at a half-penny a look. Till the fifth decade of the century, persons found guilty of high treason were cut down from the gallows when only half-hanged, disembowelled, and their entrails burned before the howling mob.[4]

Till the middle of the century, too, women, for different crimes, including arson and husband murder, were, after semi-strangulation, publicly burned.[5] And not till 1771 was the law tepealed condemning prisoners refusing to plead on capital charges, to have iron weights placed on their bare chests, and slowly be " pressed to death " : though not for three decades preceding, had this barbarous law been enforced. But well into the second half of the century, and even after its close, certain brutalising legal punishments lingered on. The pillory long remained an established institution wherein unpopular victims sometimes perished from mob assaults ; branding on the hand continued ; whipping at the tail of a cart was still a familiar sight in many communities ; while the transportation of both sexes, and the flogging of women, survived the century.

[1] *Johnson's England*, Vol. I, p. 321.
[2] Dr. George, *op. cit.*, p. 7.
[3] *Johnson's England*, I., p. 316.
[4] Andrews, *op. cit.*, p. 281.
[5] See Blackstone's *Commentaries*, IV, Chap. vi. The law read, " burnt alive." It was not actually repealed till 1790.

I

The magistrates and officials, moreover, who enforced the law were often as callous as the law itself. Fielding's Justice Thrasher, in *Amelia*, and his Justice Frolic in *Joseph Andrews* are sketched from life. "Many of the justices," Smollett pronounced, "men of profligate lives, needy, mean, ignorant and rapacious," who "often acted from the most scandalous principles of selfish avarice."[1]   In rural and small-town areas most Justices of the Peace were squires, though about a fifth or sixth part were parsons ; and the power they exercised approached that of " petty sultans." The pillory, the stocks, the scold's bridle, the whipping post, the branding iron, transportation and atrocious jail were among the means whereby they demonstrated the virtues of the Happy Constitution in " the Land of the Free." In urban centres the enormities of " trading justices " and pettifogging lawyers marked such as social pests. Johnson, in his poem *London*, attacks " the fell attorney " who " prowls for prey " ; and certainly the " justice-shops " of the trading justices, by exploiting the shortcomings of a then " highly litigious people," beguiled many to their undoing.[2] Fielding represents these contemptible judges as interested always in the side of a case from which they could extract most personal gain. Nor was this mercenary taint always confined to the lower officials of the law : during a considerable part of the century the higher judges expected, and got, large sums of money as New Year " presents " from the Bar practising under them, while the gratuities of the Lord Chancellor, at this season, long ran into thousands of pounds.

(iii) *A Barbarous Prison System*

As for the prison system which accompanied this administration of justice, its horrors, owing to the labours of Oglethorpe, Wesley and Howard, are well known. Oglethorpe's Parliamentary Committee (1728–29) found that the " gross cruelties " perpetrated even upon debtors, amounted to little less than " deliberate torture."[3]   But for decades following these revelations, there was " no public conscience " to support reform. Not till Wesley began to awaken the soul of England and till Howard, Wesley's friend and apostle, gave his life to prison reform, was any progress registered ; and even then it was appallingly slow.

[1] T. B. Smollett, *History of England* (1790 Ed.), III, pp. 330–1.
[2] See Dr. George, *op. cit.*, p. 5.
[3] J. L. and B. Hammond, " Poverty, Crime, Philanthropy " (*Johnson's England*, I, p. 324).

On February 3rd, 1753, Wesley wrote in his *Journal* : " I visited one in Marshalsea prison, a nursery of all manner of wickedness. O shame to man, that there should be such a place, such a picture of hell, upon earth ! And shame to those who bear the name of Christ, that there should need any prison at all in Christendom ! " A few years later (1758–59) Dr. Johnson published in *The Idler* a poignant arraignment of the whole prison system, and of debtors' prisons in particular. Of the " multitudes " pining in those " cells of misery " he contended that most were there not because of any wilful fraudulence on their part, but because of " the wantonness of pride, the malignity of revenge, or the acrimony of disappointed expectation " on the part of their oppressors ; while of prison conditions he said : " The lewd inflame the lewd, the audacious harden the audacious."[1] In 1759 Wesley walked to Knowle, near Bristol, to see a company of French prisoners of the Seven Years War. His report is revealing : " About eleven hundred of them, we are informed, were confined in that little place, without anything to lie on but a little dirty straw, or anything to cover them but a few foul, thin rags, either by day or night, so that they died like rotten sheep. I was much affected, and preached in the evening on (Exodus XXIII. 9.) ' Thou shalt not oppress a stranger ; for ye know the heart of a stranger, seeing ye were strangers in the land of Egypt.' Eighteen pounds were contributed immediately, which were made up to £24 the next day. With this we bought linen and woollen cloth, which were made up into shirts, waistcoats, and breeches. Some dozens of stockings were added ; all which were carefully distributed, where there was the greatest want. Presently after, the Corporation of Bristol sent a large quantity of mattresses and blankets. And it was not long before contributions were set on foot at London, and in various parts of the Kingdom. . . ."[2]

On January 2nd, 1761, Wesley wrote a long, trenchant letter to the *London Chronicle*, commending the marvellous transformation which had taken place in Bristol's Newgate. That prison, he observed, was now " clean and sweet " ; there was " no fighting or brawling " ; " contending parties " were heard " face to face " before the keeper : " no drunkenness " was suffered ; nor any whoredom, the women prisoners being " kept separate from the men." Furthermore, industry was encouraged both by the free provision of tools and materials,

[1] *Idler*, Sept. 16th, 1758, and Jan. 6th, 1759.
[2] John Wesley, *Journal*, Oct. 15th, 1759.

and by the payment to prisoners of a " moderate profit " on all articles made ; public service was provided every Sunday and a sermon was also preached every Thursday ; medical treatment was given gratis to the sick, and " a large Bible was chained on one side of the chapel, which any of the prisoners may read." So remarkable was the transformation from the "filth, the stench, the misery, and wickedness " of previous days, that Wesley declared the prison to be wearing " a new face " and called for the blessing of God and man upon its remarkable Keeper and his amazing achievement. But how different was this Keeper's prison from those up and down the country ! In the concluding sentence of this letter, Wesley asked : " Meanwhile, will no one follow his example ? " In the opening sentence he had protested : " Of all the seats of woe on this side hell, few, I suppose, exceed or even equal Newgate (London)."[1]

When John Howard, in 1773, began his historic crusade, general prison conditions, though somewhat improved since Oglethorpe's day, were still extremely nauseous. Most jailers received no pay. Like trading justices they were jobbers. Hence, being dependent for livelihood upon bribes, tips, fees, extortions and the like, their tactics were based on intrigue and cunning. Profits on the open sale of vile intoxicants and on the covert permission of prostitution, together with weekly charges for " release from chains," were among their chief sources of revenue. Many persons moreover were confined in jails for months, or even years, awaiting the Assizes ; and many were detained after being pronounced innocent, because they could not pay the accumulated jailer's-bill. Notorious prisoners, too, like Jack Sheppard and Rev. Dr. Dodd, were still exhibited to the public, usually at a shilling-a-head. Sheppard in this way brought in £200.[2]

On the revelations of Howard's amazing and selfless career we dare not here pause. One or two quotations will suggest the problem he faced. At Ely, the prison being unsafe, " the

---

[1] Though Wesley does not here mention the fact, the Bristol Newgate was run by Mr. Dagge, an early convert of the Revival. His work must have been both a challenge and an inspiration to John Howard. See Dr. E. D. Bebb, *Nonconformity and Social and Economic Life, 1660–1800*, p. 153. Praise of Dagge's reforms appears in the *Annual Register* (1761), p. 61.

[2] In 1724, Sheppard, twenty-two years old, escaped four times from Newgate, forcing on his third evasion " six great doors." But before the end of the same year he was hanged at Tyburn, " in the presence of 200,000 spectators." Dodd, as a popular London clergyman and a King's Chaplain, had violently attacked Wesley. But before death it was to Wesley he turned for spiritual comfort. His crime was forgery.

jailer had endeavoured to secure the inmates by chaining them down on their backs upon the floor, placing an iron collar with spikes about their necks, and a heavy iron bar over their legs." [1] Thetford jail was " a small dungeon down a ladder of ten steps, with a small window " ; yet " in this pit, at the Summer Assizes . . . from sixteen to twenty persons were usually confined for several days and nights, without regard to age, sex or circumstances." Of Knaresborough jail, in 1776, Howard says : " It is under a hall of difficult access ; the door about four feet from the ground. Only one room about twelve feet square ; earth floor ; no fireplace ; very offensive ; a common sewer from the town running through it uncovered . . . an officer confined here took with him a dog to defend him from vermin ; but the dog was soon destroyed, and the prisoner's face much disfigured by them." [2]

Jail-fever too was one of the by-products of the filth and stench of most prisons of the time. In May, 1750, " two judges, the Lord Mayor (of London), several of the jury and sixty persons who were present in the Session House during a trial," died of jail-fever, contracted from a batch of filthy prisoners who before entering the dock had been subjected to long and heinous confinement. [3]

A study of the eighteenth century prison exhibits in the London Museum, will reveal something of the gruesome bestiality from which our modern prison system has been redeemed. The recent researches, too, of Dr. George, Professor Halévy and other scholars have proven conclusively that the earlier half of that century in England, particularly from 1720 to 1750, was a period of social retrogression, perhaps without parallel in modern times. Yet in 1752 David Hume, the materialistic philosopher and " intellectual monarch " of the time, was blandly asserting " that the privileges of the people have, during the past two centuries, been continually upon the increase." [4] Had Hume descended from the Olympian heights of his own frigid, assuming superiority and come to know something of the life of the common people of England, he would have realised that " the privileges of the people," far from increasing, had for some decades been declining : and had he the spiritual eyes to see, he would have realised also that the soulless scepticism of which he himself was chief propagator was a primary instrument of that retrogression. Gray, the

[1] See Sydney, *op. cit.*, Vol. II, p. 318.
[2] John Howard, *State of Prisons in England and Wales* (1777), p. 372.
[3] Besant, *London in the Eighteenth Century*, p. 644.
[4] David Hume, *Political Discourses*, p. 265.

poet, said of Hume " that he has continued all his days an infant, but one that has unhappily been taught to read and write."[1]   Is not this criticism equally applicable to the combination of intellectual sophistication and spiritual atrophy which characterised the ruling cliques of most of the century ?

(iv) *A Poignant Paradox*

With all its social, economic and political perversions, however, English public life, particularly after 1750, was not so utterly retrograde as that of France.   Even in the eighth decade of the century that libertine autocrat, Louis XV, who had spent hundreds of millions of livres from the Public Treasury upon his vain, flattering and intriguing mistresses, could blatantly boast : " In my person alone is the authority ; legislative power belongs to me alone ; public order emanates from me ; I am its supreme guardian."[2]   In England, Parliament, for all its corruptions, was a real instrument of Government, expressing at least the opinions of a landed and privileged minority.   Moreover, as Lecky points out, English law at this time, for all its cruelty, knew nothing either of " arbitrary imprisonment " or of the " barbarous punishment of the wheel " ; nor indeed of any other mode of designed, exquisite, diabolical torture.[3]

Howard's investigations too, show that bad as were most English prisons, many Continental lazarettos, with their studied and ghastly tortures, were worse.[4]   Indeed while Louis XV was still boasting " that he was France," in England certain things truly majestic already were emerging amidst the surrounding chaos.   More than twenty-five years before the century's close, the national conscience of England was beginning to awaken to the enormity of the whole slave-traffic ; two years before the storming of the Bastille, inspired solely by religious and philanthropic motives, the famous Abolition Committee was formed : and were it not for the French Revolution's set-back to all social reform in England, the suppression of the slave-trade throughout the British Empire would have been an eighteenth century achievement.   Long before the conclusion of the century, too, " South Sea Bubble finance " was a closed chapter in British history : a new sense of sobriety, morality

---

[1] Matthew Arnold, *Essays in Criticism* (first series), on Thomas Gray.
[2] See J. B. Perkins, *France under Louis XV* (1897).
[3] *Op. cit.*, I, p. 505.
[4] J. Howard, *An Account of the Principal Lazarettos in Europe*, (1780).

and earnestness was everywhere appearing ; drunkenness no longer was fashionable ; the " trading justice " and his " justice-shop " were now but vaguely remembered ; the harsh crassness of the prison system was greatly ameliorated ; " patriotism " was assuming a more lofty significance ; and already British Courts of Justice were beginning to win the admiration of the civilized world. A new moral outlook and philanthropic spirit were, in fact, everywhere apparent ; a temperate, thinking, industrious and religious Middle Class was springing rapidly into being ; and an unmistakable demand for Parliamentary reform was already becoming vocal.[1]

One of the most poignant paradoxes, moroever, of this highly paradoxical century was that, though mobs frequently were exploited by their " betters " to sinister ends—not infrequently being incited to the perpetration of dastardly outrages—and though both the Wesleys and Whitefield were at times the objects of mob fury, yet, on the whole, considering the range of their travels, the singularity of their methods and the propor-tions of their programme, these Spiritual Awakeners were wondrously received by the national multitude. True, John Wesley, with his customary plainness of speech, could on occasion refer to the " beasts of the people " ; but this " beastli-ness " was generally the effect of mobs being plied with alcohol or heated adroitly to " local patriotism " by squires, magistrates, parsons, or other designing " gentlemen." This mob violence moreover, when it occurred, was always local, not national : it was the exception, not the rule. The central Government never interfered with Wesley's life-long, national crusade : and, of the Common People, whom Wesley so dearly loved, and to whom he specially ministered, it may truly be said that, despite glaring exceptions, they received him and heard him gladly.

His intrepid courage, his transparent sincerity, his utter selflessness, his directness and dignity of appeal went, generally speaking, straight to the hearts of the dispossessed throng ; the sacred flame in his soul kindled the divine spark in theirs ; and they recognised him for what he was—the Friend of the People, the Mediator of Liberty, the Prophet of God. Often on the hustings the eighteenth century mob dealt to swashbuckling politicians black eyes, cracked heads, and broken ribs. Indeed so tempestuous was its fury, when fully unleashed, that Sir Walter Besant, in his close study of this period, pronounces the

[1] See Major John Cartright, *Take your Choice* (1776). This Democratic treatise is founded squarely on Bible and Christian principles.

London Mob—" brutal beyond all power of words to describe, or imagination to understand ; so bestial that one is induced to think there has never been in any town or in any age a population which could compare with them."[1]   Yet, in Wesley's case, all serious mob assaults in time collapsed ; more than once mob leaders with clubs raised over his head, but looked in his face and retired in shame—some to find their soul, and later to become Class leaders in his Cause. As Augustine Birrell puts it : " The mob knew and appreciated the difference between a Bubb Dodington and a John Wesley."[2]   During the fifty-two years of his open-air crusade, contesting three Kingdoms for Christ, Wesley experienced no really serious injuries at the hands of the mob : and one of the amazing features of the Mighty Revival he led was the life-sustained personal influence of this restrained, immaculate, erudite Oxford don, whose speech always was classical English, and whose bearing ever was that of the Christian gentleman, upon soldiers, sailors, publicans, miners, fishermen, smugglers and the roughest industrial workers.

Even as early as the " forties " of the eighteenth century, by the mouth of the pit and the door of the workshop, vast throngs of horny-handed and face-begrimed toilers removed their hats and stood in wrapt, reverent attention as Wesley, who never stooped to conquer, spoke to their souls of the eternal verities of Earth and Heaven ; of body, mind and spirit. Hundreds of English town-commons and market places, moreover, were transfigured temporarily into Cathedrals as multitudes *kneeled* solemnly on grass or cobble-stones, turning wistfully their faces toward Heaven, or burying them thoughtfully in their hands, as Wesley, in prayer, besought the Father God, through Christ, to send pardon, power and peace to sin-stained and broken lives. Wesley probably rode more miles over English roads than any other man who ever bestrode a beast : he rode in all manner of weather, by day and by night ; yet in an era when the chief thoroughfares of England were infested with highwaymen, never once was he robbed on the road. Often also the open-air crowds to whom he was preaching dealt a peremptory quietus to drunken " gentlemen " and other disturbers, who tried to break up his services ; and before his death, he was to witness many of no religious profession at all, coming voluntarily and gratuitously, after their working day, to help " the people called Methodists " to build " Preaching Houses."

[1] *London in the Eighteenth Century*, (Preface, p. viii).
[2] A. Birrell, K.C., *Miscellanies*.

In brief, despite the cruelty and coarseness, the drunkenness and depravity of the age, the multitude could still recognise true nobility and respond to the touch of soul power ; the British sense of sportsmanship, too, though often strangely perverted, was not wholly extinct : and to Wesley's spiritual eyes, there was high majesty latent even in the moral ruins of a prodigal and degraded, though inherently mighty, people. But all this is to anticipate, while both the perspective of our subject and the facts of history compel us to pause yet a little longer on the bleaker aspects of the age : for never can the problems the Great Revival faced be understood or appraised unless first we see clearly, and in some further detail, the incredibly difficult backgrounds in which it had to work.

CHAPTER VIII

EXPIRING HOPES

" I FOUND that deaths and discharges nearly made up the whole history of the lives of the parish infant poor . . . an English Church Warden, or ' Father of the Poor,' within the Bills of Mortality, under sanction of his Office, may suffer children to be starved to death, or poisoned with noxious air. Custom authorises the practice, and he may go on in it from generation to generation . . . and yet pass with impunity."

JONAS HANWAY, *Earnest Appeal for Mercy to the Children of the Poor* (1766). pp. 68, 72.

" SHOULD the drinking of this poison (gin) be continued at its present height during the next twenty years, there will, by that time, be very few of the common people left to drink it."

HENRY FIELDING, *On the late Increase of Robbers* (1751).

" A MAD bull to be dressed up with fireworks and turned loose in the game place, a dog to be dressed up with fireworks *over* him ; a bear to be let loose at the same time, and a cat to be tied to the bull's tail ; a mad bull dressed up with fireworks to be baited."

STRUTT's *Sports and Pastimes*, p. 259.

EXPIRING HOPES

Lord Bryce, after analysing the problems of modern Democracy, relates the story of an Oriental monarch, of uncertain temper, who commanded his astrologer to ascertain from the stars the time appointed for his Royal death. The astrologer cast his horoscope, but reported that it was impossible to discover the *exact* date set for the autocratic sovereign's demise. All the stars *clearly* revealed to him was that His Majesty's death " would *follow immediately on his own.*" So, contends Bryce, it must be in the case of Democracy : if ever Hope dies, the death warrant of Democracy will immediately be signed.[1]

But not only to Democracy is Hope essential. It is vital to the faith, the co-operation, the vision without which civilisations and peoples perish. Of the epoch in question however, Dr. H. W. V. Temperley, in the *Cambridge Modern History*, writes : " The earlier half of the eighteenth century in England was an age of materialism, a period of dim ideals and *expiring hopes* : before the middle of the century its character was transformed ; there appeared a movement headed by a mighty leader, who brought forth water from the rocks to make a barren land live again."[2] Now as to the historical accuracy of Dr. Temperley's verdict that England during the first half of the eighteenth century was " a barren land," blighted by " materialism," bereft of all save " dim ideals," and threatened with the *expiration of hope*, there can be no serious doubt : that fact is backed four square by a volume of evidence too weighty, too inescapable to admit even of challenge. But the conclusion that the " character " of the century was " transformed " by 1750, is premature. " Before the middle of the century " the *process* of transformation was vitally under way. Not however at Wesley's death (1791), nor even at the end of the century, was that transformation fully achieved ; and not till far into the nineteenth century were some of the noblest fruits of the " mighty leader's " sowing completely matured.

[1] See James Bryce, *Modern Democracies* (1921), Vol. II, p. 670.
[2] *Op. cit.*, Vol. VI, p. 76.

(i) *Treatment and Mortality of Children*

Nowhere is the *hope* of a people more unmistakably or more creatively expressed than in its protection, nurture and guidance of the Kingdom of Childhood : how then fared children in this age of " expiring hopes " ?   Their death rate tells its own tragic tale.   Only for London are authentic statistics available ; but they paint a portrait of unutterable woe.   The London Bills of Mortality show that in the period immediately preceding the advent of the Great Revival three out of four of all children, born of all classes, died before their fifth birthday : the exact percentage is 74.5.[1]   England therefore was then a land full of Rachels crying for their stricken babes.   Queen Anne bore seventeen children ; but only one, the Duke of Gloucester, survived infancy, and he died when eleven years old.   The plagues of the age did not spare even the bairns of Royal households ; but among the children of the very poor, Death stalked unchecked.

Jonas Hanway (1712–86) aptly described as " the eighteenth century Shaftesbury," was the unwearying friend of pauper and parish children.   Among the scores of his published works preserved in the British Museum Library are several revealing his investigations into the treatment and death rate of the Parish Infant Poor ; and the facts they unearth present a mirror of child tragedy.   In Hanway's *Earnest Appeal for Mercy to the Children of the Poor*, he tabulates the results of his examination of *all* the Parish Registers in Greater London for the years 1750 to 1755 inclusive.   In the Parish of St. Luke, Middlesex, for instance, 53 children had been received ; and *all* had died in the institution within twelve months of entry.   Several other parishes revealed 100 per cent. of deaths.   But in most districts a considerable proportion of the illegitimate infants were removed from the workhouse by their mothers, grandparents or other relatives ; and if these " discharged " children be subtracted from the lists, nearly all the remainder died within a twelve-

---

[1] See *Lancet*, 1835–36, I, p. 692.   (T. R. Edmonds, *On Mortality of Infants in England*).   Also A. K. Chalmers, M.D., *Growth of Maternity and Child Welfare Movement in Great Britain*, pp. 1–2.

DYING UNDER FIVE YEARS PER 100 BORN.

Period.			Rate.	Period.			Rate.
1730–49	..	..	.. 74.5	1790–1809 ..	..	..	41.3
1750–69	..	..	.. 63.0	1810–29	..	..	31.8
1770–89	..	..	.. 51.5				

month.[1] St. Andrew above Bars and St. George the Martyr, during the years in question, received 284 infants; of these 222 died within twelve months; 57 were "discharged" or returned to their mothers; and only five remained alive in the institution. St. Martin-in-the-Fields received 312 children; 158 had died; 147 were "discharged"; while but seven survived the parish's tender care. And so the tragedy continues. Commenting on the conditions discovered, Hanway says: "From this view of six years it may be presumed that for ages before the opening of the Foundling Hospital for such general reception,[2] the parish officers, within the Bills of Mortality, *sported away* the lives of many thousands of children. . . . The office of Church Warden, or Father of the Poor, was become a cruel exercise of authority, the officers acting as the wolf towards the lamb in the fable. If the child brought money it was squandered or deemed no object; if no money was brought, this was a secret reason why no expense should be made upon it, and in either case the child became a sacrifice." Of St. Clement Dane's parish, where in one year eighteen infants were received and all died before twelve months old, Hanway says the nurse seemed " to understand the art of lulling children to their everlasting rest." But the real blame he traced higher up. " The Officers," he charges, " are defendant, judge, jury and executioner, and they think it to their *interest* that the prisoner *should die*."[3]

There is infinite pathos in Hanway's statement: " I found that deaths and discharges nearly made up the whole history of the lives of the parish infant poor." Little wonder then that poignantly he pointed the moral to his contemporaries: " The pagan Chinese may legally drown female children; but an English Church Warden, or ' Father of the Poor,' within the Bills of Mortality, under sanction of his office, may suffer children to be starved to death, or poisoned with noxious air. Custom authorises the practice, and he may go on in it from generation to generation; he may do all he can to undo his country and yet pass with impunity."[4] In another treatise Hanway writes: " The parish infant poor's mortality may be

---

[1] Jonas Hanway, *op. cit.* (1766), pp. 68–9.

[2] The Foundling Hospital was started by Thomas Coram in 1739, the year after Wesley's " Conversion." In 1756, with Government support, it opened its doors to all; but soon its " gates were besieged," and in 1760 it had to restrict admittance. Hanway was one of its Governors.

[3] Hanway, *op. cit.*, pp. 69, 140.

[4] *Ibid.*, pp. 68, 72.

called 80 or 90, or if you please, upon those received under twelve months old, 99 per cent."[1]

Yet even as Hanway was making his discoveries and writing his reports, the Social Conscience was steadily awakening : and he himself was one of its noblest creations. Repeatedly he compared the conditions he encountered with the teaching and example of Christ, and frequently he pointed out that it " was *not* the will of God that one of these little ones should perish." Years earlier, Thomas Coram, agitating for the establishment of the Foundling Hospital, had referred to the large numbers of " exposed " children, and declared that he had himself witnessed " the shocking spectacle of innocent children who had been murdered, and thrown on dunghills."[2]   Again, in the *Memorial* (1739), petitioning Parliament to grant a charter for the creation of the Foundling Hospital, trenchant reference is made to the prevailing " murder of poor miserable infants " ; to the " inhuman custom " of exposing newly-born babes " to perish in the streets " ; to the placing of unhappy foundlings with " wicked and barbarous nurses " who for a " trifling sum " suffer them to " starve for want of due sustenance or care " ; and to the fact that the few who survive are generally turned " into the streets to beg or steal "—some being " blinded, or maimed and distorted in their limbs, in order to move pity," thus becoming " fitter instruments of gain " to " vile, merciless wretches."

Both Defoe and Hanway make reference to the incredibly vicious custom of " saddling the spit," which meant the holding of hilarious and bacchanalian parish-feasts by child " guardians," on the lump sums paid in for the rearing of illegitimate children. " Some vestries," wrote Defoe in 1727, " are more barefaced and even make a trade of a parish. I mean those churchwardens and vestries who lump it with harlots and whoremongers and take bastards off their hands at so much per head, for which they get a *good treat*, from two guineas to five according to the circumstances of their chap, which they call ' *saddling the spit*,' besides a good sum with the bantling (child), which 'tis to be feared is entirely sunk, all being done by connivance."[3]   Hanway says the practice of " saddling the spit " did " not give a day of life to the infant " ; a " speedy release from all expense " became the dominant motive ; while " the traffic of receiving money," he urged, seemed " but

---

[1] Hanway, *Letters on the Importance of the Rising Generation*, II, p. 136 (1768).
[2] See George, *op. cit.*, pp. 43, 334 (note 61).
[3] Daniel Defoe, *Parochial Tyranny*, p. 19.

a small remove from innocent blood."[1]   Burrington, too, in 1757, declared that he had been "informed by a man *now living* that the officers of one parish in Westminster received money for more than 500 bastards, and reared but one out of all that number."[2]   Hanway's protracted crusade on behalf of foundling and exploited children was, we repeat, one of the marks of the gradually awakening Social Conscience ; and that awakening was a product of the new religious emphasis on the sanctity of *all* human life.[3]

(ii) *The Gin Age*

The incredible bestialities practised in the earlier half of the eighteenth century upon friendless children become more understandable when it is remembered that this was *par excellence* " the Gin Age " of English history, and that Hogarth's pictures, " Election Entertainment " and " Gin Lane," far from being caricatures, are, in fact, realistic side-lights on the country's plight.   Lecky pronounces the national gin-drinking habit, which reached its zenith by the middle of the century, " the *master curse* of English life."[4]   The " curse " of national drunkenness, however, like most other social plagues, had a gradual development.   After the Restoration, the custom of drinking toasts to the sovereign became universal ; and this whetted the taste for alcohol.   In 1688 the beer brewed in England, with a population of but slightly over 5,000,000, was " no less than 12,500,000 barrels."   Meanwhile, too, large quantities of French brandy were being imported.   So the Government, in 1689, partly through " hostility to France " and partly " to encourage home distilleries," prohibited all importation of spirits, and on payment of small duties threw open the distilling business to all and sundry.[5]

Little did legislators then realise what they were doing : within a generation had arrived the " Gin Age," and with it, " cheap, fiery, poisonous " alcohol was flowing everywhere. Lecky gives the following figures to show how vile spirits in this period became a national beverage, out-rivalling beer.   In

---

[1] *An Earnest Appeal* . . ., p. 39.
[2] Burrington's *Answer to William Brackenridge's Letter*, p. 23.
[3] To appraise the epochal advance in child welfare since Hanway's day, see the author's *Dr. Barnardo : Physician, Pioneer, Prophet* (*Child Life Yesterday and To-day*), fourth cheap edition.   (Allen & Unwin, 2s. 6d.)
[4] Lecky, *op. cit.*, Vol. I, p. 476.
[5] *Parliamentary History*, XII, 1211–14.

1684 only 527,000 gallons of spirits were distilled in England ; by 1714 the number was 2,000,000 ; in 1727 it had risen to 3,601,000 gallons ; in 1735 it was 5,394,000 ; by 1742 it struck 7,000,000 ; and when in 1750 it reached its peak, the consumption of spirits was 11,000,000 gallons. The resulting welter of national drunkenness, Bishop Benson declared, had made the English people " what they never before were, cruel and inhuman."[1] Wesley, consequently, was giving vent to no fanaticism when repeatedly he pronounced the liquor traffic, which meanwhile had developed titanic vested interests, an arch plague among his countrymen.

Some idea of the strangle-hold in which this traffic had engripped the nation, may be gauged by the fact that when things reached their " lowest depths " (1750), 506 of the 2,000 houses in St. Giles (Holborn), London, were gin-shops ; while in addition the area had eighty-two tuppenny common lodging houses—all of them vicious brothels—wherein " gin was the principal liquor drunk."[2]   In the entire Holborn district, one house in every five-and-a-quarter was a gin-shop ; even in Westminster, every eighth house plied the same deadly business ; gin was sold from barrows in the streets, and secretly from cellars and attics ; and before the accumulated horrors of back alleys in these gin-inflamed areas, imagination pales. The case of Judith Dufour, recorded in the Old Bailey *Session Papers* (February, 1735), is suggestive of many. This woman brought her toddling child from the workhouse where it had just been clothed, strangled it, threw the body in a Bethnal Green ditch, sold the clothes for one shilling and fourpence, and forthwith spent the money on gin, which she shared with another woman who had connived in the murder.

Henry Fielding, in 1751, as a London magistrate, affirmed gin " the principal sustenance (if it may be so called) of more than 100,000 people in this Metropolis," deploring, at the same time, " the dreadful effects " which he had " the misfortune every day to see and to smell, too." " What must become," he asks, " of an infant who is conceived in gin, with the poisonous distillations of which it is nourished, both in the womb and at the breast ? "[3]   Again his blind—but far-seeing—brother, Sir John Fielding, who on Henry's death, in 1754, succeeded him as Bow Street Magistrate, attacking " this liquid fire by which men drink their hell beforehand," declares its vendors " the principal officers of the King of Terrors," who conveys " more

---

[1] Lecky, I, pp. 479–81 ; and Fraser's *Life of Berkeley*, p. 332f.
[2] George, *op. cit.*, p. 41 ; see, too, *Johnson's England*, Vol. I, p. 312.
[3] *Enquiry into the Late Increase of Robbers* (1751), p. 19.

to the regions of death than the sword or the plague."[1]   Rev.
James Townley's protest, in 1751, is only less emphatic :

> " Gin, cursed Fiend, with Fury frought,
>   Makes human Race a Prey,
> It enters by a deadly Draught,
>   And steals our Life away."

During the national " orgy of spirit drinking " (1720-51),
crude gin was being sold from thousands of grimy dens at even a
penny a pint ; and so all-consuming was the craving for the
initial excitement and the ensuing oblivion of intoxication,
that many gin shops hung signs reading : " Drunk for 1d :
Dead Drunk 2d. : Free Straw."[2] Some dens, appealing to
the more fastidious, advertised " *Clean* Straw," Nor was this
passion for alcohol confined to the congested denizens of back
alleys and slums. Its ravages affected all classes. As early as
1708 Defoe, referring to the corruption of elections, averred
that " it is not an impossible thing to debauch this nation
into a choice of thieves, knaves, devils, anything, comparatively
speaking, by the power of various intoxications."[3] Houghton,
Walpole's country seat, was a frequent scene of boisterous
drunken revelries, whose origin is easily traced ; for when
Walpole was a young man his father used to pour into his glass
" a double portion " of wine, saying : " Come, Robert, you
shall drink twice while I drink once ; for I will not permit
the son in his sober senses to be a witness of the intoxication
of his father."[4]

A generation later, in Sir Robert's heyday—the age of
" peeping-galleries " and " drinking-bouts "—when " gentlemen," squires and judges boasted of being " four " and " five-
bottle " men, a fashionable father would not have scrupled
about his son witnessing his inebriation : for in that era " the
Mother of Parliaments," on various occasions, adjourned early
because " the honourable Members were too drunk to continue
the business of State " ; and marriages, when possible, were
solemnised in the morning to ensure the sober senses of the
contracting parties. Indeed, among the mounting thousands
of " Fleet marriages,"[5] one or other of the contracting persons

---

[1] *A Brief Description of London* (1776), p. xxiii.
[2] Lecky, *op. cit.*, I, p. 479.
[3] Wilson's *Life of Defoe*, III, p. 23f.
[4] Lecky, I, p. 478 ; W. Coxe's *Walpole*, I, p. 758f.
[5] Dr. George, *op. cit.*, pp. 314-15 ; Lecky, I, pp. 490-1. Lecky says :
" It was proved before Parliament that on one occasion there had been
2,954 Fleet marriages in four months." Lord Hardwicke's Marriage Act
(1753) put a stop to Fleet marriages.

was nearly always sodden drunk, and rarely were the " vagabond parsons " who performed such unions—generally in " pubs."— completely sober. Even lord-bishops at this time too commonly were " good fellows " among the country gentry; and when they became " over merrie," a favourite witticism was to imply that " only as lords, and not as bishops," did they imbibe so freely : for the phrase " drunk as a lord," carried then a peculiar pertinence.

An exhaustive survey of the ramifications of the liquor traffic during the ascendancy of the gin period would itself fill a volume. Increasingly " the trade " came to be associated with the landed interests; vast fortunes were amassed from the manufacture of cheap alcohol, and vicious vested interests became deeply entrenched. In many crafts, including all branches of building, the custom became established of paying wages late on Saturday night in public houses and other drinking dens; every workman was " expected " to purchase at least a quart of drink; " proper sports " of course bought more; and, as frequently the pay-desk was not opened till near midnight, many an artisan returned to his family " drunk and empty-handed," thus causing " words and blows."[1] All manner of clubs, too, met regularly in drinking quarters, many beginning as benefit fraternities and degenerating into mere drinking rabbles. Even Vestries often met in public houses; wedding and funeral services were sometimes conducted in them, while frequently convivial baptismal parties were held therein.

The whole apprenticeship system, too, was tied, almost inextricably, to the drinking habit. Every step and stage of advance in an apprenticeship exacted a levy for a drinking-bout; while every promotion of a full-fledged craftsman was the occasion of a similar carousal. Benjamin Franklin, in his *Autobiography*, records vividly his experience in 1725, when working in Watts' printing house, London, among " great guzzlers " of alcohol. His companion in the press room drank daily six pints of " muddling liquor "; the cost was about five shillings a week; generally he was in debt; " and thus," says Franklin, " these poor devils keep themselves always under." After a few weeks in the press room, Franklin was called to the composing room, where a " new " *bien venu* (sum for drink) of five shillings was demanded of him. Having " paid below," he at first withstood the demand; but this made him " an excommunicate ": so whenever he left the room " the chappel

---

[1] See Sir John Fielding, *Observations on Penal Laws* (1761). Justice Buller, Justice Colquhoun and Wilberforce were among those who led public opinion against this social curse.

ghost " mixed his type, transposed his pages and broke up his matter. In little over a fortnight he found himself " obliged to comply and pay the money, convinced of the folly of being on ill terms with those one is to live with continually " ; and often to avoid abuse or ill-feeling, he had to lend " near thirty shillings a week " to fellow craftsmen who " continued sotting with beer."[1]

Till well into the second half of the eighteenth century, it was not uncommon for publicans to be constables, or watchmen. Many Justices of the Peace, too, and Members of Parliament, as well as squires and lords, were " deeply interested " in the distilling and brewing trades. The young savages of boasted aristocratic blood who, as " Mohocks,"[2] in the early decades of the century, committed such outrages upon women and wrought such barbarities on London's streets, were always regaled with alcohol and always sallied forth on their mad " sport " from " pubs." Drinking " dives," too, were the regular quarters of crimps, touts, pliers, kidnappers, highwaymen, pickpockets, and fakirs of every description ; while commonly lawyers, physicians and merchants conducted much of their business over jugs of intoxicants, in the heady atmosphere of the public house.[3]

In a hundred ways eighteenth century liquor interests laid a corrupting hand on industry and business ; but no practice was more contemptible than that of " buying carcases," a species of guile clearly described by Dr. William Smith, the benefactor of many prisoners. In the case of an " ingenious " craftsman the publican " encourages him to drink till he gets considerably in debt." Then his note is demanded, " which the publican sells to some person in the same trade with the debtor, who is obliged to work for his creditor, or go to gaol."[4] Defoe as early as 1702 said that to be " an honest, drunken fellow " was " a character in a man's praise " ; but the " honest, drunken fellow " found many dishonest, drunken fellows ever ready to prey upon his honesty. Dr. George, in her recent research into the eighteenth century, has been driven to agree with the vast majority of disinterested and reputable contemporaries that the cardinal cause of the admitted social retrogression between 1720 and 1750, was the multi-headed liquor traffic, with its fiery spirits and strong beers, and its innumerable

---

[1] See " The Water American " (*Model English Prose*. Edited by Professor G. R. Carpenter), pp. 73–4.
[2] Lecky, I, p. 482 ; Swift's *Journal to Stella*.
[3] See Sir Walter Besant, *London in the Eighteenth Century*, p. 241.
[4] Dr. W. Smith, *Mild Punishments Sound Policy* (1778), p. 42.

ramifications in the nation's work-a-day life.[1] The number
even of eminent men whose lives in the eighteenth century
were blighted by drink is too great to cite. Bolingbroke, Oxford,
Chesterfield, Addison, Steele, Cartaret, Pulteney, Pitt, Fox,
Goldsmith and Burns, to say nothing of Walpole, are but
illustrative of its highly talented victims.[2] As for the multitude,
Henry Fielding's *Increase of Robbers* (1751) predicted that,
" Should the drinking of this poison be continued at its present
height during the next twenty years, there will by that time, be
very few of the common people left to drink it." This drunkenness, however, was an *effect* as well as a cause of social
retrogression ; it was an expression of the demoralising *Zeitgeist*
of the age.

In 1736 an Act was passed (9 George II, C. 23) designed
practically to prohibit the trade in spirituous liquors ; but having
no real support in public opinion, it was still-born. Again in
1743, despite the opposition of the bench of bishops, a Bill was
carried (16 George II, C. 8) for the suppression of the increasing
" clandestine trade." It too was futile. Not till 1751, when
the vehement temperance teaching of the Evangelical Revival
had already been heard throughout the land, and when groups
of converts in every considerable community were committed
to total abstinence, was Law of any avail. In that year the famous
Act passed by the Pelham Government (24 George II, C. 40)
marked the *legislative* beginning of Britain's emancipation from
the thraldom of the liquor traffic. Progress, indeed, was all too
slow. But never again was drunkenness in England comparable
to the bestial degradation of the preceding half-century.
Relatively, in 1751, the " Gin Age " closed.[3]

(iii) *Perverted Conceptions of Sport*

The chief sports of the time were characteristic of a rum-
inflamed mentality, cruelty, gambling and coarseness being their
outstanding marks, and the ruthless torture of animals their
pivotal allurement. Typical, for instance, of the amusements
advertised in London, in the third decade of the century, is the
following : " A mad bull to be dressed up with fireworks
and turned loose in the game place, a dog to be dressed up with

---

[1] *London Life in the Eighteenth Century.* See especially Introduction and
chapters I and VI.
[2] Lecky, I, pp. 477–8.
[3] For nineteenth and twentieth century aspects of the liquor traffic, see
Dr. J. Wesley Bready's *Lord Shaftesbury and Social-Industrial Progress*,
chapter XXI. (Allen & Unwin, fourth cheap edition, 7s. 6d.)

fireworks *over* him ; a bear to be let loose at the same time, and a cat to be tied to the bull's tail ; a mad bull dressed up with fireworks to be baited."[1] The " baiting " of bulls, bears, badgers, etc., was specially popular. Usually these " shows " took place in public house grounds or on village commons ; but not infrequently they were conducted in village Church yards or on Cathedral greens. In the case of bull-baiting the " bullard," arriving with his animal in any village, invited the patronage of all " bull-hankers." The beast then was chained to a stake and anyone who paid a shilling might set his dog at him for a specified time. Frequently, of course, the dogs were gored and killed ; more frequently they were hurled high into the air, and often their owners carried long staves to break their fall. But the condition of the tortured bull was extremely pitiable ; fighting perhaps a dozen dogs in a day, " his head and neck invariably were disfigured with scars," while raw, bleeding wounds were always in evidence.[2]

Bear-baiting was after the same order ; but for this sport an admission of at least 3d. to 6d. was charged, the bear being a rarer animal and providing a " better show." Two or three dogs were set on a bear at once, and anyone who brought a " game dog " was " admitted gratis." An advertisement in the *Daily Advertiser* (January 29th, 1747), describing a bear about to be baited as " the celebrated white sea-bear . . . arrived at his utmost strength and perfection," says : " It is not doubted from his uncommon size, excessive weight, and more than savage fierceness, but he will afford extraordinary entertainment ! " The same newspaper, on November 28th of the same year, describes a *he-tiger* about to be baited as " the largest that ever was seen here, being eight feet in length," and " one of the fiercest and swiftest of savage beasts." The journal, of course, predicted that the baiting would " afford good sport." A London attraction in 1717 advertised as its chief turn " the baiting of a tiger by *six* bull and bear dogs " ; while the lesser items, of the same entertainment included the playing at " blunts " (i.e. fighting with sticks) by six young men, " he to get the prize who broke most heads."[3] Sometimes these animal torturing shows advertised that a bear would be " baited *to death*," in which case the entertainment would begin " exactly at three o'clock in the afternoon, because the *sport continued long*."[4]

[1] Strutt's *Sports and Pastimes*, p. 259. See, too, Sydney's *England and the English*, Vol. I, p. 180.
[2] See E. D. Cuming, " Sports and Games " (*Johnson's England*, Vol. I, p. 375).
[3] See Besant, *op. cit.*, p. 440.
[4] *Weekly Journal* (June 9th, 1716).

So popular and so lucrative proved the bear-baiting sport that London alone, in the first half of the century, had four recognised " bear-gardens "—one on Bankside, Southwark, one south of Soho Square, another in Tothill Fields and the far-famed one of Hockley-in-the-Hole, where one proprietor, Christopher Preston, was " killed and devoured " by " his own bears."[1] In the case of badger-baiting, the badger was secured to a stake by " a chain passed *through* his tail," and because of the amazing strength of his jaws " he might maim or kill half a dozen dogs before he succumbed himself."[2]

Cock-fighting, however, was the universal sport ; to it all classes, from peer to cowherd, were " addicted " ; and from its peculiar parlance, have sprung such vernacular expressions as " pit against," " cut out for," " scoot " and " cock-pit." In the case of a ploughman or labourer who simply sharpened the beak and spurs of his bird with a knife, he normally would take his cock in a sack to a public house and challenge anybody present to pit one against it. Then, after all bets had been placed, the cocks would be shaken from their bags and the fight would continue for perhaps an hour, generally till one bird was killed. But more than likely some rustic would now produce a " surprise sack " and bet a roast goose or a barrel of beer that his cock could " lick " the winner. Time would then be allowed for a round of " drinks " and the arrangement of new bets, before the victor, still half-exhausted, would face his new foe. In the case of *organised* rural cockings, they commonly were held in village churchyards ; the roosters on such occasions being equipped with sharp steel or silver " heels," two to two-and-a-half inches long : and perhaps a dozen birds in turn would be set to " win their spurs," or die in the attempt.

The " great " cocking events however took the form of the Main or Welsh Main and in these tournaments, generally lasting from two to five days, county was pitted against county, town against town, peer against peer ; while the stakes not uncommonly ran as high as a thousand guineas. In order that one competitor should win a majority of battles, a Main had to consist of an odd number of cocks, forty-one being usual, and in the case of a " Welsh Main " it was customary, after several days battle, for every bird save the final victor to be killed in fight. Small wonder therefore that, at the conclusion of a cocking, it was often said that both promoters and spectators were " glutted with blood." Yet many eighteenth century clergymen bred fighting cocks and supported this " royal

[1] Besant, p. 440.   [2] Cuming, *op. cit.*, p. 375.

sport," while sometimes Church bells were rung to honour a local winner of a Welsh Main.

Cock-fighting, admittedly, was all too prevalent in England before the eighteenth century ; but it was left to the first half of that century to popularise metal spurs, to introduce " long mains " ; greatly to multiply stakes, and to make cocking a recognised and accepted school sport.[1]

Other "sports" with birds were equally brutalising. A favourite was to bind an owl tightly on a duck's back and throw them into a lake. The duck, of course, dived to free itself of its burden ; the owl floundered and fought, and often both birds were dead before the " fun " stopped. In the case of " goose-riding " a live goose with " neck well greased " was suspended by the feet from a high horizontal bough or pole, and competitors, riding beneath at a gallop, tried to snatch off its head. " Cock-throwing " expressed English antipathy to the French, then symbolised by that much-abused bird. A trained cock was tied by the leg to a peg, and from a distance of twenty-two yards you might throw at him with a broomstick for a penny a shot, or six shots for 5d. If you knocked him over and could run and seize him before he rose, the bird was yours. The setting of trained dogs, also, on domestic ducks in lakes was a favourite recreation ; hunting, in general, was excessively cruel ; while horse racing at this period, says Cuming, " was less a contest of speed than a running fight among the jockeys."[2]

An early eighteenth century race was frequently run in three heats of four miles each on the same day and represented an endurance test both for horses and jockeys. Any beast " on four legs might be entered and flogged over the course " ; crossing and jostling were quite in order ; jockies lashed, kicked and entwined legs in attempts to unseat each other, while some were not above boasting of the " eyes and teeth " they had " beat out."[3] The crowds around the course were of the same kidney. If a jockey lost a race, those who lost their bets were likely to set upon him with stones, sticks, ropes and whips, to remind him he " could not ride " : if he won, he was almost certain of like abuse as a rogue and a cheat from the large rabble who had " backed " other favourites.

Cudgel play and pugilism, again, were popular sports, known

[1] Cuming, p. 372ff ; Roberts's *Social History of the Southern Counties*, p. 421f ; Chambers's *Domestic Annals of Scotland*, III, p. 268f ; Latimer's *Annals of Bristol*, p. 140f ; Besant, *op. cit.*, p. 437f ; and Hogarth's engraving, " The Cock Pit."

[2] *Op. cit.*, p. 364.

[3] J. Lawrence, *History and Delineation of the Horse*, p. 249.

to every community.   In the former the contestant who first
clubbed blood from his opponent's head, was acclaimed winner
of the bout[1] :   the latter, as practised in the first half of the
century, has been aptly described as " downright slaughtering."
No gloves or mufflers were then allowed to interfere with the
grandeur of the " noble art " ;   and women as well as men
through this medium might court the favour of the mob.   In
the case of a pugilist who had hammered his way to fame,
he generally won the patronage of a sporting peer and became
the object of huge bets ;   but every district had its popular
local " bruisers," male and female, and all contests, " prize "
or local, till the latter part of the century, were fought on a
stage scarcely raised above the ground.   Hence backers of a
fighter who was faring badly often would " force their way
into the ring, and, with kicks and blows, strive to disable his
opponent."   Many a pugilist was so cruelly beaten-up that he
had to be carried from the ring.[2]

The noble art lent itself to all manner of occasions, and many
are the fighting challenges which appeared in the eighteenth
century press.   On October 7th, 1728, the *Daily Post*, in
announcing a " boxing match " to be held that day in an
amphitheatre in Islington Road, London, printed this challenge :
" Whereas I, Ann Field, of Stoke Newington, ass driver, well
known for my abilities in boxing in my own defence . . .
having been affronted by Mrs. Stokes, styled the European
championess, do fairly invite her to a trial of her best skill in
boxing for £10, fair rise and fall ;   and question not but to give
her such proofs of my judgment that shall oblige her to acknowledge me championess of the stage, to the satisfaction of all
my friends."   Alongside was printed Mrs. Stokes's reply :   " I
Elizabeth Stokes, of the City of London, have not fought in
this way since I fought the famous boxing woman of Billingsgate
nine minutes, and gained a complete victory, which is six years
ago ;   but as the famous Stoke Newington ass woman dares me
to fight her for £10, I do assure her I will not fail meeting her
for the said sum, and doubt not that the blows which I shall
present her with, will be more difficult for her to digest than
any she ever gave her asses."

In this gin period moreover many an " emancipated "
woman, after a round of angry argument with a man, challenged
him to strip off his coat and " prove his manhood," which
frequently he quite failed to do.   But these " mixed " fights
were generally spontaneous affairs fought off in drinking-house

---

[1] *Johnson's England*, I, p. 378.   [2] *Ibid.*, p. 376f.

" parlours " or yards, for the sole amusement or edification of those who then happened to be present. They were part and parcel of everyday brawls and rarely found their way into the press. Newspaper notices however, of formal challenges and fights between women were almost as common as those between men. In June, 1722, the *London Journal* printed this challenge : " I Elizabeth Wilkinson, of Clerkenwell, having had some words with Hannah Highfield and requiring satisfaction, do invite her to meet me on the stage and box with me for three guineas, each woman holding half-a-crown in each hand, and the first woman that drops her money to lose the battle."[1] The said Hannah, the *Journal* continued, " hearing of the resolution of Elizabeth, will not fail to give her more blows than words, desiring home blows and from her no favour." Even as late as 1768 a London paper (June 22nd) reported that : " On Wednesday last two women fought for a new shift (shirt) valued at half-a-guinea, in the Spa Fields near Islington. The battle was won by a woman called ' Bruising Peg,' who beat her antagonist in a terrible manner."[2]

For prize fights between famous male bruisers, who battled bare-fisted, with little science and few restraining rules, the Age of Reason could muster mobs of 12,000 spectators, to whom " downright slaughtering " was capital sport.

(iv) *Gambling—a National Obsession*

The gambling mania of this era—a subject much discussed both by political and general historians—is a matter of universal admission, though often the tyranny of its grip is but little understood. The Government regularly raised vast sums by popular lotteries : even the building of Westminster Bridge (1736) and the founding of the British Museum (1753) were financed chiefly by this means.[3] Parliament was full of gamblers, and the smart Clubs of West London were nearly all gaming dens. White's was the favourite centre of aristocratic Tories, and Almack's (later Brooks's) of aristocratic Whigs, while at more Bohemian centres, like the " Cocoa Tree," both met for equally high stakes. Horace Walpole, writing to Sir Horace Mann (February 2nd, 1770), says : " The young

---

[1] The idea of holding a half-crown in each hand was that the women would thus be kept from scratching each other's eyes and tearing each other's hair.

[2] Sydney, Vol. I, p. 177.

[3] See Macpherson's *Annals of Commerce*, Vol. III, p. 300.

men of the age lose ten, fifteen, twenty thousand pounds in an evening there (Almack's). Lord Stavordale, not one-and-twenty, lost £11,000 there last Tuesday, but recovered it by one great hand at hazard. He swore a great oath—' Now *if* I had been playing *deep*, I might have won millions '."[1] Lord Ilchester " lost £13,000 at a single sitting " ; the Duke of Devonshire " lost his estate, ' Leicester Abbey,' at a game of basset " ; Lord Mountford who committed suicide on New Year's Day, 1755, had spent the preceding night gambling " deep " and losing heavily at White's ; the Hon. John Damer, who also made his quietus with a pistol, was involved in gambling debts to the tune of £70,000. Miss Pelham, daughter of the Prime Minister, was but a notorious representative of the gambling intoxication among high-born women ; Lady Cowper, in her *Diary*, speaks of sittings at Court at which " the lowest stake was 200 guineas " ; even Addison relates that he won £1,000 in a lottery : and Swift says that Lord Oxford never passed White's without bestowing upon it a curse as " the bane of the English nobility."[2]

Sir John Bland, M.P., who " died suddenly abroad " in 1755, had " squandered his entire fortune " at hazard[3] : at one point in a night's play, reports Horace Walpole, Bland had " lost two and thirty thousand pounds "[4] ; while at an earlier date the Duke of Bedford forfeited almost an equal sum in a single night's fling. That gay wag George Selwyn who entered Parliament in 1747, two years after his expulsion from Oxford " for a blasphemous travesty on the Eucharist," seems to have spent most of his time around " gaming hells " and was the means of leading many a young patrician into the trap.[5] He it was who, in 1756, on seeing Ponsonby, Speaker of the Irish House of Commons, airily toss a fat roll of notes over a gaming table at Newmarket, exclaimed : " Look how easily the Speaker passes the money bills ! " George Harley Drummond, of the famous banking house of Charing Cross, dropped £20,000 at whist, and was " forced to resign his partnership in the firm " ; while, at the " Cocoa Tree," one cast at hazard awarded the

---

[1] Horace Walpole's *Letters* (Cunningham Ed.), Vol. V, p. 226.
[2] Lecky, I., p. 522f. ; Sydney, I, p. 230ff.
[3] For a vivid, though perhaps overdrawn, picture of the gambling mania on the Continent, see Thackeray's *George the First* (*Works*, Vol. X, pp. 285–307). European Princes, in " play," sometimes gambled the lives of whole regiments of their army as mercenaries for foreign service.
[4] H. Walpole, *Letters*, Vol. II, p. 425.
[5] *Chambers's Biog. Dict.*, p. 841 ; Jesse's *George Selwyn and His Contemporaries*, Vol. III, p. 137f ; *Life of Wilberforce*, by his sons, Vol. I, p. 117.

victor no less than £140,000.[1] Gay ladies, too, it was openly whispered, sometimes gambled themselves into immorality :

> " And when the Fair One can't the Debt defray
> In Sterling Coin—does Sterling Beauty pay ? "[2]

The classic gambling victim however was the brilliant Charles James Fox who, before reaching his twenty-fourth year, was committed at high interest to the Jews for gaming debts of some £100,000. Sportively Fox dubbed the retiring room where Hebrew creditors waited after his play to adjust accounts, his " Jerusalem Chamber." Gibbon drolly recalls a certain twenty-two hour spell of Fox's " recreation " at the " trifling cost of £500 per hour," and Horace Walpole wonders what the said gentleman will do when he has " succeeded in selling the estates of all his friends." Fox's passion for gambling had been implanted by his notorious father, Lord Holland. When the future statesman was but fifteen, sojourning at Spa, his father gave him a rouleau of guineas to stake on the gaming tables there ; at sixteen he was a member of Brooks's ; at twenty-four he was a dupe of " the Honourable " Mrs. Grieve, who " gave advice on all emergencies for half-a-guinea," and who persuaded Fox that she could manage a marriage for him with a certain Miss Phipps, then " on her way from the West Indies to England with a fortune of £80,000." It was only when Mrs. Grieve was arrested by another of her dupes, that Fox's dealings with her were revealed.[3]

Sir G. O. Trevelyan's *Early Life of C. J. Fox* delineates the society of the day as " one vast casino." Horace Walpole, writing to Mann in August, 1776, asks : " Can you believe that Lord Foley's two sons have borrowed money so extravagantly, that the interest they have contracted to pay amounts to £18,000 a year ? " Smaller fry often found themselves fleeced of their " little all." Oliver Goldsmith, at twenty-one, was " equipped with £50 to study law in London " ; but before ever he saw London, it all " disappeared at a Dublin gaming-table." Some four years later, " at play " in Leyden, he again lost every penny he possessed. Little wonder therefore that he " died £2,000 in debt."[4] Nor could a twentieth century gangsters' den, have taught much to the infamous " gambling hells " of the Age of Reason, concerning the use of cunning, *camouflage* and guile. In 1731, the Editor of the *St. James's*

[1] See Botsford's *English Society in the Eighteenth Century*, p. 245f.
[2] Mrs. Centilevre, *The Gamester* (1705), Epilogue.
[3] *Correspondence of C. J. Fox* (Edited by Lord J. Russell), Vol. I, p. 94.
[4] See " Goldsmith " (*Chambers's Biog. Dict.*).

Evening Post published a typical " list of officers," attached to
the more noxious gaming houses of the day : and among the
considerable band were included an " operator," who deals
the cards at a " cheating game called faro " ; " Puffs " with
" money given them to decoy others to play " ; a " Clerk,"
who checks upon the puffs " to see that they sink none of the
money given them to play with " ; a " Squib," who is a puff
of lower rank, serving at half-salary while learning to deal ;
" Flashers," who subtly move among new plungers recalling
" how often the bank has been stripped " ; a " Dunner," who
strives to recover money lost at play ; a " Waiter," to serve
wine, etc. ; an " Attorney " ; a " Captain," to handle any who
are peevish about losing money ; an " Usher," who lights
patrons up and down stairs and gives the word to the Porter,
" who is generally a soldier of the foot guards " ; an " Orderly
Man," who walks up and down outside the door, to give notice
to the porter, and alarm the house at the approach of constables ;
a " Runner," who is to get intelligence of justices' meetings ;
together with " Link-boys," " Watchmen," " Chairmen,"
" Drawers," " Affidavit men," " Ruffians," " Bailees," *cum
multis aliis.*[1]

(v) *Immorality as Sport*

Even immorality, under cloak of the " nature worship " and
" natural expression " propounded by Deism, was, during most
decades of the century, largely winked at as " sport."
George II, Walpole and the Prince of Wales were but representative of a large section of " high society " who lived in flagrant,
shameless adultery. Lady Montagu, in October, 1723, writing
to the Countess of Mar, declared that, in society " the appella-
tion of rake is as genteel in a woman as in a man of quality."
The Drury Lane district of West London was an extensive
seraglio, and such terms as " Drury Lane Vestal," " Covent
Garden Virgin " and " Newgate Saint " were ironical designa-
tions of different classes of prostitutes.[2] The Court Masquerades
moreover, which continued till the Lisbon Earthquake of
1755,[3] when the moral and religious feelings of the country
procured their suppression, were scandalously sensual ; while
the popular " subscription " Receptions and Masquerades were
copiously tarred with the same brush. " Champagne, dice,

---

[1] See Sydney, Vol. I., p. 229.
[2] See Sir Richard Steele in *Tatler* (July 26th, 1709) ; G. R. Balleine,
History of Evang. Party, p. 14 ; Sir Chas. Petrie, *The Four Georges*, pp. 74-5.
[3] See Lecky, I., pp. 503-4.

music or your neighbour's spouse," were among the contending attractions of " the midnight orgy " and " the mazy dance." Horace Walpole, writing to Mann (May 3rd, 1749), concerning a " subscription masquerade " at which George II was present, says that Miss Chudleigh, a popular maid of honour, masquerading as " Iphigenia," was " so naked that you would have taken her for Andromeda " ; and Besant, lumping together the masquerades of the time, describes them as " scenes of dissipation."[1] Yet as late as February, 1770, the House of Commons " adjourned to attend a subscription masquerade held in Soho."

Among the illiterate and outcast multitude, to such a pitch of barbarity did sensuality rise, that frequently it was seen on parade. Every new Parliament, for example, " the borough of Garret," a settlement of " straggling cottages near Wandsworth," held a mock election ; and " the qualification of a voter was that he had enjoyed a woman in the open air in that district." The occasion, with all its obscene humour and bawdry horse-play, drew swarming crowds of debauchees from London ; " and so much custom resulted to the local publicans, that they found it to their interest to contribute largely to the expense of the ceremony."[2] So utterly depraved, too, were some rural areas, that labourers actually " sold their wives by auction in the cattle market ; and Baptism registers show how rampant was immorality in the villages."[3]

Nor can it seriously be contended that the primary cause of this depravity was economic or financial. Defoe, in the early part of the century, and Arthur Young, more than fifty years later, make it abundantly clear that English wages, both rural and urban, were very substantially higher than those on the Continent; and prices were cheap.[4] The *root* cause was none other than spiritual atrophy and moral decay : for one of the most remarkable facts of the century, was the way in which multitudes of converts of the Great Revival, despite their unprecedented voluntary charity, quickly raised themselves from a condition of drunkenness, poverty and squalor to a status of decent living, economic independence and self-respect.

Of such wholesome present-day sports as baseball and Association or Rugby football, the eighteenth century knew

---

[1] *London in the Eighteenth Century*, p. 410.
[2] Petrie, *op. cit.*, p. 15.
[3] Balleine, *op. cit.*, p. 14.
[4] See Daniel Defoe, *A Tour Through Great Britain* (1724–26), and Arthur Young, *A Tour Through the Southern Counties* (1768), *A Tour Through the North of England* (1771).

nothing : while anything approaching modern cricket made
no popular appeal till well into the latter half of the century.[1]
To the general rabble, as indeed to many of " their betters,"
the baiting of bulls, bears and badgers ; the teasing and torture
of cats, dogs, rams, cocks and ducks ; the flogging of horses
over an " endurance course " ; the beastly bludgeonings of
prize fighters and local bruisers ; together with drunkenness,
gambling and sex immorality represented the basic elements
of " Sport." Even the school games of children were for the
most part, bullying, cruel and crude—a stimulus perhaps to
brawn and muscle, but an enemy both of team-work and wit.
Little wonder, therefore, that Wesley's attitude towards popular
amusements was so inhibitive as to seem unreasonable to-day.
His problem was comparable to that of the Early Christian
leaders concerning Roman gladiatorial shows. A complete
and peremptory *break* was imperative. He had to free the
masses from the cruelty and barbarism, the lust and the avarice,
then associated with the name and substance of " sport." His
high and holy purpose was to re-discover and purge the nation's
soul ; and when once that unparalleled service was wrought,
a new and elevated conception of sport duly appeared. Meanwhile, the vulgar, degrading pastimes of the early and middle
eighteenth century, reflected all too clearly the vicious *Zeitgeist*
then at work : they expressed with uncanny accuracy the soul
tragedy of " a period of dim ideals and expiring hopes."

[1] E. D. Cuming, *op. cit.*, Vol. I, pp. 378–81.

CHAPTER IX

DAWN DEFERRED

" I do not remember that our English poets ever suffered a criminal amour to succeed upon the stage until the reign of Charles II. Ever since that time the alderman is made a cuckold, the deluded virgin is debauched, and adultery and fornication are supposed to be committed behind the scenes as part of the action."

JONATHAN SWIFT, *Project for the Advancement of Religion.*

" IT is certain the apprenticeship of some parish children is as great a scene of inhumanity as the suffering others to die in infancy."

JONAS HANWAY, *An Earnest Appeal for Mercy to the Children of the Poor* (1766). p. 105.

" Here malice, rapine, accident conspire,
And now a rabble rages, now a fire ;
Their ambush here relentless ruffians lay,
And here a fell attorney prowls for prey ;
Here falling houses thunder on your head,
And here a female atheist talks you dead."

SAMUEL JOHNSON, *London,* (1738).

L

DAWN DEFERRED

LIGHT literature, including comic drama, has, in every age, striven to hold a mirror to the fashions and foibles, the habits and humours, the appetites and aspersions, the manners and morals of contemporary life. Co-ordinated imagination and artistic latitude here, of course, are freely allowed. But unless the action and atmosphere are consonant with current experience, habit, fashion or fancy, such literature has scanty hope of wide appeal. What then of the light literature of the early and middle eighteenth century? Beyond doubt, it emits an odour of scented sickliness and putridity that never would have been tolerated in a healthy or decent age. Sir Walter Besant, in his comprehensive quarto volume *London in the Eighteenth Century*, writes : " The coarseness prevalent in the eighteenth century, the gross indecency and ribaldry of its songs, of the daily and common talk, makes itself felt in the whole of its literature—in the plays, the poems, the essays, the novels . . . the grossness belonged not only to the poor wretch of a harlot, but to all classes alike."[1] Among the many characters, for example, in John Gay's sweeping success, " The Beggar's Opera " (1728), one looks in vain for a single honest person.

True, Addison, Steele, Richardson, Johnson and Goldsmith worked hard to stop the pestilential rot ; but to the vast proportion of their countrymen, they were asking water to run up hill. The taste for the pornographic was avid, if not insatiable : the drift of the era was toward the pedantic, the sensual, the vulgar. Even clergymen like Swift and Sterne could not resist the lure of the coarse and the prurient : neither could such would-be reformers as Defoe, Fielding and Smollett often succeed in keeping their pages quite clean ; while as for the " wit " of most popular scribblers—many of them women— they won and held their following by gilding and mirroring dirt. The moral standards of Richard Sheridan were far removed from anything Puritan or prudish ; yet in *The Rivals*,

---

[1] *Op. cit.*, p. 276.

written in 1774, when private and public morals had already greatly improved, he made Sir Anthony Absolute define "a Circulating Library" as "an evergreen tree of Diabolical Knowledge"; while fourteen years earlier, George Colman, in the concluding words of his drama, *Polly Honeycombe*, wrote: "A man might as well turn his daughter loose in Covent Garden, as trust the cultivation of her mind to a circulating library."

Lecky points to "the prevailing coarseness" of the literature of the first half of the century.[1] And Sir Walter Scott has recorded the experience of his grand-aunt who in old age turned again to the pages of Aphra Behn, whose novels she "had delighted in when young"; but she then found herself "unable to read without shame a book, which sixty years before she had heard read out for amusement in large circles consisting of the best society in London."[2] Goldsmith moreover maintained that most novels of his time were "no better than instruments of debauchery."[3]

(i) *General Drama and the Theatre*

John Wesley, because of his attitude to the theatre of his day, has often been lashed and lampooned as "narrow," "bigoted," "fanatical" and "Puritanical"; but if he pronounced the current stage a "sink of all profaneness and debauchery," many non-squeamish contemporaries passed judgments equally harsh. Swift's humour was both brusque and "broad"; yet referring, in 1709, to current drama he says: "It is worth observing the distributive justice of the authors, which is constantly applied to the punishment of virtue and the reward of vice: directly opposite to the rules of their best critics, as well as to the practice of dramatic poets in all other ages. . . . I do not remember that our English poets ever suffered a criminal amour to succeed upon the stage until the reign of Charles II. Ever since that time, the alderman is made a cuckold, the deluded virgin is debauched, and adultery and fornication are supposed to be committed behind the scenes as part of the action."[4]

Four decades later William Law wrote his treatise, *On the Absolute Unlawfulness of the Stage*, wherein he declared the "playhouse" of his day to be "as certainly the house of the devil

---

[1] *Op. cit.*, Vol. I, p. 519.
[2] *Ibid.*, p. 521; see, too, Lockart's *Life of Scott*, V, pp. 136–7. Mrs. Behn (1640–89) was the *first* English professional authoress. Modern critics have said of her works that "all alike are coarse." See *Dict. of Nat. Biog.*
[3] *Citizen of the World*, Letter lxxxiii (quoted by Balleine, p. 14).
[4] Jonathan Swift, *Project for the Advancement of Religion.*

as the Church is the house of God," maintaining also that every-one who attended the theatre was thereby promoting " the devil's triumph." Henry Fielding, in *Joseph Andrews*, makes Parson Adams to say of contemporary drama : " I never heard of any plays fit for a Christian to read but *Cato* and the *Conscious Lovers* "—works by Addison and Steele. Sir John Hawkins, too, in his *Life of Dr. Johnson* (1787), says : " A play-house and the regions about it are the very hot-beds of vice " ; while, with a magistrate's eye on the social problems of his time, he asks : " How else comes it to pass that no sooner is a play-house opened in any part of the kingdom, than it at once becomes surrounded by a halo of brothels ? "[1]

This pronouncement of Johnson's literary executor may seem prudish and cruel. In an age of moral and spiritual awakening high-minded men are liable to magnify the evils of contemporary life, while in times of spiritual paralysis the same, or even worse, ills may be taken for granted, and so escape censure. Yet a century after Hawkins's verdict, W. C. Sydney, reviewing, in the light of history, the middle eighteenth century drama and theatre, says : " The reader would err, and that very considerably, were he to suppose that it was the attractions of the stage that induced the majority of fine gentlemen in the last century to resort to the three principal theatres of London. Contemporary light literature bears its emphatic testimony to the fact that it was the attractions presented by the saloons of the playhouses (establishments which partook as much of the nature of brothels as they did of taverns) which filled the benches of the theatres with visitors, and the purses of those who kept them with coin of the realm. The existence of these resorts was the chief inducement for hundreds of men, old and young, to resort to Drury Lane, Covent Garden, and the Haymarket Theatres."[2] Lecky says : " The profligacy of the theatre during the generation that followed the Restoration can hardly be exaggerated."[3] That theatre, too, was the almost exclusive preserve of the aristocracy ; and according to Hallam, Steele's

[1] *Op. Cit.*, pp. 75–6.
[2] *England and the English in the Eighteenth Century*, Vol. I, p. 161. Even at the opening of the nineteenth century the theatre atmosphere was still bad. " To the right and left," writes Professor Elie Halévy, of the London theatres, " were free entrances for the light women of the neighbourhood ; for the management had devised this method of attracting the men." (*History of English People in 1815*, p. 440.) Even the 1832 *Report of the Select Committee on Dramatic Literature* refers to " a most decided objection to any man carrying his wife or sister to the theatre when he is compelled to take them through a crowd of women of notoriously bad character." (p. 27).
[3] Vol. I, p. 538.

Conscious Lovers (1722) was the " first comedy," after the Restoration, " which can be called moral."[1]　Indeed, so revolting was the general run of comedies with their smutty assortment of *doubles ententes*, that for decades " ladies of respectability and position," whose curiosity led them forth to " first nights," appeared in masks.[2]

David Garrick, admittedly, did much to raise the level of theatrical performances and to popularise Shakespeare ; but the liberties Garrick was capable of taking with the Master Dramatist are truly amazing ; and W. J. Lawrence, in his essay, *The Drama and the Theatre*, describes the theatrical atmosphere of the era as that " of malice, intrigue and caprice."[3] Most of the acclaimed actresses of the period, too, were women of easy virtue.　Anne Oldfield, buried in Westminster Abbey (1730), lived clandestinely with different men of affairs ; while the famous beauty, Peg Woffington (1720–60), whose portrait hangs in the Victoria and Albert Museum, once said to Thomas Sheridan (Richard's father) that " there were two things " her sister " should never become, by her advice—a whore, and an actress, for she had sufficiently experienced the inconveniences of those ways of life herself."[4]　The same Sheridan, in language true to the age, describing the said stage idol to William Windham, the statesman, pronounced her " a most willing bitch, artful, dissembling, lewd and malicious " ; but withal " a very captivating woman."[5]

(ii) *Ignorance, Lawlessness and Savagery*

Yet even as England's privileged and literary classes boasted the glories of their Constitution and the theatre mirrored their " liberty " ; at the very zenith of the " Age of Enlightenment," when " Nature " was God, the gross ignorance and barbarism of the general populace was rapidly increasing.　Nonconformity, representing an intelligent middle class minority, villainously segregated from social and national institutions, had been forced for its livelihood, almost exclusively, into channels of trade, commerce and craftsmanship ; a fact which bode ill to the coming Industrial Revolution.　For a philosophy of ultra-independence and individualism had been foisted upon

---

[1] Henry Hallam, *History of Literature*, Vol. IV, p. 284.
[2] See *Apology for the Life of Mr. Colley Cibber, Comedian* (Autobiography, 1740), Chap. viii.
[3] *Johnson's England* (1933), Vol. II, p. 168.
[4] R. W. Ketton-Cremer, *Early Life and Diaries of William Windham*, p. 79f.
[5] Sir Chas. Petrie, *The Four Georges*, p. 105.

Dissenters before the advent of the Factory System, with its catastrophic social effects ; and what here applied to Nonconformists was true largely of Roman Catholics and Jews. The Church of England, on the other hand, was in no real sense a National Church ; it was an assuming and superior department of State, a proud branch of the Civil Service, whose directing officers represented quite consciously the landed and governing class. The working multitudes therefore were left as sheep without true shepherds, and all manner of ravenous beasts battened upon the fold.

Till the advent of the Sunday School movement, in the seventh and eighth decades of the century,[1] little or no provision was made for the free education of the poor save the Church system of Charity Schools, dating from the close of the sevententh century ; and they commonly were a farce. Most Charity School teachers were half illiterate ; their average pay was less than that of sturdy labourers, and habitually they lived on the very verge of the " subsistence margin." But they could supervise the " dreary droning of the catechism," dogmatise mechanically on " piety, industry and thrift," teach the A.B.Cs. and lay down the " first principles " of reading and ciphering. And there their duties stopped. In Lambeth Palace Library or the British Museum Reading Room, one may still examine the *Reports* and *Accounts* of early Charity Schools. The present writer has perused many of them and repeatedly he finds that the ecclesiastical instructions issued to the masters remind them that they are to teach children " humility," " placid obedience " and a " due reverence for their superiors " ; they are to guard against all inculcation of " unbecoming airs " and against educating children " out of their station " ; while also, they are to see that their pupils are " inured to the meanest services," and taught " willingly " to perform " all labours of the lowest kind."

A typical Charity School *Report* (1714) informs us that the summer hours of instruction were 7 a.m. to 11 a.m., and 1 p.m. to 5 p.m., while in winter the schools opened an hour later and closed an hour earlier. The ages of the children ran between seven and twelve years. The teaching was " mainly from the Catechism " ; scholars wore " distinctive " hats, bands, etc., which marked them off as *charity* children ; and the ordinary cost of " a school for fifty boys, including the charge of a school-room, books, firing, master's salary, and three bands,

---

[1] In 1769, in High Wycombe, Hannah Ball, under Wesley, started a flourishing Sunday School ; but not till Robert Raikes began his work in Gloucester (1780) did the movement begin to assume *national* proportions.

one cap, one coat, one pair stockings and one pair shoes, given annually to each boy," is laid down as "about £75 a year." The annual cost of a similar Charity School for fifty girls, however, is set out at "about £60." Few of the masters received as much as £20 a year: most got six shillings to seven shillings a week. Ludicrous, nevertheless, as these schools were, an occasional teacher had an idea of his own, and some children happily learned more than was written on the blackboard or conned by rote.[1]

Charity Schools, moreover, were not found in all districts: generally they were limited to the more populous areas; and, in any case, they were designed only for the very poor. The children of artisans, farmers, traders, industrial workers, etc., if they got any education, procured it in some sort of struggling private school whose fee was anything from eighteen shillings a year, per child, with family reductions for several children. Millions of the eighteenth century populace were never inside a school of any description, and multitudes received such rough, practical training as they got in the shape of " apprenticeship " to some craft, business, industry or trade. Apprenticeship, however, at this period reached its nadir of debasement, representing often but a hollow mockery of its original intent. The contemporary revelations of Jonas Hanway and the *Old Bailey Session Papers*, together with the detailed researches of different modern scholars, reflect the incredible abuses upon which the old apprenticeship system had fallen. " Parish children," for instance, were customarily indentured from an early age till twenty-four years old; yet they could be conscripted by the Government for war at eighteen, in which case their masters could legally draw their army pay till their twenty-fourth birthday. Gin shops, gambling dens, the collapse of moral standards and the *Zeitgeist* of the age, all played havoc with the old apprenticeship basis of craft education. Some masters beat, half-starved and half-enslaved their apprentices, who commonly lived in their homes; others let them run riot on the streets at night. Many inhuman wretches of both sexes took apprentices for no other purpose than villainously to exploit them; while many debauched apprentices, on the other hand, robbed and defamed decent masters.

In the meanest " trades," too, apprentices were actually bought and sold, as was the case with Blake's little Chimney Sweep:

> " . . . my father *sold* me when yet my tongue
> Could scarcely cry, ' 'Weep ! 'Weep ! 'Weep ! 'Weep ! '
> So your chimneys I sweep, and in soot I sleep."

---

[1] Besides Charity School *Reports, Accounts* and *Sermons*, see Dr. George *op. cit.*, pp. 218–22 and 251–4.

The incessant and bitter litigation in the first half of the eighteenth century relative to masters and apprentices, proves conclusively that, as a basis of social and practical education, the prevailing system of apprenticeship was bankrupt.[1]

The vivid outline sketched by Francis Place of the life of his own immediate forebears and their associates, sheds a revealing light on the semi-savagery of the " lower orders " during the era under discussion. Going back to his maternal grandfather and to the birth of his own father (about 1717), the unfolding of the known facts of his family history records a tale of drunken brawls, violent assaults, the breaking of indentures, repeated ruinations through gambling, wife desertions, highway robbery, transportation and the like. Workhouse, jail and murder all enter into the vicissitudes of this humble family history ; when fifty-seven, Place's own mother was reduced to taking in washing to support her family, his father meanwhile retiring to Fleet prison.

This domestic history, notwithstanding its seeming incredibility, Francis Place believed fairly typical of the *early* and *middle* eighteenth century; and internal evidence makes it abundantly plain that the pre-eminent causes of such ruin, were moral and social rather than economic.[2] Place indeed continually ridiculed the notion that the lot of the toiling masses, in the late eighteenth and early nineteenth century, was growing worse. The Social Conscience, he argued, had meanwhile been fully awakened, and people then were becoming keenly sensitive to evils which, for generations, they either had accepted as inevitable expressions of a necessary social order, or had passed by unseen. Indeed many hoary social evils already were submitting to the pressure of the reforming conscience, before their existence became generally recognised. Hence the common, but fallacious, belief that such evils were new.

The plunder of shipwrecked vessels, again, is indicative of the then prevalent savagery. Lecky records how ships, particularly off the Cornish coast, were, at times deliberately " lured by false signals upon the rocks " ;[3] and Defoe relates an occasion on which a Spanish ship, observing the sinking of a British vessel and crew off the coast of Biscay, denied them any succour, its captain observing : " that, having been shipwrecked

---

[1] See Hanway's *Earnest Appeal for Mercy to the Children of the Poor*, p. 102f ; Dr. George, *London Life in the Eighteenth Century*, chap. v, and pp. 275–86 ; Sir Chas. Petrie, *The Four Georges*, pp. 86–8 ; G. D. H. Cole, " Town Life in the Provinces " (*Johnson's England*, I, pp. 220–1).

[2] Francis Place, *Autobiography*, Brit. Mus. Addl. MSS., 35,142.

[3] *Op. cit.*, Vol. I, p. 488.

somewhere on the coast of England, the people, instead of saving him and his ship, came off and robbed him, tore the ship almost to pieces, and left him and his men to swim ashore for their lives while they plundered the cargo ; upon which he and his whole crew had sworn never to help an Englishman in whatever distress he should find them, whether at sea or on shore."[1] Wesley's *Journal*, too, contains several references to this savage practice. In June, 1760, for instance, during an Irish preaching tour, he recorded the following observation : " A Swedish ship, being leaky, put into one of our harbours. The Irish, according to custom, ran to plunder her. A neighbouring gentleman hindered them ; and for so doing demanded a fourth part of the cargo. And this they said, the law allows." It should be noted, in this case, that the craft was not yet actually shipwrecked.

Professor G. M. Trevelyan pronounces Dr. Johnson " the most abnormally English creature God ever made " ;[2] and so warm in time became the Doctor's attachment to his beloved Metropolis that finally he averred anyone " tired of London " to be " tired of life " ; nevertheless, there is more than humour in Johnson's couplet from *London*, written in 1738—the very eve of Wesley's world-stirring crusade :

> " Prepare for death if here at night you roam,
> And sign your will before you sup from home."

The drunkenness and inefficiency of the watchmen, or constables, as Fielding, Walpole and other contemporaries so often point out, was notorious. Smollett in his *History of England*, referring to the year 1730, says : " Thieves and robbers were now become more desperate and savage than they had ever appeared since mankind was civilised." Footpads armed with " bludgeons, pistols, cutlasses," etc., infested " not only private lanes and passages, but likewise public streets and places of usual concourse," committing daring and dastardly outrages even at such times of day as were " hitherto deemed hours of security."[3] Often indeed constables passed by a notorious robber, not daring to apprehend him lest he give signal and " twenty or thirty armed villains " rush to his assistance.[4] In John Gay's *Trivia* (1716) the lines :

> " Yet rather bear the show'r, and toils of mud
> Than in the doubtful quarrel risk thy blood,"

[1] Walter Wilson, *Life of Daniel Defoe*, Vol. I, p. 209.
[2] Trevelyan, *The Age of Johnson* (*Johnson's England*, Vol. I, p. 6).
[3] See *Address* from Mayor and Aldermen of London (1744) to the King, imploring protection against these bandits.
[4] See Henry Fielding, *Increase of Robbers*.

represent his advice to London pedestrians never to squabble with street ruffians for the welcome shelter of the wall, but rather to let them have it. As late as 1751, Horace Walpole, writing in rather lurid style to Sir Horace Mann, complains : " One is forced to travel, even at noon, as if one were going to battle."

(iii) *Ichabod ?*

But along with ignorance, lawlessness, barbarism and godlessness went also superstition. That tyrant, King Quack, surrounded by his innumerable votaries, many of whom were " dealers in Destiny's dark counsel," reigned over no small percentage of the subjects both of George I and George II ; and the fact that many of these dupes mouthed pretty phrases about Deism, Nature Worship, Natural Religion, Natural Philosophy, Freedom, Reason, Rationality, Self-expression and Syncretism, made them no less his slaves. W. C. Sydney, writing of this period, says : " The capital and provinces literally teemed with men and women who gained a livelihood by telling fortunes and casting nativities, and by the extensive sale of their ridiculous inventions called ' sigils,' the possession of which was vulgarly supposed to avert evil and destruction from life and property."[1] Among the socially *élite*, current superstitions normally gravitated toward the astrologer, the magician, the palmist, the Nature Doctor and the ever-present army of foreign " Professors " of weird and wondrous " Natural Sciences " :[2] among the working masses, whom the *élite* commonly designated " the vile and brutish part of mankind," or briefly " the brutes,"[3] superstition naturally assumed crasser forms. One of its most humorous manifestations is seen in the fact that many rural cockers took endless pains to have their game fowls' eggs hatched in a magpie's nest ; for the magpie being the " special protégé of Satan," it followed that gamecocks so hatched would be " devilish good fighters."[4] Sir Robert Walpole, with bluff humour but grim truth, was wont to boast that he " controlled George I by bad Latin and good punch." His observation is characteristic not only of the man but of his era. The country was " controlled " by a

---

[1] *England and the English in the Eighteenth Century*, I, p. 264.
[2] See *Ibid.*, chaps. viii and ix.
[3] Henry Fielding's *Joseph Andrews* (1742) makes this prevailing custom abundantly plain.
[4] See E. D. Cuming, " Sports and Games " (*Johnson's England*, I, p. 374)

factious, aristocratic oligarchy, addicted to bad morals and strong intoxicants ; and the surest passport to the "best" society was to be a well-bred, clever rake. True, the gospel of Class Hatred—a Continental product—had not yet been propounded, but the chicanery of English Class rule and the arrogance of English Class privilege were, up to the middle of the eighteenth century, seen at their height. Among the labouring masses, too, the publican and the pawnbroker, the kidnapper and the crimp, the bookie and the quack, the fakir and the tout, the magician and the charlatan, the footpad and the highwayman, paraded in the heyday of their power. Till toward the end of the fifth decade, indeed, it seemed as though when the century had run its course, its certain epitaph would be *Ichabod* : for the glory of the land of Spencer, Shakespeare and Milton had steadily been ebbing away ; and dawn was long deferred.

(iv) *Changing Horizons*

Nevertheless, mighty, though despised, spiritual influences already were operating among the outcast masses ; and greater days than any the Anglo-Saxon peoples had previous known, lay still ahead. Survey first the age of Marlborough and Bolingbroke, of Pope and Gay, of Swift and Butler, of Walpole and Chesterfield, of Collins and Hume. Then turn to the latter half of the century and survey the age of Chatham and Clive, of Smith and Pitt, of Burke and Mansfield, of Gibbon and Blackstone, of Johnson and Goldsmith, of Cowper and Howard, of Burns and Blake. The inherited and accumulated sins of the century, are still appallingly manifest ; but there can be no mistaking the certainty that a better era was now dawning. A new moral earnestness was entering into the warp and woof of British character. A new sense of philanthropy and humanity was stirring in the blood. A new vision of justice and righteousness, of altruism and fellowship, was challenging the souls of men. The spirit of reform was in the air. It no longer smart in England to boast of being a "four" or "five-bottle man" ; nor were spiritual values any longer in the discard. The British people were becoming more worthy of the guardianship of an expanding Empire and of the world trust which it entailed. Whatever else the trial of Warren Hastings implied, his impeachment expressed a new demand for moral values in Government and a new recognition of trusteeship, even toward conquered and backward peoples. On all sides it was apparent that a new and nobler *Zeitgeist* was possessing the land. Mere smartness was fast falling into disrepute. Integrity and vision, in addition to mental acumen, were coming to be recognised as essential to true leadership. Substance and sincerity were dispelling tinsel and gloss. Already the judgment was spreading among the nations, that a Briton's word was " as good as his bond " ; and relatively speaking, that judgment was not untrue. Higher values were passing into circulation, which never could have been transmitted in the current moral coinage of the earlier half of the century. England, at last, was regaining her Soul.

True, many who manifested the unmistakable effects of this changed national outlook would have despised, had they ever suspected, its primal cause : for the ruling, privileged and educated classes, even in the latter half of the century, were loath to admit that they could be moved and moulded by the impulse of a religious revival mediated first of all through the multitude. But not so with all. Vital spiritual fire is possessed of amazing propensities for consuming Class barriers and dispelling Class snobbery. Hanway and Howard, Lady Huntingdon and Hannah More, Lord Dartmouth and John Thornton, Newton and Cowper, as much as any itinerant preacher, were among the band of fearless exemplars who carried the Torch of Faith to the very portals of the succeeding century : while among those who bore it across the threshold to purge, illumine and challenge the nineteenth century were William Wilberforce and Zachary Macaulay, William Carey and the younger Venn, Isaac Milner and Sir James Stephen, Charles Simeon and Henry Martyn, Lord Teignmouth and Charles Grant, Henry Thornton and Sir Thomas Fowell Buxton, Francis Asbury and Dr. Thomas Coke. Times were changing mightily for the better since the days when Cowper wrote of, " *one* who wears a coronet and prays."

The " conversion " of the one-time don of Oxford, which " strangely warmed " his heart toward God and impelled him forth as the friend and releaser of the outcast, vulgarised masses, was fraught with a succession of results destined finally to change the whole trend of social history throughout the British Empire and the English-speaking world. Nor was the impact of this prophet, who claimed " the *world* for his parish," confined even within those spacious limits. Millions, of many colours, climes and tongues, inhabiting the four corners of the earth, have lived richer, happier, nobler and more serviceable lives because, in 1738, fire from off the altars of God purged and illumined the soul of a downcast and disillusioned English priest.

PART II

A BAPTISM OF FIRE

CHAPTER X

THE EMERGENCE OF A PROPHET

" I knew that Christ had given me birth
To brother all the souls on earth."

JOHN MASEFIELD, *The Everlasting Mercy*

" This is the victory that overcometh the world,
even our faith."

1 *John* v, 4 (the text of Wesley's
first sermon after his soul's Great
Awakening).
See *Journal*, Sunday, May 28th, 1738.

THE EMERGENCE OF A PROPHET

CONTUMELY and persecution have been the birth pangs and growing pains of most movements which have cleansed society, and wrought deliverance to the soul of man. As for the eighteenth century Revival, commonly known as the Evangelical Movement, it was cradled and reared in an atmosphere of insolence, contempt and abuse. Yet the day was to dawn when the descendants of those who maligned it would acclaim it, " the moral salvation of England," and a mighty inspiration to all mankind. Few world movements, indeed, have ever emerged from the depths of slander to the heights of historical honour, with such consistent progress as did this remarkable revival of vital, practical religion.

(i) *Contemporary versus Historical Judgments*

John Kirkby, Rector of Blackmanstoke, writing in 1750, twelve years after Wesley's " conversion," speaks of " the horrid blasphemies and impieties taught by those diabolical seducers called Methodists." " They pray," he says, " in the language of a saint to Beelzebub himself " ;[1] and " their religion," he declares, " could be forged nowhere else but in the bottomless pit."[2] John Wesley he designates as " that mystery of iniquity " and " emissary of Satan " whose religion is " as opposite to Christianity as heaven is to hell," and whose " damnation will be just." Then, warning the public against " Methodist " meetings, he cries : " You should be as much afraid to come near their assemblies as you would be to put your hand into the den of a cockatrice."[3]

Bishop Lavington, referring to the disciples of Wesley and Whitefield, says : " Their whole conduct is but the counterpart of the most wild fanaticisms of the most abominable communion

[1] J. Kirkby, *The Impostor Detected*, p. 23.
[2] *Ibid.*, p. 51.
[3] *Ibid.*, p. 52.

in its most corrupt ages."[1] Dr. Smollett, in his *History of England* (1760), exclaims : " Imposture and fanaticism still hang upon the skirts of religion. Weak minds were seduced by the delusions of a superstition, styled Methodism, raised upon affectation of superior sanctity and pretention to divine illumination. Many thousands were infected with this enthusiasm by the endeavours of a few obscure preachers, such as Whitefield and the Wesleys, who *found means to lay the whole Kingdom under a contribution*."[2] Even as late as 1808, in the *Edinburgh Review*, Rev. Sydney Smith exhibits the same prejudice. Referring collectively to the followers of Wesley, Whitefield and the Evangelical clergymen within the Establishment, but not connected directly with the Methodist societies, he sneers : " We shall use the general term of Methodism to designate those three classes of fanatics, not troubling ourselves to point out the finer shades and nicer discriminations of lunacy, but treating them all as in one general conspiracy against common sense and rational, orthodox Christianity."[3]

For decades, too, many magistrates, squires and civic officials not only winked at the brutal and drunken attacks of mobs and gangs upon peaceful, offenceless " Methodist " gatherings, but encouraged, if they did not actually direct, these intoxicated wretches in their criminal and barbaric brigandage.[4]

But priests, bishops, historians, journalists, magistrates and squires by no means monopolised this aggressive opposition. Sir Robert Walpole the politician, Pope the poet, Fielding the novelist, Lord Northington the judge, Butler the theologian, Foote the dramatist, Hume the philosopher, Hogarth the painter, Lady Buckingham the smart society leader, Horace Walpole the literary man-about-town, and Cobbett the demagogue—these are but a few of the notabilities who enlisted as lieutenants in the solemn campaign to exorcise the hated spectre of " Methodism," which was haunting the arctic formalism of English life.

As early as 1740, more than one hundred anti-revival publications had poured from the Press ; by the close of the century, their number was Legion. And certain of their titles are as

---

[1] *Enthusiasm of Papists and Methodists Compared* (1750). Lavington later was reconciled to Wesley, whose *Journal* (August 29th, 1762) says : " I was well pleased to partake of the Lord's Supper with my old opponent, Bishop Lavington. O, may we sit down together in the Kingdom of our Father ! "
[2] Vol. XV, pp. 121-2. When, shortly before his death, Smollett wrote *Humphrey Clinker*, he had quite changed his attitude.
[3] *Edinburgh Review*, No. XXII, art. V (Ingram on " Methodism ").
[4] Wesley's *Journal* references to these attacks are far too numerous to list.

amusing as their contents are revealing. In 1743 appeared the scurrilous anonymous farce, *Trick upon Trick, or Methodism Displayed*. The worthy Dr. Faustus, in 1757, published *A Dozen Reasons Why the Sect of Conjurers, called Fortune Tellers, should have at least as much Liberty to Exercise their Abominable Art as is now granted to Methodists, Moravians, and other sorts of Conjurers*. In 1758 came, *Die and be Damned* (anonymous), the title being specially designed to " appeal to gentlemen."

S. Roe, in *Enthusiasm Detected and Defeated* (1768), charitably proposed legislative power to " cut out the tongues " of field preachers ; and the author of *The Jesuit Detected* (1769) could still prove that Wesley was a wily, " plotting Papist." *The Serpent and the Fox* (1777), by Auscultator, bore the luminous sub-title *An Interview between Old Nick and Old John* ; while Bishop Challenor's *Caveat against the Methodists* (1787) was one among scores of attacks in an episcopal succession.[1] Even the great High Church historian, J. H. Overton, points out that " among the numerous Bishops' charges, from 1740 to the end of the century, . . . there are few in which some blow is not aimed at the Methodists."[2]

The foregoing, alas, are all too representative of contemporaries who, down the ages, have so proverbially stoned their greatest prophets. To-day, however, the leaders of the eighteenth-century Revival, stoned, in more senses than one, by the polished, exclusive society of their own age, are not wanting for memorials immortalising their memory. Professor Elie Halévy, in his monumental volumes on the modern *History of the English People*, discovers in this Spiritual Awakening the only consistent explanation of the highest social and moral achievements of modern England. " In the vast work of social organisation which is one of the dominant characteristics of nineteenth-century England," says Halévy, " it would be *difficult to over-estimate* the part played by the Wesleyan revival."[3] " We shall witness Methodism," says this great French historian, " bring under its influence, first the Dissenting sects, then the Establishment, finally secular opinion. . . . We shall explain by this movement . . . what we may truly term the miracle of modern England, anarchist but orderly, practical and business-like, but religious and even pietist."[4] " Evangelical religion,"

---

[1] For a selected list of anti-Evangelical publications, see the author's book, *Lord Shaftesbury and Social-Industrial Progress* (in Bibliography pp. 422–3).
[2] Overton's *John Wesley*, p. 198.
[3] Halévy, Vol. I, p. 372.
[4] *Ibid.*, p. 339.

Halévy pronounces, " the moral cement " of nineteenth century English society. It " restrained the plutocrats who had newly risen from the masses from vulgar ostentation and debauchery, and placed over the proletariat a select body of workmen, enamoured of virtue and capable of self-restraint. Evangelical-ism . . . restored in England the balance momentarily de-stroyed by the explosion of the revolutionary forces."[1]

Professor Thorold Rogers boldly asserts that he does " not believe the mass of peasants could have been moved at all, had it not been for the spiritual and educational stimulus which they received from Methodist organisations."[2] J. R. Green claims for this Revival that it " changed, after a time, the whole tone of English society." " The Church," he says, " was restored to new life and activity. Religion carried to the hearts of the people a fresh spirit of moral zeal, while it purified our literature and our manners. A new philanthropy reformed our prisons, infused clemency and wisdom into our penal laws, abolished the slave-trade, and gave the first impulse to popular education."[3] Lecky, himself a Rationalist, avers that the Evangelicals gradually " changed the whole spirit of the English Church. They infused into it a new fire and passion of devotion, kindled a spirit of fervent philanthropy, raised the standard of clerical duty, and com-pletely altered the whole tone and tendency of the preaching of its ministers." Overton, too, writes : " Of the faith which enabled a man to abandon the cherished habits of a lifetime, and to go forth ready to spend and be spent in his Master's service, . . . which made the selfish man self-denying, the dis-contented happy, the worldling spiritually minded, the drunkard sober, the sensual chaste, the liar truthful, the thief honest, the proud humble, the godless godly, the thriftless thrifty—we can only judge by the fruits which it bore. That such fruits *were* borne is surely undeniable."[4]

The Cambridge Modern History, after enumerating some of the greatest men of the eighteenth century, adds : " But more important than any of these in universality of influence and range of achievement, were John Wesley and the religious revival to which he gave his name and his life."[5] Again, Augustine Birrell, K.C., writes : " No man lived nearer to the centre than John Wesley, neither Pitt nor Clive, neither Mansfield nor Johnson. You cannot cut him out of the national life.

[1] Halévy, Vol. III (1830–1841), p. 166.
[2] *Six Centuries of Work and Wages* (1901 edition), p. 516.
[3] *Short History of the English People*, p. 736.
[4] J. H. Overton, *The Evangelical Revival in the Eighteenth Century*, p. 131.
[5] Vol. VI, p. 77 (by H. W. V. Temperley). The Oxford *History of England* (Vol. VI, p. 386) is equally emphatic.

No single figure influenced so many minds, no single voice touched so many hearts. No other man, did such a life's work for England."[1]

Even Primates and Prime Ministers are at last awakening to the centrality of Wesley's high influence on the English-speaking world. Archbishop Davidson, in 1928, after pronouncing Wesley " one of the greatest Englishmen who ever lived," declared that, it was " not too much to say that Wesley practically changed the outlook and even the character of the English nation." He admitted also that the Primates of the revival era, " were not the men to make the right response to a magnificent enthusiast like Wesley."[2]   Mr. Lloyd George, when Prime Minister, in 1922, avowed that Wales " owed more to the movement of which Wesley was the inspirer and prophet and leader, than to any other movement in the whole of its history. . . . It civilised the people. . . . There was a complete revolution effected in the whole country." As for the wider impact of this movement, Lloyd George affirmed that, " it had given a different outlook to the British and American people from the outlook of Continentals."[3] Mr. Stanley Baldwin, commenting, as Prime Minister, on Wesley's labours, said : " I am supposed to be a busy man, but, by the side of Wesley, I join the ranks of the unemployed." He said, too, that historians of the eighteenth century " who filled their pages with Napoleon and had nothing to say of John Wesley, now realise that they cannot explain *nineteenth* century England until they can explain Wesley." Then poignantly he added : " And I believe it is equally true to say, that you cannot understand *twentieth* century America, unless you understand Wesley."[4]

(ii) *Forerunners and a Retrospect*

Now is this sweeping reversal of contemporary judgments justified ?   Are these diversified and remarkable tributes— every one, be it remembered, from men outside the Methodist connection[5]—really merited ?   In this and succeeding chapters,

[1] Essays and Reviews, p. 35. See also *An Appreciation of Wesley's Journal*, by Birrell, prefaced to Parker's abridgement of the *Journal*, pp. xiii–xxiv.

[2] See *The Times* (London), November 2nd, 1928.

[3] From his Address supporting the Renovation Fund of Wesley's Chapel (June 20th, 1922).

[4] *The Times*, November 2nd, 1928. (From an Address celebrating the one hundred and fiftieth anniversary of opening of Wesley's Chapel.)

[5] The present writer, too, is *not* a Methodist.

it will be our task to study carefully the primary documents and literature of the Evangelical Movement, together with recognised secondary authorities, and to strive impartially to ascertain the origin, the evolution and the social consequences of that amazing phenomenon.

In the chapters preceding we have endeavoured to reveal something of the social, economic, political and religious backgrounds in which the Revival was born and had to work. Before proceeding further, we pause briefly to scan its forerunners; for rarely, if ever, does any vital historic movement make its appearance as a bolt from the blue. By those who have eyes to see and ears to hear, it will be found than an ominous cloud, a pillar of fire, a beckoning star or a still small voice, heralds the advent of new days ahead.

It was over the hills and woodlands of picturesque Wales, that the fingers of dawn first cast their quickening rays.[1] Nearly two decades before Wesley's conversion, Griffith Jones, among his Celtic compatriots, had begun a valiant work. A clergyman of the Establishment, he experienced a religious renewal which brought with it a passion to serve his countrymen; so he began travelling about Wales, preaching the Gospel with great effect in whatever Churches would receive him. He had the sagacity, moreover, to see that ignorance is the arch-foe of true religion, and to overcome the power of this entrenched enemy, he founded the once-famous Circulating Schools, which, in the course of a quarter-century, taught tens of thousands of men, women and children to spell out the Bible in Welsh.

One day, as Jones was preaching in a Welsh village, he was struck by the scoffing attitude of an athletic young clergyman. Silently, without anger, he prayed that the heart of this clerical mocker might be changed. Soon afterwards Daniel Rowlands, the man in question, became an earnest, effective colleague in Jones' work; and from the day of his enlistment, his heart rejoiced greatly in the new-found liberty engendered by association with the Cause at which he once had scoffed.[2] Later, Rowlands became a friend and helper of Wesley. Another honoured leader among the Welsh forerunners of the movement was Howell Harris, whom Whitefield designated " a burning and shining light in those parts; a barrier against profaneness and immorality, and an indefatigable promoter of the Gospel of

---

[1] John Simon, *Revival of Religion in Eighteenth Century England*. (See chapter, " Dawn of Revival in Wales.")

[2] *Ibid.*, p. 136.

Jesus Christ."[1]   This young schoolmaster who, after a term at Oxford, became disgusted with the " irregularities and immoralities of the university, " anticipated in some degree the work of Wesley's itinerant preachers ; and like Rowlands he became an enthusiastic supporter of the Revival, labouring especially with Whitefield and the Countess of Huntingdon, but ever an ardent admirer of Wesley.

Not only in Wales, however, had cleansing breezes begun to blow.   In 1729, in Northampton, Massachusetts, under the leadership of Jonathan Edwards, that great but awful theologian, a revival broke out which affected profoundly the whole New England colony, and whose influence upon Whitefield and the earlier American developments of the Evangelical Movement are unmistakable.[2]   Again the Pietist movement in Germany, augmented by the missionary zeal of the Moravian Brethren, drew to itself a band of choice, mystical souls who did no small work for their own country, and who left obvious ear marks on the English revival.[3]   In England, moreover, the educational and missionary work accomplished by the Society for Promoting Christian Knowledge and also by the Society for the Propagation of the Gospel in Foreign Parts must not be ignored.   True, the initial enthusiasm of these organisations, which reached its feeble climax in the reign of Queen Anne, was short lived ; nevertheless, they familiarised the Establishment with the working of Religious Societies within the Church, thus creating a respectable and significant precedent for Wesley's procedure. Yet with all due respect to the work thus attempted or accomplished in Wales, America, Germany and England, these movements were but forerunners preparing the way for an awakening infinitely greater than they.   It was not till after the conversion of Wesley, and his acceptance of Whitefield's precedent of field preaching, that a master spirit was prepared for the central and sacrificial rôle in the farthest-reaching spiritual drama yet enacted on English soil.   And for over half a century, till the hour of death, in his eighty-eighth year, John Wesley, by his incessant labours, his prophetic vision, his boundless sympathy, his inspired leadership, his superiority to caste and cant, his self-inflicted poverty, his unswerving confidence in social progress through a regenerated manhood, his warm love of all the human family, his contagious belief in the divine

[1] Whitefield's *Brief Account of Life of Howell Harris*, p. 30.   See, too, Harris's *Autobiography*.
[2] See *Life* of Edwards, by Professor Allen (1889).
[3] The Moravians, both in America and in Hernhuth, Germany, permanently influenced Wesley, but their most vital influence was through Peter Böhler in London.

possibilities of the downmost man, and, above all, by his reasonable, but simple, joyous Faith, retained with ever increasing power the crucial place in that world crusade.

At death, Wesley left not less than 120,000 members, closely knit together in the marvellous organisation of his " Methodist " Societies. Some historians estimate the number at 150,000 ; but the all-important fact is that every member was a crusader among his neighbours for righteousness and temperance, for justice and equity, for spiritual values and popular education, for joyous fellowship on earth and holy citizenship in Heaven. The organisation carried no " dead wood." Every avowed follower felt himself a missioner of God, who one day must render an account of his stewardship. But great as was Wesley's influence in the flesh, his spiritual influence has proven even greater. To-day the Societies he founded have become the largest Protestant Church in the world. Their immediate following is at least four times larger than the population of England at Wesley's demise ; their annual *voluntary* gifts run into many millions of pounds ; their religious and social programme commands the gratuitous service of hundreds of thousands of zealous workers, and their spiritual impact has been felt on every Continent of the globe.

Nevertheless, just here lies the rub. The very proportions of world Methodism tend to press heavily on Wesley's memory. That he neither desired nor intended to create a new sect or Church, everyone knows. His ruling purpose was to rekindle spiritual and Christian influences in *every* department of life. His interests and efforts were truly Catholic. Yet many historians have dismissed him curtly as the exclusive possession of the Methodist body ; whereas the truth is that, his indirect influence has been even more vital than his direct influence. Ultimately the Evangelical Revival accomplished much of Wesley's lofty intent. Mr. Lloyd George and Lord Baldwin are not far from the mark, when they suggest that neither modern Britain nor modern America can ever be understood apart from the labours of this intrepid prophet, and inspired leader of men.

(iii) *An Apparent Failure*

But let us now pause and inquire into the origin of this man Wesley, and the remarkable movement he moulded and guided. The zeal of many to push back their family pedigree to some war lord of the Norman Conquest is at best humorous, at worst pathetic ; sometimes it has led to fetish worship, sometimes to snobbery. John Wesley was too wise to waste time or incite pride by any such fruitless pursuit. He judged men always by what they *were* and what they *did*—never by social caste or family blood. Yet, since his death, he has had admirers so obsessed by this passion for family pedigree—" last frailty of noble mind "—that they have produced genealogical tables purporting to prove that he was a direct descendant of honourable stock dating not only from the Norman Conquest, but generations before.[1]

Be this as it may, it meant nothing to Wesley, and we pass no judgment upon its accuracy. His *immediate* ancestry is however of peculiar interest, for he was, in a marked sense, a child of the Christian Church. The expulsion of Puritan divines, in 1662, drove, as we have seen, a great-grandfather and both grandfathers of Wesley from their livings. All three were Oxford graduates, men of culture and character, who dared to stand resolutely upon their convictions, and to suffer for conscience sake.[2]

Thus the Puritan fibre in Wesley's ancestry was basic. But turning to Epworth Rectory, where he was born and reared, the " old " High Church influence was completely dominant. Samuel Wesley, John's father, was intended for the Nonconformist ministry and to that end was sent to a Dissenting college. But in this institution—St. Martin's Academy—Samuel found so much sectarian and political controversy and so little vital religion, that finally he revolted against all Nonconformity, and setting off on foot for Oxford, with but two pounds, five shillings, in his pocket, sought Orders in the National Church.[3] Becoming a servitor of Exeter College, Samuel in due course graduated from Oxford, meanwhile having inbibed rigid High Church ideas ; and in 1689 he was ordained a priest, " thus reuniting his branch of the family with the Church which had expelled his father and grandfather and which afterwards looked with prejudice on the efforts of his sons."[4]

Susannah Wesley, Samuel's wife, was a daughter of the scholarly Dr. Annesley, who, after ejection from the ancient parish of St. Giles, London, came to be styled, " the St. Paul of Nonconformity." Susannah was a woman eminently qualified to be the mother of an immortal world leader. Her intellectual powers were acute, her courage was unflagging, her faith serene, while also her spiritual initiative and independence were truly

[1] See G. J. Stevenson, *Memorial of the Wesley Family.*
[2] See P. Cadman, *Three Religious Leaders of Oxford,* p. 179.
[3] *Camb. Mod. Hist.,* Vol. X, pp. 431–2.
[4] Cadman, *Three Religious Leaders of Oxford,* p. 182.

phenomenal.[1]   Though the daughter of an ejected Puritan divine, Susannah, when but thirteen years old,[2] and before meeting Samuel Wesley, had become discontented with the " stern Calvinism " then dominant in Nonconformity ; so with characteristic decisiveness, after due consideration and in the face of all consequences, she too left Dissent and joined the State Church.   Hence in the blood of the renowned missioner, to a unique degree, Anglican and Puritan coalesced—" the order and dignity of the one, the fearless initiative and asceticism of the other."[3]

On June 28th, 1703, at Epworth Rectory, John Wesley was born ;   and the teaching and example he there received, especially from his mother, remained to him throughout life a sacred heritage.   But on the tables of memory the date, February 9th, 1709, was literally branded.   For then, shortly before midnight, Epworth rectory was burned to the ground ; and as the family excitedly were assembling outside the blazing house, thanking God that at least all lives were spared, a child's piercing screams burst from the topmost chamber.   " Jackie " was within the fiery cauldron !   Awakened by the raging of flames in the thatched roof just over his head, the five year old lad, seeing the staircase ablaze, had tugged a chest to the window, and on it he stood, smashing the glass and shouting for help. An heroic rescue was speedily effected, and he who later was to move the world for righteousness was plucked, " a brand out of the burning," only a few seconds before the roof fell in.[4] Always to Wesley this rescue was a direct intervention of Providence.   The hand of Destiny, he felt, was upon him.

At the famous Charterhouse School, Wesley—from 1713 to 1719—laid the foundations of his excellent classical education. But the memory of the place was not happy.   Repeatedly has he recalled the brutal bullying of the larger boys, and also the fact that for days together he there had " little to eat save bread, and no plenty of that."[5]   His undergraduate years at Christchurch, Oxford, we pass over ;   not till he became a Fellow of Lincoln College, were certain Oxford influences woven inextricably into his habits of life.   These influences centred in

---

[1] See Wesley's *Journal*, August 1st, 1742 (after Susannah's death).
[2] See Dr. W. H. Fitchett's *Wesley and His Century*, p. 16.
[3] Cadman, *op. cit.*, p. 178.
[4] C. E. Vulliamy, *John Wesley*, p. 4.
[5] See Robt. Southey's *Life of Wesley*, pp. 22–3.   This and other quotations from Southey, are from the 1820 abridged edition.   It contains all that is vital in Southey's two volumes.   Knox's essay on Wesley, published as an *Appendix* to Southey's *Life*, shows more real insight than Southey's whole ponderous work.

" the Holy Club " of which he was the leading member. Of the organisation and purpose of this club, Wesley, in a letter to Mr. Morgan (October 18th, 1732), has left a faithful picture.[1] It was a small gathering of serious, religious Oxford men who met regularly in a " Lincoln " room to cultivate and co-ordinate their intellectual and spiritual life, and to devise means of increasing their services to their fellowmen.[2] A practical programme was soon adopted, and the members so divided their time that every moment was accounted for. They resolved to receive the Holy Communion as frequently as possible, to help in the religious instruction and education of poor, neglected children, to visit and befriend prisoners in Oxford jails, and to give freely, according to their means, to relieve necessity among the poor. Their rigorous piety and methodical exertion was soon manifest both to fellow-students and dons ; " the Holy Club " became the butt of many an Oxford jest ; and some young wag, in contempt of their methodised discipline, scoffingly dubbed them " Methodists." How little did he dream of the destined significance of the name he had coined !

Again, it is noteworthy that during Wesley's protracted associations with Oxford, which continued more than a dozen years, he erected an extensive framework of solid scholarship. As a resident Fellow of Lincoln College, he was moderator of daily " exercises and disputations " held in the college hall ; and beyond doubt his experience in this office tempered and sharpened that keen, logical acumen which makes the poet Southey, in his *Life of Wesley*, say : " No man, indeed, was ever more dexterous in the art of reasoning."[3] Certainly this training stood him in good stead during critical periods of his career, when forced to defend both himself and his followers against the onslaughts of bitter and formidable foes.[4]

But Wesley's intrepid spirit was never intended for the seclusion of college halls ; so when there came a plea for volunteers as pioneer missionaries to Georgia, to work partly among the Colonists and partly among the Indians, Wesley proffered his services, on condition that his mother, now a widow, consent. When approached, Susannah Wesley, knowing that Charles, her youngest son, was also contemplating departure on the same venture, replied : " Had I twenty sons, I

---

[1] This long letter is prefaced to the first edition of Wesley's *Journal*.
[2] See N. Curnock's valuable notes on the Holy Club in the *Standard* edition of Wesley's *Journal*.
[3] *Op. cit.*, p. 24.
[4] See, for instance, his *Earnest Appeal to Men of Reason and Religion* (1743) ; *Further Appeal*, etc. (1745) ; *The Principles of a Methodist* (1742) ; and *First Letter* to Bishop Lavington (1750).

should rejoice that they were all so employed, though I should never see them more."[1]

The rigid sacramentarianism, the ardent sacerdotal zeal, the pontifical efforts to enforce ecclesiastical discipline, the ascetic legalism, the ill-managed love affair and the community friction, which stand as ear-marks on Wesley's American missionary work, need no elaboration. The impression he made upon the Georgia community is all too faithfully reflected, alas! in the words of one of their number: "We know that we are Protestants; but as for this man, we know not of what religion he is!"[2]

Had Wesley died in his thirty-fifth year, he would have been an unremembered man—capable, methodical, hard-working, but pedantic, legalistic, irascible; unloved and wellnigh unlovable. The most charitable tribute that could then have been paid him, would have been that he was a sincere, a selfless, almost an heroic, failure.

(iv)   *A Transfigured Soul*

. After more than two years of defeat and disillusionment as a Colonial missionary,[3] Wesley was overwhelmed with perplexity and anguish. "I went to America to convert the Indians; but O! who will convert me!"[4] was the agonised cry of his soul. As he sailed homeward, the hierarchical and formalistic staff upon which he had long been leaning was sorely strained, if not already broken. Setting foot again on English soil, he knew himself a sadder and a wiser man. He was less cocksure both of himself and his ecclesiastical dogmas. The mists and fogs of defeatism and uncertainty enveloped him as a blanket of darkness. His compass, he knew, was not pointing true. Gales and tempests broke on his rugged trail. His confidence in John Wesley the priest was ebbing low. But as an intrepid pioneer—still conscious of a holy vocation—he groped on and on, through fog, haze and

---

[1] Southey's *Wesley*, p. 62.

[2] Wesley, referring in later life to this period, says: "How well have I since been beaten with my own staff!" Again, in old age, he pictures himself at this time as having "only the faith of a servant, not that of a son."

[3] Whitefield's Evangelical conversion preceded Wesley's. He first set off for America just as John Wesley returned; and it is remarkable that he was eminently successful where *both* the Wesleys had failed.

[4] Wesley's *Journal*, January 24th, 1738.

darkness, o'er crag and cliff, doubting not that the mountain peaks of vision might yet be scaled. And finally, in the sunrise of a glorious spiritual morning, the fogs were lifted, the mists were dispelled, the tempest was stilled ; the heights were attained. Wesley, elevated now to the pinnacle of spiritual experience, breathed pure and fragrant air. Alone before the Holy One he stood. And there a live coal from Heaven's altar purged his dross, illumined his understanding and sealed him as a messenger of Grace.

But what language can ever explain the mystery and miracle of a soul re-born ? Wesley, lifted to the Holy Mount, was endowed with new sensitivities ; new faculties and powers. A revealing Faith became the eye of his soul, whereby he saw Him Who is Invisible : it became to him a spiritual ear through which he heard the Still, Small Voice divine. On the Mount of Transfiguration, Wesley's spirit took wings to where the heavens rang with praise. There he peered forward, and life's horizons were strangely amplified. The wondrous awesome music of choirs celestial flooded his soul. " Peace on earth, goodwill toward men " was their swelling refrain. The very stars in the firmament reflected now the crystal purity of Heaven, where all wills are attuned into harmony with the Will Divine. Wesley, transfigured, at one with God, surveyed again that " heart-warming " scene ; and the veil of time and sense being for the moment lifted, he envisaged a human society reborn to a spiritual prototype—a society wherein the will of God is done on earth as in Heaven.

Before him there loomed the City of God, the Promised Land : within him was the harmony of a new heaven and a new earth. Wesley, in " conversion," glimpsed Eternity's strand, and in that new perspective even former enemies were now his friends in God. Love possessed and transformed his being.

Then the veil fell ; the material world returned : the air chilled. Wesley looked now, with a seer's vision, upon the England of his day. It was the England of the slave-trader, the kidnapper and the smuggler ; the England of trading-justices, South Sea Bubbles and commercial cupidity ; the England of gin-shops, sodden ignorance and incredible child neglect ; the England of bestial sports, mad gambling and parading wantonness. It was the England of corrupt politics and soulless religion : the England of " materialism," " dim ideals " and " expiring hopes."

The contrast to a now hyper-sensitised soul might seem revolting. But courage never wavered. England to Wesley, despite her sins, was still a land of immortal souls. And henceforth he knew that Christ had given him birth :

> "To brother all the souls on earth."

He knew, too, that he was now commissioned by the Father of all Love and Mercy and Truth to release England from the bondage of materialism, and point her feet toward the ways of righteousness. His peculiar mission was to restore Faith to a faithless people. No longer did doubt or uncertainty corrode his mind. He had groped his way through darkness and pain to the Mount of Transfiguration, where the shackles of serfdom fell from his soul. No longer had he the faith of a servant, but the faith of a son. His, at last, was the glorious liberty of an heir of God, anointed to perform a work of mighty deliverance for mankind.

May 24th, 1738, therefore, was Wesley's spiritual birthday. On that date "the brand plucked out of the burning" was impregnated with spiritual fire that he might set England ablaze for God. The sophisticated would mock ; vested interests and prejudice would persecute ; the general populace would resist. But this twice-born man henceforth knew his "calling." The chains of pedanticism and legalism were now snapped asunder. The priest was merged in the prophet. Wesley forthwith was a child of the spirit. Formality had given place to reality. And from that day till his spirit returned to its Maker—fifty-three years later—the divine light rarely flickered, and never left his path. Depression and defeat henceforth were strangers to him. His "spiritual birthday" came exactly four months after the agonising cry : "O ! who will convert me ! "

*   *   *   *   *

The intellectual struggles, the heart-rendings, the seething emotion associated with this period of darkness and dawn, are all recorded in the restrained but unmistakable language of Wesley's *Journal* : and there the whole story is best pursued.[1] Special mention, however, must be made of a young German, who, throughout Wesley's crisis was his counsellor and guide. Peter Böhler, a graduate of Jena University, was a convert to Moravianism. Ordained in Germany, and commissioned by Count Zinzendorf for missionary work in America, he now was sojourning in London, prior to departure for the Carolinas. John and Charles Wesley, in continued association with him, were tremendously impressed by his contagious faith and the calm, assuring power of his personality. In their benighted

---

[1] See *Journal* between January 13th and May 24th, 1738.

plight, Böhler was to clear their atmosphere, and point them to the realms of Abundant Life.

A revealing picture of the state of the Wesley brothers at this time is preserved in a letter from Böhler to Zinzendorf: " I travelled with the two brothers from London to Oxford. The elder, John, is a good-natured man ; he knew he did not properly believe on the Saviour, and he was willing to be taught. His brother . . . is at present very distressed in mind, but does not know how he shall begin to be acquainted with the Saviour. Our mode of believing . . . is so easy to Englishmen, that they cannot reconcile themselves to it ; if it were a little more artful, they would much sooner find their way into it. Of faith in Jesus they have no other idea than the generality of people have. They justify themselves ; and therefore they always take for granted that they believe already, and try to prove their faith by their works, and thus so plague and torment themselves that they are at heart very miserable."[1]

It must not be assumed, however, that during this season of bewilderment Wesley became a recluse. Contrariwise, between February 1st, when he landed in England, and the dawning of the new day in May, he preached scores of sermons in different places ; and all were the utterances of a man seeking fearlessly, even desperately, for the pearl of great price. So trenchant, indeed, was his message that most of the Churches in which he now preached, being offended at his plainness of speech, excluded him henceforth from their pulpits.

The tenor of Böhler's advice when Wesley was plumbing the deeps of his travail, was that he should exercise himself to attain to living faith in the living God, through the crucified but living mediator, Jesus Christ. Wesley, knowing his faith to be weak, turned to his counsellor with the pathetic query : " How can I preach to others, when I have not faith myself ? " Böhler's paradoxical reply was pregnant with poignant truth : " Preach Faith," he urged, " till you have it, and because you have it you will preach faith."[2] Wesley, accepted the challenge. Searching the Scriptures, he threw himself on God, and proved finally to his soul's content that the fruits of pure, living, disinterested Faith are indeed good. He discovered that Faith is the mysterious dynamic which brings divine, unsuspected

---

[1] L. Tyerman, *Life and Times of John Wesley*, Vol. I, pp. 181–2.

[2] Coleridge said of Böhler's advice that it was equivalent to saying : " Tell a lie long enough and often enough and you will be sure to end by believing it." This shallow comment reflects on Coleridge rather than Böhler, showing that he failed totally to comprehend a situation of peculiar delicacy.

energy into the soul of man, and urges him on to works of righteousness.

Far more completely than Luther, Wesley came to realise that good works are the inseparable properties of living faith, even as warmth and light are the inseparable properties of the sun : that the *nature* of true faith is to bear holy fruit. Hence, accepting Böhler's advice, he followed only after the highest, and so doing, entered into a warm, glowing communion with Christ. The mantle of the Lord was cast about him ; the water of life purged and sustained his soul ; the Holy Spirit of God possessed his being.

Two paramount experiences are linked with Wesley's conversion. One was the singing of the anthem in St. Paul's Cathedral on the afternoon of May 24th : " Out of the deep have I called unto Thee, O Lord : Lord, hear my voice. O let Thine ears consider well the voice of my complaint." And as the melodious strains reverberated from the dome of that great temple, Wesley found comfort in the words : " My soul fleeth unto the Lord : before the morning watch, I say, before the morning watch."[1]   The other, and more fructifying experience, was in the evening of the same day, when " very unwillingly " he attended " a society in Aldersgate Street." Here the Leader read Luther's preface to the Epistle to the Romans, with a result thus depicted by Wesley : " About a quarter before nine, while he was describing the change which God works in the heart through faith in Christ, I felt my heart *strangely warmed*. I felt I did trust in Christ, Christ alone, for my salvation ; and an assurance was given me that He had taken away my sins, even mine, and saved me from the law of sin and death."

" I began to pray with all my might," continues Wesley's record, " for those who had in a more especial manner despitefully used me and persecuted me. I then testified openly to all there what I now first felt in my heart."[2]

Pivotal, however, as was Wesley's spiritual birthday, and sustaining as were the springs of love, peace and power which then burst forth as a living fountain in his soul, the serene joy and irresistible gladness, which so characterised his life through all his astounding labours, came gradually—even as the opening of a flower. Wesley's Aldersgate experience was a conversion, a transfiguration : it strangely warmed his heart and filled his spirit to overflowing with gratitude, veneration and awe. Yet he could not long remain on the mountain top. Those

---

[1] See Psalm cxxx.   [2] *Journal*, May 24th, 1738.

OPPOSITION TO THE REVIVAL

1. A mob uprising against Wesley, in Wednesbury (top) (From the painting by Marshall Claxton, R.A.)

2. Whitefield preaching at Moorfields Fair Ground, London. Note man raised aloft with whip; horn-blowing from tree; and pole raised to strike preacher from behind (bottom)

moments of rapture, vision and victory were fleeting. But the inner sunshine of assurance, peace and power which they brought remained constant. And as Wesley co-related his new-found faith to his newly emerging task, an increasing sense of joy nourished and sustained his soul. After the initial transfiguration, therefore, his conversion process was of an evolutionary nature. With increasing " perfectionism " came increasing joy ; also increasing ease and power in service.

(v) *The Testing and Expression of Faith*

On the Sunday following his never-to-be-forgotten experience, Wesley preached in the morning at St. George's Chapel, Bloomsbury, London, on " This is the victory that overcometh the world, even our faith," and in the afternoon at the Chapel in Long Acre, on " God's justifying the ungodly." The *Journal* significantly adds : " The last time, I understand, I am to preach at either " ; and Wesley's only comment is, " Not as I will, but as Thou wilt." " On the evening of the same day," he notes, " I was roughly attacked in a large company as an enthusiast, a seducer, and a setter forth of new doctrines. By the blessing of God, I was not moved to anger, but after a calm and short reply went away ; though not with so tender a concern as was due to those who were seeking death in the error of their life."[1] By the second Sunday succeeding his soul's awakening, his joy was beginning to express itself, for the *Journal* reads : " Sun. 4—was indeed a feast day. For from the time of my rising till past one in the afternoon, I was praying, reading the Scriptures, singing praise, or calling sinners to repentance. All these days I scarce remember to have opened the Testament, but upon some great and precious promise. And I saw more than ever that the Gospel is in truth but one great promise, from the beginning of it to the end."

Within three weeks of his conversion, Wesley, like St. Paul who withdrew temporarily into Arabia, sought a period of retirement for meditation, observation and re-adjustment. The vistas of the new life opening up before him were so vast, so wonderful, that he must needs pause a while to get his bearings and survey the land of his inheritance. It was not unnatural that Germany beckoned him thither. She was the land of his spiritual guides—Luther and Böhler. So forthwith, on June 13th, Wesley set off for Germany, via Holland, bent

[1] *Journal*, May 28th, 1738.

particularly on visiting the Moravian settlements around Hern-huth and Marienborn. He fain would study for himself the life, habits and institutions of communities which accepted seriously the doctrine of Salvation by Faith : nor was his sojourn in vain. Referring to his Marienborn contacts, he says : " Here I continually met with what I sought for, viz., living proofs of the power of faith : persons saved from inward as well as outward sin, by ' the love of God shed abroad in their hearts ' ; and from all doubt and fear, by the abiding witness of the Holy Ghost given unto them."[1] The charity, co-operation, frugality and cleanliness of these people, too, appealed strongly to Wesley. The whole visit, in fact, among the Moravian communities afforded satisfaction ; for on leaving Hernhuth (August 14th) he wrote : " I would gladly have spent my life here ; but my Master calling me to labour in another part of His vineyard . . . I was constrained to take my leave of this happy place."[2]

Such tributes, however, are by no means applicable to all the experiences of the German tour. Wesley was three months and four days away from England. Scarcely a full month was spent among the Moravian communities : as for other parts of Germany, he frankly found them disappointing. After attending Sunday worship in a Lutheran Church at Meissen, he writes : " I was greatly surprised at all I saw there : at the costliness of apparel in many, and the gaudiness of it in more. . . . The minister's habit was adorned with gold and scarlet, and a vast cross both behind and before. Most of the congregation sat (the men generally with their hats on, at the prayers as well as sermon). . . . Alas, alas ! what a reformed country is this ! "[3] Lutheranism, as a whole, he found both rigid and frigid ; and commenting on a Rhine boat trip, he says : " I could not but observe the decency of the Papists above us who are called Reformed."[4] The pomposity, more-over, of German civic officials and the inhospitality of German cities toward foreigners, did violence to Wesley's expanding conception of human brotherhood. In more than one town he was refused lodgings, while repeatedly he was detained at city gates for hours on end, being bundled, " with the usual impertinent solemnity " from one " magistrate or officer to another." " This senseless, inhuman usage of strangers ! " is his designation of the treatment he and his friends received

[1] *Journal*, July 6th, 1738.
[2] *Ibid.*, August 12th and 14th, 1738.
[3] *Ibid.*, July 30th, 1738.
[4] *Ibid.*, July, 28th, 1738.

"at almost every German city."   "A breach of all the common,
even the heathen laws of hospitality," he again defined it.   At
Weimar, after prolonged detention outside the gate, he was
carried before some great man ("I believe the Duke") and
submitted to a regimen of further questions.   Finally came
the query, "Why are you going so far as Hernhuth?"   Wesley,
with a droll, donnish thrust, answered : "To see the place
where *the Christians* live."[1]

Even Count Zinzendorf, for all his piety, zeal and charity,
was too patronising to appeal strongly to Wesley, who, upon
reflection, questioned if the Moravians as a body were not too
exclusive, too self-righteous, and too much given to over-
magnifying their own Church.[2] Wesley's conversion had warmed
his heart, unified his personality, multiplied his sympathies, and
clarified and intensified his life purpose ; but it had in no sense
stultified his critical faculties.   Much as he loathed Deism,
he was always something of a Christian rationalist ; and never
did he disparage the God-imparted faculty of reason, as the
foundation of all critical judgment.   To him reason was an
indispensable (though not the only) handmaid of Truth.   Hence
certain aspects of Moravian mysticism were later to meet with
his rational censure.

On returning to England, September 17th, Wesley at once
began to declare "the glad tidings of salvation."   Prisons,
workhouses, society meetings and whatever Churches would
open their doors to him were the chief scenes of his endeavour.
Already, though as yet but beginning to find his stride, was
he proving that the faith which had expanded and co-ordinated
his own faculties, bringing with it harmony, peace, power and
gladness, was releasing others from the shackles of serfdom
and sin. But so far everything done was in accordance with
conservative, even High Church, precedent.   The most starchy
of his clerical brethren would admit that the holding of religious services in jails, prisons, workhouses and the like was
within the scope of the Church scheme ; although the spiritual
inertia and moral laxity of the times, had resulted in a gross
neglect of this duty.   Soon, however, "the Enthusiast" was to
take a step which shocked beyond repair the dignity and etiquette of his more stiff and formal brethren.

April 2nd, 1739, is a date of poignant significance to the
whole English-speaking world.   On the evening of March 31st,
in response to Whitefield's invitation, Wesley arrived in Bristol.
Next day, by Whitefield's example, he was persuaded of the

[1] *Journal*, July 22nd, 1738, also July 30th.
[2] See C. E. Vulliamy, *John Wesley*, pp. 88–9.

necessity of field preaching as the means most likely to reach the toiling masses, who, because of the frigid aloofness of orthodox procedure, had become virtual outcasts, untouched, and seemingly untouchable, by the Church. Wesley's own record reveals the mental dilemma with which he was here confronted : " I could scarce reconcile myself at first to this strange way of preaching in the fields, of which he set me an example on Sunday ; having been all my life (till very lately) so tenacious of every point relating to decency and order, that I should have thought the saving of souls almost a sin, if it had not been done in a church."[1] Whitefield's victory, nevertheless, was complete. For that same evening—Whitefield meanwhile having left Bristol—Wesley expounded to " a little society " in Nicholas Street from the Sermon on the Mount—" one pretty remarkable precedent of field-preaching," adds the *Journal*, " though I suppose there were churches at that time also." Less than twenty-four hours later (April 2nd, 1739) Wesley himself embarked on the new venture.[2]

"At four in the afternoon," he says, " I submitted to be more vile, and proclaimed in the highways the glad tidings of salvation, speaking from a little eminence in a ground adjoining the city, to about three thousand people." His text for this, the first of his many thousands of field sermons, was prophetic of great things ahead : " The spirit of the Lord is upon me, because he hath anointed me to preach the Gospel to the poor ; he hath sent me to heal the broken-hearted ; to preach deliverance to the captive, and recovery of sight to the blind ; to set at liberty them that are bruised, to proclaim the acceptable year of the Lord."

Having preached his first field sermon, Wesley had begun the aggressive march of his crusade for righteousness. This twice-born man was now not only in possession of the central doctrine of his campaign ; he also had discovered the chief vehicle of its expression. Other developments would follow in due course, but the redemptive and creative power of a transfigured life was now about to be manifested : a great advance movement for personal and social regeneration already was launched upon a prodigal and debauched, an unexpectant and ungrateful, land.

---

[1] *Journal*, March 31st, 1739.
[2] The splendour of Whitefield's life is commonly overshadowed by the towering majesty of Wesley's achievement. In the early phases of the Revival, Whitefield's influence over Wesley was decisive. For Whitefield's importance, see Luke Tyerman's *George Whitefield*, and Dr. A. D. Belden's *Whitefield, the Awakener*.

THE SHAPING OF A CRUSADE

" CHRISTIANITY is essentially a social religion ; to turn it into a solitary religion is indeed to destroy it."

JOHN WESLEY's *Works* (1872 Edition), Vol. V, p. 296.

" FOR opinions and terms let us not destroy the work of God. Dost thou love and fear God ? It is enough ! I give thee the right hand of fellowship."

JOHN WESLEY, *Character of a Methodist* (1742), p. 10.

THE SHAPING OF A CRUSADE

LONG has it been fashionable in rationalist circles to patronise, to ridicule or to caricature the Evangelical Movement, on the score that it made no really philosophical contribution to religious or political thought. Sir Leslie Stephen, one of the most brilliant stars in the rationalist firmament, comparing the Evangelical Revival with the great religious movement of the preceding century, delineates " the new Puritanism " as but " a faint reflection of the grander Puritanism of the seventeenth century."[1]

Now the creative capacity of the movement that threw up a Milton, a Cromwell, a Bunyan, a Hampden, a Marvell, a Baxter and a Fox, no one will question. Nevertheless Stephen's criticism, and all other criticisms based solely upon philosophical, theoretic and literary standards, are far from the mark ; for it is impossible to peruse the primary documents of the Eighteenth Century Revival, without realising that it never made any pretence of formulating a new philosophy of life ; nor had it any desire so to do. It was eminently satisfied with the doctrinal statement of religion expressed in the Articles of the Creed, while also it accepted unhesitatingly the Gospel ethic as a Revelation of life's deeper meaning, to which all Christians, of whatever denomination, if really serious, were committed.

Had not Bishops Berkeley and Butler already engaged in brilliant philosophical speculations, and were not the masses of England oblivious to their existence ? To Wesley, arm-chair philosophies had no appeal. He was, at many points, a religious pragmatist before the advent of " Pragmatism." With a sensitiveness which his conversion had made peculiarly acute, he beheld the drunkenness, the ignorance, the cruelty, the vice, the misery and the poverty of teeming multitudes of his fellows, and he had an unflagging faith that the Spirit of the living God, working through the Gospel of Christ, could restore the divine image, even in the souls of the most degraded ;

[1] Stephen's *English Thought in the Eighteenth Century*, Vol. II, p. 433.

while as for rational speculation he was utterly sceptical that
it alone could ever achieve such effect. Had not " Rationalism " already had its chance, and were not its fruits sour ?
Had it not degenerated into cackling cleverness and sophisticated
stupidity ? Was it not far removed from the sources, and hence
devoid of the sagacities of living wisdom ? Wesley's supreme
purpose was to make men vitally conscious of God. He therefore had no desire to dictate the intellectual niceties associated
with the divine work of redemption ; rather was he actuated
by an impelling passion to be used of God, as a humble but
active instrument, in the *work* of redemption. With prophetic
insight he recognised the insidious demons which were luring
millions of his countrymen into the tangled labyrinths of moral
corruption and spiritual death : and challenging the sway of
those demons, he set about to release the victims from their
woeful plight. He saw the ecclesiastical machinery of his
generation rusty and clogged with dust ; he chafed to cleanse
it and set it in motion, for the redemption of the general populace.
His purpose was not to formulate a new theology or a new theory
of Church or State, but to touch dead bones with the breath
of spiritual power, and make them live ; to release the winds of
heaven, that they might blow upon the ashy embers of religion
and kindle a purging, illuminating fire of righteousness and
truth. He would substitute for the bondage of sin, the liberty,
individual and social, of men new-born after the similitude of
Christ. He would revive creative, life-giving Faith.

(i) *The Practical Nature of the Revival*

That this passion for moral righteousness and inward freedom
was the centre and essence of the Evangelical crusade, there
can be no doubt. In his treatise, *The Character of a Methodist*,
written in 1742, Wesley says : " By salvation he means holiness
of heart and life. . . . It is nonsense for a woman to consider
herself virtuous because she is not a prostitute, or a man honest
because he does not steal. May the Lord God preserve me
from such a poor, starved religion as this. Were this the
mark of a Methodist, I would sooner be a sincere Jew, Turk or
Pagan."[1] In the same booklet Wesley emphatically and
unmistakably defines his position : " I would to God that all
men knew that I and all who follow my judgment, do vehemently
refuse to be distinguished from other men by any but the common principles of Christianity. It is the plain old Christianity

[1] J. Wesley, *op. cit.*, p. 5.

that I teach, renouncing and detesting all other marks of distinction. But from real Christians, *of whatever denomination they be*, we earnestly desire not to be distinguished at all : not from any who sincerely follow after what they know they have not yet attained. ' Whosoever doeth the will of my Father which is in Heaven, the same is my brother and sister and mother ' . . . For opinions and terms let us not destroy the work of God. Dost thou love and fear God ? It is enough ! I give thee the right hand of fellowship."[1]

This tract also affords typical evidence that the very foundations of the Movement were ethical, practical and experimental rather than doctrinal, theoretical or metaphysical. Its ideal disciple, Wesley declares, " loves every man as his own soul. He loves his enemies, yea and the enemies of God—the evil and the unthankful. And if it be not in his power to do good toward those that hate him, he ceases not to pray for them." Again : " As he has time and opportunity he does good toward all men—unto neighbours and strangers, friends and enemies— not only to their bodies by feeding the hungry, clothing the naked, visiting those that are sick or in prison, but much more does he labour to do good to their souls." Wesley's true follower, moreover, " Knows that vice does not lose its nature though it becomes ever so fashionable . . . He cannot follow a multitude to do evil."[2] And referring to the accusation that he was striving to establish a new religious sect, Wesley writes : " I should rejoice (so little ambitious am I to be the head of a sect or party) if the very name ' Methodist ' might never be mentioned more, but be buried in eternal oblivion."[3] Far from desiring to pose as the founder of a new credal or doctrinal system, Wesley says : " To all opinions which do not strike at the roots of Christianity, we think and let think."[4]

In scores of Wesley's publications and thousands of his sermons, this practical outlook of the Revival was poignantly expressed : through all his manifold teaching it ran as a guiding thread.[5] In his *Earnest Appeal to Men of Reason and Religion* (1743), a fine instance of vivid, sustained, logical argument, he says : " Love to God and to all mankind is the centre of religion. . . . This love we believe to be the medicine of life, the never-failing remedy for all the evils of a disordered world. Wherever it is,

[1] J. Wesley, op. cit., p. 10.
[2] *Ibid.*, pp. 8 and 10.
[3] *Ibid.*, p. 1.
[4] *Ibid.*, p. 4.
[5] R. Green collected 233 original publications by Wesley ; he preached, too, at least 42,000 sermons.

there are virtue and happiness going hand in hand. There is humbleness of mind, gentleness, long-suffering, the whole image of God, and, at the same time, a peace that passeth all understanding, and joy unspeakable and full of glory."[1] This social and brotherly love, Wesley taught must "express itself in every kind of beneficence, spreading virtue and happiness all around it"; while concerning the practical and imminent nature of vital faith, he here calls it "the ear of the soul, whereby the sinner hears the voice of the Son of God and lives." It is "the eye of the new-born soul, whereby every true believer in God seeth Him that is invisible."[2]

Pivotal however to Wesley's religion as was that creative faith, which needs must issue in works of service and love, he would tolerate no mouthing of cant phrases, no vain repetitions of theological formulæ. "I find more profit in sermons on either good tempers, or good works," he protests, "than in what are vulgarly called 'Gospel Sermons.' The term has now become a mere cant word : I wish none of our society would use it. It has no determinate meaning. Let but a pert, self-sufficient animal, that has neither sense nor grace, bawl out something about Christ, or His blood, or justification by faith, and his hearers cry out, 'What a fine Gospel sermon !' We know no Gospel without salvation from sin."[3]

Neither would Wesley countenance any individualistic, ex-clusive, monopolistic interpretation of religion. To him religion was the be-all and end-all of life, and to exclude it from any department of human affairs was to maim and deform it. No man, no creed, no class, therefore, dare call upon God for puny, selfish ends. "Christianity," he continually taught, "is essentially a social religion," and "to turn it into a solitary religion is indeed to destroy it."[4] In the *Preface* to the first Methodist Hymn Book (1739) Wesley wrote : "The Gospel of Christ knows no religion but *social*, no holiness but *social holiness*. This command have we from Christ, that he who loves God loves his brother also."

The current modern notion that the Evangelical Revival was ridiculously individualistic and morbidly "other-worldly" is completely false. Human fellowship, co-operation and service were at its heart, and pulsed through all its life.

In a fearless, but characteristic University sermon, preached in St. Mary's, Oxford, in 1744, Wesley pictures Christianity as

---

[1] *Earnest Appeal*, etc., p. 3.
[2] *Ibid.*, p. 4.
[3] See John Wesley's *Works* (1872 edition), Vol. XIII, p. 36.
[4] *Ibid.*, Vol. V, p. 296.

" beginning to exist in individuals," next, as " spreading from one to another," and finally " as covering the earth." Then, dramatically, he asks his congregation to pause " and survey *this strange sight, a Christian world* ! " It would be a world from which injustice, inequality, hatred, vice and war were forever banished : a world illumined by the spirit of Christ, and guided by the Golden Rule. " Where does this Christianity now exist ? " asks Wesley. " Where, I pray, do the Christians live ? . . . It is utterly needful that someone should use great plainness of speech toward you. . . . Let us confess we have never yet seen a Christian country upon the earth." Finally, challenging Oxford, Wesley queries, " Is this city a Christian city ? Are all the Magistrates, all the Heads and Governors of Colleges and Halls, and their respective Societies . . . of one heart and soul ? Is the love of God shed abroad in our hearts ? And are our lives agreeable thereto ? "[1] The sure hope of a better age, he pleaded, was a better man. Only Christ's new man, could herald Christ's new world. To Wesley, " a scheme to reconstruct society which ignored the redemption of the individual was unthinkable " ; " a doctrine to save sinning men, with no aim to transform them into crusaders against social sin, was equally unthinkable."[2] The earthly *Civitas Dei* languished for lack of builders illumined by the vision and impelled by the spirit of the Land Immortal.

Again, the *Rules of the Society of the People called Methodists* illustrate the vital, practical purposes of the movement. The Society consisted of groups of people " having the form, and seeking the power of godliness." They were " to watch over one another in love, that they may help each other to work out their salvation." And all who continued in the Society were " to evidence their desire of salvation," *First,* " by doing no harm, by avoiding evil in every kind " ; *Secondly,* " by doing good, by being in every kind merciful after their power ; as they have opportunity, doing good of every possible sort, and as far as possible, to all men " ; *Thirdly,* " by attending upon all the ordinances of God." According to Wesley's *Christian Negative,* converts were to abstain from profaning the name of God or the day of God ; from " buying or selling spiritous liquors, or drinking them " ; from " fighting, quarrelling, brawling " ; from " returning evil for evil or railing for railing " ; from " using many words in buying or selling " ; from all commerce in " uncustomed goods " ; from " giving or taking

---

[1] See sermon, *Scriptural Christianity.*
[2] Henry Carter, *The Methodist* (A Study in Discipleship), p. 174.

things on usury " ; from the use of " costly apparel " ; from " softness and needless self-indulgence " ; from " laying up treasures upon earth " and from " taking up goods without the probability of paying for them." According to his *Christian Positive*, all members of the Society were to do good to men's *bodies*, " of the ability that God giveth, by giving food to the hungry, by clothing the naked, by visiting or helping them that are sick or in prison " etc : and to their *souls*, by instructing, reproving, or exhorting " ; by setting an example of " all possible diligence and frugality " ; by " denying themselves and taking up their cross daily " ; even by their readiness for Christ's sake to be mocked, buffeted and despised " as the filth and offscouring of the world." Their spiritual life, too, was to be nourished and sustained by " attending all the ordinances of God," including " public worship," " the ministry of the Word," " the Supper of the Lord," " family and private prayer," " searching the Scriptures," and " fasting *or* abstinence."[1]

These United Societies, therefore, were inspired by a faith and schooled by a discipline comparable to that of the Early Christians. Theirs were the zeal, the humility and the courage that overcome the world : and in the Bible, which they interpreted with infinitely more imagination and sanity than is generally supposed, they found, indeed, the Bread of Life.

(ii) *Virulent Opposition*

This direct, practical nature of the Revival had no sooner dawned upon the mind of the ruling classes in Church and State, than threatening clouds began to darken the sky—portents of the tempest of opposition about to break. And to this day many intelligent people have been wholly misled by the far-reaching reverberations of that thundering bombardment of prejudice : they have never stopped to investigate the real significance of the Revival, or to examine the fruits of its sowing.

After Wesley's first field sermon at Bristol, he felt certain that his special mission was to the socially and spiritually impoverished masses. Before long, his voice had been heard by countless thousands of the dispossessed in all parts of the country—by the barbarous Kingswood colliers, by Bristol's stagnant slum-dom and Cornwall's lawless smugglers, by London drunkards

---

[1] For a poignant social elaboration of Wesley's *Rules*, see H. Carter, *The Methodist*, (1914).

and prostitutes, Liverpool sailors and navvies and by the " wild, staring blasphemers " of Newcastle. His voice had reached them ; the fervour of his personality had touched their souls ; the fire of his message was burning in their hearts. Aspirations for a new and holy life possessed their being ; the Kingdom of God was stirring within them.

Half a century before the three magic words of the French Revolution had fanned Europe into a raging and consuming blaze, Wesley already had taught the mighty doctrines of Liberty, Equality and Fraternity : but on a vastly different basis from that of the cynical, sophisticated Voltaire or the demagogical, enigmatic Rousseau. Had not their witty and spleenish gods been imported from Deistic England ? And had not Wesley revolted against the frigid rationalism and cruel materialism, to which those gods had there given birth ? Class-hatred, bloody revolution and revenge, had no place in his system of thought or faith. He came preaching not his own wisdom but the wisdom of God through Christ. Hence to him those vigorous, exhilarating doctrines were spiritual to the core. He taught *Liberty* from sin, misery and death, through the regenerating power of the living Carpenter of Nazareth, the Saviour of men ; he taught the spiritual *Equality* of collier and king, both being sinners equally in need of grace divine and both being immortal souls equally precious to their Maker : he taught the *Fraternity* of all mankind, independent of colour, race or clime, as the inevitable corollary of the common Fatherhood of a God of Love.

Such teaching being little in harmony with the deeply rooted caste privileges and chartered stagnation of eighteenth century England, it was not unnatural that tornadoes of opposition should break upon Wesley, Whitefield and other leaders. The Revival soon was stormed at from pulpit and press ; and those who knew least about its purpose or meaning, and were too proud and exalted to study its teaching or observe its effects, were loudest in their abuse. Though both the Wesleys and Whitefield were ordained clergymen of the Establishment, " Church " pulpits on all sides were closed to them, many indeed being regularly used to shower anathemas on their heads. Charles Wesley, who remained till death a passionate lover and advocate of the order and procedure of the National Church, says : " Every Sunday damnation is pronounced against us, for we are papists, Jesuits, seducers and bringers in of the Pretender."[1] Indeed at a time when social rakes were receiving the Holy Communion as a symbol of fitness for State

[1] J. H. Overton, *Evangelical Revival in the Eighteenth Century*, p. 176f.

office, these men of God repeatedly were refused it. Even Epworth Church, where the father of the Wesleys had ministered faithfully nearly all his life, turned John Wesley from the Lord's Table. "Pray tell Mr. Wesley that I shall not give *him* the Sacrament, for he is *not fit*;" were the words of the Epworth rector in the very parish where, says Wesley, "according to the strictest sect of our religion, I had so long lived a Pharisee."[1]

During the first two or three decades of the Revival the ugly, riotous interference of mobs was more or less continuous. On innumerable occasions, the meetings of the Wesleys, Whitefield and many itinerant preachers were attacked by drunken, brawling rabbles armed with such formidable means of assault as clubs, whips, clods, bricks, staves, stones, stink-bombs, wildfire and rotten eggs.[2] Sometimes they procured a bull and drove him into the midst of an open air congregation; sometimes they contented themselves by performing with bells, horns, drums, pans and such like, to deaden the preacher's voice. Frequently, when goaded by a violent leader, they resorted to every available means of attack; and not infrequently they expended their fury in burning or tearing down the houses, and destroying or stealing the furniture and possessions, of the Revival's followers. Both at the hands of Staffordshire and Cornwall mobs John Wesley was in grave danger of being done to death; Charles Wesley "narrowly escaped with his life at Devizes"; while Whitefield, "covered with blood and on the point of falling, was rescued in the nick of time from the brutal fury of an Irish crowd at Dublin."[3]

Yet the very people whose duty it was to protect these Godfearing and law-abiding citizens, frequently were those who encouraged or led the mobs in their barbarous assaults. Mr. C. E. Vulliamy, in his *John Wesley*, is within the bounds of historical accuracy when he says: "It was unquestionably the attitude of the clergy and of the landed classes which gave the mob its privilege and excuse, even when it was not led in person by gentlemen or curates."[4] Wesley's *Journal* (April 17th, 1743), runs thus: "While I was speaking a gentleman rode up very drunk; and after many unseemly and bitter words, laboured much to ride over some of the people. I was surprised to hear that he was a neighbouring clergyman!" Even Overton,

---

[1] J. Wesley's *Journal*, January 1st, 1743.
[2] Southey refers also to the use of egg-shells "filled with blood and stopped with pitch."
[3] Vulliamy's *John Wesley*, p. 231.
[4] *Op. cit.*, see chapter xvi. "The Beasts of the People."

more than once, points out that Wesley was always pleased when truth permitted him to say a word in a clergyman's praise.[1] But the *Journal* shows that the above was by no means an isolated case of attack by an intoxicated clergyman. Rev. George White, curate of Colne, Lancashire, who subsequently drank himself to death, issued in August, 1748, a proclamation inviting recruits, for " the defence of the *Church of England* and the Support of the *Manufactory* in and about Colne " ; and to ensure a roisterous anti-Methodist mob, this brave parson invited all interested to repair to a specified " pub," where " each man shall receive a Pint of Ale in Advance, and other Proper Encouragements." The outrageous violence of the Reverend George White's mob towards Wesley, Grimshaw, Mackford and certain of their helpers, suggests strongly that the " other proper encouragements " were somewhat more " spirited " than the initial " pint," and that many such had been taken " in advance."[2]

Wesley, on this occasion, was struck violently in the face and later " beat down to the ground " by ruffians, raging " like lions." Grimshaw they threw down, loading him with " dirt and mire of every kind ! " Mackford they " trampled in the mire," later to drag him about by the hair of his head. The whole congregation, " without any regard to age or sex," they pelted with " showers of dirt and stones." " Many they beat with their clubs without mercy." Some of the victims sustained permanent injury. Nevertheless, " all this time," the Reverend " Commander-in-Chief," sat " well-pleased," close to the place, " talking of justice and law," and " not attempting in the least to hinder them."[3]

As early as the middle of 1743, Wesley, who always had an amazing mastery of his emotions and never lost his head, was highly perturbed by the prevailing attitude of the clergy. " I received a full statement," reads his *Journal*, " of the terrible riots which had been in Staffordshire. I was not surprised at all : neither should I have wondered if, after the advices they had so often received from the pulpit, as well as from the episcopal chair, the zealous High Churchmen had rose, and cut all that were Methodists in pieces."[4] In 1744, James Dale, a " Methodist," applied to Dr. Borlase, the antiquarian, clergyman and magistrate, for justice against a certain anti-Methodist

---

[1] See especially his *John Wesley* (1891).
[2] See *Journal*, August 25th and 26th, 1748 ; also Vulliamy *op. cit.*, pp. 240–42.
[3] *Ibid.*
[4] See entry of June 18th, 1743.

rioter, who with a mob, had smashed into his house and stolen his goods. The response of this scholarly parson-magistrate was a prelude to the nasty Cornish riots of the following year. "Thou conceited fellow!" thundered Borlase, "What! art thou too turned religious? They may burn thy house if they will; it is no concern of mine!"[1]

One must, however, guard against the over abuse of the clergy, as such. Most of them were the hirelings, if not the puppets, of their parish squires[2]; and certainly Wesley himself traced the majority of mob riots to the doors of magistrates, squires and "gentlemen." His *Journal* literally teems with shrewd, caustic, witty references to the ungentlemanly conduct of "so-called gentlemen" and to the gross ignorance, stupidity and indecency of "the great vulgar." Even indeed among the more pious of the gentry, he commonly found little to admire. "In most genteel religious people," he remarks, "there is so strange a mixture, that I have seldom much confidence in them." Parsons therefore were often corrupted and exploited by their pompous patrons, who seldom shrank from using both them and the mobs for their own sinister ends. A *Journal* entry (May 7th, 1743), says: "The sons of Belial gathered themselves together, headed by one or two *wretches called gentlemen*; and continued shouting, cursing, blaspheming and throwing showers of stones almost without intermission." In 1765, at North Taunton, a clergyman, "with two or three *by the courtesy of England called gentlemen*," began an uproar: "they had brought a huntsman with his hounds; but the dogs were wiser than the men, for they could not bring them to make any noise at all. One of the *gentlemen* supplied their place. He assured us he was such, or none would have suspected it; for his language was as base, foul and porterly as was ever heard at Billingsgate."

For more than thirty years, references to mob interference form a distinct feature of Wesley's *Journal*: and fiercest of all "the beasts of the people" were the "lions" and "bloodhounds" "called gentlemen." Part of the record for September 19th, 1769, is both amusing and revealing: "The beasts of the people were tolerably quiet till I had nearly finished my sermon. They then lifted up their voice, especially one, called a gentleman, who had filled his pockets with rotten eggs: but a young man coming unawares, clapped his hands on each side, and mashed them all at once. In an instant he was

---

[1] See Vulliamy, *op. cit.*, pp. 150 and 236; also *Journal*, July 3rd, 1745.
[2] Throughout most of the eighteenth century at least two-thirds of the parish clergy were at the mercy of lay patrons who controlled their livings.

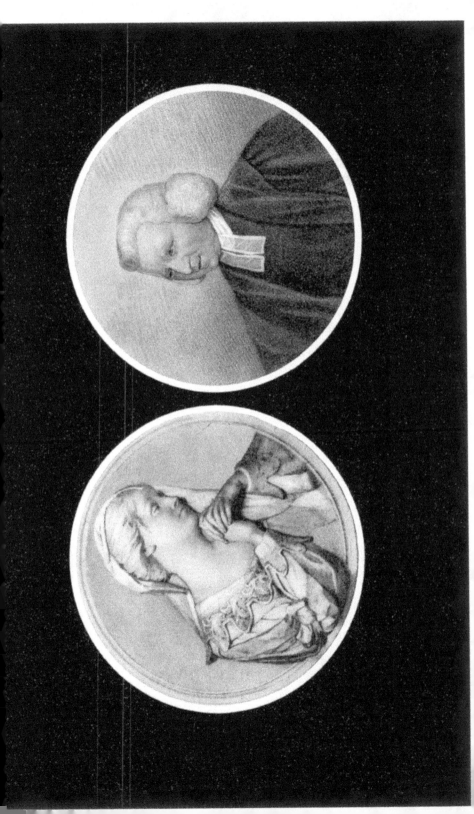

LADY SELINA, COUNTESS OF HUNTINGDON (left)
CHARLES WESLEY (right)

perfume all over ; though it was not so sweet as balsam." On another occasion " a kind of gentleman . . . hired a company of boys to shout, and made a poor man exceeding drunk, who bawled out much ribaldry and nonsense, while he himself played the French horn."[1] Some gentlemen magistrates went the length of advising mobs to " do what you will " with the Methodists, " so you break no bones "[2] ; others issued general warrants for the arrest of itinerant preachers[3] : while, more than once, strutting, fuming gentlemen contracted with mobs to drive " all that were called Methodists " out of their districts.

The *Journal* record for February 6th, 1744, is peculiarly illuminating. After months of sporadic terrorism and looting, a mob, " hired by their betters " and " bound by an oath " to " plunder all the Methodists in Wednesbury," set on Shrove-Tuesday to complete their design.[4] The attack was calculated, cowardly, wanton and ruthless. Assaulting " *all* the homes of those who were called Methodists," they " first broke *all* their windows, suffering neither glass, lead nor frames to remain therein." Then " *all* the tables, chairs, chests of drawers, with whatever was not easily removable, they dashed to pieces, particularly shop-goods, and furniture of every kind," while non-breakables, such as feather-beds, " they cut in pieces and strewed about the room." And so the valiant fellows continued. " Wearing apparel, and things that were of value or easily saleable, they carried away ; every man loading himself with as much as he could well carry, of whatever he liked best." Finally they came to the house of William Sitch, " whose wife was lying in " : " but that was all one ; they pulled away her bed, too, and cut it in pieces."

Following this valorous act, " some of *the gentlemen who had set the mob to work, or threatened to turn away collier or miner out of their service, that did not come and do his part,* now drew up a paper for those of the society to sign, importing, that they would never invite or receive any Methodist preacher more. On this condition, they told them they would stop the mob at once ; otherwise they must take what followed." The said paper " they offered to several ; but they declared, one and all, ' We have already lost all our goods ; and nothing more

---

[1] *Journal*, June 13th, 1763.
[2] See Arnold Lunn, *John Wesley*, p. 205.
[3] For an exact copy of such, see *Journal*, October 20th, 1743.
[4] Among the previous victims of this particular mob were Mr. and Mrs. Joshua Constable and their little children. On January 23rd they threw Mrs. Constable down and tried to force her. On January 30th, they smashed into Constable's house, " pulled part of it down, broke some of his goods in pieces, and carried the rest away."

O

can follow, but the loss of our lives, which we will lose, too, rather than wrong our consciences '."

So the mad orgy continued ! The " Methodists " offered no resistance, for they knew well that resistance would only jeopardise the honour of their women folk to this liberty-shouting, " gentlemen "-led mob. Before the chivalrous exploits of Shrove-Tuesday (February 7th, 1744) were concluded, the houses of " some hundreds " of Wesley's disciples in and around Wednesbury resembled a " devastated area." Not only had their houses been broken up, their furniture cut to pieces, and their portable goods looted ; even their live stock had been driven off. " Most of them " indeed were " stripped of all they had in the world."[1]

Our post-War, Dictator-ridden age is familiar with the art of doctoring and doping " news " for propaganda purposes. But was ever a war despatch, or political note, more diabolically contorted than the following " report " of the above riot ?—a report which may still be read in the British Museum Library from the files of the *London Evening Post*, February 18th, 1744. " By a private letter from Staffordshire," this " news " item reads : " We had advice of an insurrection of the people, called Methodists, who upon some pretended insults from the Church party, have assembled themselves in a riotous manner ; and having committed several outrages, they proceeded at last to burn the house of one of their adversaries."[2] This report is surely worthy of the valiant *gentlemen* who inspired and managed the Wednesbury rabble's assault ! It is the more understandable, too, when it is remembered that most eighteenth-century journalists, editors and writers, were as much " in the pockets " of gouty, irascible patrons, as were parish priests.

Wesley's superb courage and coolness, his overawing peace and composure, his humour and affability, succeeded finally in subduing even the crass, stupid bestiality of the eighteenth-century English mob. For his *Journal* note, September 16th, 1743, many parallels might be cited : " In the evening, as I was preaching at St. Ives, Satan began to fight for his King-dom. The mob of the town burst into the room and created much disturbance ; roaring and striking those that stood in the way, as though Legion himself possessed them. I would fain have persuaded our people to stand still ; but the zeal of some and the fear of others, had no ears ; so that finding

[1] See *Journal* (above date).
[2] For Wesley's comments on this " report," see the latter part of his long *Journal* entry for February 18th, 1744. Important preceding dates are included therein.

the uproar increase I went into the midst, and brought the head of the mob up with me to the desk. *I received but one blow on the side of the head ; after which we reasoned the case,* till he grew milder and milder, and at length undertook to quiet his companions."

Wesley, the Evangelist, was a man possessed of amazing grace. Never did he lose his temper ; and always was he prepared to endure a blow, if the dealing of it would relieve the hysteria of his assailant. Repeatedly, when struck by a stone or cudgel, he quietly wiped away the blood and went on preaching without so much as a frown on his face. He loved his enemies ; and do what they would, they could not make him discourteous or angry. It is no exaggeration to say that Wesley instilled into the British people, a new and highly Christian conception of bravery and courage. The swaggering, bullying, animal species of courage, so characteristic of his age, made little appeal to him ; his was entirely a product of the spirit ; and ere his earthly race was run, something of the power and majesty of that same spiritual courage was reflected even in the humblest " Methodist " Societies all over the land. In danger, Wesley had taught his followers to think of the Christ before Pilate, of the Son of God before a raging, crucifying mob. Thus it was, that Wesley's serenity first broke, and later won, the heart of many a mob-leader and ruthless enemy : thus it was, too, that many a one-time brute came to be transformed into a gentle, saintly Class-leader and understanding shepherd of souls. This miraculous Grace, was the power which finally conquered the eighteenth-century mob. Mr. Vulliamy, in words of rare insight concerning Wesley and his persecutors, says : " It was not courage alone that saved Wesley. He was preserved by a tranquil dignity, by cool, steady and courteous behaviour, by the entire absence of malice and anger ; but, above all, by those peculiar graces and powers which accompany a man of God."[1]

The attacks on the Movement by heady, superior society leaders, were more subtle but not less vicious than those of squires, clergymen, magistrates and mobs. The contemporary literature of the era bristles with demonstrations of this truth, but we need quote only the Duchess of Buckingham, an illegitimate daughter of James II. Addressing the Countess of Huntingdon, one of the few in " well-bred " society who, at an early stage, supported the Revival, the Duchess wrote : " I thank your Ladyship for the information concerning the Methodist preaching ; these doctrines are most repulsive and

[1] *Op. cit., p.* 244.

strongly tinctured with impertinence and disrespect toward their superiors in perpetually endeavouring to level all ranks and do away with all distinctions, as it is monstrous to be told that you have a heart as sinful as *the common wretches that crawl on the earth*. This is highly offensive and insulting, and I cannot but wonder that your Ladyship should relish any sentiments so much at variance with high rank and good breeding . . ."[1]

(iii) *Necessity Creates Initiative*

Persecution and scorn by Church, press and mob, by magistrates, " gentlemen " and smart society, did much to influence the practical evolution of Evangelical methods. All the bishops long opposing Wesley and Whitefield, and practically all the Churches of their communion being barred to them, field preaching perforce became their chief vehicle of expression ; but as field preaching was wholly at the mercy of the elements, it soon was found necessary to erect or procure buildings which could be lighted and heated on winter evenings, thus providing shelter for worship during inclement weather and accommodation for all special gatherings of the inner circle. If faith therefore led the movement forward, persecution pushed it forward ; and necessity stimulated its initiative.

On Saturday, May 12th, 1739, less than a quarter of the necessary funds being yet in sight, the corner stone of the world's first Methodist preaching house was laid in the Horse Fair, Bristol.[2] The famous Kingswood school and the historic London Foundery, were both opened the same year ; while in 1742 the opening of the Newcastle preaching house and Orphanage, in which the *Rules* of the United Societies were written, marks the driving of the first permanent stakes into the industrial district of the North. These four institutions were pioneer land marks ; they proved that the movement had already taken root ; while, year by year, new Societies were being formed and new Preaching Houses were springing up all over the country, with the result that ere Wesley's decease every section of industrial England and Wales could boast its " Preaching House," loved by a substantial section of the industrial population, and built by its voluntary contributions —some of them indeed by its voluntary labour.

To a lesser degree, the same development took place in Scotland and Ireland ; while, as for America, the progress

---

[1] See J. S. Simon, *Revival of Religion in Eighteenth Century England*, p. 275.
[2] See *Journal*, May 9th and 12th, 1739.

of the Revival there was phenomenal. In that age of sail-boats, when the Atlantic crossing took two or three months and every passage was a real adventure, Whitefield crossed thirteen times. He died in December, 1770, in America, leaving behind him a mighty, but largely unorganised, influence. A few years later, were heard the premonitory rumblings of the American Rebellion and the handful of Anglican clergy among the Colonials, considering themselves officials of the English Government, quickly betook themselves to their native land. Only the Revival's preachers stayed with the flock. During all the vital years of the Revolutionary War, that incredible world-ling and nepotist, Cornwallis, was Primate ; only to be suc-ceeded in 1783 by the equally mercenary Moore. Never a bishop had yet been appointed to America, and all the bishops at home refused to consecrate or recognise the Revival's preachers. Meanwhile whole communities of American Chris-tians were left without the Sacraments, which the unordained itinerant preachers were not authorised to administer ; so Wesley, in 1784, under pressure of conscience, and on the advice of several clerical friends, consecrated helpers to super-intend the American flock and ordain the most promising preachers.[1]

The pride, frigidity and paralysis of the English Church " leaders " had forced his hand, but they also had forced upon him a great opportunity. Before his demise, he had about half as many preachers in America as in Britain : he could look with joy to the work of his devoted superintendents, Francis Asbury and Dr. Thomas Coke,[2] who by their heroic selflessness and herculean labours of love, were laying deep the founda-tions of righteousness, integrity, temperance and virtue, on which the largest Protestant Church of the North American continent was to be erected ; while already it was becoming obvious that the interdenominational impact of this mighty Revival would influence profoundly the social, philanthropic and educational development of the great English-speaking Republic.

But the cruel, bigoted opposition to the Revival not only increased the amount of field preaching, dictated the necessity of building meeting houses, and compelled initiative and in-ventiveness : it also forced upon the converts the need of

---

[1] As early as August 1st, 1775, Rev. John Fletcher had recommended to Wesley a similar step. See *Journal* (Standard edition), Vol. VIII, Appendix 29.

[2] For facsimile of Dr. Coke's ordination, see *Journal* (Standard edition), Vol. VII, p. 16 ; see, too, Vol. VII, p. 2, and Curnock's notes, Vol. VI, p. 2.

cohesion, unity and organisation ; it freed the crusade of mere "hangers on" and of all "fearful spirits" who, faced by continuous persecution or contempt, turned backsliders to faith and conscience. It purged and consolidated the movement all along the line.

The study of the origin and evolution of the complex organisation of Wesley's Societies is a big subject, but it will be found upon investigation that the whole marvellous system with its local and itinerant preachers, its Band and Class Meetings, its circuits and Annual Conferences, its Sunday Schools and Quarterly Tickets, its poor relief and loan societies, its medical help and Strangers' Societies, its voluntary service and systematic finance, its Love Feasts and Watch Night services, its personal supervision and strict discipline, its religious pamphlets and Society magazine, its brotherly fellowship and family visitation, its interest in civics and its citizenship in Eternity, its local intensity and its world missionary zeal, its educational stimulus and its outburst of sacred song, its salvation by Faith and its insistence on Works, its hatred of sin and its love for the sinner, its initial autocratic leadership and its ultimate democratic influence, its demand for individual religious experience, and its emphasis on corporate service—the whole complex and variegated system was affected profoundly by the atmosphere of opposition and persecution in which the movement sprang up. Directness and intensity of purpose, coupled with efficiency of organisation, were essential to its very life. Without them, it could never have weathered the fury and contempt which raged against it : with them, it developed a corporate genius far above and beyond the capacity of its individual members. Persecution, therefore, proved a blessing in disguise. In things essential the Movement achieved Unity ; in things doubtful it granted Liberty ; in all things it mediated Charity.

(iv) *Indispensable Aids*

The Class-meeting was a unique and peculiarly interesting aspect of the Societies' development : its origin provides a glimpse of the environment in which the Revival worked. The rapid growth of the movement, with its continual demand for the erection of new meeting houses and its large monetary outlay on help for the poor, necessitated the inauguration of a sound scheme of finance. To this end certain Bristol leaders, in February, 1742, met for consultation, and on the suggestion of Captain Foy it was finally agreed : " (1) That every member of the Society, who was able, should contribute a penny a week. (2) That the whole society should be divided into little companies or classes—about twelve in each class. And (3) That one person in each class should receive the contribution of the rest, and bring it to the stewards, weekly."[1] It is noteworthy that many members were too poor to afford even a penny a week, but the leader of each class called weekly on every member of his group, took notice of the conditions in which he lived, collected the pennies of those who could afford to pay, and himself made good the deficit of the poor and unfortunate.[2]

This was the humble origin of what gradually developed into one of the world's greatest systems of voluntary finance. Moreover, it is significant that a generation after Wesley's death, when Lord Shaftesbury, Michael Sadler, Richard Oastler, Rev. R. J. Stephens, Rev. G. S. Bull, Philip Grant and John Wood—all ardent Evangelicals—were leading the epic struggle for the Ten Hours Bill, and thus winning the Magna Charta of the English worker's leisure and liberty, they financed the organisation of factory operatives by borrowing bodily the scheme of the Methodist Class Meeting.[3]

But Wesley's keen, practical eye soon discovered for these Class units a deeper and higher purpose than the raising of finance. In this Class group he found the desire of his heart—a vehicle for the personal supervision of every member of the societies. " This is the very thing," he declared ; " the very thing we have wanted so long ! " Hence it was soon arranged that the members of each Class should *assemble* weekly ; and in these *Class-Meetings*—the sexes convening separately under their respective leaders, who acted in the capacity of non-commissioned officers or lay pastors—the members discussed the most pressing and intimate problems of life, and encouraged one another to fight a good fight. Here all men were brothers ; all women were sisters ; and all members were pledged to secrecy regarding personal confessions.

Had not these Class Meetings been conducted in an atmosphere where all questions were " raised aloft," where meanness, pettiness, vanity, self-aggrandisement, animosity and revenge were unthinkable, where faith, hope and love reigned,

---

[1] *Journal*, February 15th, 1742 ; see also Fitchett's *Wesley*, pp. 221–22.

[2] The average wage of the agricultural labourer at this time was not over six shillings a week, that of the town labourer was about seven to eight shillings, and that of the artisan from ten to twelve shillings.

[3] For the full history of the Ten Hours Bill see the Fourth and Popular edition of the author's book, *Lord Shaftesbury and Social-Industrial Progress*, chapters xiii to xvi, also its Introduction by Sir Josiah Stamp.

they might easily have degenerated into centres of gossip, petulance and scandal.

> " There was an old fellow of Crewe
> Who discovered a mouse in his stew.
> Said the waiter : ' Don't shout and wave it about,
> Or the rest will be wanting one, too.' "

There certainly were " old fellows of Crewe " in those early Class Meetings. Many a mouse, too, got into the stew, but members quickly learned never to shout and wave them about. Confessions of failure, defeat and sin were heard in their respective Classes by some men and women who not long before would have gloated over the opportunities for " tongue-wagging " thus afforded ; but now, with changed hearts, in a spirit of fellowship, co-operation and service, they listened to such confessions with downcast eyes and sympathetic hearts, thinking of all that God, for Christ's sake, had forgiven them. All now were their brother's keepers ; all helped to heal the wounds of sin ; all strove together to keep running the springs of grace ; and however painful were temporary defeats, the note of triumph prevailed.

Among the ten thousand or more Class leaders whom Wesley must have personally known were surely some of the most lovely characters in England[1] : lovely because of the breadth of their Christian sympathy and the depth of their Christian understanding ; lovely, too, because of their set aspirations toward " Perfectionism," through unbroken communion with the Spirit of Christ. These humble Class Leaders were chiefly men and women at whom the smart, fashionable world long laughed ; but even blatant cynicism came in time to be hushed before their sincerity and their integrity. Their wisdom, too, was more penetrating than that of the sagacious " waiter," for it came of a regenerated heart, and expressed itself in a loving fellowship with all who " followed after what they knew they had not yet attained." The Class Meeting spirit and aspiration, are perfectly portrayed in a verse all Class members loved to sing :

> " And if our fellowship below
> In Jesus be so sweet,
> What heights of rapture shall we know
> When round His throne we meet ! "[2]

[1] There were some eight thousand class leaders at Wesley's death, and he had known throngs who had " passed on." See Warner's *Wesleyan Movement in the Industrial Revolution*, p. 262.

[2] See J. E. Rattenbury, *Wesley's Legacy to the World*, p. 283.

The stimulus afforded by these countless Class Meetings to the moral uplift, the spiritual growth, the educational development, the self-expression and the organised social endeavour of the disinherited multitudes of England, it is impossible to calculate. Professor Rogers assuredly had them in mind when he expressed his conviction that without the prior help of the Wesleyan Revival " the mass of the peasants could not have been moved at all." In the preaching services, the converts caught their vision and turned toward their goal ; in the Class Meetings, they found their spiritual *school* where, under trusted leaders, they grouped together in mutual aid to work out their salvation, and to discuss reverently and prayfully their attitude to the social, ethical and religious problems of their daily life. The Class Meeting was something wholly new to English life, and wholly beautiful ; it became a mighty civilising, as well as spiritualising, force.[1]

The creation, too, of local and itinerant preachers, was forced upon the Movement by the onward march of events. Few ordained ministers, either Anglican or Nonconformist, were at first friendly to the Revival.[2] Almost none were willing to give assistance to the man who had " the world for his parish." Wesley, Whitefield and " brother Charles " were tireless in their efforts, but the harvest was far too great for their gleaning ; more labourers had to be found. It was the old story of Jesus and the Apostles : Wesley, like his Master, had to accept the best messengers available. In the critical case of Thomas Maxfield, who became a force in the early days, Wesley's mother wielded a decisive influence. High Church as she had been all her life, her advice to her son was revolutionary : " Take care what you do with respect to this young man, for he is as surely called of God to preach as you are."[3] With the settlement of Maxfield's case, the lay preacher became an institution ; but henceforth these preachers were carefully chosen by Wesley himself, and cheerfully did they submit themselves to the rigorous discipline he imposed.

[1] Something close akin to these classes was established in the seventeenth century by the pious Frenchman and Catholic, Marquis de Renty. Even before Wesley's conversion, de Renty's *Life* had greatly appealed to him, for on January 6th, 1738 (see *Journal*) he prepared an abridgement of it, which later ran into six editions. See article, " Sharing in Former Days," by F. L. Barber (*New Outlook*, January 14th, 1932).

[2] See Dr. R. W. Dale, *History of Congregationalism*, pp. 583-4, for Nonconformist attitude.

[3] Southey's *Wesley*, p. 197ff ; Telford's *Wesley*, p. 215. Note, too, Wesley's high tributes to his mother at the time of her death (*Journal*, July 18th and 23rd, and August 1st, 1742).

Apart altogether from Whitefield's preaching disciples, Wesley finally was directing a band of some seven hundred local and itinerant preachers. And the superb heroism of those rustic missionaries forms one of the romances of history— a romance whose full significance has never yet been penned, for it is indeed an epic of adventure and achievement. If ever men were baptized in the purging fires of privation and persecution, these veterans were. A study of some of their portraits, assembled in the Standard Edition of Wesley's *Journal*, challenges acutely the imagination, and points the fact that they were men of no common mettle : by their arduous labours of love, the dross of sloth and selfishness was burned away, and the gold of the spirit was burnished bright. Of these preachers, Southey says : " St. Francis and his followers did not commit themselves with more confidence to the care of Providence, nor with more entire disregard of all human means "[1] ; and who will question this conclusion ? For these virile messengers of the Cross, no weather was too inclement, no road too boggy, no ford too swollen, no community too degraded, no mob too violent, no privation too severe—to interfere with their constant round of duty. Christ, their Master, pointed the way ; and Wesley, their captain, set them a living example. But as Wesley grew old, he became a revered, even a national, character : Mr. Vulliamy pronounces him finally the " best loved man in England." Certainly many a former enemy chose ultimately to regard him as a late Fellow of Oxford, a " fine old English gentleman," and a true bene-factor of the poor. With the humble veterans, the case was different. The fires of persecution, fanned by the winds of bigotry, still raged along their thorny trail : yet cheerful and unafraid, they laboured on. After the imprisonment of one of his preachers, Wesley wrote : " I pray you for what pay could we procure men to do this service ? To be always ready to go to prison or to death ? "

Nelson, Maxfield and other itinerant preachers were carried off by army press gangs. " Thomas Mitchell was thrown repeatedly into a deep pond till he was insensible ; then his clothes were covered with paint."[2] William Seward, who had accompanied Whitefield on his second voyage to America, was blinded in 1741 by one Welsh rabble and killed by another. Several preachers went to premature graves through the effects, direct or indirect, of injuries inflicted by mobs : others were maimed or scarred for life. Some in their excessive labours

---

[1] Southey, *op. cit.*, p. 223.
[2] J. Telford, *Life of Wesley*, p. 212.

burned themselves out : some died in harness leaving behind them from six pence to six shillings of worldly wealth. But always the gaps were filled, and always the ranks increased. Like a company of sturdy, seasoned veterans, on and on they marched. John Prichard's horse one winter became incapacitated and meanwhile, in his itinerant work, he journeyed some " twelve hundred miles " on foot.[1] Thomas Olivers travelled " not less than one hundred thousand miles " on one horse— no mean tribute to his care of the beast that shared his labours. These trail-breakers, like Wesley, rose every morning at four, and preached most mornings at five. They refrained from the use of all intoxicants, lived lives of marked abstemiousness, and commonly divided each day into three equal parts—eight hours for sleeping and eating, eight for study and meditation, eight for preaching, visitation and social labours.

Dr. Robinson, Archbishop of Armagh, once complained to Charles Wesley concerning the employment of laymen as preachers. Charles replied : " The fault is yours and your brethren's." " How so ? " inquired the astonished prelate. " Because you hold your peace, and the stones cry out ! " he rejoined.[2] " But I am told," retorted his Grace, " that they are *unlearned* men." " Some are," Charles confessed, " and so the dumb ass rebukes the prophet."[3] Yet, bearing in mind the voluntary discipline to which these preachers cheerfully submitted themselves, and the courses of reading which Wesley, the one-time Oxford don, regularly prescribed and supervised, they could not long, in their peculiar field, remain " unlearned men." Wesley's defence of them was fully justified. " In the one thing which they profess to know," he protested, " they are not ignorant men. I trust there is not one of them who is not able to go through such an examination in substantial, practical, experimental divinity as few of our graduates for Holy Orders even in the University (I speak it with sorrow and shame and in tender love) are able to do."[4]

Michael Sadler, the eminent social reformer and instigator of the classic Parliamentary Report on *Factory Children's Labour* (1831-2)," in his early treatise, *An Apology for the Methodists*, published in 1797, maintained that the " ignorance " and " uncouthness " of the Revival's preachers was studiously and

[1] *Early Methodist Preachers*, Vol. VI, p. 267 ; see, too, Fitchett, *op. cit.*, chapter vii.
[2] John Wesley, too, said : " Out of the stones (' these unlearned and ignorant men ') God raised up those who should beget children to Abraham." See Southey's *Wesley* (unabridged), Vol. I, p. 307.
[3] L. Tyerman, *Life and Times of John Wesley*, Vol. I, p. 277.
[4] P. Cadman, *Three Religious Leaders of Oxford*, p. 329.

maliciously exaggerated. Not a few of these preachers, he contended, became men of higher mental attainment than their vindictive assailants ; and certainly if Sadler himself were a fair example, they included men of rare talents. Wesley not only supervised the personal education of his preachers, but insisted also that they in turn become mediums for the spread of education among the people. " Preach expressly on education," he repeatedly insisted ; and to any who objected : " But I have no gift for this," his reply was peremptory. " Gift or no gift, you are to *do* it, else you are not called to be a Methodist preacher. Do it as you can, till you can do it as you would. Pray earnestly for the gift, and *use the means for it*."[1]

Wesley enjoined upon all his preachers the necessity of spending " at least five hours in twenty-four in reading the most useful books."[2] He warned them, too, that one could " never be a deep preacher " without extensive reading, " any more than a thorough Christian."[3] The fifty volumes of his famous *Christian Library*, were edited specifically for the general education of his preachers, helpers and followers. Scores of his own treatises, as well as the *Arminian Magazine*, were designed for the same end. Every preacher was made a distributor and seller of books, and all were expected to have mastered the contents of the publications they spread abroad. Wesley himself often was harshly censured for " pushing " his own books from pulpit and platform ;[4] but the criticism never perturbed him. He considered his ministry of writing as important as his ministry of preaching ; he knew that books, to be of value, had to be read ; and he knew, too, that people would read books for which they paid—however small the price. Hence, heedless of waspish criticism, he " pushed " and sold his books wherever he went, believing them to be an educational as well as an inspirational force : and his preachers he literally " prodded " to like efforts. " Exert yourselves in this," he insisted. " *Be not ashamed*. Be not weary. Leave no stone unturned."[5] Every itinerant, in fact, was a " Book Steward," and even Conference Minutes urged the preachers to " be more active in dispersing books." Subscriptions were taken among many societies to establish local libraries for general use, and preachers were instructed to " beg money

---

[1] Note the similarity of this advice to that of Böhler to Wesley regarding vital *faith*.
[2] Tyerman's *Wesley*, Vol. II, p. 581.
[3] Wesley's *Works*, Vol. XII, p. 254.
[4] See " Wesley," Historical Society's *Proceedings*, Vol. VII, p. 167, and *York Courant*, June 6th, 1780.
[5] *Ibid.*, Vol. II, p. 477.

of the rich to buy books for the poor."[1] "No man in the eighteenth century," says the *Encyclopædia Britannica* of Wesley, "did so much to create a taste for good reading, and to supply it with books at the lowest prices."[2] The itinerant and local preachers, however, were themselves the chief recipients, as well as the chief mediators, of that mighty educational influence; and greatly did they profit by it.

Even the maxims drawn up by Wesley for his preachers and helpers, suggest the sane, cultural influences he spread around them. " Endeavour to speak in public," he insisted, "just as you do in common conversation. . . . To drawl is worse than to hurry. . . . The good and honourable actions of men, should be described with a full and lofty accent ; wicked and infamous actions, with a strong and earnest voice, and such a tone as expresses horror and detestation. . . . The mouth must never be turned awry ; neither must you bite or lick your lips. . . . Never clap your hands, nor thump the pulpit. Your hands are not to be in perpetual motion : this the ancients called the ' babbling of hands.' "[3] Wesley's *Rules of a Helper*, issued by the Leeds Conference in 1753, are equally illuminating : " Be diligent," he admonishes. " Never be unemployed for a moment. . . . Believe evil of no one. Speak evil of no one. . . . Do not affect the gentleman. You have no more to do with this character, than with that of a dancing-master. . . . A preacher of the Gospel is the servant of all. Be ashamed of nothing but sin : not of fetching wood (if time permit), or drawing water ; nor of cleaning your own shoes, or your neighbours'. . . . Be punctual. Do everything exactly at the time." And finally he advises his preachers that, for such a high calling, " You will need all the sense you have, and to have your wits about you."[4] " Enthusiasm," therefore, was far removed from hysteria or wild emotion : it was both tutored and disciplined ; and therein lay its power.

True, a very occasional Judas found his way into the ranks of the preachers, but the proportion of such was probably closer to one in a hundred than one in twelve. John Telford is completely justified in saying : " No leader of a great religious movement was ever more happy in his helpers than Wesley."[5]

[1] See George Jackson, *Wesleyan Methodism in the Darlington Circuit*, p. 10 ; Dr. W. J. Warner, *Wesleyan Movement in the Industrial Revolution*, p. 231.
[2] Eleventh edition (*John Wesley*).
[3] See Vulliamy's *Wesley*, p. 152.
[4] *Ibid.*, p. 265.
[5] See Telford's *Life of Wesley* (chapter on Wesley's preachers).

In a vital sense, these rustic Apostles of the Cross were men of the people ; yet they were men new-born to a life high above the people, and their ruling passion was to lift the fallen and depraved to the heights of that new-born life. They had an abiding vision of the Kingdom of Christ, and their " enthusiasm " expressed itself in a holy crusade to establish righteousness in the hearts of men : their consuming desire was to see the will of God done " on earth, as it is done in heaven." Admittedly, their primary approach was the now oft-lampooned conversion of individual souls ; but converted souls, be it remembered, were " called " to be " co-labourers together with God " for the building of a society that hath foundations : a society based squarely on the rock of Christian principles, not on the shifting sands of political manœuvre, economic cupidity or class hatred ; a society wherein truth, equity, righteousness, brotherhood, purity, peace, temperance and love, should possess the souls of men and express themselves in all social institutions. To a phenomenal degree, these despised itinerant preachers were the forerunners and heralds of the principles of a true Christian democracy ; for, more than history has yet realised, did they create and release influences, which have affected profoundly the sanest movements for social emancipation throughout the English-speaking world.

The Evangelical Revival, despite Sir Leslie Stephen's verdict, assimilated all that was most vital and most heroic in Puritanism ; but it jettisoned the legalism and the quarrelsomeness of Puritanism ; it was essentially a New Testament, rather than an Old Testament, movement. Its primary appeal, moreover, was not to the trading, commercial and professional classes, nor yet to the old aristocracy, but rather to the forlorn multitudes, who earned their bread by the sweat of their brow. More than any other creative spiritual movement in modern history, it mediated a religion *of* the people, *for* the people, and *by* the people ; but its power lay in the fact that it made the people vitally conscious of God.

THE PREACHING OF SOCIAL RIGHTEOUSNESS

" GIVE liberty to whom liberty is due, that is to every child of man, to every partaker of human nature. Let none serve you but by his own act and deed, by his own voluntary choice. Away with all whips, all chains, all compulsion. Be gentle toward all men."

JOHN WESLEY, *Thoughts Upon Slavery* (1774).

" I HAVE two silver spoons at London and two at Bristol. This is all the plate I have at present, and I shall not buy any more while so many round me want bread."

JOHN WESLEY, *Letter to Commissioners of Excise*
(September 9th, 1776).

THE PREACHING OF SOCIAL RIGHTEOUSNESS

BECAUSE Wesley lived always in the consciousness of the spiritual world, and sought ever to bring individual souls into communion with God by means of individual conversions, it often is assumed, if not glibly asserted, that he had but small understanding of worldly affairs, that social questions were of little or no concern to him, and that really he turned the minds and efforts of multitudes away from the vital problems of life, to fix them upon an ethereal dream of blessedness beyond the grave.

Such an assumption represents a contortion of truth. It contains too little veracity for even the sorriest caricature. Wesley pre-eminently was a practical man ; never did he dodge the problems of life ; he was drawn into closer and longer contact with the common people, all over the kingdom, than any other character of his century ; and his vivid consciousness of Heaven and immortality, provided him with a prototype for all human relationships on earth : it gave dignity and high import to every social, political, economic and financial question surrounding and perplexing the life of man.   Those economists and social historians who airily brush Wesley aside as a fanatical enthusiast, hopelessly out of touch with the practical problems of life, are reflecting not on Wesley but on themselves : for they show clearly their ignorance of documentary evidence in which they should be versed.

(i) Wesley's Attacks on Slavery

Wesley being the central leader of the Evangelical Revival, and that revival in turn being—as later will appear—the central inspiration both of the abolition of the Empire slave trade (1807) and of the emancipation of Empire slaves (1833–4), it follows that his teaching on this subject is of peculiar and commanding interest.

In 1774, thirteen years before the famous Abolition Committee was formed, Wesley published his succinct, penetrating treatise, *Thoughts Upon Slavery* : and so direct, so graphic, so vehement, is the argument therein expressed that a sensitive reader perusing it, even to-day, must almost hear Wesley's voice and feel the throb of his heart.   After an historical and a restrained though ghastly portrayal of the inhumanity of slavery, he pierces prophetically to the moral issues involved. Countering the argument that the slave traffic was a legitimate business, he asks : " Can human *law* turn darkness into light or evil into good ? Notwithstanding ten thousand laws, right is right and wrong is wrong still. . . . I absolutely deny all slave-holding to be consistent with any degree of even *natural* justice."[1] " The whole business," he affirms, was pursued " to get money," and its excuses were " empty and hypocritical." " I deny that villainy is ever necessary," he expostulates ; " a man can be under *no necessity* of degrading himself into a wolf ! "[2] Proceeding, he dealt a timely blow at such " loyalty " as conceives Empire and patriotism in terms only of mercantile or geographical expansion, for concerning the British West Indies he urged : " It is better that all these islands should remain uncultivated for ever ; yea, it were more desirable that they were all together sunk in the depth of the sea than that they should be cultivated at so high a price as the violation of justice, mercy and truth."[3]

Wesley being bred and educated in an ultra-conservative environment, his whole tradition of life was conservative : even his conversion never completely freed him from this traditional bias. As in the famous cases of Luther and Descartes, many of the influences of early training and background survived catastrophic change ; yet when national custom or social sanction obviously blocked the road to liberty and progress, Wesley's religious convictions compelled him to become a *radical* reformer. " Are not stubbornness, cunning, pilfering and divers other vices the natural and necessary fruits of slavery ? " he demands ; and addressing the slave owners, he asks : " What wonder if they (your slaves) should cut your throats ? And if they did, whom could you blame for it but yourselves ? "[4] As for slave merchants, he reminds them that " men-buyers are on a level with men-stealers." " You know," he continues, " that your slaves are procured by means nothing near so innocent as picking of pockets, house-breaking or robbery upon the highway."[5]

Now, remembering that for decades following the printing of this treatise, the slave-trade was protected by law, and that the said merchants were eminently wealthy and " respectable " citizens, we realise that Wesley's language was scarcely " parliamentary." Indeed, two generations later his disciple, Rev.

---

[1] J. Wesley, *Thoughts upon Slavery*, pp. 34–5.
[2] *Ibid.*, p. 38.
[3] *Ibid.*, p. 40.
[4] *Ibid.*, p. 49.
[5] *Ibid.*, p. 54. See, too, the publication *Africanus* for fearful details.

J. R. Stephens, of Factory Reform and Anti-Poor Law fame, was clapped into prison for language only a few shades more provocative than that of his great spiritual father. But reverting to these slave merchants, Wesley further exclaimed : " You are the spring that puts all the rest in motion—captains, slave owners, kidnappers, murderers. . . . ' Thy brother's blood crieth unto thee.' . . . Thy hands, thy bed, thy furniture, thy house, thy lands are at present stained with blood. . . . Whether you are a Christian or not, show yourself a man ; be not more savage than a lion or a bear."[1]

Slave-ship captains and plantation owners came under a condemnation quite as castigating as slave merchants ; while some judges, Wesley protested, " are often " the slaves' " greatest tyrants."[2] " Are any laws so binding as the eternal laws of justice ? " he asks ; while as for Liberty, he proclaims it[1] " the *right* of *every* human creature as soon as he breathes the vital air."[3] Countering the inevitable excuse that English slavery was more humane than that of other countries, Wesley marshalled evidence completely demolishing this subterfuge and proving conclusively that " conditions under English masters are no better than under French or Dutch." The " grand idol " of the whole traffic, he avowed, was " the god of gain," and all its supporters he impeached as " petty tyrants over human freedom."[4] The luxurious grandeur, " of which the slave's misery forms so large a part," was under the scourge of heaven ; and it was the work of all true Christians to proclaim the Liberty of Heaven and act as instruments of God for the suppression of slavery. " Give liberty," cried Wesley, " to whom liberty is due, that is, to every child of man, to every partaker of human nature. Let none serve you but by his own act and deed, by his own voluntary choice. Away with all whips, all chains, all compulsion. Be gentle toward all men."

In other publications, where Wesley deals with the slave traffic, his denunciations are equally piquant. In his *Serious Address to the People of England with regard to the State of the Nation*, written in 1777 during the high tumult of the American Revolutionary War, he answers poignantly the lamentations over a marked loss in the slave trade. " I would to God," he thunders, " that it may never be found more ! That we may never more steal and sell *our brethren* like beasts, never murder them by thousands and tens of thousands ! O may this worse than Mohammedan, worse than pagan abomination, be removed

---

[1] *Thoughts upon Slavery*, p. 55.
[2] *Ibid.*, p. 67 ; cf. Blackstone's judgment, see chapter vi, parts (i) and (ii).
[3] *Ibid.*, pp. 76 and 56.
[4] *Ibid.*, pp. 81–2.

from us for ever ! Never was anything such a reproach to England since it was a nation as the having any hand in this execrable traffic."[1] A bit later, he breaks into a half-humorous but wholly characteristic irony : " And we can no longer sell our brethren like sheep, and pour out their blood like water. Therefore the nation is in a desperate state ! Therefore we are on the brink of ruin ! And are these the best arguments that can be brought forward to support the lamentable conclusion ? "[2] Three times, in the course of this *Address*, Wesley reverted to the national disgrace of slavery ; and, concluding, he dealt a giant blow : " With respect to trade of the West Indies, you may grant it is greatly decreased. The planters there cannot carry on their trade of buying the bodies and souls of men. God grant (for the honour of our country and religion) that they may never be able to carry it on more ! The total, final destruction of this horrid trade would rejoice every lover of mankind : yea, though our sugar islands (so the inhabitants escaped) were swallowed up in the depths of the sea. Certain it is that England may not only subsist but abundantly prosper without them— may increase in population, agriculture, manufactures, and all other articles above-mentioned, though we no more suck the blood and devour the flesh of the *less barbarous Africans*. O earth, hide not their blood, and no more cover their shame ! "[3]

In John Wesley, the negro slaves found a veritable Daniel come to judgment. Even at as early a date as the writing of ·*Thoughts Upon Slavery*, Wesley was revered by more people and influenced more consciences than any other man in England : yet every one of his followers was taught to regard the negro slave as a " brother in Christ." Nor was it any accident that the " Great Emancipator " was a spiritual son of Wesley, or that the mighty prophet's last letter, written but six days ere death, was addressed to Wilberforce :

" Unless the Divine Power has raised you up to be as Athanasius, *contra mundum*, I see not how you can go through your glorious enterprise in opposing that execrable villainy which is the scandal of religion, of England, and of human nature. Unless God has raised you up for this very thing, you will be worn out by the opposition of men and devils ; but *if God be for you, who can be against you ?* Are all of them together stronger than God ? Oh, *be not weary in well doing*. Go on, in the name of God and in the power of His might,

[1] *Op. cit.*, p. 15.
[2] *Serious Address*, etc., p. 18.
[3] *Ibid.*, p. 28.

till even American slavery, the vilest that ever saw the sun, shall vanish away before it.

" Reading this morning a tract wrote by a poor African, I was particularly struck by that circumstance that a man who has a black skin, being wronged or outraged by a white man, can have no redress ; it being a *law* in our colonies that the oath of a black against a white goes for nothing. What villainy is this !

" That He who has guided you from your youth up, may continue to strengthen you in this and in all things, is the prayer of,
Dear Sir,
Your affectionate servant,
" JOHN WESLEY."[1]

The " tract " by " a poor African," referred to in this letter, was *Gustavus Vasa*, the " autobiography of a black slave." It was the *last* secular book Wesley read. And on his death-bed, his own strength failing him, he desired both James Rogers and Elizabeth Ritchie to read aloud to him from this treatise. Even in his last hours, therefore, the burden of those tortured " black brethren " pressed heavily on this holy man's heart. An immortal emancipator was being taught by a slave.[2]

(ii) *The Insanity of War*

Save for the protests of a handful of Quakers crying in the wilderness, the arbitrament of the sword in Wesley's day was universally accepted as the final court of appeal in all international disputes. The great English evangelist could never be described as an out-and-out pacifist ; yet war he believed to be the foulest curse men knew—the denial, even the crucifixion, of all the higher attributes of civilisation : it was rebellion against humanity and God. " War," says Wesley, " is a horrid reproach to the Christian name, yea, to the name of man, to all reason and humanity.[3] In all the judgments of God," he avers, " the inhabitants of the earth learn righteousness. Famine, plague, earthquake, the people see the hand of God. But when war breaks out God is forgotten."[4] " So long as this monster stalks *uncontrolled*, where is reason, virtue, humanity ? They are utterly excluded."[5]

---

[1] See Professor Coupland's *William Wilberforce*, p. 141 ; also Vulliamy's *Wesley*, p. 346.

[2] See *Journal*, Vol. VIII, p. 135 (footnote). See, too, Elizabeth Ritchie's *Account of Wesley's Last Days*.

[3] See *Doctrine of Original Sin* (1756).

[4] *Works* of Wesley, Vol. XII, p. 327.

[5] *Ibid.*, Vol. IX, p. 221.

In 1758, the Seven Years' War being then at full tide, with France and Austria fighting England and Prussia, and with Central Europe, Canada and India a far-flung field of battle, the Wesleys published *Hymns of Intercession for all Mankind*. And the tenor of their teaching the following couplets reflect :

> " Our earth we now lament to see,
> With floods of wickedness o'erflowed.
>
> .   .   .   .
>
> " Where men, like fiends, each other tear,
> In all the hellish rage of war.
>
> .   .   .   .
>
> " Father of everlasting love,
> To every soul Thy Son reveal.
>
> .   .   .   .
>
> " And bid the fallen race arise,
> And turn our earth to paradise."[1]

As the trouble with the American Colonies began to brew, Wesley wrote to Rankin and other of his preachers in America, imploring them to use their influence " for peace."   In March, 1775, he wrote to " brother Charles," saying : " I am of neither side, and yet of both : on the side of New England and of old. . . . We love all and pray for all with a sincere and impartial love."   And he besought Charles to be " like-minded."[2]   A few weeks later, Wesley penned his famous warning to Lord North, the Premier : " In spite of my long-rooted prejudice, I cannot avoid thinking, if I think at all, that an *oppressed* people asked for nothing more than their *legal rights*, and that in the most modest and inoffensive manner that the nature of the thing would allow.   But waiving all considerations of right and wrong, I ask, is it common sense to use force toward the Americans ?   These men will not be frightened ; and it seems they will not be conquered as easily as was first imagined—they will probably dispute every inch of ground ; and if they die, die sword in hand."[3]

Lord Dartmouth, the Colonial Secretary, was a friend of Wesley and a devoted convert of the Revival.   In Wesley's letter to him on 14th June, 1775, he pleaded strongly for pacific and conciliatory efforts ; nor did he shrink from the use of utilitarian as well as spiritual arguments.   The Americans, he insisted, believed they were fighting for their homes—not for pay.   France and other European nations, he predicted, would almost certainly

---

[1] See Henry Carter, *The Methodist*, pp. 170–1.
[2] M. Edwards, *John Wesley and the Eighteenth Century*, p. 72.
[3] See L. Tyerman, *Life and Times of J. Wesley*, Vol. III, p. 198.

enter the struggle and extend the field of carnage ; and whereas the Americans were largely united, many Britons, he warned, were " ripe for rebellion " at home. In conclusion came Wesley's memorable, prophetic plea : " For God's sake, for the sake of the King, of the nation, of your lovely family, remember Rehoboam ! Remember Philip II ! Remember Charles I ! "[1] In the light of later events, were ever admonitions more apt ?

The following year, when the Revolutionary War was at its height, Wesley wrote his *Seasonable Address to the More Serious Part of the Inhabitants of Great Britain respecting the Unhappy Contest between us and our American Brethren.* That treatise portrays vividly Wesley's utter abhorrence of war. Picturing the armies of the revolution rushing together in conflict, he asks : " But what are they going to do ? To shoot each other through the head or heart, to stab and butcher each other ? . . . Why so ? What harm have they done to each other ? Why none at all. Most of them are entire strangers to each other. But a matter is in dispute relative to the mode of taxation. So these country-men, children of the same parents, are to *murder* each other with all possible haste—to *prove* who is in the right. What an argument is this ! What a method of proof ! What an amazing way of deciding controversies ! " Then, suggesting impartial arbitration instead of bloodshed, he inquires : " Are there no wise men among us ? None that are able to judge between *brethren* ? But brother goeth to war against brother, and that in the very sight of the heathen. Surely this is a sore evil among us ? How is wisdom perished from the wise ! What a flood of folly and madness has broke in upon us ! "[2]

But meanwhile, in the autumn of 1775, had appeared Wesley's *Calm Address to our American Colonies.* This treatise everyone has heard of, and on ten thousand occasions has it been used as a stick with which to beat Wesley's back. Certainly it represents a marked change of front as to the " oppression " of the Colonials and the " legal right " of their demands. He here tells the Americans that the laws against which they were revolting are just, and that the taxes they refused to pay are both moderate and fair. Here Wesley's subconscious and traditional Toryism reasserts itself in robust form. Yet his changed attitude represents more than traditional prejudice or patriotic fervour. It is a remarkable fact that a large volume of recent and disinterested research, both American and English, is completely overthrowing the long dominant delusion that the American rebels were wholly in the right and that the

[1] *Journal,* Vol. VIII, Appendix 27.
[2] *Works,* Vol. XI, p. 122.

English Tories, then controlling Parliament, were all vindictive tyrants.[1]

But dropping this thorny problem, what caused Wesley's altered attitude? Did he arbitrarily change front? Were the numberless charges of inconsistency and even of sycophancy now hurled against him rooted in truth? First of all, it must be remembered that, when the *Calm Address* was written, every last chance of pacific settlement had passed. War had come, and war to men of action means Yea! or Nay! Meanwhile, too, Wesley had read Dr. Johnson's *Taxation no Tyranny* and was profoundly impressed. Indeed his main thesis in the *Calm Address* is a popular adaptation of Johnson's argument. But if Wesley had received "light" from Johnson's treatise, and thought it his "duty to enlighten others," it must not be imagined that this was the sole cause of his changed demeanour. Daily was it becoming more obvious that the American slogans had been quite misleading, and that, presuming upon the new geographical safety won for them by the Seven Years War, Rebellion and Independence had become the Colonial leaders' real, but covert, intent. Though the American watchword was "Liberty," the actual situation had largely drifted into the hands of demogogues and mobs. Tom Paine, who had gone to America in 1774, already was showing his hand, and in 1776 was to appear his *Common Sense*. Lawyers, for some time past, had been openly threatened with mob murder, if they brought any case before a British judge. "Loyalist" neighbours, in considerable numbers, had been "tarred and feathered." Smuggling long had been openly encouraged as an honourable trade. And while the revolutionaries all shouted "Liberty" and "Independence," their armed forces were being commanded by a slave-owning planter, who entertained never a thought of freeing his own human chattels. "Liberty" was not for "blacks"; nor had the leaders of "Independence" a thought of granting the franchise to any save a favoured minority among the whites.

When therefore the crisis came, Wesley's love of "law or order" made him a staunch defender of Parliament. England's protracted bungling of a delicate situation, he still deplored; but the madness of mobs was a phenomenon with which he was all too familiar: and the provocative outrages of the Colonial mobs, he deemed wholly unpardonable. Hence the famous *Calm Address*.

As for the countless charges of plagiarism and sycophancy, they need not detain us. Dr. Johnson, far from being offended

---

[1] See Jeudwine's *Religion, Commerce, Liberty, 1683-1793*, chapters xi and xiv.

at Wesley's use of his arguments, was highly flattered. " To have gained such a mind as yours," the Doctor wrote to Wesley, " may justly confirm me in my own opinion. . . . The lecturer was surely in the right, who, though he saw his audience slinking away, refused to quit the chair *while Plato stayed*."[1] Concerning the sycophancy charges, Wesley's letter to Lloyds *Evening Post* is highly illuminating. The said *Address*, he answered his assailants, was written : " Not to please any man living, high or low. I know mankind too well. I know that they who love you for political service, love you less than their dinner ; and they that hate you, hate you worse than the devil."[2] The American revolt, Wesley averred, had been largely " incited by letters from England." The rebels had been " advised " by political malcontents in the Home Land, to " seize upon all the King's officers," and were told that, if they " stood valiantly " for six months, there would be " such commotions in England," that they might have their " own terms." The flame of disloyalty, Wesley contended, " rages " all over England ; many were " pouring oil into the flame " : he wrote to " contribute his mite " toward " putting out " the fire.[3]

Wesley's prediction that an American rebellion would spread to war with France and Spain proved correct. He knew well, that such an event would threaten every foundation of British influence throughout the globe. And he believed that England, for all her sins, was more worthy to guard the high seas and to exercise far-flung colonial influence than either France or Spain, her then envious rivals. His abhorrence of war was unchanging. He did everything in his power to prevent the outbreak of the American Revolution. But when once the war came, he supported the Government. His *Calm Address* and his co-related treatises ran into a circulation of many scores of thousands.[4] And this support to an England honeycombed with Whig dissention at home, facing rebellious colonies in America, and pushed to the wall by France, Spain and Holland at Gibraltar as well as in East and West, did much to save the Empire from complete disruption. Little wonder, therefore, that Wesley was violently lampooned as a " Government pensioner." The Man of Peace, by raising the morale of the issues and by radiating the spirit of national confidence and honour in England, proved a mighty bulwark of defence in time of war : but all war he continued to loathe ; and certain

---

[1] *Gentleman's Magazine*, Vol. XVII, Part I, p. 455.
[2] *Journal*, November 27th, 1775.
[3] *Ibid.*
[4] See, too, Wesley's *Observations on Liberty* and *Calm Address to the Inhabitants of England*.

of his publications, it must be admitted, made the war-time situation doubly difficult for his preachers on American soil.[1]

(iii) *The Use and Abuse of Money and Privilege*

" The Church," cried St. Bernard in the twelfth century, as he gazed at the wonders of Gothic architecture, " is resplendent in her walls, beggarly in her poor. She clothes her stones in gold and leaves her sons naked."[2]   Wesley, six centuries later, " was to protest in terms equally eloquent and vehement, against the extravagances of wealth : and that protest he formulated into a very definite doctrine concerning the use and abuse of money and privilege. The acquisition of knowledge, taught Lord Bacon, was for " the glory of the Creator and the relief of man's estate." Just so, taught Wesley, regarding the gaining of money and the use of all economic and financial power. " The earth is the Lord's and the fulness thereof," was the central aspect of his economic faith. Hence the cardinal articles of his financial creed were the Divine proprietorship of all wealth, property and privilege, and the responsible stewardship of man. All talents, of whatever nature, were to Wesley a temporary trust from God. " Occupy till I come," was God's commission to man. The " Christian " use of wealth, therefore, anticipated and postulated a spiritualised and socialised will. The delusion of " irresponsible ownership " represented the crassest idolatry ; avarice and cupidity were soul-killing sins ; while as for parasitic wealth, it carried within itself its own fearful Nemesis—a death-dealing sting.

To Wesley, therefore, any enduring antithesis between business and religion was unthinkable. For him the vital question was not, " Should religion interfere with business ? " but rather, " How can business avoid going to the devil, if it is not permeated with religious values, and dedicated to religious ends ? "   Riches, taught this modern prophet, were made for man, not man for riches. Economic ambition, he believed to be a good servant but an accursed master. The acid test of the economic and commercial life was the query, " To what *purpose* do the wheels go round ? "   And unless they moved for the common good, they obviously were out of gear. All " snatching to hoard, and hoarding to snatch " Wesley considered utter insanity. No more than sex appetites, should the acquisitive economic appetites be stimulated, or pampered :

[1] Edwards's *Wesley* has a suggestive chapter on " The War of American Independence." But despite all recent research in this field, he assumes throughout that the American cause was wholly just and the English unjust.

[2] See Professor G. G. Coulton *A Mediæval Garner*, pp. 68–73.

rather should they be curbed, and sublimated to social and spiritual ends. The injunction in *Proverbs*, " Give me neither riches nor poverty, but enough for my subsistence," was to Wesley a law of reason. Men who strove to " corner " the fruits of the earth were not only robbing God, but grinding the face of the poor : they were as ravenous wolves, whom any decently ordered society should seek to hold by the ears, till they learned neighbourliness. No department of life, Wesley insisted, dare be surrendered to the " powers of darkness." The remedy for bad law was good law, not lawlessness : but the foundation of all good law, in turn, he believed to be the socialised conscience and the really " changed " heart.[1]

" Luther's utterances on social morality," says Professor Tawney, " are the occasional explosions of a capricious volcano, with only a rare flash of light amid the torrent of smoke and flame, and it is idle to scan them for a coherent and consistent doctrine."[2] Wesley himself refers to Luther's writings on Salvation by Faith as " muddy and confused."[3] The leader of the " Second Reformation " was too systematic by nature and too keen a logician by training, to fall into Luther's error. Whatever were Wesley's shortcomings, system and coherence were at the centre of his life and teaching : his warm, stout heart was directed by a cool, reflective head.

Though Wesley always was suspicious of accumulated " fortunes," though commonly he avoided the rich and worked generally on the principle " the poor are the Christians," yet he was too practical to despise or underrate the value of money, if controlled by a humane, sensitive conscience for the common good. In his sermon *The Good Steward*, he speaks of " that precious talent which contains all the rest—money." Indeed he pronounces it " unspeakably precious if we are wise and faithful stewards of it."[4] But always he proclaimed wealth an inevitable curse if once it became an end in itself, or a means of self-aggrandisement. " In what manner," he asks, " didst thou employ that comprehensive talent, money ? Not in gratifying the desire of the flesh, the desire of the eye or the pride of life ? Not squandering it away in vain expenses, the same as throwing it into the sea ? Not hoarding it up to leave behind thee, the same as burying it in the earth ? But in first supplying thine own reasonable wants, together with those of thy family ; then restoring the remainder to God, through the

---

[1] See Dr. W. J. Warner, *Wesleyan Movement*, etc., chapter iii.
[2] R. H. Tawney, *Religion and the Rise of Capitalism*, p. 88.
[3] *Journal*, June 15th, 1741.
[4] *Ibid.*, p. 8.

poor ? "[1] Industry and thrift, he demanded of all his disciples as indispensable marks of Christianity : but the purpose of these must be service to God and man, not vainglorious indulgence. "Wast thou accordingly a general benefactor of mankind ? " he asks. "Didst thou *labour to improve all outward works of mercy and means of saving souls from death* ? " If so, " it remains that thou be rewarded to all eternity, according to thy *works*."[2] But if contrariwise, we forget that God is the Creator and Proprietor of all, and fail to use the money entrusted to us as stewards of His Kingdom, we are certain to become entangled in the enticing meshes of sin, and lose whatever lingering faith remains in our souls. Wesley's injunctions in this regard are emphatic and unmistakable. "Give all you can. Hoard nothing. I defy all the men upon the earth, yea all the angels in heaven, to find any other way of extracting the *poison* from riches." Any who squander or hoard wealth for self-gratification, Wesley taught are " robbing God, continually embezzling and wasting their Lord's goods, and, by that very means, corrupting their own souls." Nay worse ; in so doing, we are " keeping money from the poor, to buy poison for ourselves."[3]

Wesley's famous money rule, the world knows. " Gain all you can. Save all you can. Give all you can." But it was circumscribed by the strictest limitations, which frequently are forgotten. The Christian, guided by " love toward God and man," must do " no harm "[4] to his neighbour ; he " must not sell anything which tends to impair health " ; he must disassociate himself from all " hazardous and unhealthy employments." He must *gain* only by means which render true and honest service to his fellow men. Neither must he *save* to the extent of endangering the physical, mental or moral health of his dependants or himself. Finally, if he failed to *give all*, beyond what was necessary for the Christian support of his family, the running of his business, and a reasonable provision for his dependants—if he piled up " treasures on earth "—then he was flouting " a flat, positive command, full and clear as ' Thou shalt not commit adultery '."[5] Similarly, Wesley urged parents not to " seek riches for your children by their marriage." To call such a union a " good match," he protested, is " by parity of reason," to " call hell a good lodging."[6]

---

[1] *Op. cit.*, p. 20.
[2] *Ibid.*, pp. 20–2.
[3] J. Wesley's *Works*, Vol. V., p. 375.
[4] See *Rules* of Wesley's Societies.
[5] See Sermons, *The Use of Money, The Danger of Riches, Dives and Lazarus, Causes of the Inefficiency of Christianity, Wheels within Wheels*, etc.
[6] See Wesley's *Works*, Vol. VII, p. 85.

Emphatic was Wesley's teaching that the human body, being " the temple of God," should be kept healthy and clean ; no financial exploits therefore should be permitted which undermine men's physique. But yet more emphatic is his teaching concerning the supremacy of personality over all considerations of property and profit. " All cheating and overreaching in business, all pawn-broking and usury," he sternly denounced. " We cannot, consistent with brotherly love," he says, " sell our goods below market price ; we cannot study to ruin our neighbour's trade, to advance our own. . . . None can gain by swallowing up his neighbour's substance, without gaining the damnation of hell."[1] Though Wesley often used the word " hell," it was generally in a metaphorical sense. He was not given to the employment of " sulphurous " language ; but the hottest fires of the deepest hell, he would have deemed necessary to *purge* the sins of some modern " cornering trusts." Nevertheless, as to the worst of sinners " grace abounds," he would have said with Anatole France, " The mercy of God is boundless : it can save even a rich man ! "

Southey contends that Wesley's uncompromising teaching regarding wealth alienated the sympathy of the privileged classes. " The rigid doctrine which Wesley preached concerning riches," he says, " being only one degree more reasonable than that of St. Francis, prevented Methodism from extending itself as it otherwise might have done, among those classes where these notions would have been acted upon by zealous mothers."[2] It must be remembered, however, that this is the criticism of a highly privileged man. When Southey, in 1820, wrote his *Life of Wesley*, his place was established as a literary idol of exclusive and wealthy society ; already for seven years had he been Poet Laureate : and his youthful dreams of establishing a pioneer Utopia in America, which once he had shared with Coleridge, were now but a faint and fantastic memory. His publications were paying him handsomely ; he was living on the fat of the land ; and he left behind him £12,000.[3] Hence the prejudices of the wealthy had become his own ; he was in no position to intrepret the heroism or the selflessness either of St. Francis or Wesley. He desired no hard sayings regarding the snares of wealth. With peculiar insight has it been said of Southey's *Wesley* : " He had nothing to draw with, and the well is deep ! " The criticism is not applicable to the whole work ; but it is a sagacious rejoinder to Southey's

<hr>

[1] See section, " Gain all you can," in *Use of Money* ; also J. A. Faulkner, *Wesley as Sociologist, Theologian and Churchman*, pp. 7-35.
[2] Southey's *Life of Wesley*. p. 326.
[3] See *Dict. of Nat. Biog.* ; also *Chambers's Biographical Dict.*

denunciation of Wesley's teaching regarding wealth. The prophet-evangelist would not sugar coat the doctrines of his conscience and his Christ, to make Salvation easy for the rich and proud : so the pill was too bitter for Southey's "refined" taste.

That Wesley's life-long practice squared exactly with his money teaching, there can be no possible doubt. In 1743 he wrote : "If I leave behind me £10 . . . you and all mankind bear witness against me that I lived and died a thief and a robber."[1] In 1776, he received a communication from the Commissioners of Excise, saying they "cannot doubt but you have *plate* for which you have hitherto neglected to make an entry." Wesley's reply was succinct : "I have two silver spoons at London and two at Bristol. This is all the plate I have at present, and I shall not buy any more *while so many round me want bread.*"[2]

The income from the almost unprecedented sale of Wesley's tracts, pamphlets and books was sufficient to make him a rich man : but never did he spend more than £30 a year upon his personal needs. Always he wore cheap clothes ; and always he dined on the plainest fare. In a single year he gave away as much as £1,400 :[3] which meant that he kept one forty-seventh of his earnings, and gave away nearly ninety-eight per cent. Increased income therefore, had no effect on his personal expenditure. He supplied his humble needs in the most modest manner, and gave away *all* the rest—or rather returned it to God, its Owner, "through his brethren, the poor." Yet, giving his time, his talents, his love, his money, his *all*, he was given in return, the pearl of great price : for, amidst all his unparalleled labours, happiness and composure possessed his soul and were mirrored in his benign and saintly face. On the eve of death, Wesley closed his Account Book with the words : "For upwards of eighty-six years I have kept my accounts exactly, I will not attempt it any longer, being satisfied with the continual conviction that I save all I can, and give all I can— that is *all I have.*"[4]

Never did Revolutionist or Communist give of his all so utterly unreservedly as did John Wesley : yet he gave it not in the spirit of envy, pride, hatred or revenge, but in the spirit of fellowship, service and love ; for he hated no man, but loved, and sought fellowship with, every soul on earth.

[1] Tyerman's *Wesley*, Vol. I, p. 436.
[2] This letter (September 9th, 1776) is preserved in the library of Heading-ley College.
[3] See *Encyclopædia Britannica*, "John Wesley" (Telford).
[4] *Journal* (Curnock edition), Vol. VIII, p. 80. See, too, facsimile of a page from Wesley's *Diary* (August 5th, 1790), *ibid.*, p. 85.

CHAPTER XIII

THE REASSERTION OF THE CHRISTIAN ETHIC

" NEITHER may we gain by hurting our neighbour in his body. Therefore we may not sell anything which tends to impair health."

WESLEY's sermon, *The Use of Money.*

" So wickedly, devilishly false is that common objection, ' They are poor only because they are idle '."

WESLEY's *Journal,* February 9th, 1753

THE REASSERTION OF THE CHRISTIAN ETHIC

THAT Wesley's conversion changed his outlook from a dominantly priestly to an aggressively prophetic interpretation of Christianity, is a fact pregnant with the strongest ethical implications. Throughout Britain, and far beyond, this transfigured man and the Revival of which he was the dynamic centre, caused purging Light to shine in deep darkness : and though for long the darkness comprehended not the Light, finally a new day broke. And among the manifestations of the new dawning, which made Christ real and imminent to an apostate people, was a vehement reassertion of the wisdom and potency of the Christian ethic, and of its applicability to the practical concerns of every day life. A new faith therefore was gradually creating a new conscience, and a new conscience was gradually creating a new awareness of moral evil and social sin, which long had been accepted, if not condoned or even extolled, as normal and necessary expressions of the " natural order " of things.

(i) *Wesley and the Liquor Traffic*

Something of the vitiating influence of the liquor traffic on the social conditions in England when Wesley began his crusade we have already seen.[1] Lecky, a rationalist, in his classic *History* of the period, refers repeatedly, and in different volumes, to this traffic as " the master curse " of England's social life. Dr. M. D. George, in her recent economic and social researches into the life and labour of the general populace in the eighteenth century, is driven to be no less emphatic concerning the centrality of this traffic as a source of corruption, stagnation and death. Referring to the appalling social and moral decadence " between 1720 and 1750," she says it was " almost certainly due to an enormous consumption of very cheap, fiery and adulterated spirits."[2] But what Dr. George and most other social and economic historians, of purely secular outlook, have quite failed to recognise, is that not till the challenge of the

[1] See chapter viii (section (ii).
[2] *London Life in the Eighteenth Century*, p. 20 ; also pp. 27–42, 56, 288–304

Evangelical Revival had touched the hearts and directed the lives of great numbers of people in all parts of the country, did any semblance of redemption appear. Liquor control legislation, challenging perforce deeply rooted personal appetites, before it could effect any real reform had to be backed and vitalised by strong moral and spiritual convictions : and of such convictions, prior to the great Revival, England was almost bankrupt. From the very beginning, however, the Revival, in the face of much contumely and contempt, marshalled all its forces in direct attack upon the organised liquor traffic, as the unmistakable source of a vast volume of personal and social degradation. And that John Wesley became ultimately the most effective temperance advocate the English-speaking world has yet reared, is a claim which will square with facts.

If to Wesley the traffic in human life was " the execrable sum of all the villainies," the traffic in intoxicating liquors fell easily into second place : and the vested interests behind the latter he lashed quite as unsparingly as those behind the former ; for to him wealth gained by the distilling and distribution of beverage intoxicants, was scarcely less " stained in blood " than wealth gained through slavery. In his sermon on *The Use of Money*, for instance, after emphasising the Christian duty to practise industry, frugality and thrift, when defining the sphere of legitimate *gain*, he says : " Neither may we gain by hurting our neighbour in his body. Therefore we may not sell anything which tends to impair health : such is evidently all that liquid fire, commonly called drams or spirituous liquors." Then he continues : " Those who prepare and sell them only for *medicine* may keep their conscience clear. But who are they who prepare and sell them only for this end ? Do you know ten such distillers in England ? Then excuse them. But all who sell in the common way, to any who will buy, are *poisoners general*. They murder his majesty's subjects wholesale ; neither do they ever pity or spare. They drive them to hell like sheep ; and what is their gain ?—is it not the blood of these men ? Who then would envy their large estates and sumptuous palaces ? A curse is in the midst of them. The curse of God cleaves to the stones, the timber, the furniture of them. The curse of God is in their gardens, their walks, their groves ; a fire that burns to the nethermost hell. Blood, blood is there ; the foundations, the floor, the walls, the roof are stained with blood ! And canst thou hope, O thou man of blood, though thou are clothed in scarlet and fine linen, and farest sumptuously every day ; canst thou hope to deliver down the fields of blood to the third generation ? Not so, for there is a God in heaven ;

therefore thy name shall be rooted out. Like those whom thou hast destroyed, body and soul, ' thy memorial shall perish with thee '."[1]

That this relentless opposition to the liquor traffic was nothing accidental or sporadic, but held a crucial place in Wesley's teaching needs no demonstration. In season and out of season, he attacked the whole traffic as the foe of all progress and the antithesis of true liberty. In his *Thoughts on Present Scarcity of Provisions* (1773), he asks : " Why is food so dear ? " and proffers this answer : " The grand cause is because such immense quantities of corn are continually consumed in distilling. . . . Nearly half of the wheat produced in the Kingdom every year is consumed, not in so harmless a way as throwing it into the sea, but by converting it into deadly poison, poison that naturally destroys not only the strength and life but also the morals of our countrymen." Then, lashing the age-old argument that the traffic affords indispensable State revenue, he indulges a characteristic satirical thrust : " Oh, tell it not in Constantinople that the English raise the royal revenue by selling the flesh and blood of their countrymen." The " trade's " stock arguments concerning " Personal Liberty," Wesley believed utterly hollow and insincere. To him they were but smoke-screens behind which Avarice and Cupidity, while mouthing pretty phrases about " freedom " and " patriotism," attacked the foundations of social welfare. On humanitarian and social grounds, therefore, Wesley pleaded for the complete abolition of the manufacture and sale of all spirituous liquors for beverage purposes, as a duty of State.[2]

His letter to the Prime Minister, William Pitt, dated September 6th, 1784, is, in this connection, illuminating. " Suppose your *influence*," he wrote, " could prevent distilling by making it a *felony*, you would do more service to your country than any Prime Minister has done these 100 years. Your name would be precious to all true Englishmen as long as England continued a nation. And what is infinitely more, a greater Monarch than King George would say to you : ' Well done, good and faithful servant.' "[3] Remembering that Pitt himself was a struggling victim of the liquor traffic, this letter is doubly courageous. Always Wesley recognised the importance of educating public opinion and of sensitising the public conscience. But he was no sentimentalist. He knew that Legislation— including certain prohibitive enactments—was absolutely essential, in an imperfect world, to safeguard and consolidate

---

[1] *Use of Money* is among Wesley's " Standard " Sermons.
[2] See *op. cit.*
[3] See Wesley's *Letters* (above date).

such moral victories as faith, vision and conscience alone could initiate : and he believed the prohibition of the mercenary traffic in distilled liquors, as essential to human welfare and balanced happiness, as the prohibition of the slave traffic. Hence the above letter to Pitt.

In the "*Rules of the Society of the People called Methodists*" we read : " It is therefore expected of all who continue therein, that they should continue to evidence their desire for salvation, *first*, by doing no harm, by avoiding evil in every kind ; especially that which is generally practised. Such is . . . Drunkenness ; buying or selling spirituous liquors, or drinking them, unless in cases of extreme necessity."[1] And among the special instructions laid down by Wesley for the guidance of his local and itinerant preachers, was the injunction that they were to taste intoxicating liquors " on no pretext whatever." Finally, too, it is notable that Wesley's *Primitive Physic*, which ran into nearly forty editions, was in part designed to free the English populace from the vulgar delusion, that alcohol is the universal medicine for most diseases which afflict mankind.

(ii) *Legal, Political and State Affairs*

It cannot be over emphasised that to Wesley religion was the " be-all and end-all " of human life. The soul of reformation, to him, was ever the reformation of the soul. But human life being itself a social process, dependent for its existence upon the complex institutions of law and order, it follows that in a truly Christian community those institutions should be permeated with the spirit, and guided by the ethic, of the Gospel of Christ. Religion to Wesley therefore was not in the nature of an external crown or apex, superimposed upon the social structure : rather was it a health-giving elixir, which alone could bring harmony, purpose and dignity to all the variegated but co-related organs and members of the body politic. Concerning matters of law, politics and statecraft, accordingly, he repeatedly struck notes of no uncertain key.

The monotonous reiteration of words together with the irksome padding of legal documents, as an excuse to multiply lawyers' fees, have often been attacked, but rarely with greater pungency than by Wesley. " I called on the solicitor whom I had employed in the suit lately commenced against me in Chancery," he notes in 1745, " and here I saw *that foul monster, a Chancery bill* ! A scroll it was of forty-two pages in large folio, to tell a story which needed not to have taken forty lines ! and stuffed with such stupid, senseless, improbable lies (many

---

[1] See section 4 of *Rules*.

of them, too, quite foreign to the question) as, I believe, would have cost the compiler his life in any heathen court either of Greece or Rome. And this is Equity in a Christian country ! This is the English method of redressing their grievances."[1] The great evangelist was perhaps hyper-critical of the legal profession of his day : he refers to an honest lawyer as a " black swan,"[2] and repeatedly he condemns the " villainous tautology of lawyers." Indeed his famous " Form for the Settling of Preaching Houses," which eminent solicitors have pronounced one of the tersest and clearest of legal documents, was compiled to eradicate the bewildering phraseology and tantalising repetitions, customary in such legal documents. " I wrote a form for settling the preaching houses," he explains, " without any superfluous words, which shall be used for the time to come, verbatim, for all the houses to which I contribute anything. I will no more encourage that villainous tautology of lawyers, which is the scandal of our nation."[3]

Yet, if Wesley was unduly suspicious of lawyers, his aversion was inspired by humane motives. He felt that Law, instead of acting as a medium of equity and a protection to the poor, frequently was being used to pervert equity and to embezzle the poor ; and to him perverted law, like perverted religion, was a loathsome, diabolical thing. We quote *in extenso* a case in point : " We returned to York, where I was desired to call upon a poor *prisoner* in the castle. I had formerly occasion to take notice of an hideous monster, called a Chancery Bill ; I now saw the fellow to it, called a Declaration. The plain fact was this : Some time since a man who lived near Yarm assisted others in running some brandy. His share was near four pounds. After he had wholly left off that bad work, and was following his own business, that of a weaver, he was arrested, and sent to York gaol ; and, not long after, comes down a Declaration, ' that Jac. Wh—— had landed a vessel laded with brandy and Geneva, at the port of London, and sold them there, whereby he was indebted to his Majesty five hundred and seventy-seven pounds and upwards.' And to tell this worthy story, the lawyer takes up thirteen or fourteen sheets of treble stamped paper. O England, England ! will this reproach never be rolled away from thee ? Is there anything like this to be found, either among Papists, Turks or heathens ? In the name of truth, justice, mercy and common sense, I ask : 1. Why do men lie for lyings sake ? *Is it only to keep their hands in* ? What need else, of saying it was the port of London, when

[1] *Journal*, December 27th, 1745.
[2] *Ibid.*, October 2nd, 1764.
[3] *Ibid.*, June 8th, 1790.

everyone knew the brandy was landed above three hundred miles from thence? What a monstrous contempt of truth does this show, or rather hatred, to it! 2. Where is the justice of swelling four pounds into five hundred and seventy-seven? 3. Where is the common sense of taking up fourteen sheets to tell a story that may be told in ten lines? 4. Where is the mercy of thus grinding the face of the poor, thus sucking the blood of a poor, beggared prisoner? Would not this be execrable villainy, if the paper and writing together were only sixpence a sheet, when they have stripped him already of his little all, and not left him fourteen groats in the world?"[1]

No man of his century attacked the common practice of smuggling more stoutly or more effectively than Wesley. Yet in this case he obviously considered the representatives of the Law more criminal than the imprisoned smuggler.

Purely party politics, received from Wesley no support. Repeatedly, at election times, he convened the enfranchised members of his Societies and urged them to vote for the candidate of nobler character who would support humanitarian and Christian principles—for a lover " of God and the King." And by the King, he meant the symbol of a united nation, not the head of a faction or class. But each elector, he insisted, must conscientiously settle the choice for himself, refraining always from ill word or ill deed toward those who voted on the other side. Wesley coerced the political conscience of none of his followers. He contented himself with the application of Christian principles to public life, and avoided factional or partisan association. Nevertheless at one point he was adamant: he threw all his weight against " bribery and corruption " in elections. No members of his Societies should even " eat or drink " at the expense of him for whom they voted. Complete integrity and probity, he demanded in public as much as in private affairs.[2] Every elector, he urged, should use his franchise, as though the moral results of the Election " depended on his vote alone."[3]

Rotten boroughs to Wesley were a stupid anachronism, which more than once he exposed. On October 2nd, 1754, he wrote : " I walked to Old Sarum, which in spite of common sense, without house or inhabitants, still sends two members to Parliament."[4] " In spite of common sense," in the mouth of Wesley, was a phrase of biting condemnation. Later he derided the political injustice which allowed Looe, a town

---

[1] *Journal*, July 3rd, 1671.
[2] *Ibid.*, October 6th, 1774.
[3] Cf. Kant's " Rule of Duty," in *Critique of Practical Reason.*
[4] See *Journal* (above date).

" near half as large as Islington," to send " four members to Parliament," though the largest *county* in North Wales sent but one ;[1] while in 1778, with his country at war, he pointed the absurdity of Queensborough containing " above fifty houses," sending " two members to Parliament."[2] Already we have had occasion to notice Wesley's abhorrence of Press Gangs, so common in his day ; we also have noted his attacks on magistrates for encouraging mob violence and on judges for defending slavery. But on numerous other public abuses, he turned the searchlight of truth. The toll-gate system of public revenue, he censured as " saddling the poor with the vile imposition of turn-pikes."[3] Concerning the notorious scandal of pluralities and sinecures in the State Church (often the fruit of political intrigue) he cried : " Oh what a curse in this poor land are pluralities and non-residence." As for prison administration, he prepared the way for the coming of John Howard and Mrs. Fry, his spiritual children. How familiar he was with contemporary prisons, may be gauged from the fact that " in one period of nine months " he " preached at least sixty-seven times in various gaols,"[4] and Marshalsea was by no means the only prison he depicted, " a nursery of all manner of wickedness." Indeed the more carefully one studies Wesley's prison associations, the more obvious it becomes that his fearless criticism of such public institutions, rather than the doctrine he preached, was the real reason why, for long, he was " forbidden to go to Newgate for fear of making them wicked, and to Bedlam for fear of driving them mad ! "[5]

Wesley's mind was too systematic and his study of history too comprehensive, to despise the vehicles of government and order. Contrariwise, his conception of society being organic and not mechanical, he cherished for them instinctive respect ; but when such organisations, political or ecclesiastical, degenerated into a dress parade, behind which stalked injustice and tyranny, he was quick to tear off the mask—and not always with a gloved hand. His numerous comments on Ireland, after intimate association, are highly illuminating. A Protestant of Protestants and an Englishman to the bone,[6] his heart burned at the pompous injustices he saw perpetrated in that unhappy land. " Nor is it any wonder," he thunders, " that those who are born Papists generally live and die such, when Protestants

---

[1] See *Journal* (Curnock), Vol. IV, p. 129.
[2] *Journal*, November 4th, 1778.
[3] *Journal*, June 15th, 1770.
[4] Dr. Warner's *Wesleyan Movement*, etc., p. 237.
[5] *Journal*, February 22nd, 1750.
[6] Though Wesley by ancestry was partly Irish, in temperament and outlook he was ultra-English.

can find no better way to convert them, than Penal Laws and Acts of Parliament."[1] Again, in a quaint tract, wherein he suggests a "short and sure" way of converting Ireland to Protestant Christianity, after emphasising and commending the high veneration in which Catholics hold the lives of the Apostles, he tilts subtly at the worldliness and arrogance of Anglican officialdom in Ireland. "Let all the clergy of the Church of Ireland," he advises, "only live like the Apostles and preach like the Apostles, and the thing is done ! "[2] Often, too, Wesley denounced vehemently the laws restraining the free importation of Irish products into England, while he approved with zest nearly every effort for co-operation and understanding between the two countries. But in one regard, he was surely bigoted. Believing that all Catholics were under immediate dictation from Rome, he opposed sternly the repeal or modification of the repressive legislation that, in his day, kept them from holding any public office in England.

(iii) *Economics and Religion*

The true purpose of all creative economic theory and organisation being the advancement of "human material well-being," it becomes at once obvious that to Wesley all economic problems were primarily ethical, and therefore religious. Moreover, as religion encompasses the whole of life, and as the question of earning a livelihood for one's self and one's dependants occupies most of the waking hours of normal adults, it becomes equally obvious that the realm of economic associations affords at once the largest and the most immediate field for the cultivation of brotherhood and co-operation, of character and virtue. This constantly was Wesley's position. He was an economic "realist" because he believed spiritual values the only ultimate "reality" : hence those values he would cause to permeate and control, every material relationship of man.

It is not surprising therefore that Wesley showed an alert, intimate and life-long interest in the "bread and butter" problems of life. The people among whom his mission chiefly lay, were those compelled to struggle grimly with stern economic difficulties : he was more familiar with the life of the poor than any other man of his age ; he knew that many of them dwelt in cellars and attics, amidst verminous surroundings, lacking warmth, raiment and decent victuals. Yet never did he assume a fatalistic attitude : never did he accept a "law" of indifference and drift. Certain doctrinaire aspects of *laisser*

---

[1] *Journal*, August 15th, 1747.
[2] J. Wesley, *A Short Method of Converting all the Roman Catholics in Ireland.*

faire, indeed, would have made his blood boil ; while, as for the crasser interpretations of the Malthusian and Ricardian theories regarding food, disease, poverty, population and wages, he would have declared them diabolical. " Man's inhumanity to man," he believed, " made countless thousands mourn " ; and to excuse or condone that inhumanity by any sophisticated appeal to " predestinations of Providence," or to the " nature of the Universe," was to him hypocritical sacrilege. Often, therefore, Wesley felt himself " called of God " to proclaim righteousness, temperance and forthcoming judgment to Power, Avarice and Luxury, in all their arrogance and sloth : for they, by perverting the gift of Free Will, and by " embezzling " the talents of God, not only thwarted temporarily the Divine purpose, but robbed mercilessly their fellow men. Wesley emphatically was a Constitutionalist and an anti-Revolutionist ; but unless both government and economic organisation strove sincerely, resolutely and intelligently to serve the Common Good, he believed them wholly at variance with the Christian ethic and a hollow mockery of their true intent.

On February 8th, 1753, Wesley wrote : " In the afternoon I visited many of the sick ; but such scenes, who could see unmoved ? There are none such to be seen in a pagan country. If any of the Indians in Georgia were sick (which indeed rarely happened till they learned gluttony and drunkenness from the Christians), those that were near him gave him whatever he wanted. Oh, who will convert the English into honest heathens ! "[1] The following day he notes : " I visited as many more as I could. I found some in their *cells* underground ; others in their garrets, half starved both with cold and hunger, added to weakness and pain. But I found not one of them unemployed, who was able to crawl about the room. *So wickedly, devilishly false is that common objection, ' They are poor, only because they are idle.'* If you could see these things with your own eyes, could you lay out money on ornaments and superfluities ? "[2] A fortnight later, his *Journal* reads : " I visited more of the poor sick. The industry of many of them surprised me. Several who were ill able to walk, were nevertheless at work ; some without any fire (bitterly cold as it was), and some, I doubt, without any food ; . . ."[3] Wesley, with Shakespeare, was crying : " Something is rotten in the state of Denmark ! " Ceaselessly he called upon the rich to " visit the poor," as " their brethren " ; and among his strict injunctions to his followers, was the warning : " Give none that asks relief, either

[1] *Journal* (above date).
[2] *Journal*, February 9th and 10th, 1753.
[3] *Ibid.*, February 21st, 1753.

an ill word or an ill look. Do not hurt them.''[1] '' Treat every poor person,'' was his constant rule, '' as you would God Almighty should treat you!''

Wesley never was a theorist; his economic principles were forged by the action of his religious faith, on the anvil of social experience. Yet certain very definite economic proposals he did put forward. Great estates, in his day, were the centre and symbol of power and influence, nevertheless he suggested the radical reform of permitting '' no farm above one hundred pounds a year.'' This proposal in fact was revolutionary; Wesley had no sympathy with a land system of vast domains hedged off as private preserves; recognising that '' the earth is the Lord's and the fullness thereof,'' he would use the soil for the national good—to provide wholesome food, at cheap prices, for *all* the people. And lordly, luxurious estates both decreased the amount, he believed, and raised the price, of the workers' bread. '' The rich,'' he complained, '' consume so much, they leave nothing for the poor.''[2] A favourite epigram of Wesley's was: '' An ounce of love, is worth a pound of compulsion.'' He loathed the '' Decrees '' of predestination and fatalism. Continually he propounded the '' free grace of God '' and the '' free will '' of man. His life, too, incarnated the robust Englishman's love of Liberty; yet he indulged no sentimental effusions about Liberty. He saw what many English theorists have commonly failed to see—that most laws are themselves inhibitions! Hence when institutions, habits or customs became a public nuisance or a social plague, and their perpetrators failed to respond to the appeals of reason, conscience, sympathy, or faith, he was quite prepared to support legal restrictions and positive prohibitions. The distilling of, and traffic in, spirituous liquors, as we have seen, he would completely prohibit. Slavery, '' gambling hells '' and such like '' curses,'' he would submit to the same fate. Wanton luxury, he would repress both by '' laws and example.'' Upon every '' gentleman's horse,'' he would place a '' tax of £5 ''; while '' useless pensions '' he would abruptly abolish, '' especially those ridiculous ones given to some hundreds of idle men, as governors of forts and castles; which forts have answered no end for above these hundred years, unless to shelter jackdaws and crows.''[3]

It is notable, too, that Wesley supported fair prices, a living wage and honest, healthy employment for all. No one disliked mob action more than he: yet in his *Journal*, in 1758,

---

[1] Wesley's *Works*, Vol. VIII, p. 262.
[2] See Wesley's *Thoughts on Present Scarcity of Provisions*; also J. A. Faulkner, *The Socialism of J. Wesley*.
[3] *Works*, Vol. XI, pp. 58–9.

he records with obvious admiration a high-handed work of economic justice, achieved by the rabble. " The mob," he says, " had been in motion all the day ; but their business was only with the *forestallers* of the market, who had bought up all the corn far and near *to starve the poor*, and load a Dutch ship, which lay at the quay ; but the mob brought it all out into the market, and sold it for the owners at the common price. And this they did with all the calmness and composure imaginable, and without striking or hurting anyone."[1] In Wesley's occasional experiments in providing employment for the unfortunates, it may fairly be presumed that he was dealing mostly with second or third class workmen, who had to be patiently instructed in the craft set them. But they, too, had souls ; so a definite principle guided his efforts. The produce of their labour he sold at the standard rate ; and that being insufficient for a decent livelihood, he made it up to a reasonable living wage ; for while there was plenty in the land, he regarded it a national disgrace that any should be denied the material necessities of a healthy and self-respecting life. How basic was this principle to him, may be gauged from the fact that as late as August, 1789, we again find him condoning, if not justifying, the direct action of a mob. In Truro, on his way to the society's preaching house, he found the street completely blocked by " numberless tinners," stampeding for higher pay. He was compelled to retire, and so preached at " the other end " of the town instead. Now a peevish man, in his eighty-seventh year, might have reacted bitterly to this industrial mob, which had thus upset his plans. Not so Wesley : his *Journal* entry depicts it as " a huge multitude," who, " being *nearly starved*, were come to beg or demand an increase in their wages, without which they *could not live*."[2] Obviously, therefore, he believed these workmen, like the African slaves in resisting the suppression of their " natural " liberty, to be but asserting their " natural rights."

In brief, Wesley's ethical and social teaching, the product of his religion, was based upon the following articles of faith :

    1. The spiritual brotherhood of man under the Fatherhood of a loving and moral God, who, with high Purpose, has granted to His children a large degree of free will.

    2. This free will, though utterly necessary to the moral and spiritual development of man, is capable of dire abuse, thus causing perplexing social problems.

    3. All social problems are fundamentally spiritual and

[1] Curnock edition, Vol. IV, p. 268.
[2] *Journal*, August 18th, 1789.

ethical ; and persons who fail to dedicate mental equipment and material power to spritual-ethical ends, are enemies of the Kingdom of God—anti-social citizens, who needs must be restrained by humane law.

4. In a really Christian society, men will recognise that they are stewards of God, the Creator and Owner of all : human " possessions," accordingly, are a self-acquired delusion, and private " riches " a subtly dangerous snare. Service, not material acquisitions, being the real standard of human attainment, fellowship, co-operation, and a truly equalitarian spirit, are the genuine marks of a Christian society ; wherein the strong, motivated by sympathy and love, will rejoice to assist their weaker brethren, even as parents rejoice to assist their children.

5. Faith in the ultimate justice of God, in Heaven, and in the immortality of the soul, are essential inspirations of any stable and happy society on earth : all human institutions, therefore, including those of politics and economics, must be impregnated with spiritual values, if they are to serve the highest interests of man, and fulfil the will of God.

6. If men persist in perverting the grace of free will, refusing to recognise that they are stewards of God and their brothers' keepers, then Divine Providence must necessarily resort to catastrophic means to upset their vain, pompous plans and force them, in chastened mood, to build anew.

Wesley, even more than Shaftesbury, his spiritual descendant, was a mighty social reformer ; for by initiating and directing a marvellous spiritual movement latent with moral imperatives, he opened the springs of human sympathy and understanding, which in turn inspired and nourished a glorious succession of social reforms. Ostrogorski, the Continental political writer, in his *La Democratie*, has glimpsed something of the high humanitarian influence of Wesley, and the heroic succession of Christian crusaders whom the Evangelical Revival raised up. " They appeal always and everywhere," he says, " from the miserable reality, to the human conscience. They make one see the man in the criminal, the brother in the negro." They " introduced," he avers, " a new personage into the social and political world of Aristocratic England—*the fellow man.*" And that fellow man, Ostrogorski predicts, " never more will leave the stage."[1]

[1] See French edition, p. 10 (the above version is from an unpublished English translation by William Jones, M.Sc., by kind permission).

THE SPIRIT OF EQUITY AND FELLOWSHIP

" We need great grace to converse with great people !
From which, therefore (unless in rare instances), I
am glad to be excused."

> JOHN WESLEY, after dining with Lady ——
> in Dublin, April, 1758.

" Do nothing as a gentleman ; ye are the servants
of all."

> JOHN WESLEY (among Rules and Maxims
> to his helpers).

THE SPIRIT OF EQUITY AND FELLOWSHIP

INCREASINGLY has it become a fashion to judge bygone historical periods, by economic and social theory fashioned long after their close; for Marx, to many, has become the touch-stone of all social criticism. Now even were this questionable procedure justifiable, by no possible leap of the imagination, could Wesley's teaching and example be reconciled to the tenets of Marxian Communism. From the soulless materialism, the economic determinism and the ruthless class-hatred of Marx's " philosophy," his every sensitivity would have recoiled.

Albeit, like Marx, Wesley's primary interest was in the working multitude: like Marx, he believed in the dignity of labour, for labour he conceived the chief—though *not* the only—source of human material wealth. Scarcely less than Marx, he believed the poor frequently were exploited and " robbed " by the rich; while no whit less than Marx, did he consider social justice to the worker the foundation of any true society. But their differences in temper, spirit and outlook were colossal : the two men were as diametrically opposite as Love and Hate. Marx was a militant, dogmatic Atheist, the prophet of " No-god," whom he worshipped with vociferous acclaim : to Wesley, God—" the source of all insight, confidence, justice and truth " —was closer than breathing. The individual man, to Marx, was a materialistic animal, who at death perished like a rat : to Wesley, he was an immortal spirit with infinite latent capacity for infinite growth. Marx, in the name of " Science," harping always on the " inexorable laws of economics," sought social justice by revolution : Wesley held that men's first step towards emancipation, was to find their souls, by entering into communion with the spiritual world ; and then, having the proto-type and essence of social justice *within* them, they would be social builders indeed. His primary medium of expression, therefore, was conversion, not revolution. To Marx, all religion was a priest-concocted opiate, a pernicious, paralysing soporific, which at any cost must be destroyed : to Wesley, true religion was the eye of the soul, the source of liberty, the fountain head of every worthy aspiration, the sustaining power behind every exalted attainment of man ; it was the Mighty Indispensable. Brotherhood, to Marx, was a mechanised " comradeship," forced upon " the workers of the world " in self-interest and self-defence, that, as a vast army, they might wreak vengeance upon their hated exploiters—the capitalist class : to Wesley, it was a spiritual affinity, a social fellowship, which one day, in love and co-operation, would embrace all mankind.

Even Professor Laski admits that Marx " hated too strongly ; he was jealous, and he was proud." From the day of his conversion, Wesley hated no man ; jealousy had no discoverable place in his life ; and his only pride was in the things appertaining to the Kingdom of God. Laski again says of Marx : " The seeming logic of his attitude is deceptive, for it in part rests upon . . . an abstract view of human nature with which the totality of facts is in direct contradiction. . . . He was often wrong, he was rarely generous, he was always bitter."[1] Wesley, like all mortals, at times was wrong, but always he was generous, and never was he bitter : few mighty leaders of men, indeed, have ever been so severe with themselves, or so chivalrous with their foes. Wesley, in brief, would change society by " changing men " ; for really changed men, becoming endowed with sensitised consciences and socialised wills, must perforce be workers for the Kingdom of Righteousness on Earth : Marx " scientifically " would marshal the proletariat for the day of World Revolution, when, in ruthless, long-cherished vengeance, they would strike down their " enslavers " and proceed to mould their social Utopia, according to their own materialistic desires. To Wesley, the true Society was organic and evolutionary : to Marx, be it emphasised, it was mechanical and revolutionary. Wesley, too, knew individual men—including thousands of the " proletariat "—as his brethren and friends : Marx, who lived for thirty years an alien on a foreign strand, knew few workmen individually ; nor did he wish so to know them ; the " workers," to him, were abstract beings fitted neatly into his own theoretic, doctrinaire plans. The Gospel of Christ to Wesley was a Revelation of God, containing an inspired ethic, whose application pointed the way to social equity and fellowship, among all peoples. Christ, to Marx, was a fanatical idiot, whose Gospel was worse than foolishness. He taught the proletariat

[1] H. J. Laski, *Karl Marx*, pp. 28, 48.

to despise not only religion in general, but Christianity in particular.

The High Priest of Communism knew what to omit. Astutely, he does not explain *just how* the proletariat, after stimulating for generations the lust for blood, would, following their Revolution of Revenge, at once settle down into peaceful co-operative " comrades " and friends. He who scoffed at the possibility of miracles, blandly assumed that, after the great proletarian banquet of blood, long nourished tiger appetites would forthwith give way to those of the lamb ; that the beast of prey would at once, and by choice, become a vegetarian, delighting to feed and frolic in the common pastures of the Communistic Utopia. But One wiser than Marx has said : " Of thorns men do not gather figs, nor of a bramble bush gather they grapes."[1] From that Wiser One, Wesley drew the inspiration of his social teaching and example. And not least among the reasons why Marxian Communism, with its gospel of hate, has cast no deep root into the mental soil of the English-speaking world, is the fact that Wesley started a movement which largely revived vital, practical Christianity, and made it a moral and social force.[2]

(i) *Dress and Station*

Wesley was not a sociologist. As a prophet of God and an ordained ambassador of Christ, he did not conceive it his task to formulate economic, political or social theories ; nor did he judge himself competent so to do. His " calling " he believed far more sacred, and more thorough-going : it was to lead men into contact with spiritual reality, to enable them to possess their souls and enter the realm of " abundant life." For if once men, in sufficient numbers, were endowed with an illumined conscience and a spiritual insight, they, collectively as well as individually, would become possessors of the " wisdom that passeth knowledge " ; and in that wisdom social problems gradually would be solved. Ultimately, therefore, the movement guided by Wesley became a far-reaching social leaven : for no sociologist has yet lived, with the exception of Marx, who has exercised such direct and intimate influence upon the social activities of great multitudes of men ; and no sociologist, including Marx, has yet inspired such *voluntary,*

[1] St. Luke vi, 44.
[2] For Marx's teaching, see *Communist Manifesto* (1848) and *Das Kapital* (1867).

R

cheerful, creative sacrifice, on the part of his disciples. But though Wesley's cardinal purpose remained spiritual, and though he elaborated no comprehensive theory of social organisation, never did he shirk the duty of striving to apply the Christian ethic to the most pressing social problems that crossed his path. Had he not done so, he believed he would have betrayed his trust. Perhaps, on occasions, he was rash ; but "rashness," as Professor Tawney reminds us, is surely "a more agreeable failing than cowardice, and, when to speak is unpopular, it is less pardonable to be silent than to say too much."[1]

Dress to Wesley was an expression of the inward man. His own habit always was neat, tidy, shapely, but severely plain and cheap : his linen was spotless, and his shoes regularly were shined, however wet the weather, or however muddy the road. No frill or flounce found any place in his attire, and in an age of powdered and monstrous wigs, he was content always with his natural hair : yet from a hundred sources it is clear that immaculateness and simple comeliness were outstanding marks of his person. Wesley's teachings concerning dress exhibit an interesting combination of his native, Oxford-nourished conservatism, and his radical religious convictions. In studying his writings and records, one quickly discovers the arch-instance of his conservatism. It is the British Kingship—ever, to him, the emblem of the people's corporate life. English royalty, to Wesley, was a divinely sanctioned institution ; hence, never do we find him criticising the "ruling sovereign." George II, though possessed of undoubted physical bravery, was a weak King, maintaining an immoral Court. Yet, sagacious and observant as Wesley in most matters was, he seems never to have suspected the sensual conditions surrounding that monarch's life ; and more than once, he applauds him as a just and generous prince. Thus, accepting without question this exalted view of Kingship—as did most other Englishmen of his age[2]—Wesley does not condemn a high degree of grandeur and gorgeousness in royal attire. Yet even as he states his case, his conscience is ill at ease. "It is *doubtful*," he writes, "if Scripture forbids those in any nation that are vested with supreme authority, to be arrayed in gold and costly apparel ; or to adorn their immediate attendants

---

[1] R. H. Tawney, *Religion and the Rise of Capitalism*, p. 287.

[2] It must be remembered that to this day English royalty is largely immune from criticism by the contemporary generation. Criticism of kings is the prerogative of *later* generations. For Wesley's severe criticism of Elizabeth, Charles II and James II see his *History of England*.

or magistrates, or officers with the same."[1] He also admitted
that there might be " a moderate difference of apparel between
persons of different stations."   But quickly forging on to the
conviction upon his heart, he exclaims : " These Scriptures
manifestly forbid ordinary Christians, those in the lower and
middle ranks of life, to be adorned with gold or pearls or costly
apparel."[2]

Gay, gorgeous, gaudy attire, Wesley taught, " engenders
pride, and where it already is, it increases it " ; it " breeds
and increases vanity " ; it " begets anger," and directly tends
to " create and inflame lust."   " Every shilling," he says,
" which you save from your own apparel, you may expend in
clothing the naked and relieving the necessities of the poor " :
and " everything about thee that costs more than Christian
duty required thee to lay out, is the blood of the poor ! "[3]
Then, pointing the tenor of his message—for always there is
a piquant directness in Wesley's teaching—he asks : " Is not
your dress as gay, as expensive as theirs, who never had such
warning ? Are you not as fashionably dressed as others of
your rank that are not Methodists ? "   " But I can afford it,"
comes the reply.   " O lay aside that idle, nonsensical word !
No Christian can afford to waste any part of the substance
which God has entrusted to him."   " Let me see before I die,"
he pleads, " a Methodist congregation full as plain dressed as
a Quaker congregation. Only be more consistent. Let *your*
dress be *cheap as well as plain*. Otherwise you do but trifle
with God, and me, and your own souls. I pray you let there
be no more costly silks among you, how grave soever they may
be."[4]   Just here, to Southey and his soberly superior set, lay
the rub.   They were too refined to desire loud, foppish apparel :
they wanted a habit " rich not gaudy," but always costly as
their purse could buy. To Wesley, by such indulgence, they
were " making themselves accountable for all the want, afflic-
tion and distress, which they may, but do not, remove."[5]

Moreover, even the special privileges which Wesley, somewhat waveringly, conceded to royalty, were not without limitations. Five years before the demise of George II, he was " in
the robe-chamber, adjoining to the House of Lords, when
the King put on his robes."   The *Journal* records his impression : " His brow was much furrowed with age, and quite

[1] Sermon on *Dress*, p. 5.
[2] *Ibid.*, pp. 5, 6.
[3] *Ibid.*, pp. 7-10.
[4] *Ibid.*, p. 10.
[5] Wesley's *Works*, Vol. V, p. 375.

clouded with care. And is this all the world can give even
to a King? All the grandeur it can afford? A blanket of
ermine round his shoulders, so heavy and cumbersome he can
scarce move under it! An huge heap of borrowed hair, with
a few plates of gold and glittering stones upon his head!
Alas, what a bauble is human greatness! . . ."[1]

Wesley's subconscious and recurrent Toryism, was the " hang-
over " of the natural man : his spiritual being revolted against
all pompous, parading display. The fashionable dress of his
period now seems preposterous. Certainly its more flamboyant
styles achieved the grotesque : for periwig-pated males, sported
fringe, ruffles and fluff, gold and silver lace and braid, silks,
satins and velvets of gaudy hues, colourful tassels, garters and
bows, together with huge bejewelled buckles and, perhaps, a
dozen glistening, garish buttons, each the size of a small sun-
flower. The wardrobe of an eighteenth-century fop cost
hundreds of pounds—if paid for. Even the proverbially slouchy
Dr. Johnson, who declared that " fine clothes are good only
as they supply the want of other means of procuring respect,"
for his visit to Paris in 1755 " spent £30 on a new suit and
a new bourgeois wig."[2] Smart feminine fashions were on a
par with those of male dandies. Women achieved incredible
hairdressing and incredible millinery, while hoops, bustles,
open bosoms and wasp waists, together with abundance of
flashy jewellery, augmented the ravishing allurements and
embellishments of their attire. Nevertheless, while the rich
paraded all their feathers and fripperies, exhibiting often their
vulgarity no less than their wealth and pride, multitudes of
the hard-working poor eked out their existence in tatters and
rags. No wonder, therefore, that Wesley placed strong emphasis on the moral significance of dress. He despised all
garnished gaudiness. He would have every man, woman and
child to be clothed in raiment at once comfortable, neat, modest,
shapely and clean : and to him such raiment was more comely,
than any " daubed with gold."[3]

---

[1] *Journal*, December 23rd, 1755.
[2] *Johnson's England*, Vol. I, p. 384.
[3] For the fashionable dress of this period, see collections in Victoria
and Albert Museum and London Museum. See, too, T. T. Osserhyn,
Costume in the Time of George II. Many of Hogarth's paintings reflect
the meaner garb of the times. Illustrations in Besant's *London in the
Eighteenth Century*, in Sydney's *England and the English*, and in *Johnson's
England* are also revealing.

(ii) *The True Nobility*

Having touched upon Wesley's conservative attitude toward Kingship, it is noteworthy that even to royalty he could at times speak with a boldness few of his contemporaries approached. In his *Address* to George II (1744), assuring him of the loyalty of the Methodist Societies, and repudiating the current, though absurd, accusation that they were allied to the Pretender, he reminds his Majesty that the loyalty of his societies must be based on Scriptural principles. " We cannot indeed do either more or less," he says, " than we apprehend consistent with the written Word of God ; but we are ready to obey your Majesty to the utmost, in all things which we conceive to be agreeable thereto."[1] In this *Address*, moreover, Wesley takes opportunity to remind his sovereign of the eternal supremacy of the " Prince of all the Kings of the earth," to whom all men, whether princes or peasants, must one day render account. So Kings, too, were subservient to the proprietorship of God. Their elegance and pomp, though granted as a concession to traditional custom, and to the people's love of the spectacular, were but external trappings : their souls, if hidden to men, were naked to God.

Whitefield repeatedly has been accused of a fawning, subservient demeanour toward the genteel and titled ; though his thirteen Atlantic crossings in days when Johnson described all ships as " floating prisons," and the fact that always he was happier on the American frontier than in England, tend sharply to modify this criticism. Charles Wesley was a noble, generous character possessed of sympathy and love for all mankind : yet there can be little doubt that after his sons became musical prodigies, performing in exclusive drawing-rooms before nobles, princes and Kings,[2] the glitter of the brilliant society in which he not infrequently found himself, dulled, in some degree, his zest for the national service of humble folk. No such accusation could sanely be levelled against the guiding genius of the Revival. His supreme mission was to the Common People, whom he specially loved ; and

[1] *Journal* (Standard), Vol. III, March 5th, 1744. Owing to the pressure of Charles Wesley, this address was not presented, lest it might encourage the tendency to look upon the societies as separate bodies outside the Church. The Moravians did send such an address.

[2] It is said that after playing for George III and his party, a son of Charles Wesley was greeted by the King with the words : " To your uncle John Wesley, to your father Charles Wesley, and to Mr. Whitefield, the Church of this realm owes more than to all others."

his glorious life record shows not a trace of any subserviency toward titled, élite or wealthy society. Outside the sphere of Kingship, with its unique symbolism, he judged men entirely on the basis of character and service ; and, by such standards, he was convinced that dress and station, wealth and titles, were no dependable recommendation to honour. His prejudices (and no man is without them) were distinctly in favour of the poor ; rarely did he turn to a rich man for financial support : the Common People financed his crusade. To Wesley, as to Burns :

> " The rank is but the guinea's stamp,
> The man's the gold for a' that."

And the chief reason why, after his conversion, he jettisoned *The Whole Duty of Man* as a religious text, was the fact that it taught a nauseating, pagan servility on the part of the poor toward the " rich and great " ; for pseudo-religious jingo he could not endure.

Far, then, from fawning or crawling before the rich, the aristocratic or the famous, Wesley commonly avoided them. " They do me no good," was his conviction, " and I fear I can do none to them." Even Dr. Johnson, who came to admire Wesley because he " could talk well on any subject," complained that he could not enjoy more of his company. " Wesley is never at leisure," repined the renowned literary monarch ; " he is always obliged to go at a certain hour. That is very disagreeable to a man who loves to fold his legs and have out his talk, as I do." In June, 1739, when Wesley came to Bath the air was full of threats, and the general excitement drew " many of the rich and great " to his preaching. Grasping the opportunity, he " told them plainly the Scripture had concluded them all under sin—high and low, rich and poor, one with another." After his sermon, an electric curiosity charging the atmosphere, several fine ladies followed him to his lodging, desiring conversation with him. The ensuing interview was brief, for he read their motives. " I do not expect," he told them tersely, " that the rich and great should want either to speak with me, or to hear me ; for I speak the plain truth—a thing you hear little of, and do not desire to hear."[1]

Not seldom, when invited to dine with the high and mighty, Wesley politely declined, and went on his way. A casual *Journal* memorandum (February 10th, 1758) reads : " The judge, immediately after sermon, invited me to dine with him. But having no time I was obliged to send my excuse. . . ."

[1] *Journal*, June 5th, 1739.

After dining with the Governor of Guernsey (August 18th, 1787), he was "well pleased to find other company." Having spent "an agreeable hour at a concert" rendered by his nephews, he poignantly adds : "But I was a little out of my element among lords and ladies. I love plain music and plain company best."[1] On another occasion he writes : "I spent an hour agreeably and profitably with Lady C—— H—— and Sir C—— H——. It is well a few of the rich and noble are called. Oh, may God increase their number ! But I should rejoice if it were done by the ministry of others. If I might choose, I should still preach the Gospel to the poor."[2] In Dublin (April, 1758), after dining with Lady —— Wesley noted : "We need great grace to converse with great people ! From which, therefore (unless in rare instances), I am glad to be excused. . . . Of these two hours I can give no good account." "O how hard it is," he again muses, "to be shallow enough for a *polite* audience ! " while further, he refers to "the learned, rich and honourable heathens, commonly called Christians."[3]

On Sunday, March 16th, 1788, Wesley, now a national character, preached by invitation before the Lord Mayor of London and "most of the aldermen." He "applied" the "awful" history of Dives and Lazarus—a subject chosen for very "plain speaking." Always he treated Selina, Countess of Huntingdon, the sincere, wealthy, zealous patron of the Revival, with courtesy and respect ; but his attitude to her was not a whit different from the gracious fellowship he invariably extended to the humblest lay preacher, or the most obscure Class leader ; and generous character as Lady Huntingdon was, it is doubtful if she quite relished Wesley's habitually equalitarian mood. Indeed, it is probable that the customary, if unconscious, subservience Whitefield commonly manifested toward her, was by no means distasteful. Her conversion in many respects was catastrophic ; but never did it wholly remove from her the proud consciousness that she was a peeress of the realm. And to this prophet-evangelist even a converted peeress was, like himself, but a sinful mortal, in constant need of grace divine.

Repeatedly Wesley speaks of the "ignorance," even the "gross ignorance," he "had observed in rich and genteel people throughout the nation."[4] "Gentlefolk, so-called," were

---

[1] *Journal*, January 25th, 1781.
[2] *Ibid.*, November 17th, 1759.
[3] See Wesley's *Thoughts on the Earthquake at Lisbon*.
[4] *Journal*, July 4th, 1757.

the subject of his constant irony; and once, in exasperation, he permitted himself the licence of referring to " *things* called gentlemen."[1] With succeeding years, too, his suspicion of accumulated riches only increased ! " I saw a very rare thing," he remarked in 1776, " men swiftly increasing in substance and yet not decreasing in holiness " ; but eleven years later, after a similar observation, he adds : " If they continue so, it will be the only instance I have known in above half a century. I warned them in the strongest terms I could."[2] After addressing a fashionable company, including " the chief men of the town," he notes : " I spared neither rich nor poor. I almost wondered at myself, it not being usual with me to use such keen and cutting expressions : and I believe many felt that for all their form they were but heathens still."[3]

The same fearless, independent spirit is exhibited in Wesley's reply to a Bishop, who had " forbidden all his clergy to admit any Methodist preacher to the Lord's Supper." " But is any clergyman obliged," asks Wesley, " either in law or conscience, to obey such a prohibition ? By no means. The *will* even of the King does not bind any *English* subject, unless it is seconded by an express law. How much less the will of a bishop ? But did you not take an oath to obey him ? No, nor any clergyman in the three kingdoms. This is mere vulgar error. Shame that it should prevail almost universally."[4] Wesley, like every true and effective prophet, was something of a rebel. If a deep-lying strain of recurrent Toryism occasionally forced its way to the surface, it is well to remember a dictum of Overton's, that Wesley surely was " the most revolutionary Tory who ever lived." To him, true nobility was a thing of the soul, superseding all rank, station, colour and class : yet the fact that he had deep conservative instincts, perhaps enabled him the better to understand the real genius of the English peoples, and the better to serve the English-speaking world.[5] For rarely have the Anglo-Saxon peoples, despite their long quest for Liberty, bestowed their allegiance upon any rebel, or leader, who has striven abruptly to break the continuity of History, or whose hatred of individuals, classes or institutions, has obscured the higher ideals and deeper humanities, which alone can justify radical or revolutionary change in organic institutions.

[1] Compare with Defoe's satire, *The Compleat English Gentleman.*
[2] *Journal*, August 27th, 1776, and March 31st, 1787.
[3] *Ibid.*, June 10th, 1757.
[4] *Ibid.*, June 1st, 1777.
[5] For a thoroughgoing—though occasionally misleading—attempt to elaborate Wesley's " Toryism," see M. Edwards's *John Wesley and the Eighteenth Century* (1933).

(iii) *Constructive Social Work*

Scarcely is it an exaggeration to say that Wesley's *Sermons*, *Journal*, New Testament *Notes*, *Appeals* and *Letters*, together with his occasional and miscellaneous publications, contain either definite teaching or suggestive reflections on practically every recognised social problem of his time. A few of his most representative utterances, we have brought together : it remains briefly to survey certain of his constructive social labours among the poor—labours to which such contemporaries as Hume and Gibbon, Voltaire and Rousseau, Paine and Cobbett were totally blind. Their outlook on life was agnostic, deistic, materialistic or egotistic. Wesley's was spiritualistic, though experimental and pragmatic. Hence, lacking the faintest comprehension of Wesley's standards, and accepting prejudiced ridicule at face value, they naturally despised or ignored his endeavours ; and many of the sophisticated and cynical of the twentieth century, following their verdict, as embellished by the later raillery of Rev. Sydney Smith, Leigh Hunt and William Hazlitt, have mediated the same supercilious contempt.[1] Disinterested investigations, however, point increasingly to an opposite conclusion. Mr. A. E. Dobbs, in his scholarly book, *Education and Social Movements*, says : " The part which the Evangelical Revival played in the political education of the masses has been *often misrepresented or ignored*. An exceptional degree of intelligence and attainment was not uncommon among the Methodists in humble station and those who had been raised in Methodist homes ; " while of the Class Meeting, he declares : " It was the starting point of serious friendships, and often contained an inner circle of companions, more intelligent than the rest, who would meet to converse on religion and matters of general interest, and who occasionally entered on a course of reading."[2] " A circle of labourers or mechanics led in worship or conference by one of their own rank," Dobbs also reminds us, " was a great step for Democracy." Fairburn, moreover, claims that " the local preacher and not the secularist lecturer has formed the mind of the miner and the labourer," with the result that when " the politician addresses the English peasantry he has to appeal to more distinctly ethical and religious principles

---

[1] Smith's " Liberalism " did not apply to ecclesiastical affairs. He stoutly opposed the reform of the " Rotten Boroughs " of the State Church, and used the *Edinburgh Review* to lampoon the Evangelical Revival, which insisted on their reform. Hazlitt, too, used the *Examiner* to ridicule the Revival.

[2] *Op. cit.* (1919), p. 119f.

than when he addresses the upper and middle classes." But Wesley's social initiative and example, as well as his teaching, lay behind all such influences.

If education means character building and the imparting of ability to live nobly, usefully and co-operatively, Wesley, beyond comparison, was the greatest educationist of his century, and one of the greatest of all time. He and his preachers "found many of the people in a semi-barbarous state, deeply sunk in ignorance and vice, and almost lost in dirt and wretchedness." Albeit, wherever the Revival "took deep root, cleanliness and order, with personal and domestic comfort, followed in the trail of vital Godliness."[1] As an *adult* educationist Wesley, throughout history, has had few peers. His movement, long despised by the "cultured" and the "great," was compelled to find and educate its own leaders : and considering the social conditions of the age, it rose magnificently to the task. Of the thousands who during Wesley's day attained to the position of preachers, teachers and leaders, the overwhelming majority served a mental, moral and spiritual "apprenticeship," passing with democratic mobility and by natural selection from stage to stage, without any barriers of class, wealth or sex. Self-help and mutual service were outstanding marks of the movement : and the attainment of ability for greater usefulness, was the recognised passport to higher opportunity. "Do nothing as a gentleman," was one of Wesley's axiomatic precepts to his army of lieutenants. "Ye are the *servants* of all."[2] To character, initiative, ability and consecration, every avenue of the Revival was open ; and before the close of Wesley's long life, not a few from the middle, professional and upper classes were serving cheerfully under the leadership of those who had sprung from the humblest labourers' homes.[3]

But the amazing educational results of the Revival, were not achieved without commensurate causes, paramount amongst which was Wesley's genius for creating, editing and distributing literature specially adapted to the mental, moral and spiritual needs of the abandoned multitude. Wherever the Spiritual Awakening spread, there was generated a persistent craving for popular instruction, and that craving Wesley, the one-time don, was determined to satisfy. His religion was a Bible religion ; and Bible religion demanded a knowledge both of the Scriptures and co-related ethical books. Wesley himself taught

[1] Wm. Entwistle, *Memoirs of Rev. Joseph Entwistle*, p. 28.
[2] See *Wesley Historical Society Publications*, "John Bennet's Minutes of 1744."
[3] See Dr. W. J. Warner, *op. cit.*, p. 257ff.

that one could never be a " thorough Christian " without extensive reading.[1] The duty therefore of acquiring knowledge was obvious, and this set thousands of converts to the task of *teaching themselves* to read, so that they might " search the Scriptures " and peruse other works designed to strengthen their moral and spiritual life. Such auxiliary publications, Wesley, with incredible energy, set himself to place before his people at the lowest possible cost : hence the previously un-paralleled dissemination of simple, direct, didactic Christian literature, to satisfy newly created but unmistakable needs ; hence the fifty volumes of *The Christian Library* gleaned and edited from a very wide field ; hence Wesley's " Book-room " ; hence the endless stream of pamphlets, tracts, appeals and text-books ; hence the *Arminian Magazine*, the various hymnals and the ceaseless use of the printing press, to augment and strengthen the preachers' spoken word. Tens of thousands must have taught themselves to read from the Revival's publications ; and perhaps chief among the spelling and reading texts were the collections of hymns, for when once people knew hymns by heart they soon learned to spell them out and read them. Then rapidly they proceeded to devour Wesley's prose, for his vivid, chaste, logical Saxon style was specially adapted to the people's immediate needs. Every home deeply affected by the Revival, had its little collection of much-pondered books, and almost every convert helped to distribute the printed message. Most publications were sold at a small price, but for those too poor to buy, funds were forthcoming to provide literature.

Mr. G. D. H. Cole in a recent essay says : " We get an im-pression throughout Wesley's *Journal* that he is appealing to persons incapable of an intellectual response, whose souls must be saved by other and more ferocious means . . ." ; while of the Revival in general, he suggests that, " setting out to catch men's souls by all means, it used methods of approach which played upon the fears of the uneducated and the illiterate without qualm or remorse. And it was able to do this with the less compunction because from the outset it would have no truck with political democracy in any form."[2] It is unfortunate that a man of Mr. Cole's eminence, learning and influence, should, at this late hour, be reflecting the spleen of a Cobbett or a Hazlitt. Indeed, such remarks force one to doubt if Mr. Cole has ever really studied Wesley's *Journal*, *Sermons* or

[1] Wesley's *Works*, Vol. XII, p. 254.
[2] G. D. H. Cole, " Town Life in the Provinces " (*Johnson's England*, Vol. I, p. 222).

other publications. He, like many another theoretic agitator, is annoyed with the Revival, because its huge following refused to be exploited by the Paines, Cobbetts or other " Democratic " demagogues of the era, for semi-revolutionary ends ; but that it laid the foundations of " Self-Help " and prepared the way for later and saner democracy, is, nevertheless, indisputable. Moreover, who can deny that the Movement itself was a democracy of service, fellowship, aspiration and attainment ?

Wesley's immediate contribution to popular education, however, extends far beyond the stimulation and satisfaction of an adult desire for literature and knowledge. Wherever his teaching sank deep, parents desired education first for their own children and then for neglected youngsters around them. The result was a steady increase in schools, some supported by converted individuals of means, some by local societies, some, like Kingswood seminary, by the United Societies. In London both West Street Chapel and the Foundery ran schools.[1] The first preaching-house in Halifax was used also " as a day school," which was taught by a local preacher. The Bradford Society, in 1766, built a school chapel ;[2] and so on all sides the re-birth of religion advanced efforts for education, which Wesley everywhere encouraged. One instance at least is on record of *orphan* children for many years, by society efforts, being " fully maintained and taught."[3] The Revival, too, was the mother of the world Sunday School Movement. Eleven years before Robert Raikes began his famous work in Gloucester, Hannah Ball, Wesley's disciple, was conducting Sunday School work in High Wycombe : and Wesley himself lived to examine local Sunday schools with nearly one thousand children in attendance, and about one-tenth that number of voluntary teachers.[4] But this great movement will demand our later attention.

Wesley's interest in the physical welfare of the underprivileged was of a piece with his zeal for their spiritual and mental emancipation. In 1746 he founded the first really free medical dispensary in England. " I mentioned to the society," he notes, " my design of giving physic to the poor. About thirty came next day, and in three weeks about three hundred. This we continued for several years, till the number of patients, still increasing, the expense was greater than we could bear : meantime, through the blessing of God, many who had been ill for months or years were restored to perfect health."[5] In 1747

[1] John Telford, *Two West End Chapels*, p. 72.
[2] W. H. S., *Proceedings*, Vol. III, p. 102.
[3] E. M. North, *Early Methodist Philanthropy*, p. 99.
[4] See *Journal*, July 27th, 1787, and April 20th, 1788.
[5] *Journal*, December 4th, 1746 ; *Ibid.*, June 16th, 1747.

appeared Wesley's *Primitive Physic (An Easy and Natural Method of Curing Most Diseases)*, a compilation which for over a century has been the butt of endless ridicule. But recently that " beloved physician," Sir George Newman, long the " official guardian of Britain's public health," has bestowed upon it high praise. Pointing to the remarkable improvement in household sanitation, personal cleanliness, domestic hygiene and general health which followed in the Revival's wake, Sir George places Wesley among the vital pioneers of the national health movement, and the long-despised *Primitive Physic* among the effective instruments to that end.[1] Certainly the book contains some odd remedies ; for the approaching infirmities of old age, it prescribes " tar water," or a " decoction of nettles." " But remember ! " it quaintly warns, " the only *radical* cure is wrought by *Death.*" A deal of needful information was mediated through this treatise : plain foods, abundance of fresh air, daily exercise and contented spirits, were medicines on which Wesley placed the highest store ; and to ensure the purity of drugs, he advised people, where possible, to procure them " at the Apothecaries Hall."[2]

Wesley had a special and practical interest in electricity. Writings by Franklin, Priestley and other authorities, he avidly devoured ; and his own experimentation convincing him of its healing power, he forthwith established free electrical treatment for the poor. " Having procured an apparatus on purpose," he writes in 1756 : " I ordered several persons to be electrified who were ill of various disorders, some of whom found an immediate, some a gradual, cure. From this time I appointed, first some hours in every week, and afterwards an hour in every day, wherein *any that desired it* might try the virtue of this surprising medicine. Two or three years after, our patients were so numerous that we were obliged to divide them : so part we electrified in Southwark, part in the Foundery, others near St. Paul's, and the rest near the Seven Dials : the same method we have taken ever since ; and to this day, while hundreds, perhaps thousands, have received unparalleled good, I have not known one man, woman or child who has received any hurt thereby : so that when I hear any talk of the danger of being electrified (especially if they are medical men who talk so), I cannot but impute it to great want either of sense or honesty."[3]

[1] See Sir George Newman, *Health and Social Evolution*, p. 41.

[2] The author has seen copies of *Primitive Physic* even on the frontiers of Canada, which have been passed down as heirlooms. Before Wesley's death it ran into twenty-three editions, and many afterwards.

[3] *Journal*, November 9th, 1756 ; see also Tyerman's *Wesley*, Vol. I, p. 525.

Free electrical and dispensary service, together with the distribution of " health literature," were, however, but typical of the humanistic initiative which, on all sides, the Revival kindled. On occasions, following marked calamities, Wesley and his followers, by co-operative methods, were feeding from one hundred to one hundred and fifty persons a day in a single place.[1] Constantly in conjunction with their amazing systems of prison, sick and poor visitation, they raised money to clothe and relieve prisoners and to buy food, medicine, fuel or tools for the stricken and unfortunate ; while the universal collection of warm raiment for the helpless-aged and the half-naked, was so continuous and persistent a feature of their work, that generally it passed unobserved. The renaissance of vital religion in their hearts, had made this despised people their brothers' keepers indeed ![2] And " brother " to them had a comprehensive significance.

Wesley also, according to his opportunity, was a promoter of co-operative industry among the poor. He had no sympathy with an industrial and economic procedure which, in the sweat shops of cellar and attic, or in the dark, damp depths of the mine, could reduce the bodies of men, women and children to the resemblance of walking skeletons, finally to hurl them on the scrap-heap—when no longer the source of gain. His persistent teaching concerning the use and abuse of money, contained at least a germinal answer to this gross inhumanity. But meantime, the slave trade had first to be abolished ; and the hour had not yet struck when Lord Shaftesbury, in complete religious devotion, would consecrate his life to the epic task of " converting Parliament " and " emancipating the workers of industrial England." Wesley, the initial pioneer, had, in this sphere, to be content with doing *what* he could, *as* he could ; but the problem he did not shirk. On November 25th, 1740, he wrote : " After several methods proposed for employing those who were out of business, we determined to make a trail of one which several of our brethren recommended to us. Our aim was, with as little expense as possible, to keep them at once from want and from idleness ; in order to which we took twelve of the poorest, and a teacher, into the society room, where they were employed for four months, till spring came on, in carding and spinning of cotton. And the design answered : they were employed and maintained with very little more than the produce of their own labour."[3] This was but one of Wesley's endeavours

---

[1] *Journal*, January 21st, 1740 (concerning an area near Bristol).
[2] *Ibid.*, May 7th, 1741.
[3] See *Journal* (above date).

to provide wholesome, remunerative employment for the needy. His efforts in this realm extended to women as well as men. Part of his *Journal* jotting for May 7th, 1741, reads : "My design, I told them, is to employ, for the present, all the women who are out of business, and desire it, in knitting. To these we will give first the common price for what work they do ; and then add according as they need. Twelve persons were appointed to inspect these, and to visit and provide things necessary for the sick."

The chief value of Wesley's industrial undertakings, however, lies not in the size of his experiments, nor yet in their material success, but rather in the humane spirit by which he approached the problems involved. To him such industrial terms as "hand" and "boss" were pagan and degrading. Unswervingly did he believe in the nobility of toil and the fraternity of man. All faithful, productive "workers" to him were honourable ; while, contrariwise, no one commanded his respect who did not engage in some honest, creative service for the common weal. For wilful idleness and assuming arrogance, he could not cloak his contempt ; and that perhaps is the reason his *Journal* is so loaded with biting references to "the great vulgar" and to the "gross ignorance" and "paganism" he had so often observed among the "rich and genteel." "Polite triflers," so characteristic of his age, were Wesley's chief aversion. Never did he hear the modern maxim, "From each according to his ability : to each according to his need." Yet both his example and his teaching, endorse the social principle therein implied.

Wesley's Benevolent Loan Fund and his Strangers' Friend Society, are specially interesting. Always it was his purpose to stimulate the expression of initiative and independence on the part of the under-privileged, and that of social responsibility on the part of the privileged. These two schemes are symptomatic of that double aim. In January, 1748, he wrote : "I made a public collection towards a lending stock for the poor. Our rule is to lend only twenty shilling at once, which is repaid weekly within three months. I began this about a year and a half ago : thirty pounds sixteen shillings were *then* collected, and out of this no less than 255 persons have been relieved in eighteen months."[1] By later collections the capital of this fund was raised in 1772 to £120, and the borrowing limit to £5 ; and certain business romances, including that of Lackington, who became a famous bookseller, owe their origin to its initial aid.[2] The Strangers' Friend Society was one of the last of

[1] *Journal*, January 17th, 1748.
[2] See J. Telford's *Wesley*, p. 334f.

Wesley's social creations. Not till 1787 was it founded ; yet, even prior to Wesley's death, it had its branches in every populous centre of the country. A casual *Journal* memo in 1790 explains its purpose : " In the morning I met the Strangers' Society, instituted wholly for the relief *not* of our society, but of poor, sick, friendless strangers. I do not know that I ever heard or read of such an institution till within a few years ago. So this also is one of the fruits of Methodism."[1] Without the new spirit and the new humanity created by the Revival, the utterly selfless efforts of this Society would have been unthinkable. Yet by the turn of the century, public tributes, in populous centres, were being paid to its work. " This Society," says J. Smith's *History of Liverpool* (1810), " originated among the Methodists of this town, and is in a great measure supported by them. The principles upon which it rests are liberal in the extreme, and reflect the greatest honour on the sect. It includes the wretched of every religious persuasion except their own, who are relieved from another fund. The only recommendation is distress."[2]

Still more important, with the assisting genius of " brother Charles," Wesley caused the masses of England to break forth into song. Carlyle, in his essay on Burns, says : " Let me make a nation's songs, and I care not who makes its laws." His epigram, if exaggerated, is not devoid of truth. Charles Wesley made the songs of the more earnest of the working populace of his day, and John Wesley's marvellous organisation taught the people to sing and love them. Multitudes, up and down the land, including many who once had been drunkards, prostitutes, wife-beaters, bruisers, gamblers, smugglers, sluggards and thieves, as they joined in the refrain :

> " My chains fell off, my heart was free,
>   I rose, went forth, and followed Thee,"

were singing from the depths of a miraculous personal experience. Thousands, too, who struggled stoutly for mean raiment, and scanty bread, rose in ecstasy on the wings of faith as they sang :

> " Riches unsearchable in Jesus' love we know,
>   And pleasures from the well of life our souls o'erflow."

---

[1] *Journal*, March 14th, 1790.
[2] Quoted in Edwards's *Wesley and the Eighteenth Century*, p. 153.

WESLEY'S DEATH BED
(After painting by Marshall Claxton, R.A.) Charles
Wesley's widow is kneeling at foot of bed. Most of
the others present are itinerant preachers

John Wesley (inset)
(after painting by Frank Salisbury, A.R.A.)

Such flaming, triumphant songs, even if they infuriated the Lavingtons and Warburtons, the Paines and Cobbetts, the Places and Owens, the Hunts and Hazlitts of the time, were no opiate, no soporific ; rather were they the portents and harbingers of better days on earth—the invigorating strains of a cloud of witnesses whose conception of social reform started with the purging of their own motives, and the moral reformation of their own lives. The popular hymns and choruses of the Revival contained no trace of ranting jingo or syncopated clamour : they bore no kinship to the uproar and fury of modern jazz, to the stupid insipidity of radio "crooning," or to the sombre, sullen rumbling of Proletarian chants of hate.[1]

On the contrary, this new hymnody, born of a new and vital experience, was expressive of noble aspirations : it strove to penetrate the purpose, the meaning and the end of life ; it pointed the relationship between Earth and Heaven, between Time and Eternity ; it radiated an atmosphere of peace and progress, of harmony and co-operation ; it fostered human fellowship and gladness ; it symbolised the Fatherhood of God and the Brotherhood of Man : the triumph of faith and the immortality of the soul. And it was expressed in music at once lyrical, dignified, soulful and sweet. The Evangelical Movement gave to the whole English-speaking world, its richest heritage of sacred song.[2]

Such songs, nevertheless, were an effect, rather than a cause ; the renewed life created by the Revival *had* to express itself in the ecstasy of sacred praise, but it by no means stopped there. The significant fact is, that Wesley and the movement of which he was the impelling centre, brought to the neglected masses of Britain the priceless boon of hope and aspiration, of self-respect and self-control. They removed from the working multitude the dead hand of an inferiority complex ; yet they indulged no stupid superiority complex. Without the sobriety, the discipline, the joyous fellowship, the love of knowledge, the training in co-operation and the new consciousness of human dignity and divine purpose, which the Revival brought to countless numbers of humble folk, the vigorous Self-Help and Social Reform movements, following in steady succession, could never have been born. England, be it reiterated, without the

---

[1] For an excellent treatment of the early hymnody of the Revival, see J. E. Rattenbury, *Wesley's Legacy to the World*, pp. 257–301.

[2] Charles Wesley *published* several thousand hymns. John wrote some, but made many excellent translations, especially from German. The Revival, too, in its wider impact, created a great company of hymn-writers, whose productions have become the common heritage of Christendom.

S

moral cleansing, the mental stimulus, the spiritual vision, which this mighty Spiritual Awakening brought to her, was ripe for social disintegration and soulless chaos ; with them she began gradually—if all too falteringly—to lead the world in humanitarian achievement.

THE PASSING OF A PROPHET

" Till glad I lay this body down,
   Thy servant, Lord, attend ;
   And O ! my life of mercy crown
   With a triumphant end."
                              CHARLES WESLEY

" A larger soul I think, hath seldom dwelt in house
of clay ! "
(Cromwell's valet, six months after his master's death)

THE PASSING OF A PROPHET

WESLEY's eight octogenarian years were a prolonged and glorious evening, terminating in a golden sunset. If the face of the very young man had been ascetic, rigid and slightly overweening, that of the very old man was mellow, gracious and beatific. His white, silken, wavy locks, his expansive brow, his aquiline nose, his firm jaw and his expressive mouth, together with his clear, ruddy complexion, his penetrating, kindly eyes and his radiant, permeating cheerfulness, combined to give him an appearance resemblant more of heaven than of earth. Still would the cynics sneer : but no sensitive person could look deeply into Wesley's age-worn face and fail to behold in it the tokens of a man of God. He was, as one of his latest biographers puts it, " so truly human and so truly divine."[1] Christian—though not sinless—" Perfection " was the goal to which he long had aspired ; and though he himself was acutely conscious of his shortcomings, the marks of his high aspiration were written unmistakably in the beauty and strength of his countenance, and reflected unmistakably in the graciousness of his spirit and manner. The vital, incarnate saintliness of Wesley's old age, was a thing of winsome and irresistible charm.

Though from his " spiritual birthday," late in his thirty-fifth year, unbroken peace and increasing joy had reigned within, nevertheless for at least four decades following, he had encountered a succession of violent tempests without. But ere the termination of his eightieth year, cloud and storm had well nigh passed from his horizon, and the veteran prophet henceforth moved largely in an atmosphere of serenity, veneration and awe. Many indeed who once had cursed him, now were praying for him. Not a few parsons who long had thundered against him from their pulpits, now were imploring him to preach from those same pulpits. The stiff-necked—ecclesiastical and lay—continued to put on airs and expatiated on the " folly of enthusiasm " and the " madness of the masses " ; but to multitudes Wesley finally was an honoured and matchless

[1] C. E. Vulliamy, *John Wesley*, p. 349.

prophet. The tide had turned. The latter years of the great Evangelist's itinerary were a series of triumphal tours. Commonly, as this veteran campaigner for God passed through towns and villages, the streets were lined with excited crowds gazing with stark admiration and wonder, " as if the King were going by."[1] Clergymen—Nonconformist and Anglican— turned out everywhere to hear him preach.[2] Even bishops stole sheepishly into his open-air congregations. The fury of the anti-Wesley mobs was no more.

(i) *A Last Retrospect*

This patriarch-preacher's virility as an octogenarian is one of the marvels of recorded history. Still he rose regularly at four a.m., and generally he preached at five. Still his manifold labours were unabated, and still his mental and physical powers matched—or all but matched—the vigour of his indomitable soul. Increasingly, but particularly on successive birthdays and other commemoration occasions, he praised God for sustained powers of body and mind. On his eighty-fifth birthday, for instance, he breaks forth in a typical strain : " What cause have I to praise God !—as for a thousand spiritual blessings, so for bodily blessings also ! How little have I suffered yet by ' the rush of numerous years ! ' It is true, I am not so agile as I was in times past. I do not run or walk so fast as I did : my sight is a little decayed . . . I find likewise some decay in my memory, with regard to names and things lately past ; but not at all with regard to what I have read or heard twenty, forty, or sixty years ago ; neither do I find any decay in my hearing, smell, taste or appetite . . . nor do I feel any such thing as weariness, either in travelling or preaching : and I am not conscious of any decay in writing sermons ; which I do as readily, and I believe as correctly, as ever."[3] His famous letter to Wilberforce, written three years later, in the last week of his life, exemplifies the sustained richness and clarity of his mind.[4] Wesley's life extended into all the decades of the eighteenth century. To many of his followers it must have seemed incredible that ever he should leave them. His very person appeared to them the symbol and embodiment of all that was immortal. Yet the days even of holy men are numbered, and

[1] See *Journal*, August 17th 1789.
[2] *Ibid.*, October 19th, 1790.
[3] *Ibid.*, June 28th, 1788.
[4] See chapter xii, end of section (i).

the sands of his life were fast running out. On Tuesday, February 22nd, 1791, he preached in the City Road Chapel and conferred with his leaders ; but he was not well. Up at four the following morning, he travelled to Leatherhead, where, in the home of a magistrate, he preached from the text, " Seek ye the Lord while He may be found." It was his last sermon. On Thursday, he visited an old friend, Mr. Woolf, at Balham, spending the night with him. On Friday, he was hurried back to his London rooms in the City Road,—a stricken man. With difficulty he mounted the stairs to his chamber. Premonition told him he would mount those familiar stairs no more. Immediately Bessie Ritchie had a blanket about him and he was seated in an easy chair. Friends already were clustering around, desiring to serve him. Calmly and graciously he bestowed upon them his blessing. Then, emphatically, he requested to be left alone. For at least " half an hour," *no one* must enter his chamber—not even his faithful confidant Joseph Bradford, or Dr. Whitehead, his physician.

For fifty-three years past, the central doctrine of Wesley's preaching was that men are saved by faith : but the corollary of that doctrine, he taught, was that they would be judged by their works. And now he who had spent his long life in leading a nation to God, was himself about to stand before the Eternal Judge. No sooner was the chamber door closed, than the deeper impressions of his life began to surge in rapid sequence across his mind. As with one in a trance, time and space were gone : now subjectively, now objectively, all passed in fleeting review. Again a child of five, the old man felt himself a " brand plucked from the burning," staring wildly from his rescuer's arms to see the blazing roof of the Epworth parsonage crash into a furnace of flames. . . . Again he heard his mother's soft voice, explaining to him the mysteries of the Spirit. " Your rescue from the fire, Jackie, was wrought by the hand of God ! Providence has sealed you for his own ! "—How often had he heard those words from his mother's lips ! . . . The scene changed. Charterhouse school . . . Oxford . . . the Holy Club, loomed before him. The Holy Club !—Very sincere had been that band of legal zealots, struggling, with monkish ardour, to hammer out their salvation by ascetic habits and rites ! Their faith was that of servants—not sons. His mind sped on to Georgia . . . Sophy Hopkey—that capable, sprightly, lovely girl. Little had he understood her ! . . . and his squabbles with his parishioners . . . and his stern sacerdotalism . . . " How well have I since been beaten with my own stick ! " he mused. . . . The panorama swept back to England . . . a soul in anguish—groping for light. Then appeared Peter Böhler, with his tender patience, and his quiet communion with Christ. . . . "Preach Faith till you have it!" implored the young Moravian missionary of the donnish priest, whose sophistication and sacerdotalism had obscured the simple truth. . . . Aye, Böhler's example and advice, had indeed been a lamp to his feet. For the thousandth time, he thanked God that the youthful Pietist had crossed his path. . . .

And now once more it was May 24th, 1738—the day of his spiritual baptism : the day of his rebirth. . . . Again the anthem in St. Paul's was ringing in his ears . . . again he was with the little society in Aldersgate Street. The eternal glory and power of *Faith*, now flashed afresh as a mighty revelation athwart his soul . . . Anew, his heart was " strangely warmed," and vividly he saw himself impelled to " testify," concerning the marvellous " experience " that there first filled his being. . . . Struggles and difficulties were ahead ; but worry, morbidity, corroding doubt—these (Heaven be praised !) were nightmares of the past. . . . Sin still would tempt him, but never again could it conquer him ; he had glimpsed the glory of the " transfigured life " : a new Power possessed him. Henceforth he knew himself an approved ambassador of God. . . . And now, as his life's work really began, the Church that had ordained him, began to disown him. " Go hence ! " was Bishop Butler's advice. " Pretending " to any special guidance of the Holy Spirit, was " a horrid thing—a very horrid thing."[1] . . . The visit to the Moravian settlements at Hernhuth and Marienborn, confirmed his faith : but blind, leaden officialdom, ever more obdurately, blocked his path. . . . It was Whitefield who cast down the barriers. His open-air preaching to the disinherited had illumined the example, and revealed the will of Christ. Was not the Sermon on the Mount preached by the Son of God, in God's open-air, to God's wandering sheep ? . . . The brooding man now saw himself preaching on the Horse Fair, Bristol. In the benighted multitude's dumb woe, he had heard the call of God. . . . A national crusade had been forced upon him. Henceforth, the market place, the town common, the open field, the dock, the factory yard, the mouth of the pit, ·were to him the Temple of God. . . . And how the Holy One had sealed his witness ! Strong men, by the hundred, had wrestled violently with the demons of sin, and, by the grace of Christ, had prevailed. . . . Presently, the dreamer was in the saddle, riding in sunshine and rain, o'er plain, fell and bog—now jotting down notes for a sermon, now

[1] See J. H. Overton, *John Wesley*, p. 100.

planning a pamphlet, now perusing a well chosen book, now dismounting, to extricate his horse from the mire. . . Once more, he saw the mobs—" raging as lions " ; sticks and stones again were hurtling round his head : " Satan was fighting furiously for his kingdom " . . . But how the arm of the Lord had been revealed ! What wondrous deliverances had he known ! Even mob leaders, had turned defenders and friends. Persecution assuredly had proved a blessing in disguise ! . . .

Abruptly then, the chambers of memory opened upon the itinerant and local preachers, upon the Class leaders and teachers of the crusade. They now were to be numbered in thousands—" a cloud of witnesses " to the redeeming power of grace. . . . The stones which the builders rejected, had become a living edifice of truth. Ah, the ways of God put the pride and snobbery of man to shame ! . . . The kaleidoscope moved on to Scotland. Twenty-two times, he had visited the land of the " North Britons." Increasingly had he come to admire the Scots ; but never quite, could he understand them : the seed, however, had been faithfully sown—with what result the Great Reaper would know. . . . And so to Ireland : during his twenty-one tours of that island, he or his associates had repeatedly been assaulted by wild, howling hordes . . . Nevertheless, they were a lovable people—the Irish ; and his mission to them had not been in vain. Even now, he could see the vast multitude falling reverently upon their knees, on the docks, as, from the deck of his departing ship, he invoked upon them—for the last time—God's blessing and peace. . . . Reverie glided on to America. Where he had failed, Whitefield had prepared the way for his disciples . . . Oh, the encouraging letters from Asbury and Coke ! In ten years, the preaching circuits within the young Republic had increased five fold ! He himself, had hoped to visit America again ; but well had his place been filled ! If the English colonies had separated from " the Motherland," thank Heaven they had not separated from Him who, once more, was being acknowledged and worshipped, as the Motherland's God ! . . .

Anon came a group of old friends . . . Whitefield—dear George ! With what holy abandon had he placed his life on the Altar of God ! " Oh, the tragedy," thought the brooding man, aloud, " that ever we had bickered ! As though any creed or doctrine, could encompass the wisdom or ways of God ! Ah, here our hearts were purged, but, hereafter, our brains also will be purged." . . . and brother Charles : already his hymns were proving a blessing in far-flung ends of the earth . . . and Lady Selina : she too, had been wondrously used. . . .

and that sturdy Yorkshireman, Grimshaw . . . Henry Venn
. . . and the eccentric, lovable Berridge. . . . Grace Murray.
. . . Mary Bosanquet . . . and his wife : her lot had not
been easy. Should he not have remembered, ere he married,
that a wife reasonably might expect a husband's companionship.
And how could he grant that, when his life was spent so largely
on the roads ? . . . and the serene, reflective Perronet . . .
the promising young Simeon . . . and Fletcher—the saintly
John Fletcher : he had preached " Perfection " ; but Fletcher
had come nearer to its attainment, than he. Even in controversy, that gracious, godly man had breathed but tender love
toward his adversaries. . . . The Holy One however was
merciful : he claimed no merit ; he had made many mistakes :
but, without presumption, he trusted he had not been altogether
an unprofitable servant. . . . God knew, he had striven to do
all for the glory of His Kingdom, and the welfare of His children.
. . . Soon now, he would join his friends departed. . . . His
life's work was done. He was ready—to go. . . .

But England ! . . . True, the Revival had made religion
once more vital, and God, through Christ, both personal and
real. True, routing cynicism, fatalism, and paganism, it had
established the sovereign merit of goodness and truth, in countless
souls . . . But England's need of spiritual vision, was still
great . . . The poor ! How misunderstood were the poor !
How neglected, and how abused ! How very, very much
remained to be done—in England. . . . And the African slaves !
Their appalling wrongs cried aloud to Heaven, for redress !—
Oh, man's inhumanity to man ! Yet (God be thanked !) the
National Conscience was gradually, if slowly, awakening.
Widespread spiritual forces had been released. Something
approaching a moral revolution, was under way. Already, there
were Wilberforces, Clarksons and Sharps spending their lives
for the Negroes' Cause. " The world is my parish ! " had not
been preached for naught. . . . But hark ! The brooding,
stricken man roused himself, as from slumber. The great clock
was striking. His " half-hour " of solitude was more than up.
Someone was vigorously tapping on the door. Anxious voices
were heard without. Wesley's musing, ceased.

(ii) *Crossing the Bar*

The veteran preacher's end was wholly beautiful. The Last
Enemy for him had no sting, the grave no victory. For five
days the silver cord was loosing : but in Death, as in life,

Wesley's example was one not only of spiritual triumph, but of continued fellowship with the poor. During his half-century crusade, he never claimed for poverty any peculiar virtue ; while, on the other hand, he said much regarding the value of money—if properly used. Yet despite the fortune accruing from his publications, never did he retain more than a few odd pounds. All went to the needy. During no single year, did he expend an average of twelve shillings a week upon himself. Never did he wear other than the cheapest, as well as the plainest, clothes ; and always he dined on the humblest fare. To the end, he gave his time, his talents, his means, his all, that he might gain Christ and make Christ real to England.

> " His life was gentle, and the elements
> So mixed in him, that Nature might stand up,
> And say to all the world : ' This was a man ! ' "

And now when Time, in last farewell, had shaken him by the hand, and Death was beckoning him to Eternity's brink, being full of years, yet full of hope and gladness, his parting words, his funeral instructions and his last will, reflect the undimmed splendour of his majestic spirit. Often had he prayed, " Lord let me wear out, not rust out ! Let me not live to be useless ! " That prayer was literally fulfilled. Though in the ninth month of his eighty-eighth year, he was preaching and writing even into his last week on earth. And now, on his death-bed, his spirit " all love " and " breathing the air of paradise,"[1] he called out : " Where is my sermon on *The Love of God* ? Take it, and spread it abroad. Give it to everyone ! "[2] Then he broke into song :

> " All glory to God in the sky,
> And peace upon earth be restored."

But the strength of his body being spent, long periods of sleep ensued. Once or twice, as the fever reached its zenith, he was wafted into a gentle delirium, and imagined himself preaching to the multitude or conferring with his preachers. As the fever waned, his countenance would kindle and his eyes sparkle, as though beholding some wondrous vision, afar. And as full consciousness returned, he would bid his friends, " pray and praise." No murmur, no complaint, escaped his lips. With the humility of saintliness, several times he cried :

> " I the chief of sinners am,
> But Jesus died for me."

[1] From the *Account* of Elizabeth Ritchie, who attended Wesley before his death. See, too, Standard edition of *Journal*, Vol. VIII, p. 132.
[2] Many thousands of copies of this sermon were gratuitously distributed.

The lines, however, which focussed his consciousness, and which again and again he sang, were :

> " I'll praise my Maker while I've breath,
> And when my voice is lost in death,
> Praise shall employ my nobler powers."

On the evening preceding his translation, he smiled benignly on all about him, and with great effort, raising his hand, exclaimed calmly and clearly, " *The best of all is—God is with us !* " The night brought slumber. About ten o'clock, on the morning of March 2nd, 1791, casting his eyes again slowly from person to person around his bedside, he whispered : " Farewell ! " Instinctively, all present fell on their knees : and as Joseph Bradford led in prayer, the holy man's soul, without struggle or groan, sped forth to the spirit centre of the Kingdom of God— the Kingdom which had provided the inspiration and the dynamic for his abundant labours on earth.[1] In death, his countenance reflected the supreme gladness of his exultant soul. A winsome smile enwreathed his face.

Thus, the man who had preached more than forty-five thousand sermons, who had travelled (mostly on horse-back) a distance equivalent to nine times round the world, who had written two hundred and thirty-three books and pamphlets, and helped with the writing of fully one hundred more[2]—the " grand old man " and noblest prophet of the English-speaking world—passed to his Long Home. No sooner was his spirit released, than those who had come " to rejoice with him," burst into an anthem of praise.

Among Wesley's funeral instructions, was the request that his body be buried in nothing more costly than wool. No silk or satin was to adorn the corpse from which his spirit had fled. And his last will and testament gave final seal to the Gospel he had so long and so courageously preached—in " darkest England." " Whatever remains in my bureau and pockets, at my decease," he directed, was to be " equally divided " among four poor itinerants, whom he named. To each of the travelling preachers within the connection six months after his death, he bequeathed copies of the eight volumes of his sermons. Then came a clause expressive both of his solicitude for the unemployed and of his efforts for funeral reform. Specially requesting that neither hearse nor coach take any part in his

[1] See *Journal*, Vol. VIII, p. 139.
[2] R. Green, in his collection of Wesley literature, prints the titles of 17 publications by John and Charles Wesley.

funeral, he desired that six poor men, in need of employment, be given a pound each to carry his body to the grave. His statement on this point is emphatic. " I particularly desire," the will reads, that " there be no hearse nor coach, no escutcheon, no pomp, except the tears of those who love me, and are following me to Abraham's bosom."[1]

For several days, Wesley's body lay in state in his City Road Chapel, where multitudes filed silently by, each reverently pausing a moment over the now cold, lifeless face, which so often they had seen aflame with a living fire, divine. Thousands in that multitude shed tears, as they thought of all they owed to him who, in the deepest sense, was their " father in God." But to avoid any final blockade, the actual hour of interment was kept secret to the inner circle. The funeral, on that memorable winter's morning, was conducted by torchlight, and was concluded before dawn of day.

All Wesley's burial instructions were punctiliously observed. Dr. Whitehead, his faithful medical adviser and loyal disciple, delivered the funeral address : an itinerant preacher performed the last rites. The solemn comrades, looking on, knew well that " Earth to earth, ashes to ashes," referred only to the body. Wesley already was in the Land of the Immortals, where always he will occupy a foremost place among the world's very worthiest leaders of men. " Do you think we shall see John Wesley in Heaven ? " once inquired an over-aggressive Calvinist of Whitefield. " I fear not," replied the fellow evangelist, musing. " No !—he will be so near the throne, and we at such a distance, that we shall hardly get a sight of him."

Though this great gentleman and mighty prophet died without material estate, he nevertheless left behind him a heritage which has enriched, beyond computation, the real and abiding wealth of all mankind. For if spiritual values and spiritual attainments be the ultimate standard of greatness, few greater than this little English preacher have yet trodden the earth ; and none greater, has spoken the English tongue.

[1] Wesley's will may still be seen at Somerset House, London. See, too, *Journal*, Vol. VIII, p. 343

A PEOPLE FINDS ITS SOUL

" For is not God . . . the principle of coherence in the universe ? (' In Him all things consist ') and is not religion the supreme synthesis in which all lesser syntheses are brought together into a coherent whole ? . . .

PROFESSOR FREDERICK TRACY, *Broken Lights*, p. 139.

" At a time when Bishop Butler asserted that Christianity was wearing out of the minds of men, Wesley kept the English people Christian. . . . It is certain that into the moral fibre of the English people, even in the classes most anxious to repudiate the debt, were woven new strands by the abiding influence of Methodism."

SIR C. GRANT ROBERTSON, *England Under the Hanoverians* (in *A History of England*, Edited by Sir Charles Oman, Vol. VI, p. 386.)

1. GREAT BUST OF LORD SHAFTESBURY
presented by the Factory Workers of the North
of England to his wife, in 1859 (top)

2. SHAFTESBURY MEMORIAL (Eros Monument),
Piccadilly Circus, London. Erected by the con-
secrated pennies of the Emancipated Industrial
Workers of Britain (bottom)

A PEOPLE FINDS ITS SOUL

OFTEN, after the manner of Sydney Smith, has it been assumed that " Methodism " and " Evangelicalism " are purely synonymous terms. And though this assumption frequently has been born of a desire to stimulate ecclesiastical prejudice or to confuse the popular mind, nevertheless so close is the historical relationship between the two that they are inextricably joined. Almost, they may be considered as cause and effect. The " Methodist " crusade, initiated by the efforts of the Wesleys, Whitefield and the Countess of Huntingdon, was the vital nucleus from which emanated ever expanding zones of spiritual quickening, moral renewal and social zeal. But the baptising fire of this mighty Revival overleapt all " society " and denominational barriers. Soon it permeated the dry and dying body of Old Dissent and, injecting into it a pulsing life, created a new and Evangelical Nonconformity.[1] Similarly, despite contumely and persecution, it revived religious vision and kindled religious initiative among thousands within the National Church ; while, yet more important, reclaiming multitudes of religious outcasts who long had been quite beyond the pale of any immediate spiritual influence, it finally transformed the whole tone and tenor of the National life. With that larger, interdenominational and truly Catholic Evangelicalism, this study is chiefly concerned.

(i) *The Streams O'erflow*

Constantly must it be remembered that harsh as was the treatment they received from the National Church, the Wesleys and Whitefield were ordained clergymen of the Establishment, who struggled against heavy odds to keep their followers within the Anglican communion. They insisted that, save in cases of special and extreme necessity, their societies should never meet during the hours of Church worship ; they urged all their members to attend Church services, particularly the Holy Communion ; and sternly did they insist that the societies

---

[1] Dr. E. D. Bebb's *Nonconformity and Social and Economic Life* (1935), throws light on the influence of the Evangelical Revival over the Old Dissent. See Chapters II, III and X. Professor Elie Halévy, too, in different volumes of his *History of the English People* substantiates this truth.

should not be called a Church. True, the expulsion of the six Evangelical students from Oxford in 1768, the repeated refusal by parish priests of the Lord's Supper to " Methodist " preachers and class leaders, and the vindictive persecution of Methodists (under long dormant Conventicle Acts) for meeting in unlicensed places,[1] caused endless annoyance, and finally forced both Wesley and the Countess of Huntingdon reluctantly to license their preaching houses, under protection of a statute " exempting Protestant Dissenters from the penalties " of the said Acts.[2] But if it is certain that the relationship of the societies to the Establishment was never cordial, and equally certain that most of the ecclesiastical potentates continued to caricature and lampoon the " Methodists " as " wild," if not " mad," " enthusiasts," it yet is none the less certain that the impact of these Societies upon the long suspicious and resentful mother Church, had, within half a century, greatly mitigated the initial prejudice of her more earnest and tolerant lay members ; while also, it had convinced many of them that Evangelical endeavour, with its spiritual motives, its missionary fervour and its strong sense of stewardship, could alone save England from moral turpitude and social disintegration. Consequently, the influence of the movement grew steadily within the State Church. For thousands of Anglicans who never dreamed of joining the Methodist societies, nevertheless found in the Revival a new vision of life, a new love for God and man, a new passion for service—a new yearning to be used of God in building the Kingdom of Righteousness on earth.

The names of such men as Fletcher, Romaine, Newton, Scott, the Venns, the Milners, Grimshaw, Berridge, Hervey, Walker, Perronet, Clarke, Jones, Adam and Charles Simeon indicate something of the hold which the Revival began to exercise over the clergy of the Established Church, even before the close of Wesley's century[3] : while the mere mention of such pioneering zealots as Wilberforce, the Emancipator ; Zachary Macaulay, the Governor of the freed slave colony at Sierra Leone ; Cowper, the poet ; John and Henry Thornton, the eminent banker philanthropists ; James Stephen, the famous advocate and Under Secretary to the Colonies ; Lord Dartmouth, the Colonial Secretary ; Lord Teignmouth, the Governor-General

---

[1] See G. R. Balleine, *History of the Evangelical Party in the Church of England*, pp. 46, 58, 88, 125 and 245–6.

[2] The Countess of Huntingdon resorted to this protection in 1782 and Wesley in 1787.

[3] For an excellent survey of the labours of such men, see Balleine, *op. cit.*, pp. 50–143 ; also Bishop Pilcher's *Evangelical Movement and Oxford Movement*.

of India ; Charles Grant, Chairman of the East India Company ; and Hannah More, friend of the poor, and most noted literary woman of her day, affords some idea of the inspiration which the Movement had provided within the ranks of the Anglican laity. Yet most of the prelates remained sullen, or hostile ; and had not these " Enthusiasts " abode in the ship, it is doubtful if the National Church could have been saved.[1]

The practical influence, however, of the Evangelical group within the Establishment was altogether disproportionate to its numbers. Canon Overton, with his High Church outlook, is scarcely liable to be prejudiced in this direction. Yet, reviewing the effects of the Evangelical Movement, he says that, in the sphere of religion, " to be *serious* and to be *Evangelical* were only different ways of saying the same thing."[2] And concluding his able survey, he adds : " In short, it would be no exaggeration to say that, morally and spiritually, though by no means intellectually, the dominant religious power, both inside and outside the Church of England, at the close of the eighteenth century, was that which had been evoked by the Evangelical Revival."[3] Nevertheless, contrary to general belief, not more than five or six per cent. of the clergy of the Establishment were at this time avowed Evangelicals. Mr. Gladstone (*British Quarterly Review*, July, 1879) estimated that, at the close of the eighteenth century, the proportion of Evangelical clergy within the State Church was " about one in twenty " ; but Balleine considers this as, " probably an over-estimate."[4] Certainly any suggestion of appointing " an Evangelical " as a Bishop at this time, would have been viewed by the Episcopal Bench as utterly preposterous : indeed, with the close of the century, no real preferment had been proffered to any Evangelical, with the solitary exception of Isaac Milner, who in 1788 was appointed President of Queens' College, Cambridge, and in 1791 Dean of Carlisle. But so brilliant had been his mathematical attainments, that the University examiners had appended to his name the word " *Incomparabilis*." With Milner's Presidency of Queens' College, came the Evangelicals' first opportunity to have their candidates for Holy Orders educated at one of the ancient universities without violence to the principles of their Faith.[5]

" At a time when Bishop Butler asserted that Christianity was wearing out of the minds of men,"[6] says Sir C. G. Robertson

---

[1] See Bishop Inskip's *Evangelical Influence in English Life* (Preface, p. viii).
[2] Overton's *Evangelical Revival in the Eighteenth Century*, p. 160.
[3] *Ibid.*, p. 161 ; see also pp. 131–160.
[4] *Op. cit.*, p. 134.
[5] Balleine, p. 124ff.
[6] See Butler's Preface to his *Analogy*.

in the Oxford *History of England*, " Wesley kept the English people Christian, and shamed the Church, which had closed her pulpits to him, into imitating his spirit, if not his methods. . . . It is certain that into the moral fibre of the English people, even in the classes most anxious to repudiate the debt, were woven new strands by the abiding influence of Methodism."[1] This conclusion is incontrovertible : but those hardest to " shame " and " most anxious to repudiate the debt," were the eighteenth-century prelates.

That this leavening effect was produced in the Nonconformist bodies as well as in the Established Church, is indubitable. No less an authority than Dr. R. W. Dale, writes : " The fires of the Revival had been kindled from heaven, and before the accession of George III the Congregational Churches had caught the flame. Their ministers were beginning to preach with a new fervour, and their preaching was followed by a new success. The religious life of the people was becoming more intense. A passion for evangelistic work had taken possession of church after church, and by the end of the century the old meeting houses were crowded ; many of them had to be enlarged and new meeting houses had to be erected in town after town, and village after village, in every part of the country."[2] The extent of this Nonconformist quickening was positively phenomenal ; and the fact that all Dissenting places of worship had to be registered under the Toleration Act of 1689, provides the historian with a ready gauge of its effects. In 1690, the total number of " permanent " places of Dissenting worship, including those of Quakers, in all England and Wales, was 251, while the number of " temporary " places (private houses, barns, sheds, etc.) was 927. By 1740, the " permanent " places of such worship had dwindled from 251 to 27, and the " temporary " from 927 to 506. By the end of the eighteenth century, however, the " permanent " places of Dissenting worship had leaped from 27 to 926, and the " temporary " from 506 to 3,491.[3] Both the Congregationalists and the Baptists meanwhile had copied much of the Methodist system, including that of local preachers and central organisation, while also the Disesnting outlook had quite shifted from a rational-political and individualistic emphasis, to a Christo-centric and more social-religious approach.

Under the permeating influence of the Evangelical Revival, Nonconformity became again a power in the land. This " New

---

[1] *Op. cit.*, Vol. VI, p. 386 (" England under the Hanoverians ").
[2] R. W. Dale, *History of English Congregationalism*, p. 585.
[3] *Parliamentary Papers*, 1852–53, pp. 78–9, 82. See, too, Bebb's *Nonconformity and Social and Economic Life* (Appendix I).

Nonconformity " represented a smaller proportion of the privileged and landed classes than did the Puritanism of the seventeenth century, and its primary emphasis was on the New Testament and the Spirit of the Gospel, rather than on the Old Testament and the sanctity of the Law. Nevertheless silently, peacefully, it now was sowing the seeds of a mighty quickening throughout the English-speaking world : and not yet, despite the researches of Professor Halévy, Dr. Bebb, P. A. Brown[1], and many others, has that influence been duly appraised. In the struggle for a sane Democracy and a balanced Liberty, its contribution was invaluable. The Nonconformist Conscience has been a poignant dynamic in British history ; yet the rebirth and true effectiveness of that Conscience were inextricably associated with the eighteenth-century Revival of " vital practical religion." Wesley's societies, as Dr. Priestley and other contemporaries frankly acknowledged, were the spear head of the general spiritualising and civilising advance,[2] but the self-governing tradition of Dissent enabled it the more effectively, at certain points, to apply the new enthusiasm and power to the problems of social, economic and political life. Perhaps, too, almost as many of the newly " civilised " were tutored and found their souls within the revived Chapels of Dissent, as within the Preaching Houses of Methodism or the " Evangelical " Churches of the Establishment. The new Christo-centric emphasis of the Revival, as the forthcoming great Missionary and Bible societies soon would reveal, made all Evangelicalism much of a piece, for it was in essence a unifying emphasis.

As for the Church in Scotland, Wesley and Whitefield wrought upon it more effectively than ever they knew. The original design of the Revival was to quicken the dead bones of the National Church in England, to breathe into her the breath of spiritual sensitivity, and thus kindle the fire of religious energy. The blindness, the lethargy, the pomposity of the English hierarchy thwarted this design. Not so in Scotland. One of the most amazing revelations of Wesley's *Journal* is the quiet, respectful, and even reverent hearing, which almost invariably was afforded him in " North Britain." Repeatedly there, he was invited to preach in College Chapels, Town Halls and prominent Kirks, and to dine and confer with Presbyterian ministers. His work among the Scots was accompanied by comparatively few phenomenal conversions, by little excitement and not many highly successful Societies. Hence, adroit as

---

[1] *The French Revolution in English History*, (1918).
[2] See Dr. Warner, *op. cit.*, pp. 170–180.

Wesley was, he never properly gauged the effects of the Revival upon the Scottish Kirk and people.

Large numbers of Presbyterian ministers were, at this time, keenly aware that all was not well with the National Church of Scotland. Sadly they had observed the dour effects of frigid Deism and Socinianism in their own lives, and upon the Kirk they loved. Like Wesley, before his conversion, not a few of them had eaten the bread of disillusionment ; they were penitent, and groping for light. More than he himself ever dreamed of, Wesley, indirectly if not directly, was a Peter Böhler to scores, perhaps hundreds, of Presbyterian ministers ; bringing faith, hope, courage and joy to their heavy, if not weary hearts. He saw no great expansion of his societies, and thought the Scots over canny and critical. Little did he realise that actually he was accomplishing for the Church of Scotland, much of what he set out to do for the Church of England. But this he achieved not so directly through the Scotch multitudes, as through the Scotch clergy. Largely he had converted the Presbyterian ministry from a glacial, latitudinarian rationalism to a warm Christo-centric zeal, while they, independent of his societies, in their own semi-philosophical way, carried the Evangel throughout the length and breadth of Scotland, and from Scotland to many a distant clime. The renewed faith, vision and vigour of the Church of Scotland, soon to manifest itself in an adventurous missionary and philanthropic enthusiasm, can never be explained apart from the expanding influence of the Evangelical Revival. In the light of all the facts, indeed, it is not surprising that Scotland was the first part of the Kingdom to begin to honour Wesley by conferring upon him the Freedom of prominent corporations and cities[1] ; and the influence of Presbyterianism was by no means disassociated from these public tributes. Yet here, too, the new wine of " enthusiasm " finally proved too strong for the old bottles of formalism, and for many a decade the " Free Kirk," turning its back on endowments and patronage, chose to tread its own pioneering and heroic path.

This, however, is but half the story. The influence of Whitefield in Scotland has not yet been fully recognised. His mildly Calvinistic theology was more in harmony with Scottish backgrounds than was Wesley's Arminianism. Nowhere, save in America, was his influence more triumphant than amongst the

---

[1] When Perth, the old capital of Scotland, on April 28th, 1772, conferred this honour upon Wesley, his only *Journal* reference reads : " They did me an honour I never thought of—presented me with the Freedom of the City." A few days later (May 6th, 1772), the magistrates of Arbroath did likewise, and Wesley notes : " I value it as a token of their respect, though I shall hardly make any further use of it."

Scots,[1] and, beyond question, the credit for the steady renewal of deep religious life in Scotland was as much due to Whitefield[2] as to Wesley.[3]

In Ireland, for obvious reasons, Wesley's task was hard. Often there, he and his preachers found themselves the centre of tempestuous and violent mobs. Yet his love both for Ireland and the Irish people is well known, and highly merited was his pride in his band of Irish itinerant preachers, including the memorable Thomas Walsh. For despite poverty and persecution, they created influences which not only brought insight, education and uplift to large sections of Ireland, but, voyaging in the spirits of thousands of Irish emigrants, enriched the life of numerous frontier settlements, both in the British Empire and the United States. Indeed the *first* Local Preacher in the New World was an Irish immigrant.

(ii) *New Birth, New Character, New Moral and Social Zeal*

Mr. G. W. E. Russell, a Liberal Under-Secretary and a wholly detached observer, reviewing the characteristics of Evangelical religion as he encountered it in the latter part of the nineteenth century, writes : " I recall an abiding sense of religious responsibility, a self-sacrificing energy in works of mercy, an evangelistic zeal, an aloofness from the world, and a level of saintliness in daily life such as I do not expect again to see realised on earth. Everything down to the minutest details of action and speech were considered with reference to eternity. . . . Money was regarded as a sacred trust, and people of good positions and comfortable incomes habitually kept their expenditure within narrow limits that they might contribute more largely to objects which they held sacred. The Evangelicals were the most religious people whom I have ever known."[4]

This type of character and service grew naturally out of Evangelical faith, which sought to bring all mankind, independent of race, sex, class, wealth or station, into abiding personal communion with God, through Christ. The Revival proclaimed " the infinite latent value of even the downmost

[1] See Belden's *Whitefield—the Awakener* (Part III, chapter ii).

[2] Had Whitefield, who died in 1770, lived but a few years longer, he, like Wesley, undoubtedly would have had honours conferred upon him by the Scots.

[3] On June 23rd, 1772, Wesley notes : " What a difference between an English and a Scotch congregation ! These judge themselves rather than the preacher ; and their aim is not only to know, but to love and obey." On numerous occasions he refers to the Scotsmen's love of plain, direct speech and frank dealing ; on others he criticises them for their lack of zeal and their intellectual pride. His criticisms of Scotland, however, are often repeated ; his *many* tributes are generally forgotten.

[4] Russell's *Household of Faith*, p. 232.

soul." Different from the Puritan Movement preceding, and the Oxford Movement succeeding, the Evangelical Movement centred religion neither in the state nor in the church, but in the individual and the home. True religion, it taught, is " the life of God in the soul of man, bearing fruit in every good work for human betterment." Yet, as suggested in Cowper's noble poem, *The Task*, from the individual and the home this Movement finally spread the faith, vision, fellowship and power of vital religion to the furthermost corners of the earth.[1] Its ideal was to cause the spirit and ethic of Christ to permeate *all* departments of life. Not only the individual, the home and the Church, therefore, would it claim for the Kingdom of God ; but the world of business, economics and education ; all social relationships, all national and international affairs— these, too, would it bring under the lordship of Him Who, when on earth, " went about doing good."

The Bible, to the Evangelical Movement, was " the book of books " ; and if the Revival's staunch belief in " the all-sufficiency of the Scriptures " tended sometimes towards " Bibliolatry " and " Sabbatarianism," it tended always toward high purpose, self-restraint, and a noble serenity of character. If Evangelical theology often was narrow, it at least had the depth of its narrowness : a depth contrasting acutely with the shallowness of much boasted modern breadth. Wherever the Revival spread, its first avowed aim was to dispel religious illiteracy, and in so doing it became a mighty and ennobling educational force. To the individual convert, his much-underlined personal Bible was his handbook of moral and spiritual guidance ; to the Evangelical household, the Family Bible was not only the sacred register of births, baptisms, marriages and deaths, it also was the medium of " family worship " wherein parents and children were daily lifted together to the Throne of Grace : to all Evangelical society, the Bible was both chart and compass in the voyage of life. Nor is it any accident that out of this Movement sprang The British and Foreign Bible Society which, to date, has circulated the Scriptures in hundreds of millions of copies in every quarter of the globe, while also it has translated them, in whole or in part, into over seven hundred different languages and tongues.[2]

The Movement placed little emphasis on æsthetics, and less on æsthetic symbolism. It shunned as superficial all " art for

---

[1] For Cowper's place in the Revival see Gilbert Thomas, *William Cowper and the Eighteenth Century* (1935).

[2] See *The Master-Light* (Report of British and Foreign Bible Society, 1937), p. 40 ; also Bishop Inskip's *Evangelical Influence in English Life*, p. 205.

art's sake" theories of thought, expression or conduct. Its worship was simple almost to the point of austerity ; but tense reverence was at its heart, and where reverence dwells, decency and order are never absent. In most branches of the Revival, the Sacraments were esteemed as special and divinely appointed means of grace, to be administered only by duly ordained shepherds of Christ : but in all branches, priestly assumption and sacerdotal domination over the consciences of fellow Christians were quite discountenanced. To this "Second Reformation"—which certainly was more deeply spiritual than the first—" the priesthood of all believers " bore a vital significance : for was not every " convert " a mediator and missionary of the Cause of Christ ? Hence the spiritual character of all true greatness was strongly emphasised, with results that often cut clean athwart a hundred hoary and hampering social prejudices. To the soul of this Movement there was neither Greek nor barbarian, neither male nor female, neither bond nor free ; for " all were one in Christ." Women accordingly were treated as the equals of men ; the cause of the slaves was championed because the " black chattels " were all immortal souls and " free men in Jesus Christ " ; while missionaries were dispatched over the Seven Seas to proclaim even to the fiercest cannibals, the Fatherhood of God, the Brotherhood of Man and the Evangel of Goodwill. On all sides, the Movement breathed a more soulful conception of the purpose and goal of life, thus engendering new standards of " attainment " and " success." And one of its most marked manifestations was its capacity for creating " lay saints," to whom prayer and spiritual meditation became instinctive, and to whom Christian altruism became the necessary concomitant of Christian faith. Indeed, for all the importance which the Revival attached to the " converted," " regenerated " or " recreated " individual, always it emphasised that he was reborn to a social end ; and two maxims of Wesley were indelibly impressed upon all true Evangelical tradition :

(1) " The Gospel of Christ knows of no religion but social, no holiness, but social holiness."[1]
(2) " I look upon all the world as my parish ! "

Moreover, never should it be forgotten that if the Revival implied marked inhibition, it yet insisted that the content and purpose of pure religion is positive. Inhibitions, therefore, represented but the pruning of the branches that the tree might bring forth more and better fruit : they were the necessary

[1] See Wesley's Preface to his 1739 *Hymn Book*.

discipline of body, mind and soul that, being kept clean and
healthy, they might increasingly merge into a unified personality
—the temple of the living Spirit of God. Nor, despite its intensity, was this "new Puritanism" as narrow as it is often
portrayed. Vehemently did it believe in freedom of conscience,
and if some of its representatives opposed Roman Catholic
Emancipation, it was because they honestly thought that the
consciences of vast masses of Roman Catholics were "priest
ridden" and therefore "not free." It is poignant, however,
that whereas many of the old High Church leaders continued
to the end to oppose Catholic Emancipation, most of the leading
Evangelicals came to support it. From 1813 to the end of his
Parliamentary career, Wilberforce spoke in favour of Catholic
Emancipation in the House of Commons. "Persecution for
religious opinions" he pronounced "not only one of the
wickedest, but one of the most foolish things in the world";
while "to give the Catholics the vote and go no further"
(keep them out of Parliament) he insisted, "was to let them
out of prison and keep them in their convicts' dress."[1] When
this question came to its final issue, in 1829, all three Evangelical
bishops (Ryder and the Sumner brothers) supported Emancipation in the House of Lords : in the Commons such stalwart
Evangelical leaders as Lord Ashley (Shaftesbury), then in his
twenty-eighth year, Buxton, Thornton and the Grants all voted
for Catholic liberty ; while the now aged Simeon bestowed
upon the Catholic Emancipation cause his approbation, and
Rev. Daniel Wilson wrote a pamphlet favouring the Bill.[2] In
the case of the famous Reform Bill of 1832, Evangelicals as a
body were largely behind this political advance, not so much
because the Bill was "Democratic"—for still they retained
haunting memories of what had happened in the name of
"Democracy" under the Rule of Terror in France—as because
it was "anti-oligarchic," and because they believed it would
clear the ground for the reform of "rotten boroughs" within
the Church.[3]

(iii) *Wilberforce and the Clapham Sect*

The case of William Wilberforce is but an outstanding
instance of the character transformation which the Evangelical

---

[1] See Professor R. Coupland's *Wilberforce*, pp. 444–5 and 369–70.

[2] Balleine, *op. cit.*, pp. 210–11. If Wesley and most of the eighteenth
century Evangelicals opposed Catholic representation in Parliament, it
must be recalled that they remembered the Jacobite Rebellions and feared
the possibility of a Catholic succession to the throne.

[3] Dr. W. L. Mathieson's *English Church Reform, 1815–1840*, is illuminating
on this subject. See, too, Dr. J. H. Rose's *Christianity and the French
Revolution.*

Revival wrought on a grand scale. A child of wealth, endowed with wit, brains, charm and the singing " voice of a nightingale," he was the centre of a gay set during his Cambridge days. In 1780, at twenty-one years of age, having spent nearly £9,000 upon the election, he was returned M.P. for his native city of Hull, receiving as many votes as the two opposing candidates.[1] Exactly the same age as Pitt, he soon became his most intimate friend, Pitt often spending weeks on end at his country house. The " political game," too, was dear to his heart ; he loved its urbanity, its repartee, its satire, its banter, its innuendo and its thrusts ; while nothing afforded him keener delight than an opportunity " to tear the enemy to pieces." In every sense, he was a smart young " man-about-town " ; membership in five of the most exclusive London clubs affording him opportunity for much frolic and some dissipation. He could drink as deeply and gamble as suavely, as most dandies in his set ; and all the while the shady antics and sensuous excitement of " night life " were gaining hold on him.

Then casually in 1785, he fell upon Dr. Doddridge's book, *The Rise and Progress of Religion*.[2] Discontent with his manner of life, at once began to scourge his conscience ; a wistful yearning plumbed the depth of his being : an ordeal of months ensued. During that ordeal Isaac Milner, his one-time teacher at Hull, and John Newton, the one-time slave-ship captain, were his spiritual guides, and from it, after burning anguish of soul, he emerged " a new man." Even Pitt—much as Wilberforce loved him—could not shake his new found faith. No longer, had mere party politics their old appeal ; no longer would the gaming table, the drinking bout or the night club, dissipate his energies or fritter away his time : no longer would he consider either his wealth or his talents his own. A new world had opened up before him ; new standards of judgment forthwith would control his mind ; new motives would energise his life.

Henceforth be believed himself a steward of God : and if many were to mock him as a " budding saint," his own deepest desire was that he might approximate, ever more nearly, toward the object of their raillery. But there are " saints " and " saints "; to Wilberforce, and to the religion he typified, sainthood was a highly practical and highly useful state of life. Moreover, if the all-night ball and the smart set would know him no

---

[1] Coupland's *Wilberforce*, p. 10.
[2] Doddridge was President of a Nonconformist Theological Academy at Northampton. His interest in Wesley and the Revival is evidenced by the fact that as early as 1745 he got Wesley to address his theological students. See Wesley's *Journal*, September 9th, 1745.

more as a boon companion, as years passed there were those even among the glittering friends of early days who would yet declare that the cheerfulness and serenity of " the saint " were more utterly charming than the swagger and dash of the gay young sinner. His love, too, for his intimate friends of early Parliamentary days, never abated. True, Pitt as Prime Minister could scarcely pour out all his heart on such twilight questions, for instance, as party finance to the highly sensitised conscience of his " converted " comrade. But if complete intimacy was broken, Pitt's veneration for the character and integrity of " the saint " only increased ; and the one occasion on which that cool, restrained, masterful statesman was ever known to bury his head or to shed a tear in the House of Commons, was when his revered friend, conscience-bound, opposed him sternly on a major moral issue of his policy. Yet, when such rare occasions occurred, Pitt knew well that the cleavage pained his old friend no less than it pained him. " The saint " was no prig, and all semblance of pharisaism was obnoxious to him.

Long after his " transfiguring ordeal," Wilberforce wrote : " I devoted myself for whatever might be the term of my future life, to the service of my God and Saviour and, with many infirmities and deficiencies, through His help I continue until this day."[1] So strong, however, was the odium with which " Methodist " convictions were held by the ruling classes, even as late as 1785, that many associates on learning of his " conversion," actually thought the young parliamentarian had gone mad. " Strange reports," writes Wilberforce, " were now raised about me. I was said to be out of my mind and melancholy mad. These reports were conveyed to my mother and to my relatives in Yorkshire, and for some time made them very uneasy, but on my going down to visit them, which I soon did, I took particular pains to be cheerful and pleasant and kind in the society of my friends. My natural disposition was irritable, and it had often caused them much pain. They were exceedingly struck by my altered deportment—they found me so much more kind and patient—so much more forbearing and considerate than formerly, that one of them remarked, " *if such were the effects of becoming ' melancholy mad,' it would be well if many of our acquaintance would take the infection.*"[2]

Of the more positive effects of his soul's " awakening," Wilberforce speaks in no uncertain words. In his famous

[1] Travers Buxton, *William Wilberforce—the Story of a Great Crusade*, p. 38.

[2] *Ibid.*, pp. 40–1.

book, *A Practical View of the Prevailing Religious System of Professed Christians in the Higher and Middle Classes in this Country contrasted with Real Christianity,*" which ran into some forty editions and several translations, and for decades was judged a sort of Manifesto of Evangelical Christianity, he objects strongly that religion is too frequently " suffered to dwindle into a mere matter of police."[1] But " to the real Christian," he bluntly affirms, " the doctrines of the Gospel constitute the centre to which he gravitates ! " They are " the very sun of his system ! —the soul of the world !—the origin of all that is excellent and lovely !—the source of light and life and motion and genial warmth and plastic energy ! " " Dim," says Wilberfore, " is the light of reason, and cold and comfortless our state, while left to her unassisted guidance."[2] Again, the directing power of his religious convictions over his public life, is clearly expressed in a letter to his mother :

" It is not, believe me, to any imagination, or to any system formed in my closet that I look for my principles ; it is to the very source to which you refer me, the Scriptures. . . . All that I contend for is that we should really make this Book the criterion of our opinions and actions. . . . Some men are thrown into public life, some have their lot in private life. . . . What I have said will, I hope, be sufficient to remove any apprehensions that I mean to shut myself up in my closet in town, or in my hermitage in the country. No, my dear mother, in my circumstances this would merit no better name than desertion ; and if I were thus trying to fly from the post where Providence has placed me, I know not how I could look for the blessing of God upon my retirement, and without this heavenly assistance, either in the world or in solitude, our own endeavours will be equally ineffectual."[3]

How thoroughgoing was Wilberforce's sense of stewardship and how deep his generosity, are illustrated by the fact that in 1801, a year of dire necessity and unemployment, his " gifts to the poor " were of such proportions that, when he came to take stock, he found they had exceeded his entire income " by £3,000."[4] That, of course, could not long continue ; but he

---

[1] Wilberforce, *op. cit.*, p. 1.
[2] *Ibid.*, p. 24.
[3] Buxton's *Wilberforce*, p. 41. This book, written by a man who for many years was Secretary of the Anti-Slavery Society, is essential, along with Coupland's, to an understanding of Wilberforce. The original tomes executed by Wilberforce's sons are a tomb in which their father lies embalmed.
[4] Coupland, *op. cit.*, pp. 265 and 43.

disposed of property, eliminated luxuries, lived simply, and besides manifold and generous benefactions to scores of causes at home and abroad, rarely did he give less than a quarter of his income to the poor. To Hannah More's schools, for years he subscribed £400 per annum. With two friends, he provided an annuity for Charles Wesley's widow; and to hundreds of Lascars stranded around the London Docks, his purse was never closed.[1] In old age, Wilberforce lost nearly all his means: but refusing the proffered help of six friends who wanted to replenish his loss, he said good-bye to his beloved little estate and went to live alternately with two of his parson sons, where, he believed, God prolonged his life to show him "that a man can be as happy without a fortune as with one."[2]

To certain of the wilder Radicals, notwithstanding, this man was "an ugly epitome of the devil" whose "grandiose humanity" was all expended upon "fat, lazy niggers" overseas, while Englishmen were "enslaved" or "starved" at home: he was a "ranting hypocrite" whose religion was a "hollow sham." Cobbett, who had no sympathy whatever with the African "niggers," who lauded bull-baiting, prize-fighting and the like as "manly sports," who aggressively encouraged the "rotten-egging" of "Methodists," and whom even Place pronounced a "mountebank," always had Wilberforce in the pillory of his *Political Register*. "If all that was published about me was true," said "the saint" as early as 1816, "nothing but a special Providence can have prevented me being hanged thirty years ago."[3]

Wilberforce however was but typical of that remarkable group of men historically remembered as "The Clapham Sect." So dubbed by Sydney Smith, because many of them lived around Clapham Common, and because their chief haunt was the spacious, Chatham-designed library of Henry Thornton, in Clapham, this group included statesmen and men of affairs, whose daily contacts extended to the ends of the earth. Among them were a Governor-General of India, a Chairman of the East India Company, the "King" of the Colonial Office, several Members of Parliament, a Governor of Sierra Leone, the head of a great banking house, and philanthropists and publicists, whose ceaseless, sacrificial labours benefited millions of their fellow men. Among them were Anglicans, Nonconformists and Quakers; Conservatives, Liberals and Indepen-

---

[1] Coupland, pp. 42-3 and 377.
[2] *Ibid.*, p. 507.
[3] Coupland, pp. 456 and 421-2. For Cobbett's poisonous venom against the Abolitionists and his smug praise of slave-owning planters who had just pulled down a Methodist Chapel in Barbados, see *Political Register*, Vol. XLVIII, pp. 514, 559, 583, 591, 673, 677, and Vol. XLIX, pp. 31, 34.

dents. Their common bond was Evangelical Christianity and their common " enthusiasm " the application of the ethic of Christ to personal, social, political, national and international affairs. None of them claimed to be theologians ; nearly all were laymen ; but all were Bible students, and men of prayer ; all accounted themselves stewards and missioners of the Kingdom of God ; and all devoted themselves with amazing initiative to the practical application of the Faith they professed. Something altogether new to the British Empire, was this coterie of powerful Christian statesmen and philanthropists, giving so freely of their time, talents and means, that public life might be Christianised, and that the very Empire might become an instrument of moral and social welfare to all peoples. Most of the " Clapham brethren " were members of the Church of England ; all, being fervent Evangelicals, were Protestants : but the most amazing feature of their lives, was the true Catholicity of their Christian sympathy, and of their humanitarian crusade. The Clapham Sect was directing influences which ennobled the life of coloured and primitive peoples the world over, before ever " an Evangelical " was elevated to the Episcopal Bench : and were it not for the influence of such " lay saints," Evangelical Christianity might have been quite cold-shouldered from the National Church.

A business man's ledger affords a revealing commentary on his mode of life. Many years after his death, a granddaughter of Henry Thornton, the banker, published figures from his accounts which show that, during the years 1790 to 1793, he gave to charity no less a sum than £20,408, while his total expenditures for *all* other purposes whatsoever, were but £6,964. On different years, before his marriage, Thornton consistently gave away as much as six-sevenths of his entire income ;[1] and such devotion was but characteristic of all the Clapham " brethren." Granville Sharp, though " too poor for a Parliamentary career," gave lavishly of his time, talents and means in the negroes' cause. Zachary Macaulay faced fever and bore labours sufficient to kill half a dozen ordinary mortals, in establishing the freed-slave colony at Sierra Leone ; while later, he laboured for years without pay, as editor of the famous Evangelical magazine, the *Christian Observer*. James Stephen turned his back on a most brilliant and lucrative career as " advocate in prize cases before the Privy Council " to serve quietly as Under-Secretary for the Colonies—a post later occupied with equal distinction and devotion by his son, Sir James. The consecration of Clarkson's life, was equal to that of Wilberforce. As for other members of this " Christian Brotherhood," they

[1] See *Guardian*, June 19th, 1907 ; Balleine, p. 149 ; Coupland, p. 251.

included Lords Teignmouth and Glenelg, Charles Grant, William Smith, John Venn and Edward Elliot, together with Gisborne, Milner, Babington and Bowdler; while for all practical purposes, Hannah More also was a member of the " Sect." All regarded their vocations as sacred " callings " ; all conceived their time, abilities and possessions, as naught else than stewardships held in trust for the God of Righteousness—the Lord of Heaven and Earth.

The " Clapham Sect " rose splendidly above the ordinary barriers of party, class, creed, colour and nationality. Inspired by a common faith, humanitarian and philanthropic questions, they saw with a single eye; and concerning them they spoke with a single voice. No exclusive, theoretic pietists, were these " lay saints " ; in projects which they believed for the common good, they would, and did, co-operate with Catholics, Unitarians and Utilitarians. In Parliament, their influence was out of all proportion to their numbers. Into the whole Indian and Colonial Administration they injected a new moral leaven, conceiving of the Overseas Empire not as a vast gold mine for British exploitation, but as a solemn, sacred trust to be developed for the highest good of the different peoples concerned. At home, they furthered schemes of education and self-help among the poor; abroad, they created and sponsored missions of a highly practical mould, especially in the most savage and benighted communities. Everywhere they stood for honourable peace and co-operation among all peoples of goodwill.

Whatever the limitations of the Clapham fraternity, this Christian coterie, in proportion to numbers, achieved perhaps more than any other group in English history to impregnate the British Empire and British policy with Christian ideals of service and helpfulness, particularly as they applied to backward and underprivileged peoples, who, up to this time, were being exploited and enslaved by vast mercenary interests for sordidly selfish ends. Paine, Place, Cobbett, Hazlitt, Hunt and company, would, of course, continue to rail at them as arch-hypocrites and master-pharisees : but the concentrated fury of the assault, attested the wide influence " the saints " were exerting over the soul and conscience of the realm.

(iv) *The Wider Impact*

If, however, Wilberforce was but intensely characteristic of the Clapham Sect, that Christian brotherhood, in turn, was but intensely characteristic of a new moral and spiritual earnestness which affected not only the tone and temper of the entire English-speaking world, but, spreading through the English tongue and through a purged and invigorated Anglo-Saxon civilisation, brought hope and blessing to peoples of many tongues and climes. The Evangelical Revival, despite the surge of many materialising forces, was making the Gospel of Christ a new and highly pervasive leaven, not only in the life of individual men and women, but in the world of practical affairs. Like early Christianity, it had begun chiefly among the outcasts of society ; it now was impregnating the lives of men governing nations and leading world-stirring crusades. Even royalty, would one day experience its power.

Turn first to the realm of poetry. Can anyone even half-familiar with the teachings and impact of the Evangelical Movement, fail to recognise in the most soulful poems of Cowper and Blake, of Crabbe and Burns, of Wordsworth and Coleridge of Southey and Hood, of Browning and Tennyson, of Whittier and Bryant, of Longfellow and Elizabeth Barrett Browning, or even of Kipling and Masefield, the permeating influence of that mighty re-creation of soul and conscience ? In prose literature, the impress is scarcely less pronounced. The pages of Hannah More and Harriet Beecher Stowe, of Scott and Reade, of Ruskin and Carlyle, of Irving and Hawthorne, of Dickens and Thackeray, of Jane Austen and the Brontë sisters, of Emerson and Stevenson, of Macaulay and Green, of Besant and Stead, of Drummond and Helen Keller—all owe much to the same purging and ennobling source. Some of these authors, admittedly, were girded when they knew it not : but their sincere reverence for purity, truth, temperance, virtue, integrity, justice, honour, bravery, liberty and the quest for righteousness (individual and social) marks them as men and women whose ideal of life was largely coloured or shaped by the " plain, vital, practical Christianity " which Wesley had preached and lived, and which he had mediated to the multitudes. Their appreciation of spiritual values, moreover, their knowledge of the Bible, their belief in prayer, their homage to sterling character, and, above all, their unswerving faith in the high Destiny of man, separates them by a wide gulf from the " post-war " shoal of morbid " realists," whose sex obsession, moral cynicism, spiritual defeatism and utter futility, plunging their whining and snivelling course through dirt, despair and death, succeed only in deleting all manliness from man and obscuring all purpose in life. From these " emancipated " worldlings, comes the illuminating verdict that : " Man is a parasite, crawling on the vertebræ of the pigmy among the planets."[1] To them and to their set, Wesley and all his followers were simply fools.

---

[1] This is the dictum of a smart American " intellectual," whose name matters not. He is but a little bolder than hundreds of English and American novelists who suggest a similar " philosophy of life."

U

Turn next to the immortal social emancipators of modern times. Wilberforce and Clarkson we have already mentioned. Peruse the lives and labours of Lord Shaftesbury and Abraham Lincoln, of John Howard and Fowell Buxton, of Elizabeth Fry and Florence Nightingale.[1] and soon it becomes evident that the Evangelical Revival stands to them in the direct relation of cause and effect. Shaftesbury, who constantly described himself as " an Evangelical of Evangelicals," when pressing in the House of Commons for the emancipation of women and children from " white slavery " in the mines and collieries of Britain, declared : " For my own part I will say, though possibly I may be charged with cant and hypocrisy, that I have been bold enough to undertake this task, because I must regard the objects of it as being created, like ourselves, by the same Master, redeemed by the same Saviour, and destined to the same immortality."[2] Words of similar import, might be quoted from the mouths of every one of these heroic liberators of men. The depth, sincerity and intensity of their Christian Faith, made them the doughty emancipators they were.

Proceed, however, to other creative crusaders and pioneers in the sphere of social achievement, and the story is much of of a piece. Live awhile with the careers of Barnardo and Booth, of J. B. Gough and Frances Willard, of Oastler and Plimsoll, of Stephens and Loveless, of Orsman and Kirk,[3] of Toynbee and Jane Addams, of Agnes Weston and Evangeline Booth, and quickly the truth emerges that the source of their vision and the dynamic of their efforts was vital, practical Christianity. Radicals would spin out plausible social theories, and sacerdotalists would argue much concerning religious ceremonies, sacred symbolism, " Apostolical Succession " and patristic orthodoxy ; but the very faith of sincere Evangelical Christians constrained them to put their hand to the plough, and to cultivate the vineyard of the Lord. The first article of Dr. Barnardo's will reads : " Death and the grave are but temporary bonds ; Christ has triumphed over them ! I hope to die as I have lived, in the humble but assured faith of Jesus Christ, Whom I have so imperfectly served, and Whom I acknowledge to be my

---

[1] Even the brilliant—sometimes satirical—paradoxes of Lytton Strachey do not remove the religious dynamic from Florence Nightingale's life. See his *Eminent Victorians*, pp. 115–175. See, too, Sir E. Cook's *Life of Florence Nightingale*.

[2] See Hansard (H. of C.), August 4th, 1840 ; Shaftesbury's *Speeches*, p. 28 ; Bready's *Shaftesbury*, p. 269.

[3] Orsman and Sir John Kirk are but typical of many thousands of Evangelical zealots who, in all the great industrial centres of Britain, have served the poor through the Ragged School Union. They symbolise, too, thousands who to-day are serving under " The Shaftesbury Society "—the new name of that organisation.

Saviour, my Master and my King."[1]   Herein is reflected the central inspiration behind the truest tradition of philanthropy and social reform among the English-speaking peoples. These intrepid pioneers, beholding in faith a better country, laboured for a society which hath foundations, whose maker and builder is God. Believing themselves to be surrounded by a great cloud of spiritual witnesses, and enduring as seeing Him Who is invisible, they sought to save their fellows because they knew themselves saved by Christ. They lived heroically, adventurously, gloriously on Earth, because their abiding citizenship was in Heaven. The social fruits of their lives, were nourished by the deep roots of their faith.

Again, the mighty nineteenth century preaching tradition throughout the British Empire and the United States, drank deeply from the same fountain head. Moody and Spurgeon, Beecher and Brooks, Chalmers and Guthrie, Robertson and Dale, Westcott and Ryle,[2] Talmage and White, Hughes and Jowett, Parker and Cadman—all were mighty expository preachers of the Bible, which the Evangelical Revival had not only opened to the multitudes but had made the Book of Books to the Anglo-Saxon peoples. All, too, were fired by a consuming passion to mediate Christ not only as the Saviour of individual men and women, but as the Saviour of the world. Even Newman and Keble, owed more to the Evangelical Revival than is generally imagined. In his *Apologia* Newman pronounces Thomas Scott, author of the famous Evangelical *Commentary*, " the writer who made a deeper impression on my mind than any other, and to whom, humanly speaking, I owe my soul."[3]   And Hurrell Froude, the eager disciple of Keble who captured Newman for the Tractarian Movement, scented " Methodism " in his spiritual father's *Christian Year*.

Come next to the splendid world missionary efforts of Protestantism. Not only are Coke and Asbury, Carey and Livingstone, Moffat and Martyn, Morrison and Paton, Johnson of Sierra Leone and Smith of the West Indies, Alexander MacKay and Mary Slessor inextricably associated with this mighty outpouring of spiritual power, but the whole Protestant " world movement," with its great succession of foreign missionary societies, is a lineal descendant of the Evangelical Revival. Or proceed to the pioneers of popular education, and once more

[1] See the author's *Dr. Barnardo*, p. 259.
[2] If Bishop Ryle is little heard of to-day, it should be remembered that his religious tracts once sold in millions, and were translated into twelve languages. Ruskin said of them : " The pleasantest and most useful reading I know, on nearly all religious questions whatever, are Ryle's tracts." See letter quoted in *Churchman*, July, 1900 ; also Balleine, p. 279.
[3] Cardinal Newman, *Apologia pro Vita Sua* (chapter I).

the far-reaching impact of this baptism of fire is unmistakable. Hannah Ball and Silas Told, Whitefield,[1] and the American Tennents, Raikes and Lancaster, Lucas and Bell, Hogg and Williams, Arnold and Ryerson,[2] Mott and Kagawa, are all children of the same spiritual succession, confessing constantly the lordship of Christ. Their educational efforts, indeed, grew out of their vision of the Kingdom of God on earth. Nor even on the hard and stony ground of statecraft and public affairs, is this soulful succession quite broken. Pitt and Burke were better men because of the character influences it shed abroad. But consider the lives of Perceval and Liverpool, Queen Victoria and the Prince Consort, Gordon and Lawrence, Gladstone[3] and Bright, Keir Hardie and Arthur Henderson, Woodrow Wilson and Theodore Roosevelt, or again of Mr. Lloyd George and Lord Baldwin, and it will be found that the powerful influence of that Spiritual Baptism has been branded deeply upon their lives. It is fatally easy to satirise Queen Victoria's famous message to two African chiefs : " England has become great and happy by the knowledge of the true God and Jesus Christ."[4] Yet even the very partial application of that knowledge, has been the saving salt not only of England, but of the British Empire and English-speaking realms.

Some of the more creative and far-reaching *Movements* which flowed from this amazing outpouring of soul power, we shall examine in succeeding chapters. Meantime, we pause to consider certain of the attacks commonly levelled against Wesley and the mighty Revival so closely connected with his life's work.

[1] The influence of Whitefield as a promoter of education in America, is too little known. See Belden's *Whitefield*, pp. 236–8.
[2] Egerton Ryerson, a Methodist minister, was the virtual founder of popular education in Canada. See Chapter XXIII, Section (ii).
[3] Though Gladstone was a Liberal High Churchman, the marks of the Evangelical Revival were written indelibly upon his life, and Evangelical Nonconformity rendered him mighty support.
[4] J. T. Inskip, *op. cit.*, p. 200.

THE PERENNIAL CRITIC

" From scheme and creed the light goes out,
  The saintly fact survives ;
  The blessed Master none can doubt,
  Revealed in holy lives."

(See Professor FRANCIS PEABODY,
  The Christian Life in the Modern World, p. 199.)

" He that loveth his brother abideth in light, and
there is none occasion of stumbling in him."

1 *John* ii, 10

THE PERENNIAL CRITIC

CAPTAINS and conquerors commonly depart this world leaving but " a little dust," while kings and emperors are remembered only by " a dubious legend of their reign " ; but the greatest seers, prophets and spiritual leaders, by making men vitally conscious of their divine origin, and by causing the deeps within them to respond to the Deeps Eternal, release soul forces and create movements which abide : for, transcending the ravages of time, and triumphing over the dead weight of materialism, cynicism and inertia, they incarnate the divine fire and the latent grandeur of man's imperishable soul. They make men to feel and know that they are not puppets of fate, created only to be resolved to dust, but rather that they have a high destiny to achieve ; and greatest of all, they open to them the springs of faith, vision and courage which, despite all temporary rebuffs, enable them ever to labour steadfastly for the attainment of that High Destiny.

That Wesley and the Evangelical Revival represent such undying spiritual forces, is surely beyond dispute. Yet, for obvious reasons, they are easy targets of ridicule and attack. Their initial appeal having been chiefly to the outcast and the untutored, they not unreasonably fostered various self-imposed inhibitions and disciplines ; indeed such, during the early stages of the Revival, proved quite indispensable. But also they laid down rules and precedents, not a few of which were designed to apply only to immediate and particular situations. And, being human, they of course made mistakes : while furthermore, as so often happens in human affairs, rules and inhibitions, codes and precedents, organisations and ceremonies tended too frequently to assume a sanctity rightly belonging only to the living Spirit of Truth. Nevertheless, beneath and above all that was sporadic, impulsive, incidental and transitory, there continued to be manifested the pulsing power of the Eternal, which created and mediated abundant life.

(i) *Recreation, Education, Emotion*

Perhaps the fiercest of all stock attacks upon Wesley, has been aimed at his attitude toward amusement and sport. Repeatedly has it been contended that he was intolerant of all recreation. This at best is but a half-truth; for only can we appreciate his attitude when we recall the nature of the then prevailing popular " sports " and inquire candidly whether " cocking," bear, bull and badger-baiting, bare-fisted prize-fighting, smutty comedy, fakir-ridden and prostitute-infested fairs, drinking bouts and innumerable gambling games, could make any possible contribution toward the " abundant life " he sought to mediate to needy men. Were such diversions capable of " re-creating " spiritual, mental or physical health? True, he prohibited all games at his Kingswood School, but it was planted in the midst of what, before his efforts, was one of the roughest collier districts in England; and practically the only " games " which the youngsters knew how to play were coarse, crude and bullying. Then, too, he retained haunting memories of his own residence at Charterhouse School, where the chief " games " and " sports " of the larger boys were hounding, beating and half starving the smaller, and especially the more sensitive, lads. This, undoubtedly, was his reason for the Kingswood rule that the pupils always must be under the inspection of a master. For he knew from bitter personal experience what crass, bullying tyrants some unimaginative and insensitive school-boys can be; and at that time bullying in many forms was rife. But if all sport was prohibited at Kingswood, if discipline was far too stern and the days were much too crammed with lessons and routine, at least it should be recalled that the curriculum was anything but monotonous. Indeed, it was decidedly too diversified, and such recreating exercises as singing, gardening and walking were part of the daily round. Wesley, too, was personally very fond of riding, swimming and the observation of natural phenomena : and such organised, co-operative games as present-day football, cricket, hockey, lacrosse, basket-ball and baseball, it must be remembered, were quite unknown in the England of his day.

Wesley's *Journal*, moreover, provides inescapable evidence that he was by no means opposed to such clean, innocent diversions as sharpen the wit, quicken the mind, renew the spirit and strengthen the body. He rejoiced greatly at the singing performances of the children in his numerous Sunday schools; he recorded the pleasure afforded him on hearing different concerts given by his highly talented nephews ; and after attending a students' dramatic performance at Westminster School he wrote : " I saw the Westminster scholars act the *Adelphi* of Terence, an entertainment not unworthy of a Christian. Oh, how do these heathens shame us ! Their very comedies contain both excellent sense, the liveliest pictures of men and manner, and so fine strokes of genuine morality as are seldom found in the writings of Christians."[1] Are these the judgments of one opposed to all recreations ? Do they smack of the persistent " joy-killer," or the proverbial " prophet of gloom " ? Admittedly, Wesley had no sympathy with " time-killing " sports ; for time to him, as much as money, was a precious talent and a sacred trust. Neither would he encourage children's " games " which pandered to mob brutality or savoured of hooliganism. But of his great love for children and their sincere love for him, there can be no room for doubt ; and Curnock, in his notes to the Standard Edition of the *Journal*, does well to point that fact. Often large bands of children flocked forth to meet Wesley as he entered their town. Commonly, as he preached in the open air, groups of youngsters were to be seen perched on walls, or on the stouter branches of overhanging trees, and the simple, direct vividness of his message frequently went straight to their hearts. Contemporaries, too, have left touching impressions of how Wesley would take the smaller children tenderly in his arms and kiss and bless them ; while always he was greatly delighted to see them clean, neat, courteous and happy.

Commonly has it been stated or inferred that Wesley expressly *prohibited* his followers from all association with amusements, entertainments and sports. This is an unwarranted assumption. Moral and spiritual values, admittedly, always coloured his outlook, and certainly he took pains to explain to his people the evil influences so generally associated with the prevailing " pass-times " of his day. But never did he anathematise all lighter diversions as harmful in themselves. His actual prohibition was that his followers " cannot join in or countenance any diversion, which has the least tendency to vice of any kind."[2] " A Methodist," he insisted, " cannot even follow a multitude to do evil." The use of intoxicating liquors, as a beverage, he did prohibit because of their iniquitous personal, family and social effects. All betting and gambling amusements he proscribed, because they excited an anti-social and immoral desire to get something for nothing, and because frequently they robbed children of bread. Cock-fighting, bear-baiting and the

[1] *Journal*, December 14th, 1768.
[2] Wesley, *Character of a Methodist*, p. 10.

ilk he tabooed, not only in consequence of their brutalising effect on human character, but because of their cruelty to dumb animals, toward which—different from many of the contemporary political agitators—he taught his followers always to show mercy and kindness. Toward diversions in general, his converts were free to follow the dictates of conscience. But the awakened conscience of this " peculiar people " was highly sensitised. Many of Cobbett's " manly sports " were as revolting to them as were gladiatorial " games " to the early Christians. " What doest thou here, Elijah ? " was to them an interrogation written large on the whole eighteenth-century arena of " popular " amusement and sport.

Wesley certainly would not have discouraged clean, wholesome, re-creating diversions. He himself delighted in the open spaces, the vernal woods and the beauties of nature, and he taught his people to delight in them. But they all were enlisted in a crusade incomparably more thorough-going and more truly revolutionary than the reformation of sport. Far better, Wesley mediated spiritual forces which re-created the inner being ; he set his followers singing at their work ; he made familiar " the medicine of a merry heart." Aye, more ! He opened to his people the windows of heaven, and let in a flood of healing and transforming light ; he made even the most arduous and prosaic toil to assume a sacred dignity and purpose ; he linked men and women into such human fellowship as was to them a veritable paradise on earth ; he enabled scores of thousands of humble, hard-working " Methodists " to find more exhilaration and truer " recreation " in their daily duties and their Christian service, than soft, cynical, pampered idlers found in their " time-killing " play. If the Methodists and Evangelicals gave little time to sport, time, assuredly, never " hung " on their hands. Pre-eminently were they a busy and a happy people. Their high and holy " Enthusiasm " was not born of gloom ; rather was it the child of vision, energy and ecstasy. Constantly by scoffers were these enthusiasts dubbed " fool optimists " : yet, perchance, even their foolishness was wiser than the wisdom of most of their critics. Certainly, out of their poverty, they raised such voluntary funds for spiritual work, as England never before had known.

Again, repeatedly it has been objected that Wesley and the Movement he guided were hyper-emotional and manifested a sublime disregard for " higher " education. As this is a criticism lurking usually in the tail of a hazy and generalised interpretation of the Revival, by those who have never deigned to study the documentary evidence involved, it would be well for such as harp on it to pause and ask themselves a few questions. If Wesley were averse to higher education, why was he made a fellow of Lincoln College? Why did he spend some thirteen years at Oxford?—most of them in the capacity of a resident don. If suspicious of broad learning, why did he take pains to write grammars in five languages—not to mention histories and other texts—for his Kingswood seminary? Why did he insist upon his itinerant preachers spending five to eight hours every day in concentrated study? Why did he inform his local preachers that the only means whereby they could strengthen and deepen their sermons, was the mastery of deep, difficult books? Why was he himself a prodigious reader of the widest range?[1] Why was he concerned to study the works of men so diametrically opposite to his outlook as Gibbon, Smollett, Dryden, Pope, Machiavelli, Mandeville, Rousseau and Voltaire? Why so frequently and so approvingly did he quote from the classics? Why did he read all the literature he could find on electricity, and become a student of medical writings? These scarcely are the marks of one opposed to higher education. In sympathy, charity and regard for rugged honesty, Wesley was a man of truly Catholic mind. Of all persecuting instinct he was completely free; and Marcus Aurelius he believed certain of a place in heaven, whereas multitudes of professing Christians would be shut out. His Protestantism, however, protested vehemently against all priestly domination of the individual conscience, and at many points he can only be described as a Christian rationalist, for his faith, he emphasised, required him to believe nothing which could do violence to his God-given reason; while a similarly rational religious attitude he commended to all his followers. Wesley was a logician to the bone, and reason he never would decry. Whence then sprang the popular misconception in question?

Its source, located in contemporary circumstances, is not difficult to trace. Deistic rationalism in the eighteenth century —like Gnosticism in the first century and materialistic Secularism in the twentieth—was putting on intellectual airs. Humility it had quite disowned, and the self-hypnotism of pride, arrogance and conceit were carrying it to ridiculous lengths; it was intoxicated with the heady wine of its assumed superior sagacity. As Butler complained, Christianity no longer was considered a subject even worthy of inquiry; rather was it assumed to be "fictitious." And just here was Wesley's quarrel with the then current trend of "higher education." Much of it he believed a stilted and sterile process, offering stones for bread. Faith

---

[1] The number of books referred to and criticised in Wesley's *Journal* is quite remarkable.

and revelation being sneered out of court, and frigid, isolated reason being elevated into a heartless deity, a false antithesis was established whereby the rational faculty was severed from other human faculties necessary to the upbuilding and sustaining of a healthy, coherent, harmonious personality.[1] Religion, therefore, which to Wesley was the " supreme synthesis " of all true life, and which found incarnate expression in the person of Christ, was discounted or cast aside, while to the hungry souls of floundering men Deistic rationalism offered but a barren, intellectual husk.

Far, then, from opposing higher education, Wesley strongly favoured it, but he saw clearly that extended education divorced from Christian ethics and from spiritual values was really not " higher " at all, but " lower "; for he perceived the latent powers of evil with which its materialism was fraught. To Wesley all " man-discovered " truth was equally " God-revealed " truth. He was wholly sceptical of the growing economic and " scientific " doctrine of " enlightened self-interest."[2] Though he desired not less higher-education but vastly more, he insisted that it be really " higher," for he held to the truly Catholic doctrine that all knowledge and science should be tempered by a social, ethical, spiritual solvent—religious love—which alone, he believed, can refine knowledge into wisdom and provide the key to understanding. " To what purpose ? " was the question Wesley would ask of all education. And it is notable that since his day the students, the world over, who have received higher or professional education in institutions founded, financed and directed by his followers, can be numbered only in hundreds of thousands.

Nevertheless, the sort of Deistic rationalism against which Wesley revolted dies hard. When, seventeen years ago, the present writer began his social researches into this period, neither the library of University College, nor that of King's College, of the University of London, contained even a volume of Wesley's *Journal*—or any other publication from his hand. The *literati* of his time, the politicians, the economists, the radicals, the Encyclopædists, the " philosophers " of the French Revolution and the Utilitarians were all amply represented and allowed to speak for themselves. The man who restored to a nation its soul, and started a Movement which has brought blessing to tens of millions of people in many lands, was allowed

---

[1] See Professor Fred Tracy's *Broken Lights*, chapters viii and x.
[2] This was the essence of the *laissez-faire* theory, which increasingly, even from Restoration times, was becoming the accepted economic gospel. Adam Smith's *Wealth of Nations* (1776), far from creating *laissez-faire*, modified at many points its cruder expressions.

no word on his own behalf. Wesley at least read the works of those he criticised. Moreover, are not our *Universities* supposed to implant a *universal* respect for Truth? One is here reminded of the protest of a great Minister of Education, Augustine Birrell : " Our standard historians," he complains, " have dismissed him curtly ; the fact is, Wesley puts your ordinary historian out of conceit with himself."[1] But if this is true of many historians, is it not more true of many tutors, lecturers and professors who, guarding jealously the scientific, economic or psychological deities of their own design, desire no " religious fanatic " to disturb the spell of the doctrinaire creeds they propound ?

As for emotionalism, often has it been charged that Wesley turned the balance from the intellectual to the emotional side of Christianity. This criticism is aptly answered by Dr. Parkes Cadman. What Wesley " really did," says Cadman, " was to demonstrate the values of spiritual experience to such a degree that *philosophy was compelled to acknowledge them.* That he did this unwittingly does not detract from its importance, and the latest modern thought has confessed that this movement re-enthroned a religious consciousness which must be recognised and respected."[2] Wesley's real conflict was with the frigidly non-moral and non-spiritual assumptions of a Deistic and pagan rationalism.

(ii) *Further Attacks*

Another perennial thrust at Wesley and the Evangelicals, is that they were ultra-conservative and credulous. And at certain points this judgment must stand. In his attitude toward kingship, as we have seen, and in his *Calm Address to our American Colonies,*[3] Wesley undoubtedly was ultra-conservative ; while also his habitual desire to discover and develop the best in people, made him at times unduly credulous. Yet, this being fully admitted, in certain other respects he was a dauntless radical. In his trenchant attacks upon slavery and the mercenary liquor traffic, in his withering condemnation of war as a final " settlement " of international disputes, in his denunciation of the Government's policy in Ireland and of its system of press gangs ; in his proposals regarding the leasing of land, the taxing of gentlemen's horses, and the restriction of luxuries ; in his revolt against the scandalous tautology of legal documents

[1] See Birrell's *Appreciation*, prefaced to Parker's abridgement of Wesley's *Journal*, p. xv.
[2] S. P. Cadman, *Three Religious Leaders of Oxford*, p. 375. On this subject see also Wm. James's *Varieties of Religious Experience*.
[3] See Chapter XII, (ii).

and his broadsides against bribery, smuggling and political corruption ; in his exposure of prevalent economic shibboleths and his castigation of pluralities and sinecures ; in his abhorrence of " gentlemanly " idleness, his teaching regarding the use of wealth, time, property and privilege, together with his onslaughts upon vested interests in social iniquity—in *all* these matters, his moral and religious convictions made him (despite his theory of Government and his warm patriotism) a progressive radical, far in advance of his age, and, at some points, far in advance of his modern critics.

Moreover, as for his itinerant lieutenants and local preachers, including such of his spiritual " grand-children " as Oastler, Stephens, Wood, Sadler, Brotherton, Loveless and Standfield, some were considered so " dangerous " that they were pilloried, imprisoned, kidnapped by army press gangs, or even transported ;[1] while others laboured under the continual suspicion of the Home Office. And it is a revealing fact that when, in 1818, Parliament voted £1,000,000 for the building of State churches, that expenditure was designed, at least in part, to wean the industrial population from the " too-radical " influence of " Methodism " and its increasingly co-related forms of Dissent. As early, indeed, as 1792, the Mayor of Liverpool wrote to the Home Office enforcing this argument ; Arthur Young in his *Inquiry into the State of Mind among the Lower Classes* (1798) strongly re-enforced it ; and certainly the Government's expenditure for the new churches was defended, both in and out of Parliament, on this very ground.[2]

The charge again has been hurled against Wesley, as against most mighty leaders, that his colossal labours were motivated by personal ambition and a lust for power. This is the insidious kind of attack so easily made without proof, and depending entirely upon the insinuations and assumptions of innuendo, for effect. Of all Wesley's biographers, Southey, in this respect, is most blameworthy. Repeatedly he hints at Wesley's inordinate ambition and his thirst for power, yet never does he substantiate his inference. Indeed, it seems certain that he is but reflecting, however unconsciously, a deeply-rooted prejudice of his time and class. Greatly is it to Southey's credit, nevertheless, that, years after the publication of his *Wesley,* he frankly admitted

[1] For the story of Loveless and his fellow Tolpuddle " martyrs," see Owen Rattenbury's *Flame of Freedom* (1931).

[2] Young's *Inquiry* stimulated existing official anxiety. The Napoleonic wars, in turn, augmented it ; so by 1818 it was not difficult to pass this Church Building Bill. The most Radical group of Methodists were the Primitive Methodists, who, under the leadership of Hugh Bourne and William Clowes, broke from the " Wesleyans " in 1810. They were avowed Democrats.

he had been wrong. The cause of his reversal of judgment was an essay by Alexander Knox, an intimate friend, but in no sense a follower, of Wesley.[1] After pondering this essay, Southey wrote : " A long and intimate paper has convinced me that I was mistaken in supposing ambition entered largely into Wesley's actuating impulses."[2] " In estimating John Wesley," says Knox, " I am not conscious of any partiality. For his singularities as a public teacher I had no predilection. I loved and revered him for his cheerful piety, his resistless amiability and his perfect superiority to every vulgar feeling and selfish motive. . . . My conviction is that he never consciously swerved from what he considered his ' heavenly calling.' "[3] At other points Knox, notwithstanding his High Church outlook, is equally emphatic. " Where the highest interests of men were concerned, Mr. Wesley," he affirms, " made no account of precedent, or public opinion, or maxims of human or even ecclesiastical prudence. The Church of England appeared to him to have fallen into a state of stupor like that of the ancient Jewish Church ; and it was his persuasion that a kind of second John the Baptist, ' a voice crying in the wilderness,' was necessary to awaken it ; to this duty he conceived himself providentially called, and he engaged in it with as firm a purpose as if he had been commissioned by a voice from heaven."[4] Regarding " pride, ambition, selfishness and personal gratification of whatever kind," Knox records it as his " deep impression " that " since the days of the Apostles there has not been a human being more thoroughly exempt from all those frailties of human nature than John Wesley."[5]

Numerous other aspersions have been cast at Wesley. Commonly it is averred, or assumed, that he was devoid of any grain of saving humour ; that the phenomenal physical manifestations frequently accompanying his preaching were nothing other than fanatical hysteria, and that his famous *Primitive Physic* represented sheer medical quackery. Now if the charge that Wesley lacked humour means that he was not a comedian, striving sardonically to stimulate jocularity, it assuredly is well founded. Too profoundly was he in earnest, to treat serious problems facetiously or to seek out causes of mirth ; but he had an all-embracing interest in human affairs, and whenever he was confronted with a situation either amusing or preposterous, he

---

[1] Knox for a very brief period had been attracted towards " Methodism," but his instincts were all in the High Church direction, and he became a sort of forerunner of the Oxford Movement.
[2] See Appendix to the 1903 abridgment of Southey's *Wesley* (p. 394).
[3] *Ibid.*, p. 365
[4] *Ibid.*, p. 370.
[5] J. H. Overton, *John Wesley*, p. 91.

was by no means immune from humorous response. Indeed, contrariwise he often revealed a wit that was spontaneous, playful and sharp. Some of his keenest satires are close akin to humour, and his *Journal* affords innumerable instances of a dry, droll, donnish pleasantry of mind. He refers, for instance, to a certain " gentleman " trying to create confusion at one of his preaching services, as hailing from " another parish " and *therefore* under no obligations of civility or courtesy. Recalling the outrages of a certain drunken rabble, he inquires what their victims had done to deserve such furious onslaughts, and dryly he answers : " Why, they were mad ; they were Methodists. So to bring them to their senses," the mob " would beat their brains out."[1] The biographer of St. Catherine, he says, " *aggrandised* her into a mere idiot," making her " a fool of a saint."[2] Or picture a congregation of " two or three thousand people " listening " as for life," and note Wesley's delineation of a certain individual therein : " Only one big man, exceeding drunk, was very noisy and turbulent, till his wife seized him by the collar, gave him two or three hearty boxes on the ear, and dragged him away like a calf. But at length he got out of her hands, crept in among the people, and stood as quiet as a lamb."[3] Was the narrator of this incident devoid of humour ? Recall, too, his comment when informed that he may no more minister at Newgate Prison : he is kept from preaching at Bedlam, he sagely surmises, " lest he drive the inmates mad," and at Newgate " lest he make them wicked." Or finally, having declared that in Ireland fashion had " almost " as much to do " with medicine as with head-dress," he avers that, " Now the grand fashionable medicine for twenty diseases is *mercury sublimate* ! " and continues : " Why is it not a halter or a pistol ? They would *cure* a little more speedily ! "[4]

The " fits of hysteria " which at times accompanied Wesley's preaching must be viewed in relation to their environment. Constantly must it be remembered, that he was instrumental in effecting thousands of lasting conversions among notorious sinners. The inner change accordingly which took place in the lives of those who once had been drunkards, robbers, blasphemers, adulterers, fornicators and scandalmongers, can only be described as catastrophic. Is it surprising then, that catastrophic phenomena frequently accompanied the release of these poor victims from the clutches of bestiality and sin ? Wesley's *Journal* records the evidence of more than one medical doctor whose preconceived mockery and wrath were hushed to

[1] *Journal*, August 30th, 1766.
[2] *Ibid.*, December 3rd, 1761.
[3] *Ibid.*, June 12th, 1780.
[4] *Ibid.*, June 14th, 1773.

awe, by the manifestations which met their eyes. Were the proprieties of drawing-room deportment, however, to be expected when, under Wesley's restrained, realistic, compelling preaching, and in an atmosphere of prayerful reverence, even hardened criminals, convicted of sin, sought and found the releasing grace of God ?

As for *Primitive Physic*, its very compilation and publication bear eloquent testimony to Wesley's keen, practical interest in the problems of private and public health. To him it was a religious duty to keep the body functioning up to the highest possible standards of efficiency. The directing genius of the Evangelical Revival was not a doctor of medicine, but a minister of religion ; hence some of his prescriptions in *Primitive Physic* may, to physicians, seem crude. Yet it is well to recall that this compilation—like his electrical treatment—was designed to help the suffering poor, whom the medical profession had so grossly neglected because they could not pay, and that the remedies therein prescribed were those which Wesley himself used, though rarely did he miss a night's sleep in sixty years. Nevertheless, it is doubtful if all history can provide a parallel to the boundless labours and achievements, compressed by this saddle-bag preacher within a life's span. Certain it is therefore, that if Wesley's medical remedies had any relation whatever to his indomitable spirit, his boundless energy and his awe-inspiring attainments, those remedies were not quite so crude, or so ridiculous, as some critics and satirists would suggest. But be this as it may, one thing is certain : the most marked decrease in the death rate, and the most marked increase in public health known to British history, synchronised completely with the expanding influence of the Evangelical Revival. Between the fourth decade of the eighteenth century and the second decade of the nineteenth, the mortality of London children under five years of age dropped from 74·5 per cent. to 31·8.[1] Various causes, admittedly, were at work in producing this salutary effect : but the greatest single cause, by far, was the *moral reformation* which the mighty Revival had wrought for the masses of England. Laugh, if one will, at Wesley's *Primitive Physic*, the fact remains that wherever the spirit of the Revival spread, there also, with an intensity vital religion alone could provide, were spread the accompanying influences of temperance and abstemiousness, of cleanliness and sanitation, of sick-visitation and domestic hygiene, of self-respect and self-restraint, of personal purity and family sanctity, of gracious fellowship and sociability ; as well as the effects of a salutary thirst for knowledge, and a

[1] *Lancet*, 1835–36, I, p. 692. (T. R. Edmonds " On the Mortality of Infants in England.")

hunger for abundant life.[1] And this all contributed mightily to mental and physical, as well as spiritual health. The Revival was both a " moral bath "[2] and a civilising tonic to a pagan, vulgarised England, long floundering toward a spiritual abyss.

(iii) *A Belated Assault*

One of the latest, and perhaps the most brilliant, of all the literary critics of the Evangelical Movement is Dr. J. L. Hammond. In his celebrated book, *The Town Labourer*, having dubbed this Movement " a storm in a tea-cup,"[3] he says : " It taught patience where the Trade Unions taught impatience. The Trade Union movement taught that men and women should use their powers to destroy the supremacy of wealth in a world made by men ; the Methodist that they should learn *resignation* amid the painful chaos of a world so made, for good reasons of His own, by God."[4] It surely would be hard to conceive of a statement more abortive of the true spirit and meaning of that amazing Revival, than is contained in this colourful contrast. Wesley assuredly was not a promoter of strife ; on the contrary, many great historians, from Lecky to Halévy, believe that the spiritual Revival he initiated and guided, saved England from revolutionary bloodshed. But be that much-mooted point as it may, in a real sense the Revival was itself an effective ethical revolution—a revolution against the injustice, the unrighteousness, the immorality and the irreligion of the *status quo*. To argue that Wesley taught " resignation amid the painful chaos " of a disordered world, is woefully to misunderstand and misinterpret the general tenor and trend of a silent, but mighty, leavening Movement. Such a portrayal indeed is less than a caricature : it is repudiated not only by Wesley's life and teaching, but by a hundred purging, reviving, life-giving streams of influence, traceable, through manifold tributaries, to the same Spirit source.

Far from teaching " resignation " regarding the prevailing and selfish use of wealth, for instance, Wesley expounded a doctrine concerning the employment and function of money, more exacting and more deeply revolutionary in its social implications,

---

[1] For a very great doctor's tribute to this influence, see Sir. Geo. Newman, *Health and Social Evolution*, p. 41f.

[2] The phrase is that of Wm. James in the Preface to *Varieties of Religious Experience*.

[3] *Op. cit.*, by J. L. and Barbara Hammond, p. 221.

[4] *Ibid.*, p. 283.

than any ever advocated by Trade Union organisations.[1] That doctrine, moreover, was cheerfully accepted and acted upon by Wesley himself, whose mode of life, as we have seen, was modest and abstemious to the last degree[2] : whereas Cobbett, the capable but bludgeoning, egotistical, quarrelsome and semi-revolutionary Trade Union firebrand, despite his pious *Advice to Young Men* and his flaunted altruistic airs, lived (whenever possible) in comparative pomp, defended the enslavement of " niggers," ranted vociferously in his *Political Register* to advertise his own profit-making wares, and died leaving no mean estate.[3] Do Wesley's vehement attacks upon slavery and all its promoters savour of " resignation " or " patience " ? Is " resignation " an epithet applicable to his titanic bombardments of the liquor traffic, of bribery and smuggling, of legal, political and ecclesiastical corruption ? Was Wesley resigned to the *status quo* when he launched his piquant assaults upon war and all its barbarities ? Is " resignation " at all compatible with his caustic strictures on the fashionable and snobbish boarding-schools of his day ?[4] Can " resignation " be applied to his repeated and piercing thrusts at the perverted administration of justice to the poor, or at the inhumanity and " falsity " of certain metallic economic maxims ?[5] Did " patience " with prevailing conditions or " resignation " to the Powers-that-Be, inspire this incomparable leader, for more than half a century, to labour sixteen to eighteen hours a day, for the individual and social salvation of England and mankind ? Was it " resignation " that inspired his disciples, braving danger and death, to start a missionary crusade in every quarter of the globe ? Serenity of spirit and obedience to the will of God, the Evangelical Revival assuredly mediated in marked degree ; but these enabled it to battle with moral and social evils with greater assurance, persistence and power. Real Evangelical serenity, was not that of apathy : it was, as Sir Josiah Stamp points out, " the serenity of utter warfare, of which the final issue is never in doubt, so vested is it in the justice of God."[6]

Only doctrinaire prejudice, or utter misconception, could

[1] See, for instance, sermons on *The Use of Money, The Good Steward, Wheels within Wheels*, and various discourses on *The Sermon on the Mount.*
[2] See Wesley's *Earnest Appeal to Men of Reason and Religion*, p. 40.
[3] No modern English or American magazine advertisements equal the superlative braggadocio splashed throughout the *Political Register* to advertise Cobbett's pamphlets, etc. It certainly is no tribute to the type of mentality at which Cobbett aimed his appeal.
[4] *Journal*, April 6th, 1772.
[5] *Journal*, July 3rd, 1761 ; December 27th, 1744 ; February 8th, 1753 and Tyerman's *Wesley*, Vol. II, p. 160.
[6] See Sir Josiah Stamp's Foreword to the cheap editions of the author's *Lord Shaftesbury and Social-Industrial Progress*, p. 6.

delineate this Spiritual Awakening as born of, nurtured by, or tending toward, Resignation. Never will "resignation" explain the labours of Wesley or the meaning of his Movement. Indeed it would appear that Dr. Hammond's underlying objection to this "new religion," as he styles it, is that it did not overthrow the selfishness of one social class and enthrone that of another and, as yet, wholly untutored class. The Evangelical Revival was in fact a revolution : but it was a revolution which had at its heart love of humanity, not hatred of class. True, this "peculiar people" contemplated continually the love of God, the goodness of God and the purpose of God. But their sublime faith in the Deity, far from reconciling them to the injustices of men, made those injustices the more intolerable ; for it provided them with an ever-challenging vision and prototype of what human society should, and might, be. It made them faithful builders of a better social order ; for their supreme desire was to be co-labourers with the Great Artificer, in hastening the advent of that longed-for era, when the Divine will shall be done on earth, as in Heaven. This movement, moreover, preceded any vital Trade Union movement ; and by its aspiration, its foresight, its Sunday and week-day schools, its class and band meetings, its lay and street preaching, its financial organisation, its democratic co-operation, its genius for fellowship and its boundless faith and energy, it laid the foundations of self-discipline, self-help and self-government on which the Trade Union structure was itself largely built—foundations without which any worthy Trade Union development would have been wholly impossible.[1] New moral character, was the most pressing need of the new industrial age : that, this despised "new religion" proceeded steadily, despite new difficulties, to build ; and it is no coincidence that many of the noblest Trade Union leaders and industrial welfare pioneers, were themselves local preachers. All laboured efforts, therefore, to place the Evangelical Revival in opposition to a sane Trade Union movement, result only in a forced and false antithesis.

In a memorable passage, Mrs. Sydney Webb says : "It is assuredly to the credit of the English working man that numerous associations, both for trade union and industrial purposes, should have existed continuously for half a century with no other security but the personal honour of members and the personal honesty of officials."[2] "The *personal* honour of members," "the *personal* honesty of officials !" Herein lay the crux and key of all early efforts for industrial emancipation.

---

[1] See Jack Lawson, M.P., *A Man's Life* (chapter x, " Little Bethel ").
[2] Beatrice Webb, *The Co-operative Movement*, p. 52.

And these sterling *character* qualities " the gin-age," economically honeycombed and corrupted by the powerful, monopolistic, expanding slave-trade, intellectually dominated by a shallow, faithless Deism, and politically and ecclesiastically ruled by worldling, nepotistic cliques, could never on a considerable scale have produced. Such character attributes are not the products of chance. Nor are they—as often to-day is naïvely assumed—the inherent, exclusive possession of the " working classes," as such. Whence then came they ? And whence their influence on the workers' just aspirations ? Only one explanation is commensurate with the deepest underlying facts, and that is—the purging moral and spiritual influence which this Baptism of Fire brought to the toiling masses. Made conscious of their own eternal worth, and given the means of moral reformation, they first learned to rule their own souls ; and that achieved, they gradually fitted themselves for the exercise of economic, social and political power, which subsequently could not long be withheld.[1] " To you," said Dr. Priestley in An Address to the Methodists, " is the civilisation, the industry and sobriety of great numbers of the labouring part of the community owing."[2]

So chagrined, however, is Mr. Hammond that this " storm in a tea-cup " won the support of the industrial population and thus averted a ruthless class war, that he complains : " It diverted energy from a *class struggle* at a time when wise energy was scarce, and money when money was still scarcer. It would be supremely interesting to know what sum was spent on this religion by a class that was thereby diverting its resources from a *war* for independence."[3] The present writer, as his book *Lord Shaftesbury* will prove,[4] offers no word of apology for the dire miscarriage of social and industrial justice which Mr. Hammond so graphically depicts. But when (true to the

[1] As late as 1755, a Manchester philanthropist described the " labouring poor " as possessed of " an abject mind . . . a mean, sordid spirit, which prevents all attempts of bettering their conditions. They are so familiarised to filth and rags as renders them in a manner natural ; and have so little sense of decency as hardly to allow a wish for it a place in their hearts." (John Clayton, M.A., *Friendly Advice to the Poor*, and Luke Tyerman, *Oxford Methodists*, pp. 52–3.) Dr. D. George's researches point to similar conclusions relative to the first half of the eighteenth century. Yet Mr. Hammond, by repeated inference, assumes this period, preceding 1760, to be a sort of industrial golden age.
[2] Joseph Priestly, *Original Letters to the Rev. John Wesley*, etc., pp. xvii–xviii. (Also Dr. W. J. Warner, *The Methodist Influence in the Industrial Revolution*, p. 175.)
[3] *The Town Labourer*, p. 285 (the italics are ours).
[4] See chapters xiii to xix and xxii.

stereotyped Marxian thesis)[1] he comes to suggest that this Religious Revival perverted the progress and liberty of the industrial masses, has he not quite lost perspective, and is he not doing violence to Truth? Revolution, or class war, initiated by the English "workers" at the period in question, could have resulted merely in brutal suppression. They lacked not only the sobriety, discipline and articulateness, but also the coherence, organising ability and co-operative experience, without which their cause assuredly was doomed to failure. Wesley and the Evangelical Movement, as Professor Elie Halévy in four monumental volumes of his modern *History of the English People* repeatedly has emphasised,[2] brought all these qualities in more intense and abiding degree than any other movement Britain has known. They brought them moreover, at as small a monetary outlay as that at which any practical school has even been conducted.

True, the outrages of American Revolutionary mobs and the bloody "Terror" of the French Revolution, together with the flagrant, swashbuckling arrogance of Voltaire, Rousseau, Paine, Cobbett and the like, long made the Revival forces less progressive and more suspicious of the new "Democracy" than otherwise would have been the case. But the substantial fact remains, that the Revival's character-building influence provided the solid foundation upon which the social and industrial emancipation of the English masses was reared, while also it gave to women their first extensive opportunities of serving the common weal.

The books most read by the more turbulent section of the industrial populace, in the later decades of the eighteenth century, were those of Tom Paine:[3] yet Paine, far from possessing self-control, himself died a drunkard. The incredible moral degradation with which the Revival was long confronted, including the bestiality of straw-littered, vermin-ridden, "drunk-for-a-penny" pubs, we have already explored.[4] Most of the workers' class-war agitation, however, was conducted in the stagnant, depraving environment of these mercenary, liquor-vending, and gambling dens. So long therefore as the industrial multitudes were thus stupefied with alcohol and excited with gambling, in the lairs of their wily, though unrecognised, foes

---

[1] Marx advocated not only relentless class war and revolution, but the abolition of *all* religion and *all* morality. (See *Manifesto of the Communist Party*.) Again, "Christian Socialism," says Marx, "is but the holy water with which the priest consecrates the heart burnings of the aristocrat." (*Ibid.*, p. 30.)

[2] See especially Vol. I, Book III ("Religion and Culture").

[3] See his *Common Sense* (1776) and *Rights of Man* (1791).

[4] See chapter viii, especially section (ii).

what hopes could they cherish for successful revolution ? Their very manner of life, evolved its own Nemesis. They were as lambs bleating for Liberty, while all the time the paw of the lion was suspended over their heads : they were as opium slaves who dream of Paradise, only to awaken in Hell.

In all Mr. Hammond's brilliant work, notwithstanding, this vital character element is practically ignored. Purporting to champion the workers' cause, scarcely a word has he to say regarding their half-depraved moral life when the " Industrial Revolution " began, and their incredible readiness to exploit their own children, often for the satisfaction of vitiated appetites and lusts. Caricaturing and satirising Wilberforce and Hannah More, Mr. Hammond bemoans the money expended by the industrial toilers on the Evangelical Movement ; but he is blind to the basic fact, that this money was largely rescued from the acquisitive " capitalism " of distillers, brewers, crimps, gamesters, brothel keepers, bull-baiters, fakirs and exploiters of a hundred varieties, who, like guileful vampires, coquetted pertly with all the highest aspirations of industrial England, even as they sucked her life-blood. He fails to perceive that this lamented money was not only diverted from the grinding coffers of the workers' subtlest suppressers, but that it was expended in creating and mediating the insight and idealism, the temperance and resourcefulness, the integrity and per- severance, the brotherly fellowship and organising ability, the powers of co-operation and agitation—the qualities, in short, of character and spirit—which alone could lead them from bon- dage into their Promised Land. As Mrs. Sidney Webb's statement suggests, *personal* character values were at the very heart of the workers' emancipation problem ; and the long- maligned Evangelical Revival did more to transfigure the moral character of the general populace, than any other movement British history can record.[1]

---

[1] It is significant and pleasing to note that in later writings, Mr. and Mrs. Hammond have shown themselves much more sympathetic toward the Evangelical Revival. See the new Preface and Appendix to the fourth edition of their *Lord Shaftesbury*. Their criticisms have in these pages been focused upon, only because they represent a very large and influential school of thought, and because, in the opinion of the present writer, their attacks have seemed the most plausible as well as the most devastating.

PART III

SOME FRUITS OF FAITH

CHAPTER XVIII

THE ABOLITION OF SLAVERY

" But to understand the delight with which the emancipation of the negroes was greeted, the rejoicings which took place on a large scale throughout the entire country . . . we must remember that the abolitionist campaign had been first and foremost a Christian movement. What the liberal bourgeoisie of contemporary France failed to do for the slaves of the West Indies, the Evangelical middle class dared to accomplish in England . . ."

PROFESSOR ELIE HALÉVY, D.LITT., *A History of the English People* (Vol. 1830–1841), p. 85.

" I BELIEVE that this country (Britain) when it stands before history, will stand, when all else has passed away, not by her fleets and her armies and her commerce, but by the heroic self-denying exertions which she has made to put down this iniquitous traffic."

LORD ROSEBERY (*See* Sir John Harris, *A Century of Emancipation*, p. 263.)

CHAPTER XVIII

THE ABOLITION OF SLAVERY

" ONE of the turning events in the history of the world "—is
the designation applied by Professor George Macaulay Trevelyan
to the success of the mighty agitation which freed the British
Empire first of the slave-trade and, twenty-six years later, of
the monstrous " institution " of slavery. Pondering the centrality of that immortal achievement, Trevelyan avers : " It
was only just in time. If slavery had not been abolished before
the great commercial exploitation of the tropics began, Africa
would have been turned by the world's capitalists into a slave-
farm so enormous that it must have eventually corrupted and
destroyed Europe herself, as surely as the world-conquest
under the conditions of slavery destroyed the Roman Empire."[1]
    So emphatic is Dr. Trevelyan on this point that four times
in his *British History in the Nineteenth Century* alone, does he
revert to it.[2] If his verdict is correct, it follows that the Evangelical Revival not only saved Britain and the Empire, but
actually averted the corruption and destruction of " Europe
herself." The suppression of the traffic and the " institution "
which made chattels of multitudes of human beings was the
indispensable foundation upon which any social development,
worthy of the name, had perforce to be built. Indeed the arch
tragedy of the modern world is that the Industrial Revolution,
which with its machine power transformed the face of Western
Europe, took place at a time when the economics of a revived
slavery were colouring, if not actually controlling, the commercial and financial life of the most adventurous, inventive
and influential peoples. To assume moreover—as some schools
of thought to-day do—that modern slavery became economically
unprofitable and simply " wore itself out," is to fly blandly in
the face of Truth.

(i) *The Far Flung Boon of British Emancipation*

    On August 1st, 1834, the Emancipation Act, passed twelve
months previously, came into force throughout the British

[1] Trevelyan's *British History in the Nineteenth Century*, p. 51.
[2] *Ibid.*, pp. 51, 116, 254-5, 411. See also his *History of England*, p. 599.

Empire. In the West Indies it was a never-to-be-forgotten date, for then three-quarters of a million negroes were acclaimed " free men." In England, for weeks following, Sir Thomas Fowell Buxton, who, in 1823, had moved in Parliament " that the state of slavery is repugnant to the principles of the British Constitution and of the Christian religion "[1] and ought to be abolished, waited anxiously for news of the vital day. Troops and warships had been sent out " in case of disturbance." On September 10th Buxton was in receipt of a " large pile " of letters from the West Indies ; and deep was his " gratitude to God " for the intelligence they contained. Throughout the Colonies, on the evening of July 31st, " the Churches and Chapels had been thrown open and the slaves had crowded into them." As midnight approached, they fell on their knees, awaiting the solemn moment, " all hushed in prayer." On the first stroke of twelve from the chapel bells, " they sprang upon their feet, and through every island rang the glad sound of thanksgiving to the Father of all, for the chains were broken and the slaves were free."[2]

From the Churches and Chapels in all the British West Indian Islands the emancipated negroes, in company with their beloved missionaries, proceeded directly to the highest hill-tops, " to watch for the sun to rise." For its first rays would bear to them a sacramental significance, betokening the dawn of a new era to the whole negro race. On that day of liberation and thanksgiving, " the Churches and Chapels were thronged from eleven in the morning to eight in the evening " ; and, according to the reports of Governors, Police Superintendents and magistrates, the conduct of the negroes was marked by order, temperance and " universal reverence." All prophecies of insurrection and bloodshed, therefore, were falsified ; the despatching of troops and warships had proved but a waste of money. The festivities of August 2nd were almost as peaceful and orderly as the thanksgivings of August 1st : the much-maligned and oft-persecuted Evangelical missionaries, who long had laboured heroically among the slaves, had prepared them for the reception of liberty. True, in all save two of the islands, four years of semi-purgatorial " apprenticeship " was to ensue, before the negroes' legal freedom should be complete. But the patience, fortitude and courage of the negroes, under much cruel and callous provocation from many of their ex-owners, is a high tribute both to the potential qualities of their

[1] See Hansard (H. of C.), May 15th, 1823.
[2] See Buxton's *Life*, by his son ; also Sir John Harris, *A Century of Emancipation*, p. 52.

race and to the Christian principles which had been engendered in their souls.[1]

With sacramental thanksgiving in their Chapels, and with boundless hope on the hill-tops, the freed slaves of the West Indies greeted the dawn of a new era for their long-tortured race. But far overseas, in the jungles of unexplored Africa, the darkness comprehended not the Light which had dawned. Few among the teeming millions of the ex-slaves' brethren in Africa "understood or regarded" what had transpired on August 1st, 1834. "Yet it was that continent," Trevelyan rightly insists, "whose future was most deeply affected. Before its exploitation by Europe had well begun, it had been decided by the most powerful of its future masters that slavery should not be the relation of the black man to the white."[2]

By one of the most humane and disinterested acts in the whole history of nations, the British people, through its Parliament, cheerfully paid £20,000,000 in advance, to the West Indian planters to secure freedom for British slaves. Nor was this all the money thus expended : £700,000 was paid by England to Spain and Portugal to gain even their wavering co-operation in suppressing the slave-trade. The British Navy was enlarged and not a few of its vessels were engaged for years, at no small cost, in police work against slave-smuggling boats, and against the subterfuges of recalcitrant nations which persisted in profiting by the slave traffic. After 1787, vast voluntary sums were raised throughout the country for the support of the epoch-making propaganda of the Committee for the Abolition of the Slave Trade ; after 1823 again, vast sums were raised for the support of the Anti-Slavery Society ; and these were but the chief of many organisations of like intent. The British Parliament, too, came finally to stand on guard against slavery ; British diplomacy was used to thwart it ; the Colonial Office, under "King Stephen," became its sworn foe ; the numerous British Foreign Missionary Societies attacked it as the antithesis of all vital Christianity ; the better organ of the Press opposed it ; the conscience of the nation at length was stirred to its depths, and all that was best in the British people cried out against "the accursed thing."

After Britain had abolished the slave-trade and purchased the emancipation of the Empire's slaves, a hundred ways were found of putting pressure upon France, Holland, Portugal,

[1] Dr. W. L. Mathieson's balanced study, *British Slavery and Its Abolition*, makes it abundantly clear that the influence of the large number of Evangelical missionaries among the West Indian slaves was of cardinal importance to the final success of the British anti-slavery crusade. See especially chapters iii and iv.

[2] Trevelyan, *op. cit.*, pp. 254-55.

Spain and other slave-holding peoples. Her command of the seas, her far-flung Empire, her mounting industrial power, her commercial supremacy, her inventive genius, above all her increasing moral stature and her expanding spiritual vision, won her a place of unique leadership among the nations. She was hated, she was dubbed a Pharisee, she was cursed ; but more than any other great nation in the middle of the nineteenth century, she was worthy of world power ; and nations which most maligned her, not only feared her, but secretly respected and envied her.

With Britain's abolition of slavery throughout her Empire, even the vast and deeply-entrenched " Institution " of American slavery received a staggering blow. Innumerable were the points of contact by which the victorious Emancipationists in England encouraged their fellow zealots in the United States. And such encouragement, naturally, was little appreciated by the ave-owning states.[1] In 1853, for instance, two years after Lord Ashley, on his father's death, went to the House of Lords as the Seventh Earl of Shaftesbury, he headed a strong declaration of encouragement to the American Abolitionists. By way of retort, a Southern newspaper, in the sublimity of its ignorance, burst forth : " Who is this Earl of Shaftesbury ? Some unknown lordling ; one of your modern philanthropists suddenly started up to take part in a passing agitation. It is a pity he does not look at home. Where was he when *Lord Ashley* was so nobly fighting for the Factory Bill, and pleading the cause of the English slave ? We never even heard the name of this Lord Shaftesbury *then*."[2]

(ii) *Modern Slavery and the Forces Arrayed Against It*

The establishment of Colonial Slavery in Christendom, centuries after the slow and painful eradication of the deeply-rooted remnants of " Classical slavery," represents the most tragic and monstrous aberration in the annals of the modern world. At the very time when all the " liberated " *intelligentsia* of Europe were satirising the ecclesiastical tyranny of the " Dark Ages " and glorifying the " liberal culture " of the old Classic World—which economically was based squarely on slavery— the dragon's teeth of a new and awful tyranny were being sown. With the dawning of the Modern World, ruthless

---

[1] With the gradual awakening of the Social Conscience in England, it was increasingly recognised that she was originally responsible for the planting of American slavery in Colonial days, and therefore now was morally bound to encourage the Abolitionists within the Republic to eradicate the curse.

[2] Hodder's *Shaftesbury*, II, p. 439 ; Bready's *Shaftesbury*, p. 412,

Nationalism was raising its head ; the statecraft of Machiavelli was guilefully at work in the counsel chambers of Statesmen and Kings ; the iconoclasm of the new and intoxicating " freedom " was subverting all Christian authority.   The flamboyant eulogy of pagan literature, philosophy and institutions, was creating an intellectual and political atmosphere highly favourable to the enslavement of weak and defenceless peoples.   It was no accident that the period of the Renaissance coincided with the introduction of modern slavery ; and far more than is generally recognised, must the licence and paganism of the Renaissance era be held accountable for encouraging the advent of the blackest tragedy which has befallen the modern world —a tragedy which was to prove the nursing mother of a vast retinue of social and industrial ills.[1]

In passing it should be noted that, at the end of the sixth century, Pope Gregory the Great, in his struggle against the continuance of " ancient slavery," had declared that " inasmuch as the Redeemer of men had taken upon himself Humanity, to restore us to liberty, so it becomes us to restore those men whom nature had made free, but the law of nations had made slaves, to their natural condition—namely, liberty."[2]   Moreover, when the gruesome institution of " modern slavery " was beginning to manifest itself, Pope Leo X (1513-22) protested in a bull that, " not only the Christian religion, but nature herself, cried out against a system of slavery."[3]

If Britain was the last of the great maritime powers of Christendom officially to sanction and organise the slave-trade,[4] after the Asiento concession of 1713 she became by far the most deeply involved in its guilt.   Nevertheless she it was who, under the inspiration of a mighty spiritual baptism, was to set in motion moral and humanitarian forces which finally would break the backbone of modern slavery.   When English slave-trading began with Hawkins, in Elizabeth's reign, it was in the nature of a sporadic and semi-piratical adventure.   But under Charles I chartered African trading companies began to be formed ; and soon royal households, as well as commercial magnates, became vigorous propagators of this lucrative traffic in human blood.   For almost two centuries following the formation of the first African company, Britain's association with the slave-trade and slavery was to cast a contaminating influence

[1] See articles on " Slavery " in *Ency. Brit., Ency. of Rel. and Ethics*, and *Cath. Ency.* ; also articles on " Renaissance."
[2] See C. L. Brace's *Gesta Christi* (seventh edition), p. 229.
[3] *Ency. of Rel. and Ethics* (" Slavery ").
[4] Ancient slavery and slave-trading has never been suppressed in the Mohammedan world.   In Christendom it had been almost eradicated by the end of the tenth century, though the system of serfdom remained.

over the whole economic and social fabric of the nation's life.

The honour of the initial corporate stand against slavery, both in England and in America, must of course go to the Quakers. Even in the seventeenth century they began to protest against " this negation of Christianity." In 1724, they passed a resolution condemning both the slave-trade and slavery : " in 1758, in step with their brothers in Pennsylvania, they proceeded to warn, and in 1761 to disown, all Friends who continued to participate in the Trade."[1] Richard Baxter, the Puritan, too, in his *Christian Directory*, had pronounced " slave-pirates " the " common enemies of mankind." Defoe, the Nonconformist, both in verse and prose, had taken up the cudgels. Godwyn, an Anglican clergyman, who had lived in Barbados, had predicted vengeance upon the " inhuman authors " of slavery ; while in 1766 the redoubtable Bishop Warburton was to stigmatise from the pulpit " the infamous traffic." Such isolated and occasional protests, however, represented but so many voices crying in the wilderness. Britain was profiting tremendously from the slave-trade ; enormous and powerful vested interests were being established ; and so far, the conscience of the nation had scarcely been touched. Indeed the mighty spiritual Revival which already was spreading quietly over the Kingdom, and which finally was to achieve the miracle of abolishing—without revolution or bloodshed— both the British slave-trade and British slavery, was not yet really awakened either to the nature and proportions of modern slavery, or to the moral and spiritual issues involved.

At this stage, early in 1772, Wesley noted in his *Journal*, that he had just read " a very different book," by an " honest Quaker," depicting " that execrable sum of all the villainies " —the Slave Trade. The book was by Anthony Benezet, and its effect on Wesley was overpowering. This British slave-trade, the peerless evangelist concluded, " infinitely exceeded in every instance of barbarity what Christian slaves suffer in Mohammedan countries."[2] With characteristic intensity Wesley now began to accumulate all the information he could, both concerning the slave-trade and slavery. Two years later (1774), appeared his *Thoughts Upon Slavery*. That booklet proved to be perhaps the most far-reaching treatise ever written against slavery. Wesley already was much the most beloved and influential religious leader in the world of that day. His own eyes had been opened with a shock by Benezet, and later investigations but increased his revulsion. His *Thoughts upon Slavery*

---

[1] R. Coupland, *Wilberforce*, p. 77.
[2] See entry for February 12th, 1772. No one who has pondered Wesley's *Journal* can fail to note his numerous contacts with Quakers.

was the Revival's Manifesto, declaring spiritual warfare against the " execrable sum of all the villainies." It immediately committed the thousands of his followers to active and sacrificial effort in the " holy cause." But more : it was a trumpet call to every professing Christian, yea, to every lover of man. Dared *any* honourable person stand neutral while Freedom, Justice, Mercy and Truth were being trampled under foot, for blood-stained gain?

Meet it was, moreover, that on this great issue the whole Evangelical Revival should have been influenced by the teaching and example of the Friends. When, by the fifth decade of the eighteenth century, the spiritual power of the Revival began to manifest itself in every quarter of the realm, the Quakers, like the other Nonconformist denominations, were a dwindling body struggling desperately for life in the asphyxiating atmosphere of Deism ; but their remnant was vital. And like the other Nonconformist bodies, they, too, began to experience new life, hope and vitality from the new faith which the Revival was shedding abroad, while, true to their peculiar genius for Christian Friendship, they expended their new-found power to the most practical ends. Remarkable affinities indeed existed between the Revival and Quakerism. Consecrated *lay* leadership, including that of preaching, teaching and spiritual supervision, was at the heart of both. Both gave a pronounced place to the initiative and peculiar gifts of women, opening up for them special avenues of leadership and service. Both placed the strongest emphasis on Christian peace and forbearance, on Christian neighbourliness and goodwill ; and both insisted that Christian faith must always be tested by its ability to create the fruits of love. Both, moreover, felt that their ultimate citizenship was in Heaven ; yet both believed that Heaven could only be reached by striving faithfully to establish the Kingdom of God on earth.

But the Evangelical Revival, more than Quakerism, more than any branch of Puritanism, more indeed than any other religious movement the English-speaking world has yet known, emphasised the " equal and priceless value " before God of "*every* immortal soul." The full implications of this central doctrine were not at first wholly apparent. But from the beginning the movement entertained hope for the hopeless ; it proclaimed the sanctity of the humblest serviceable labour ; it was possessed of a crusading missionary enthusiasm, and proclaiming " the World as its parish," it could not discriminate against any colour or race among its parishioners. When once the slavery question then was squarely raised, and fairly faced, the Revival could do none other than proclaim the negro a child of God, a brother-man, an immortal soul " for whom Christ

Y

died," that he might be *free*. The slave therefore was as worthy of Evangelical effort as any potentate or prince. " The Clapham Sect " was symbolic of something entirely new in English social and public life. It represented a "lay brotherhood" of highly talented and privileged men who consecrated wealth, power and time to the things of the Kingdom of God ;[1] it became the nerve-centre of the epic movement against slavery ; it was a typical child of the far-reaching Evangelical Revival.

(iii) *Abolitionists and Emancipationists*

The abolition of the British slave-trade in which for many years more than two hundred English ships were constantly engaged, was the first essential objective in the valiant and long-protracted struggle against modern slavery. The progressive stages which led to the Abolition Act of 1807 are too well known even to be outlined here. To recall but the names of the sacrificial leaders who through more than two decades bore the heat and burden of the campaign is itself suggestive. As long as free men pay tribute to the champions of liberty, the names of William Wilberforce and Thomas Clarkson, of Granville Sharp and Zachary Macaulay, of Henry Thornton and James Stephen, of Lord Teignmouth and Charles Grant, of John Newton and William Cowper, of James Ramsay and Lady Middleton, of Hannah More and John Venn, stand assured of fame. All derived their initial inspiration and their sustaining perseverance in the Abolition struggle from their Faith ; most of them were " members " of the " Clapham Sect " : all were within the fellowship of the Evangelical Movement. From Wesley's preachers and leaders they derived the fullest support ; the Quakers quietly, but persistently, afforded them an arm of strength ; other Nonconformist bodies rallied increasingly to " this Christian Cause " ; nevertheless most prelates of the State Church remained cold till victory was assured, while some, like the rigid Bishop Phillpotts, who, through the famous Gorham Case was to strive doggedly to kill all Evangelicalism within " the Church,"[2] would actually remain slave-owners till " Emancipation " was finally forced upon them.[3]

[1] See Sir James Stephen, *Essays in Ecclesiastical Biography*.
[2] For Phillpotts and the Gorham Case, see Balleine's *Evangelical Party*, pp. 222–7.
[3] Bishop Phillpotts (Exeter) who owned 665 West Indian slaves, received from the Compensation Fund " about £11,000." See *Parliamentary Papers*, 1837–8, Vol. XLIII, and Mathieson's *British Slavery*, p. 275 (note). The old S.P.G., too, was a slave owner on two West Indian estates. It admitted to the use of the " driving whip " on its property as late as 1829. See Sir J. Harris, *A Century of Emancipation*, p. 10, and Mathieson, *op. cit.*, p. 216.

A group of gifted Humanitarian Rationalists, too, rendered memorable aid in the work of abolishing the slave trade. Pitt, in his early days, under Wilberforce's influence, proffered the cause yeoman's service ; though in later days, under Dundas's impact, his enthusiasm waned. The Abolition question was specially upon Fox's heart when he died. Grenville, as head of the Government, " in consultation with Wilberforce,"[1] introduced the final and successful Bill through the House of Lords. To Sir Samuel Romilly's big heart this question was ever dear ; while both Bentham and Gibbon rendered the movement no mean support. But most Humanitarian Rationalists were under no delusion as to who initiated, organised, financed, sustained and really carried to victory, the epoch-making agitation against the slave-trade. Jeremy Bentham, in this connection, once exclaimed : " *If to be an anti-slavist is to be a saint, saintship for me. I am a saint !* "[2] Again, Romilly's noble tribute to Wilberforce on that triumphant night in the House of Commons (February 23rd, 1807), when the Abolition Bill was carried to victory, is applicable in no small degree to the untiring host of Christian zealots who upheld his hands :

" When I look," said Romilly, " to the man at the head of the French monarchy, surrounded as he is with all the pomp of power and all the pride of victory, distributing kingdoms to his family and principalities to his followers, seeming when he sits upon his throne to have reached the summit of human ambition and the pinnacle of earthly happiness—and when I follow that man into his closet or to his bed, and consider the pangs with which his solitude must be tortured and his repose banished, by the recollection of the blood he has spilled and the oppressions he has committed—and when I compare with those pangs of remorse the feelings which must accompany my honourable friend from this House to his home, after the vote of this night shall have confirmed the object of his humane and unceasing labours ; when he retires into the bosom of his happy and delighted family, when he lays himself down on his bed, reflecting on the innumerable voices that would be raised in every quarter of the world to bless him, how much more pure and perfect felicity must he enjoy, in the consciousness of having preserved so many millions of his fellow-creatures. . . ."[3]

[1] Coupland's *Wilberforce*, p. 336.
[2] Halévy's *English People in 1815*, p. 510 (note) ; also Bentham's *Works* (Bowring edition), Vol. X, p. 508.
[3] Romilly, nevertheless, was one of the many Englishmen who had greeted the dawn of the French Revolution with exuberant joy.

In the valiant struggle leading to the Emancipation Act of 1833, the mantle of Wilberforce was cast directly upon the shoulders of that intrepid Evangelical Whig, Thomas Fowell Buxton. During the concluding ten years of this later crusade the conflict was herculean, but the final passage of the Emancipation Act was certainly accelerated by the enactment of the First Reform Bill in the preceding year, which at one stroke had cut away the Rotten Boroughs—the special Parliamentary preserves of the slave-owning interests. This preliminary victory had been won chiefly by Radical Whigs, but its deeper cause was the rapid creation of the great Middle Class of England ; and here again the Evangelical Revival had been mightily at work, for more than any other force that purging spiritual baptism had begotten or nurtured the education, the sobriety, the character, the self-discipline, the self-expression and the self-help which, working together with the new economic opportunities afforded by the Industrial Revolution, produced the sturdy, hard-working and capable Middle Class, henceforth —despite all later abuse—to prove the backbone of Britain. In preparing the way for the onslaught on the Rotten Boroughs and the success of the greatly extended franchise, the influence of the Revival was incalculable.

The vanguard roll-call in the struggle against slavery itself, is as suggestive as that against the slave-trade. No single band of Buxton's supporters was more important than the heroic company of West Indian missionaries, all of whom were Evangelicals and half of whom were Methodists.[1] Richard Watson, Secretary of the Wesleyan Missionary Society, proved to the cause a tower of strength. The indomitable William Knibb, who in common with a dozen of his fellow Baptist missionaries had his Church burned to the ground and his life threatened by infuriated planters, afforded titanic service both in the West Indies and in England. John Smith, a courageous Congregational missionary, was done to death for his heroism in the negroes' behalf ; while Austin, the Anglican " chaplain to the garrison at Georgetown," was hounded from the colony because he dared to give evidence in Smith's support. It is memorable too that Sir James Stephen, Lord Glenelg, Dr. Lushington, Sir James Mackintosh, Joseph Sturge and the famous Governors, Lord Sligo and Sir Lionel Smith, worked under the strongest compulsions of Evangelical religion ; while of the multitude of Petitions sent to Parliament nearly all were initiated by " the Saints," and most of the hundreds of thousands of signatures came from co-operating Evangelicals—Methodist, Noncon-

---

[1] See Mathieson, *op. cit.*, p. 111 ; Hansard (1823), IX, p. 315 ; and Edwards's *Wesley*, pp. 126–7.

formist and Anglican. In Parliament, however, Emancipation owed no small debt to the brilliance of Brougham, the radical, and the eloquence of O'Connell, the Catholic.[1]

The boiling fulminations poured on the heads of the anti-slavery leaders by many of their contemporaries, make to-day strange reading for Anglo-Saxon people. " I was bred in the good old school," wrote Lord Nelson from the *Victory*, " and taught to appreciate the value of our West Indian possessions, and neither in the field nor the Senate shall their just rights be infringed, while I have an arm to fight in their defence, or a tongue to launch my voice against the damnable doctrine of Wilberforce and his hypocritical allies."[2] James Boswell, so full of eulogy for Dr. Johnson, addressed the following lines to Wilberforce :

> " Go, W——, with narrow skull,
> Go home and preach away at Hull.
> No longer to the Senate cackle
> In strains that suit the tabernacle ;
> I hate your little wittling sneer,
> Your pert and self-sufficient leer.
> Mischief to trade sits on your lip,
> Insects will gnaw the noblest ship.
> Go, W——, begone, for shame,
> Thou dwarf with big resounding name."[3]

When men like Nelson and Boswell could sink to such vituperation, it is scarcely surprising that the hireling pamphleteers of the " West Indian Interest " fumed against the " Pestilent doctrines of those hot-brained fanatics who, under the vile pretence of philanthropy and zeal for the interests of suffering humanity, preach up rebellion and murder to the contented and orderly negroes in our territories."[4] Cobbett's virulence against Wilberforce, his blind but sustained fury against the Methodists and Evangelicals as " the vilest crew God ever suffered to infest the earth," his representation of the West Indian slaves as " fat and lazy " and " laughing from morning till night," and of their owners as " men as gentle, as generous and as good as ever breathed," together with his direct encouragement of the burning and demolition of West Indian " conventicles," we have previously suggested.[5] Cobbett certainly would not have indulged all this vituperation had it not helped to sell his *Political Register* and his *Twopenny Trash.*

[1] The volumes of the *Anti-Slavery Monthly Reporter*, especially from 1831 to 1834, are highly illuminating on the whole Emancipation question.
[2] Lady Knutsford's *Life of Zachary Macaulay*, p. 258.
[3] Quoted in " A Lesson from History " (*New Outlook*, September 6th, 1933).
[4] Sir John Harris, *op. cit.*, p. 4.
[5] Mathieson, *op. cit.*, p. 137.

He, perhaps above all others, was responsible for broadcasting the delusion that the state of the workers in England had nothing whatever to do with the slave-trade or colonial slavery. In 1832, nevertheless, when victory was certain, " he gratified his political hatred "[1] by temporarily joining the Emancipationists and, as though bereft of memory, proceeded to state that : " these slaves are in general *the property of the English borough-mongers* . . . and that the fruit of the labour of these slaves abroad, has long been converted into the *means of making us slaves at home.*"[2] In that moment of unguarded insight, Cobbett, though denying the settled policy of his life, gave expression to a poignant truth.

(iv) *America's Emancipation Problem*

The paradoxes and difficulties associated with the overthrow of American slavery, were both numerous and involved. The " Institution " of slavery in the Southern States had been established under British rule, and for generations it had been fed by the British slave-trade. Washington, commander of " the armies of Liberty " and " Father of his Country," was a Southern planter and slave-owner ; while the traditions and myths which gradually entwined themselves around his name, tended unfortunately to attach enhanced respectability to the Institution of slavery. The sacrosanct American Constitution, moreover, by its ample latent concession to the slave-owning States, became itself a stumbling block to Emancipation, many good and godly citizens believing that this solemn instrument of Union had guaranteed the foundation of slavery, in all States where previously it existed. Hence to have joined direct issue with the slave interest on this question would, they feared, have threatened the solidarity of the nation : and the astute political leaders of the " Confederate States " were not slow to exploit such fears. Indeed, for long the Southern politicians wielded a quite disproportionate power in formulating the national policy of the young republic. Not a few of the slave-owners were men of leisure, social prestige and substantial wealth ; they were skilled in the subtleties and casuistries of partisan politics and diplomacy ; and they finally represented slave property valued at " over *two thousand millions of dollars.*"[3] The power attending this enormous wealth, accordingly, was colossal. Prominent statesmen, prior to Lincoln, shrank from open combat with the greatest vested interest in the realm. So pervasive,

[1] See Halévy, *op. cit.* (1830–41), p. 82.
[2] *Political Register*, August 4th, 1832.
[3] Brace's *Gesta Christi*, p. 378.

in truth, was its pressure that it divided even great religious bodies, compelling them to temporise or to compromise. Not till the cupidity of the slave interests began to force " the Institution " upon new and free-labour territories, did many of the friends of freedom realise that their hands at last were unbound ; for then only was it wholly apparent, that their " Charter of Liberty " was being wantonly prostituted into an engine of slavery.

Wesley's direct influence in America furthermore, particularly in heated political circles, was long curtailed and discounted because of the outspoken and unflattering character of his *Calm Address to Our American Colonies* on the outbreak of revolution. He therein had revealed himself as too much of an Englishman to suit the American mood, and his *Thoughts Upon Slavery* never received a national hearing in the United States, as it did in England. Again, the persistent English crusade against slavery was all too easily lampooned in the eyes of innumerable Americans, because England long was remembered by them as their old overlord and oppressor. The British anti-slavery campaign, consequently, was decried as guileful humanity-mongering, a mere cloak with which to cover " child slavery " in English factories ; a club with which first to browbeat the " defenceless " West Indian planters and then to force British Imperial policy upon weaker peoples, outside the Empire. And such Englishmen as Cobbett, furnished the American slave interests with abundant grist for this busy mill.

The American expression of the Evangelical Revival, more-over, though finally it was to affect profoundly the whole republic's life and destiny, was, on the whole, far more individualistic in character, than was the case in England. True, the heroic labours of such tireless Methodist pioneers as Asbury and Coke were to leave an abiding concern for righteousness within countless souls throughout the land ; true, too, in the United States as in Britain, the Revival kindled spiritual fires which profoundly influenced all Protestantism, including Unitarianism. But this spiritual fervour was commonly far too denominational in expression, and the rampant demon of American slavery could never be laid low, save by the co-operative endeavour of all the moral and spiritual forces within the realm. It was unfortunate that the Evangelical Revival in America was long in producing anything comparable to the moral, spiritual and social leadership afforded in England, on a non-party and interdenominational platform by the " Clapham Sect." The deplorable fact, too, that Whitefield had owned slaves for the running of his Georgia Orphanage proved a dire tragedy to the abolitionist cause. It afforded an argument that a man might be a veritable prince of God, and yet a slave-owner : and the argument was worked to the full. Slave planters did not bother to explain that Whitefield had died in 1770, before the ghastly truth about the slave trade and slavery was generally known, and before the social conscience of the Revival had yet been quickened against it. They conveniently forgot that as early as 1739 he had attacked certain inhumanities which he had learned of the slave trade,[1] that he was a bitter foe of all harsh treatment of slaves and an advocate of their religious education, and that his orphanage slaves were both given religious instruction and treated as servant-members of a large Christian household. Whitefield, in brief, had held the popular delusion that the savage natives of Africa would profit finally by being brought within the influence of Christian lands, wherein ultimately they would *purchase* their freedom by special faithfulness. He did not reckon with a central fact of history, that slavery, by its very nature, tends spiritually to enslave the enslavers. Such considerations, however, meant nothing to the American slave interests. Enough that Whitefield, the revered evangelist, had owned slaves for the running of a great Christian philanthropy. The " Institution" of slavery, therefore, they argued, was indubitably both Christian and humane.

Nevertheless, despite all the paradoxes, difficulties and disappointments confronting American Abolitionists, the constant and tireless pressure of the unwarped Christian conscience finally prevailed ; for increasingly it was felt by truly religious people that where the Spirit of Christ is, there must be outward and visible, as well as inward and invisible, Liberty. In 1823 for instance, when the slave interests were trying to foist their " Institution " on Illinois, " at one meeting of the Friends of Freedom in St. Clair County, more than thirty preachers of the Gospel attended and opposed the introduction of slavery into the State."[2] " The pulpit," says a contemporary authority, " thundered anathemas against the introduction of slavery. The religious community coupled freedom and Christianity together, which was one of the most powerful levers used in the contest." Indeed, " the clergy of Illinois," says the biographer of Governor Coles, " were almost without exception opposed to the Convention (which favoured the making it a Slave State)," and they " exerted great influence in securing the rejection at the polls."[3]

---

[1] See Tyerman's *Whitefield*, Vol. II, p. 132 ; Coupland's *Wilberforce* p. 77. The *Political State*, in 1739, published letters from Whitefield, attacking cruelties too commonly inflicted upon slaves.
[2] Washburne's *Governor Coles*, p. 136.
[3] *Ibid.*, p. 171.

It was shortly after his return from the first of his three visits to England, that William Lloyd Garrison, following the British Evangelical example, founded in 1833 the American Anti-Slavery Society. And if, in the ardour of his righteous crusade, he was at times to grow weary of ecclesiastical prudence, caution and compromise, there can be no doubt that it was a simple Evangelical faith in Christ which upheld and sustained him. " I call upon the spirits of the just made perfect in heaven," cried Garrison in 1832, " upon all who have experienced the love of God in their souls here below, upon the Christian converts in India and the isles of the sea, to sustain one in the assertion that there is power enough in the religion of Jesus Christ to melt down the most stubborn prejudices, to overthrow the highest wall of partition, to break the strongest caste, to improve and elevate the most degraded, and to equalise all its recipients."[1] Garrison's appeal is here more explicitly directed to Christians, than was Wesley's appeal in his *Thoughts Upon Slavery* fifty-eight years earlier; and the reason for this, marks a pronounced Christian advance.

Again, when we come to the execrable Fugitive Slave Law of 1850, the " tremendous defiance " of that great liberal Evangelical preacher of Plymouth Congregational Church, Brooklyn, is suggestive of the rising tide of righteous wrath which everywhere, outside the slave-ridden areas, was possessing the mind of American Evangelical Protestantism.[2]

" But as for those provisions," protested Henry Ward Beecher, " which concern aid to fugitives—may God do so to us, yea, and more also, if we do not spurn them as we would any other mandate of Satan ! If, in God's Providence, fugitives ask bread or shelter, raiment or conveyance at my hands, my own children shall lack bread ere they ; my own flesh shall sting with cold ere they shall lack clothing ; and whatsoever defence I would put forth for my own children, that shall these poor, despised, persecuted creatures have at my hands and upon the road. The man who would do otherwise, *who would obey this law to the peril of his soul and the loss of his manhood*, were he brother, son or father, shall never pollute my hand with grasp of hideous friendship, nor cast his swarthy shadow across my threshold."[3]

[1] Johnson's *Life of W. L. Garrison*, p. 106.
[2] Unitarian ministers, too, like Channing, played an important part in the American struggle for emancipation. But most of them, at this time, were as Evangelical in spirit, as those who professed a Trinitarian creed.
[3] See *Metaphors, Similies and other Characteristic Sayings of H. W. Beecher*, p. 19.

Little wonder that Lincoln pondered Beecher's sermons! And what need be said more? That most vitally effective of all novels, Harriet Beecher Stowe's *Uncle Tom's Cabin*, first published serially in 1851, was no " art for art's sake " production : rather was it a creative Evangelical treatise exposing the total incompatibility of slavery and Christianity. The same may be said of Whittier's numerous and effective anti-slavery poems : what Cowper was to the negroes' cause, in England, that, later, was Whittier to the negroes' cause, in America. As for Abraham Lincoln, there is no understanding his life apart from the practical values of vital Christianity which the Evangelical Awakening had so largely revived and diffused throughout the English-speaking world. The first influences which moulded his boyish mind, were his mother's reverent Scripture reading and her simple Evangelical piety, together with the occasional ministrations of Methodist and Baptist itinerant preachers, which he never failed to attend, despite the mud, slush or snow of frontier trails, through which so often he had to trudge. The Bible, throughout life, remained to Lincoln "the Book of Books." Always, was it on his Presidential desk ; daily, he perused its pages ; his spiritual outlook was formed and coloured by it ; his great heart was warmed by its prophetic utterance ; his tender human sympathies were kindled at its sacred fires : and who would deny that the clear, tense, glowing imagery of his trenchant speech, derived from this intimacy with Holy Writ? Lincoln was as much a product of the Revival's impact in America, as was Wilberforce of its impact in England.

* * * * *

Not yet, is slavery completely banished from the face of the earth. The " Mui Tsai " system in China, under guise of " adoption," still holds in its toils some two million Chinese girls, as domestic and often as sexual slaves.[1] Prior to the Italian subjection of Abyssinia, on the disinterested evidence of the most trustworthy witnesses, nearly a fifth of her 10,000,000 inhabitants were undisguised and saleable slaves. Even apologists of the late Abyssinian Empire, admitted the existence of " about a million " slaves—Abyssinians enthralled by Abyssinians.[2] In Arabia, slavery survives as " a normal social institution," not less than a tenth of her 7,000,000 inhabitants being thoroughgoing slaves, while in Mekka, her holy city,

[1] For much information on " Mui Tsai," see issues of *Anti-Slavery Reporter and Aborigines' Friend* (quarterly), 1935-8 ; also Harris, *op. cit.*, pp. 237, 239.
[2] See Max Grühl, *The Citadel of Ethiopia* (1932) ; Sir Arnold Hodson, *Where Lion Reign.*

human chattels are actually displayed for sale.[1] Liberia, founded in 1847 as a free African Republic for freed negroes, is another culprit state. Though only negroes vote, Liberia, as the 1931 International Commission of Inquiry under the League of Nations proves, has degenerated into a land exercising a slave economy.[2] Again, the peonage system of the more backward republics of South America, under cover of " labour for debt," is but one remove from positive slavery, the peon being subjected to abysmal ignorance and a brutish existence, as well as being bought and sold with the land on which he toils.[3]

Nevertheless, despite these revolting facts, the truth remains that Britain's Abolition of the Slave Trade in 1807 and her Emancipation Act of 1833, together with Lincoln's Proclamation of Emancipation of January 1st, 1863, and the thirteenth Amendment to the United States Constitution (1865), outlawing all slavery within the Union, forecast the end of modern slavery. With these epochal humanitarian victories, the final doom of the " dehumanising institution " was sealed ; for they proved both the foundation and the Magna Charta of innumerable liberating movements. Yet, the sorry fact that far into the twentieth century this mocking monster can still rear its head and show its poisoned fangs, betokens the tragic tenacity of man's inhumanity to man ; it demonstrates challengingly that constant vigilance is the price of progress.

That vigilance, however, is now increasingly being organised on a world scale such as earlier generations, for lack of adequate communications, found impossible. All the great missionary organisations of Christendom, Protestant and Catholic, are to-day steadfastly set against slavery. The British Anti-Slavery and Aborigines Protection Society, co-operating with like organisations in other lands, stands constantly on guard against the exploitation of defenceless races and peoples. While, however incomplete and maladjusted has proven the membership and working of the League of Nations, and however lamentable in many respects have been its practical failures, its International Labour Office, nevertheless, has done, and is doing, excellent work in striving to rally the conscience of all civilised peoples against the surviving remnant of slavery. Indeed, if Faith remains among men, and the rapidly increasing means of modern communication can be so consecrated as to create a really intelligent public opinion, is it too much to hope that peacefully, by international effort, the last lingering remnants of this cardinal social plague shall speedily be uprooted from the earth ?

[1] See E. Rutter, *Holy Cities of Arabia* ; Harris, p. 254.
[2] Besides the League's Report, see Sir Harry Johnston, *Liberia*.
[3] For a general survey of surviving slavery, see Lady Simon, *Slavery*.

THE FOUNDATIONS OF POPULAR EDUCATION

" A STRIKING tribute to the sterling qualities of self-help and religious earnestness which were so characteristic of the Early Victorian period . . ."

Encyclopædia Britannica,
    " Education (England) " concerning the Newcastle Commission's *Report on the State of Popular Education in England* (1861).

THE FOUNDATIONS OF POPULAR EDUCATION

As long as the slave trade and slavery were permitted to flourish and expand, so long all efforts for social reform in other spheres were doomed to abortiveness. Wesley had not overstated the case when he pronounced slavery, " the execrable sum of all the villainies ! "[1] By reducing men and women to marketable chattels, it cheapened all human life ; by its system of forced and unpaid labour under the lash, it vulgarised and degraded all labour ; by offering fortunes to the unscrupulous, it contaminated all economic and financial relationships ; by its monopoly purchase of Rotten Boroughs, it multiplied political bribery and corruption ; by its crucifixion of the basic decencies of civilised society, it tended both persistently and consistently to poison the milk of human kindness, and even to dehumanise human nature. This degradation by " Christian " peoples of millions of their fellow-humans, had a baneful and tragic reflex on every aspect of the social and industrial structure.

To strive, therefore, for *any* measure of creative social reform while leaving the slave trade and slavery to mock at all the sanctities of a Christian society, was simply to beat the air. Slavery affected the social problem *per totum*. So manifold and so subtle, moreover, were its impacts that nothing save a regenerated social conscience could challenge its domain : and the regenerated social conscience, in turn, waited upon the Baptism of Fire which gave it birth. But when once the spiritual renewal had come, and slavery finally began to be adjudged the diabolical perversion it was, then the marks of the lesser thraldoms, which it bred or fed, were seen in perspective : and man, independent of colour, race or tongue, being now increasingly recognised as an immortal soul, the humanitarian cause began gradually to advance on many fronts, including that of popular education.

(i) *Ill-omened Backgrounds*

In the late fifteenth century, as we have seen, under the " free morality " of the Renaissance influence, modern slavery began to establish itself within the outskirts of Christendom :

---

[1] See chapter vi (i).

in the early eighteenth century, under the "naturalism" of Deistic Rationalism, the slave traffic leapt to such proportions that it diseased the very vitals of Christendom. During this latter period, English popular education sank to its nadir, and the reasons will now be obvious. The Anti-Puritan purge and the expulsion of Non-Jurors had muzzled both Puritan and Old Catholic culture. Roman Catholicism was held at bay. And the much-vaunted "natural philosophy" of Deism resolved itself chiefly into shibboleths and pretty prattle, without sincerity or soul. Nepotism became as dominant within the Church as in politics, and was there more easily disguised. The new gospel of "Natural Rights," being emphasised apart from "natural duties," degenerated rapidly into a cloak for unnatural cupidity and lust. The curse of sinecures and pluralities, with their accompanying non-residence, honeycombed the whole National ecclesiastical system. Parish livings, like rotten boroughs, were advertised for sale. The "higher" clergy were the worst pluralists, and many of the prelates were worldlings. The Church, while boasting that it was conquering Deism "with its own weapons" and "on its own ground," had become almost as deistic as the Deists. Its distinctively Christian message had been rationalised into a frigid paganism : it had become a choice preserve of the ruling caste, a stern and unbending guardian of the *status quo*.

This State Church, indeed, was the most extensive, the most jealous and the most assuming of all the privileged "chartered companies" of the eighteenth century ; yet in its hand was the key to the problem of popular education throughout the nation. Is it surprising, then, that the era of Deistic religion and slave-trade economics, saw the morality and culture of the common people of England sink to its lowest ebb ?

Before the impact of the Evangelical Revival began to make itself nationally felt, the only vehicles for the general education of the populace were charity schools, privately endowed schools, dames' schools and a few struggling institutions run by Non-conformists to save their faith and independence from utter extinction. All alike, suffered from the soul-paralysis of the prevailing *Zeitgeist*. The Charity Schools were designed for only the poorest of the poor. They were under the control of the Church and were staffed generally by half-starved and half-illiterate teachers. Their curriculum was simple reading and ciphering (which few youngsters mastered), the unintelligible droning of the Catechism by heart, and stereotyped lessons on the "docility" and "deportment" of the poor before "their betters." Though numbered in hundreds and distributed in different parts of the land, their total annual income

SOME GREAT CHRISTIAN LABOUR LEADERS

Thomas Burt   Joseph Arch

Keir Hardie

Ramsay MacDonald   Arthur Henderson

was less than that of certain single hierarchical families who had mastered the then current art of ecclesiastical nepotism. Endowed schools commonly fell easy prey to sinecure hunters, who pocketed the endowments and let the schools degenerate into perversions of their true intent.[1] Dames' Schools were private ventures conducted in private houses, sometimes by spinsters in genteel poverty, but more often in poverty not genteel. The few surviving Nonconformist schools struggled valiantly to preserve some standard of education and of faith, but they had to row desperately against the stream and were losing heart. The rich and privileged, on the other hand, educated their children either by private tutors at home or at one of the great boarding institutions known as " Public Schools," which perhaps were the most exclusively " private " on the face of the earth.[2]

To understand the real foundations of England's popular educational system, no less than six separate and distinct stages of advance must be clearly defined. These are represented by the Sunday School movement, the Royal Lancastrian Institution which developed into the British and Foreign School Society, the National School Society, the Factory Schools, the Ragged School Union, and finally the famous Board School Act of 1870 which, supplemented by the Acts of 1876 and 1880, established universal and compulsory education throughout the land. To the brief exploration, therefore, of these successive pioneering endeavours, we needs must turn.

(ii) *The Initial Advance*

" The Sunday schools established by Mr. Raikes of Gloucester," says John Richard Green, " were the beginnings of popular education."[3] Robert Raikes's Gloucester Sunday school, however, established in 1780 with the help of Rev. Thomas Stock, was not the first experiment in the education of neglected children on Sundays. Hannah Ball, eleven years previously, with Wesley's backing, had established a flourishing Sunday school in conjunction with her day school in High Wycombe, and Silas Told, the life friend of criminals, had on Sundays long taught poor children at Wesley's Foundery, London, to read the Bible. Nor had either of them established a precedent. Isolated enthusiasts, both Catholic and Protestant, in different lands, had from time to time instructed needy

---

[1] See *Johnson's England*, Vol. I (introductory chapter).
[2] The above conditions do not apply to Scotland, where since 1696 all but universal popular education had prevailed.
[3] *Short History of the English People*, p. 740.

children on Sundays. Yet Raikes is an historic character. When he opened his Gloucester Sunday school, the Evangelical Revival had already created an atmosphere favourable to the rapid national reception of the educational enthusiasm that warmed his own heart. Being a prominent newspaper proprietor, moreover, and a man of influence, Raikes, by the success of his scheme, attracted public attention ; and backed not only by the weight of Wesley's organisation, but also by the mighty influence of Wesley's voice and pen,[1] the Sunday School Movement, which at first taught both reading and writing as well as Bible knowledge, was soon on the high road to national and even international significance.[2]

Raikes's first teachers were paid ; but the Evangelical Revival quickly embracing the whole Sunday school plan, zealous voluntary teachers were soon forthcoming, and the amazing development of the Sunday school system affords one of the most wholesome and creative romances in the whole history of education. As early as 1784 Wesley reports that he finds these schools springing up " wherever he goes," and certainly his much coming and going was to them a source of encouragement and strength. In 1785 the *London Society for the Establishment of Sunday Schools* was formed, with the famous philanthropists, Henry Thornton and Jonas Hanway, on its managing committee ; while in 1803, the movement being already nation wide, a *Sunday School Union* was created for the *whole* of England. Meantime, so well had the soil been prepared, that by 1786 no less than 200,000 English children were regularly attending Sunday schools. In 1791 the movement was planted in America. In 1831, when Lord Shaftesbury unveiled a statue to Raikes, it was claimed that already in Great Britain alone 1,250,000 children were attending Sunday schools. When the Sunday School centenary was celebrated in 1880 the movement had taken root in every continent, and its voluntary *teachers* far exceeded a million.[3]

Not yet, has the debt been fully realised which English-speaking democracies owe to the great army of young men and women, who received their first training in Christian and social service as teachers in Sunday schools : many of them, have been the salt of the earth. Nor again is it commonly remembered that, quite independent of Rousseau, such capable Sunday school enthusiasts as Sarah Trimmer, Hannah More and Mary

[1] Wesley not only wrote in his *Arminian Magazine,* supporting the founding of Sunday Schools, but also he opened its columns to Raikes himself to explain the movement.

[2] See A. Gregory, *Robert Raikes.*

[3] See " Raikes," in *Dict. of Nat. Biog.* ; also " Sunday Schools " in *Ency. of Rel. and Ethics* and in *Ency. of Education.*

Sherwood created the beginnings of a splendid English literature for children.[1]

(iii) "*British and Foreign*" and "*National*" *School Societies*

The central character associated with the second stage of popular education in England, was the impulsive and adventurous Joseph Lancaster. Born in a fervent Evangelical home, he was intended for the Nonconformist ministry; but his restless nature would not wait for training. Mature beyond his years, and burning with missionary zeal, at fourteen he secretly left home and made his way to Bristol, bent on sailing for Jamaica " to teach the poor blacks the Word of God."[2] At Bristol, the stripling found his plans frustrated for lack of funds. Six years of variegated adventure ensued; but the impulse to teach could not be suppressed, so in 1798, having meanwhile become a Quaker, he opened a small school where he began experimenting with " new methods " of education. Then, in 1801, he took " a large room in Borough Road," London, over which he inscribed the somewhat humorous notice : " All who will may send their children and have them educated freely, and those who do not wish to have education for nothing may pay for it if they please."

Lancaster's novel methods, including the monitorial system of pupil teachers and a complex scale of " honours and humiliations," attracted wide attention. By them, he claimed, " one master could teach a thousand, or even a greater number of children, not only as well, but a great deal better, than . . . by the old methods, and at an expense of less than five shillings a year for each."[3] Here, it was contended, was an educational invention comparable to the wondrous " labour saving " factory machines : not only would it educate children wholesale, but also it would turn out teachers for the entire countryside. Soon young Lancaster had a duke and a lord among his patrons. Then, to crown all, in 1805, George III sent for him and became both a subscriber and a patron, the interview being concluded by the King's famous statement : " It is my wish that every poor child in my dominions, should be taught to read the Bible." This royal patronage was the beginning of Lancaster's undoing. A reckless financier, he now extended beyond his means, and

---

[1] See T. Bernard, *Education of the Poor*, p. 112 ff. ; also Roberts's *Memoirs of Hannah More*.

[2] *Dict. of Nat. Biog.* (" Joseph Lancaster ") ; also Lancaster's *Life*, by Wm. Corston.

[3] *Edinburgh Review*, " Education of the Poor" (November, 1810).

with the close of the year 1807, despite his " economical system," he found himself £3,000 in debt.

Supporters, including the Quakers, William Allen and Joseph Fox, came to the rescue, took over the finances, and organised the *Royal Lancastrian Institution*. This Institution quickly expanded, producing many " teachers " for provincial schools ; but Lancaster was an autocrat, and could not brook committees. His peremptory methods and extravagant expenditures caused endless friction ; so in 1814, his directors and chief supporters, despairing of controlling him, ejected him, forthwith rechristening the whole organisation, the *British and Foreign School Society*. This important educational instrument was interdenominational in its conception and range. The new Evangelical Nonconformity was the soul of the whole movement ; but, as in the fight against the slave-trade and slavery, certain eminent radicals, including Bentham, James Mill, Place and Brougham, joined the good work.[1] The Lancastrian Institution and its successor, the British Society, used the Bible as an obligatory reading text ; but no doctrinal exposition was permitted, nor was any catechism allowed. Indeed, it was the boast of this historic organisation that its schools, which soon mounted to thousands, were " schools for all," and not simply for Churchmen or Nonconformists of any particular brand.

Yet just here, to most High Churchmen and to not a few Anglican Evangelicals, was a rock of offence. Wilberforce who, in high emotion, persuaded Pitt to scrap his drafted Bill against the Nonconformists, and who was one of the creators of the very practical and truly educational *Society for Bettering the Conditions and Increasing the Comforts of the Poor*,[2] refused, after prolonged consideration, to accept the Vice-Presidency of the Lancastrian Institution. He remained friendly toward it, but to him its moral and religious teaching was too intangible, too nebulous. It was, however, chiefly to aggressive " Church " suspicion of this dominantly Nonconformist organisation, that the third advance of popular education owed its being. Mrs. Sarah Trimmer, kind soul though she was, began denouncing Lancaster as " the Goliath of schismatics." Coleridge, who had swung around from practical Unitarianism and become the High Church philosopher, in a public lecture, after reading a paragraph from a treatise by Lancaster, denounced his schools as " prison stations," and contemptuously flung his booklet on the floor.[3] The Episcopate, if more discreet, was

[1] Halévy, *Formation du Radicalisme Philosophique*, Vol. II, p. 247ff.
[2] See *Reports* of this Society (1798–1808), five vols.
[3] *Quarterly Review* (" Bell and Lancaster's System of Education "), October, 1811.

like-minded. So, in 1811, was created the *National Society for the Education of the Poor in accordance with the Principles of the Church of England.*

The dominant character behind the National Society was a Scotch Anglican, Dr. Andrew Bell, twenty-five years the senior of Lancaster. In 1787 he had sailed, almost penniless, as a chaplain to India : soon he was holding eight chaplainships concurrently, while at the same time he was Superintendent of the Madras Male Orphanage Asylum, where, prior to Lancaster in England, he had introduced a form of monitorial teaching.[1] Thanks to pluralities, plus Scottish business acumen, Bell, within ten years, was back in England with a fortune of more than £25,000. The enormous growth of the Lancaster schools and the rising suspicion of " the Church," caused Bell's hour to strike. Given a rich sinecure, and proclaimed the " real founder " of the monitorial method, he was made the virtual Director of the National Society, with a roving commission to found Church schools throughout the land. How much the officialdom of the Established Church had awakened from its century of gout and slumber, is symbolised by the fact that in the twenty years between the formation of the National Society and the burial of Andrew Bell in Westminster Abbey, in 1831, nearly 13,000 " National " schools had been formed.[2]

(iv) *Factory Schools and Ragged Schools*

The fourth landmark in the long educational march must be recorded not because of its direct educational attainment, but because, by *State legislation* it forced upon the " captains of industry " some personal responsibility for the mental, moral and social status of the factory child.

The 1833 Factory Act—the first of far-reaching significance— was, by common consent, a forced measure. The Government, to side-track Lord Shaftesbury's comprehensive Bill, simply brought forward, on their own behalf, the irreducible minimum of his demands. Nevertheless more was achieved than Lord Althorp, who introduced this Government sop, desired to concede. Disinterested and efficient factory inspection was henceforth established in English industry. Children under nine were protected from factory employment, thus giving educational institutions a free hand to work for their welfare. No child under thirteen was permitted to toil in the " key industries "

---

[1] Bell published his *Experiment in Education* in 1797, the year before Lancaster opened his first school.

[2] See *Ency. Brit.*, and *Dict. of Nat. Biog.* (" Bell ") ; also Meiklejohn's *An Old Educational Reformer.*

more than nine hours in a day, or more than forty-eight hours a week. And *during these working hours*, school facilities had to be provided by the factory owners, whereby two hours of education was afforded daily to all employees under thirteen.

Factory Schools, at best, were but sorry educational institutions, and not a few factory owners strove to make them ludicrous. Yet Britain was richly blest by the fact that for fifty years following the passage of this 1833 Act, the trusted Parliamentary leader of the industrial workers was a prince among men. The hero of the classic succession of emancipating Factory Acts, was not only a non-party statesmen who repeatedly refused Cabinet Office and other lucrative posts, the better to serve his "Cause"; he also was an unfaltering and passionate advocate of the mental, moral and spiritual culture of the humblest toilers in the land. "If there is one man in England more devoted to the interests of the factory people than another," said an official delegate of the Workers' Committees in 1836, "it is Lord Ashley (Shaftesbury)—we may always rely upon him as a ready, steadfast and willing friend."[1] Shaftesbury saw to it that the factory inspectors, introduced in 1833, were men of character, integrity and independence. He saw to it also, that the principle of daily education even for the humblest factory child, as conceded by Althorp's Act, was kept constantly before Parliament and the nation. But, all important, he piloted the epic succession of legislative enactments which, freeing the industrial child from the early tyranny of factory, workshop and mine, gave Education its chance. Indeed, the sheer majesty of Shaftesbury's achievements in this regard, has commonly blinded historians to the fact that he also was a valiant pioneer in educational schemes.[2]

Two principles central in Shaftesbury's incomparable crusade of social reform were, (1) that women should be freed from the tyranny of industry, and educated to raise home-making to the standard of a Christian art, (2) that children should be likewise freed, and educated nobly to take their place as intelligent, useful, healthy and happy citizens in a Christian State.

Fifth in the succession of pioneer educational movements, comes the Ragged School Union, a direct offshoot of Sunday School endeavours. Its purpose was to catch, befriend and educate, "human eels in the mud." As early as 1798, in Southwark, London, Thomas Cranfield, a pious tailor, branched from orthodox Sunday School work into special efforts, Sunday and week-day, for slum-ridden children *too ragged* to attend

---

[1] *Manchester and Salford Advertiser*, July 9th, 1836.
[2] See Bready's *Shaftesbury*, chapter xi ("The Problem of Popular Education").

Sunday Schools. But though he founded several schools for such urchins and was supported by Rev. Rowland Hill, his work was not destined to continuity. The same was true of the godly Portsmouth shoemaker, John Pounds, whose heroic efforts among ragged youngsters might have been quite forgotten had not Dr. Thomas Guthrie eulogised his memory. Again, the London City Mission, founded in 1835, soon established several schools, " exclusively for children raggedly clothed." But it was not till 1844 that a group of forty voluntary " ragged school " teachers banded together into the *Ragged School Union*, and urged Lord Shaftesbury to become their president : which gladly he did.

From that moment, ragged schools were assured of continuity. The *Union* became a unique educational force, and in time the mother of certain of the most Christian and most creative social-welfare movements modern Britain can boast. Theoretic educational treatises are disposed, on professional grounds, quite to ignore the Ragged Schools : indeed, many of the authors of such treatises—though continually idealising the nebulous sentimentalities of Rousseau, who left his own children to be reared in orphanages while he preached " natural " affection—are apparently wholly ignorant of their work. Yet consider some of the national characters who worked in, or for, Ragged Schools. Besides Lord Shaftesbury, were Dr. Barnardo and Quintin Hogg, General Gordon and " Rob Roy " Macgregor, Judge Payne and the Baroness Burdett-Coutts, Charles Dickens and Samuel Smiles, Archbishop Sumner and Dean Farrar, Canon Barnett and Dr. Parker, Dr. Guthrie and Charles Spurgeon, Lord Aberdeen and Sir Thomas Chambers, Judge Hughes and Sheriff Watson, Sir Robert Carden and Professor Leone Levi, Newman Hall and Hugh Price Hughes. What group of completely secular school boards or school masters, can be compared with this group ? Nevertheless, the genius of such men co-operated freely with the labours of thousands of humble religious enthusiasts, in creating that Christian " Democracy of Service " which gave both spirit and body to Ragged Schools.

The programme of the Ragged Schools, when not ignored, has often been subjected to the passing sneers of superior critics. Certainly, from purely academic standards, their attainments were modest ; but, to grapple with the peculiar social conditions for which they were created, they were uniquely adapted. And later, State schools in slum areas, though always loath to admit their debt, had to learn the social and humanitarian aspect of their task from these despised institutions. For its more orthodox educational purposes, the Ragged School Union conducted day and Sunday schools for small ragged children, evening and Sunday schools for youths and adults engaged in daily occupation, women's classes " for improving character and extending domestic usefulness," and industrial classes which taught both tailoring and shoemaking. But it was through its humane and experimental efforts, that the Ragged School Union made its most original contribution. Never was it, in Shaftesbury's phrase, " stiff, starched and in buckram." By virtue of its elasticity of organisation and its sensitivity to need, it established boys' institutes, youths' clubs, cripples' aid parlours, mothers' meetings, coffee-rooms, playing fields, recreational classes, bath houses, facilities for distributing food and clothing to the destitute, holidays in the country for sick children, annual " treats," maternity centres, temperance guilds, garden clubs, flower shows, efficiency prizes, and numerous other social activities. Nor was its economic interest less than its social. Besides its craftsmanship classes, it founded employment tests, Colonial emigration schemes, emigration farms, mercantile training ships, shoe-blacking brigades, allotment gardens and industrial tests ; while to such were added, penny banks, soup-kitchens, coal, clothing and shoe clubs, as well as cooking, sewing and knitting instruction.

The soul of the Union, however, was its religious and cultural work. The Bible was its central text : the larger schools each evolved a Ragged Church ; all had Sunday Schools, Bible classes, mission services, prayer meetings and Bands of Hope. Early the Union created its own Magazine ; lending libraries, reading-rooms and public lectures, were part of the common programme ; choral singing, children's choirs, drum-and-fife bands, and general concert parties, were objects of the Union's pride ; while the Christian spirit and influence, permeated everything the Ragged Schools undertook.[1]

(v) *The State Fills the Gaps*

The sixth and final stage, in the long and circuitous route to universal Education in England, is too well known even to be outlined here. In W. E. Forster's own words, the purpose of the Board School Act (1870) was, " to complete the voluntary system and fill up the gaps," but " not to supplant the voluntary system " ; and Gladstone, under whose Administration the Act was passed, consistently took the same attitude.

---

[1] For the fullest treatment of the Ragged Schools, see C. J. Montague, *Sixty Years in Waifdom* ; for a brief, but fully documented, treatment, see the author's *Shaftesbury*, chapter xii.

The initial " voluntary system," in truth, was expressive of the new genius which had penetrated British blood, and it was closely related to the Evangelical Revival. Rivalry, experimentation and some animosity, entered into the making of England's popular education ; but faith, nonetheless, was its guiding star ; and slow as was its evolution, it was a natural growth, rather than a bureaucratic system imposed from above. Which fact, has saved England from the robot educational methods prescribed by some modern states.

The famous Newcastle Commission (1858–61) in its " Report on the State of Popular Education in England " found that about 2,500,000 children were already receiving some kind of daily education, which meant that nearly one-seventh of the *entire* population was attending day schools. In France the proportion was one-ninth ; and in Prussia, where compulsory education was already in force, one-sixth. Much of the English voluntary education, admittedly, was open to criticism : nevertheless, the *Encyclopædia Britannica* is expressing but sober sense when it pronounces the Newcastle Commission Report, " a striking tribute to the sterling qualities of self-help and religious earnestness, which were so characteristic of the early Victorian period."

Again, Sir Thomas Chambers, after the advent of Board Schools, asked : " Who are they that have brought about this marvellous improvement in the amount of Education given, and in the Educational machinery involved ? Who but the members of all the Evangelical Churches throughout the country ? Who have filled the Sunday Schools, and the Ragged Schools, and the British and Foreign Schools, and, to a great extent, the National schools, with teachers ? Who but the men who have acted from religious motives, and whose conduct has been influenced by the teaching of the Gospel ? "[1]

Both Utilitarianism and Rationalism contributed to the broad and winding stream of England's popular educational system, but the main source and chief sustenance of the system, was the persistent, creative, adventurous impact of vital, practical, Evangelical religion. Moreover, certain remarkable social and cultural movements remain to-day, as impressive witness to the spiritual values which inspired popular education. The Sunday School movement now has no less than 33,000,000 scholars the world over ; its schools number 350,000, and its voluntary teachers and officers 3,600,000.[2] The present Shaftesbury Society and Ragged School Union, the lineal descendant of

[1] Montague, *op. cit.*, p. 310.
[2] These figures are from the *Report* of the International Sunday School Convention, 1928.

the original Union, is to-day one of Britain's noblest social philanthropies : while again, both Barnardo's Homes, whose beneficient child-welfare influence has extended to every continent, and the Polytechnic Institute, the parent of technical education throughout the Empire, were born in humble Ragged Schools. Practical religion not only pioneered the movement for popular education in England : it injected purpose, power and poise into the very concept of education.

PARALLEL CREATIVE VICTORIES

" THE anti-slave trade movement was the first success-ful propagandist agitation of the modern type, and its methods were afterwards imitated by the myriad societies and leagues—political, religious, philanthropic and cultural—which characterised Nineteenth Century England."

GEORGE MACAULAY TREVELYAN, O.M., *History of England*, p. 599.

PARALLEL CREATIVE VICTORIES

EDMUND BURKE, in his noble *Guildhall Speech* (Bristol, 1780), when exposing certain anomalies and injustices of the penal code as it affected debtors, paid memorable tribute to the unique endeavours of John Howard. " I cannot name this gentleman," said Burke, " without remarking that his labours and writings have done much to open the eyes and hearts of mankind. He has visited all Europe—not to survey the sumptuousness of palaces, or the stateliness of temples ; not to make accurate measurements of the remains of ancient grandeur, nor to form a scale of the curiosity of modern art ; not to collect medals, or collate manuscripts—but to dive into the depths of dungeons ; to plunge into the infection of hospitals ; to survey the mansions of sorrow and pain ; to take the gauge and dimensions of misery, depression and contempt ; to remember the forgotten, to attend to the neglected, to visit the forsaken, and to compare and collate the distresses of all men in all countries. His plan is original ; and it is as full of genius as it is of humanity. It was a voyage of discovery ; a circum-navigation of charity. Already the benefit of his labour is felt more or less in every country . . ."[1]

(i) *The Humanising of the Prison System*

Howard certainly was among the most heroic of the eighteenth century products of the Revival. In his Evangelicalism, as was the case with Wilberforce, and many other vital characters, the influence of Dissent, Methodism and Anglicanism coalesced in marked degree. Born in a pious Independent home, he himself continued a Nonconformist ; but he had no enthusiasm either for denominationalism or dissent, as such : he was a zealous disciple of Wesley and a warm supporter of the Revival's work ; yet married twice, both his wives, to whom he was in

---

[1] This speech is printed at length in Professor G. R. Carpenter's *Model English Prose*, p. 323.

turn devoted, were " Church " women. And though a
Dissenter till death, Howard revered vital, practical Christianity
—Protestant or Catholic—wherever he met with it ; while so
great was his appeal to the soul of the British people, that his
was the very first statue admitted to St. Paul's Cathedral.[1]
And it was raised by public subscription.

In reminiscent vein, Howard once made known to a group
of Wesley's preachers the challenge and lasting inspiration he
had derived from a sermon preached by Wesley at his seat in
Bedfordshire on the text, " Whatsoever thy hand findeth to
do, do it with thy might."[2] After an interview with Wesley
in Dublin, he related to Alexander Knox how satisfying and
sustaining he found the fellowship and conversation of his
great friend. About to set off on one of his prolonged tours of
prison inspection, he called on Wesley to present him with an
inscribed copy of his famous book and to say good-bye. It was
a " profound disappointment " to him to learn that the evangelist had left London, *en route* for Ireland, not long before he
arrived at his rooms. Wesley's admiration for Howard, moreover, was equally keen. Following an extended conversation
with him in 1787, he expressed the belief that the heroic
prison reformer was surely " one of the greatest men in
Europe."[3]

Howard's immediate precursors, as friends of the debtor,
the felon and the murderer in their enforced haunts of wretchedness and despair, were those of spiritual outlook much akin to
his own. As, during the worst years of the Persecuting Code,
hundreds of Quakers and other Puritans died in vile gaols,[4]
the Nonconformists naturally developed a sympathetic interest
in the welfare of prisoners ; but under the blighting spiritual
conditions of the early eighteenth century, that interest soon
lagged and waned. Wesley, too, as we have seen, was a constant
friend of prisoners ; Newgate, London, he considered, the
nearest possible earthly approach to hell ; he raised money to
procure clothing and blankets for the French prisoners of the
Seven Years War, detained in English gaols ; and he encouraged
all his preachers, when they were permitted to do so, to visit
and to minister to the needs of prisoners. Charles Wesley
expended much tender and gracious effort upon prisoners ;
Silas Told, one of Wesley's most heroic teachers and preachers,
served them faithfully all his life ; and Mr. Dagge, who transformed the face of the Bristol Newgate years before Howard

[1] *Dict. of Nat. Biog.* (" John Howard "). This fact was verified for the
author by the librarian of St. Paul's.
[2] Wesley's *Journal* (June 28th, 1787) (see note, Standard edition).
[3] See Edward's *Wesley*, p. 150.
[4] Graham's *William Penn*, p. 172.

began his life-work, was one of the earliest products of the Revival, converted under the preaching of Whitefield.[1]

Nevertheless it was left to the moral chivalry of John Howard the country gentleman, whom Green pronounces " the most energetic and zealous of reformers," so to challenge the emerging social conscience as to make sanitary, humane and redemptive prison conditions a matter of public concern. Prisoners, next to slaves, are the most hapless of mortals ; and being confined from public scrutiny, their lot, especially in a society dominated by factions or oligarchies, may easily degenerate into a condition of living death. When Howard in 1773, after his appointment as high sheriff of Bedfordshire, began the investigation of English prisons, he found the whole system of confinement a wilderness of cruelty, immorality and graft. Few jail keepers got any stated stipend : hence, being dependent upon guile and extortion for their livelihood " fees," they commonly represented the basest type of manhood. County jails alone, were under the control of sheriffs, while on all sides sections of counties, municipal corporations, liberties, franchises and even private individuals ran jails : some of them old towers or castles, some the dungeon-rooms under court-houses or town-halls, some even the dark, filthy cellars of public houses : and the insecurity of many of these incarceration quarters, afforded nominal excuse for the use of irons, strait-jackets and chains.[2] Men, women and children frequently were huddled together in common dens of despair ; disease, prostitution, drunkenness and general debauchery, were rife ; semi-starvation was common ; and sometimes only the generosity of felons, who legally could claim " county bread," saved luckless debtors from actual starvation. Indeed, the chief hope of the prisoner lay in the fact that, owing to the over-crowding of jails, the Legislature frequently was " obliged to make a general arbitrary gaol-delivery, and at once to set open, by its sovereign authority, all the prisons in England."[3]

It was well for the cause of prison reform that spiritual fire had possessed the soul of a county gentleman, a man of social position, financial independence, physical hardihood, indomitable will and amazing pertinacity of purpose. If Howard was both a teetotaller and a vegetarian—an odd creature in the age of gluttony and gout—he nevertheless was a country squire, and, as such, had to be respected. Hence, though when Wesley

[1] See *Annual Register*, 1761, p. 61 ; also Bebb's *Nonconformity and Social and Economic Life, 1660–1800*, p. 153.
[2] See S. Webb, *Prisons Under Local Government*, pp. 2–9 ; Howard, *State of Prisons in England and Wales*, p. 20f.
[3] Edmund Burke, *op. cit.*, p. 322.

and his itinerant preachers criticised prison conditions, they, in many quarters, could be laughed out of court as "ranting fanatics," with Howard the case was different ! He, moreover, had access to many gaols from which they were completely excluded, and when once the challenge presented itself, he was in a position to make prison reform an exclusive mission, and to finance his own life-crusade.

Early in his investigations, Howard discovered among the most pitiable inmates of English prisons, persons languishing for months without even having been brought to trial, persons in court declared " not guilty," persons whose prosecutors had failed to appear, and persons against whom grand juries could lay no charge. They were detained because unable to pay the jailer's " fees."

Rising commonly about three a.m., four times during his seventeen years of solitary crusade, did Howard inspect the jails of the entire United Kingdom. Repeatedly, amidst incredible travelling difficulties, he visited, note-book in hand, the principal prisons, hospitals, lazarettos and workhouses of a dozen European countries, though in more than one quarter admission was gained only by disguise. Before Howard, on January 20th, 1790, died of malignant fever at Kherson, in Southern Russia, he had travelled more than 50,000 miles in the prisoners' cause ; refusing Government assistance, he had expended some £30,000 of his own fortune ; he had shut himself up in dingy dungeons that he might experience something of the anguish of his fellow creatures ; without reserve, he had given his time, his talents, his means, his all : he had made sensitive souls in many lands to feel for the criminal a new sympathy as a fellow mortal, who, by humane treatment, practical education and spiritual guidance, might be reclaimed to an upright and useful life.

In a unique sense, Howard remains the father of all modern prison reform. For his " humanity and zeal," he received the official thanks of the House of Commons. As a direct result of his labours, different reforming Acts were placed on the Statute Books[1] ; and scores of decently constructed prisons were reared to take the place of previous dungeons and dens.[2] Yet so great were the " interests " and contradictions involved, that effective prison reform remained, for many decades, a crying problem : nor even to-day is it quite achieved.

Howard's labours were the immediate inspiration of Jeremy Bentham's " Panopticon " scheme ; and if that mechanical contrivance was to prove futilitarian rather than utilitarian, it was for no lack of ardour on Bentham's part. One of his many

[1] See 14 George III, c. 20 and c. 59.   [2] Webb. *op. cit.*, p. 51.

FOUNDERS OF CREATIVE MOVEMENTS

General Booth   Sir George Williams

Doctor Barnardo   David Nasmith

Rev. Benjamin Waugh   Frances Willard

Panopticon tracts opens thus : " Morals reformed, health preserved, industry invigorated, instruction diffused, public burdens lightened, economy seated as it were upon a rock, the Gordian knot of the poor laws not cut but untied, all by a simple idea of architecture." Bentham assuredly was over optimistic regarding the possibilities of his circular institutional structures, wherein warders seated in the administrative centre could " see all, without being seen." Nevertheless so sincere was the humanitarian desire for prison reform, that Bentham's scheme won the warm support of such influential characters as Wilberforce and William Allen, the Quaker proprietor of the *Philanthropist*.   Finally, too, so great became the political prestige of his Utilitarian school, that under the constant pressure of James Mill and Sir Samuel Romilly, Bentham in 1813 became the personal recipient from Parliament, on its abandonment of his Panopticon scheme, of the seemingly extravagant sum of £23,000 as indemnity for losses incurred. Despite all his theoretic talk of the *summum bonum* and of " the greatest happiness to the greatest number," the Utilitarian Bentham was much more money-minded, than the Evangelical Howard.[1]

The real successor to Howard was of course the Quaker minister, Mrs. Elizabeth Fry. Though a daughter of John Gurney, Quaker banker at Norwich, as a girl she " loved gaiety " and eschewed all religious enthusiasm ; but under the influence of William Savery, an American Quaker preacher, she began to thirst for spiritual life. On becoming a Quaker minister, at twenty-nine, she experienced such " incomings of love, joy and peace " that all doubts fled her soul. Already the mother of several children and finally to be mother of eleven, she nevertheless found time for works of mercy on every hand. But not till 1813, when thirty-three years old, did she launch forth upon the heroic labours that have immortalised her name. If the French " Terror " and the ensuing Napoleonic wars, retarded *all* social reform in England, prison reform it specially retarded. When a nation believes that it is fighting for its very *being*, its *well-being* is forgotten. All prisoners—male or female— who can serve the State are commonly released and put to " national " tasks. War-time prison inmates, accordingly, are reckoned incorrigible enemies of society—traitors unworthy of mercy or care.

Such was the case when Elizabeth Fry, in 1813, was introduced to Newgate, London, the most notorious prison in the realm ; indeed to read certain of her records one might imagine that during the long succession of war years, the good effects of

[1] See Bowring's *Life* of Bentham in *collected Works* ; Halévy, *op. cit.* (1815), p. 503f. ; *Dict, of Nat. Biog.* (" Bentham ").

Howard's life-work had been almost obliterated. She concentrated upon the care of women prisoners, many of whom were desperate and depraved, and the results of her courage, sympathy, patience, faith and far-sighted plans, afford one of the most beautiful manifestations of Christian grace. "I have seen the greatest wonder in England," observed an American visitor ; "I have seen Elizabeth Fry in Newgate, and I have witnessed there the miraculous effects of true Christianity upon the most depraved of human beings." As Mrs. Fry read the Bible and prayed with the women of Newgate, the hardest and most impervious criminals melted into reverence and love. But not only did she teach these abandoned women that they had souls, and were capable of aspiration and worship, she opened for them successful prison schools ; she had matrons appointed instead of male superintendents ; by her example and precept, she inspired the "Association for the Improvement of Female Prisoners in Newgate " ; she created the "Ladies Association for visiting Gaols " ; she interested different Christian statesmen, including Wilberforce, in the great problem ; and she sowed the seeds of an order of "nursing sisters " which Florence Nightingale later carried to such rich fruition. The Evangelical Revival created a noble succession of practical women saints, and Elizabeth Fry was one of the noblest in that truly Apostolic line.[1]

(ii) *The Reform of the Penal Code*

If in the heroic struggle for prison reform the Evangelicals took the lead and the humanitarian rationalists fell into line, in the protracted campaign to reform the penal code it was chiefly the humanitarian rationalists who led the march, while the Evangelicals accompanied with stalwart support. But here again, the French Revolution was the deadly stumbling block. Prior to that prolonged holocaust, humanitarian reform in England was gaining headway on many fronts. Indeed thousands of high-minded Englishmen, like Wordsworth, greeted the dawn of the Revolution with exuberant joy, but after the blind blood-bath of the Reign of Terror, turned from it with loathing unutterable. This revulsion completely obsessed Pitt ; it incited Wilberforce, in utter sincerity, to agitate for the miserable Combination Laws (1799 and 1800), fearing that Trade Combines would degenerate into secret revolutionary societies ; it was the immediate cause of making still more fearful an already ferocious criminal code. In fact the only

[1] See Elizabeth Fry, *Observations on . . . Female Prisoners* ; *Life*, by her daughters ; Janet Whitney, *Elizabeth Fry, Quaker Heroine* (1937).

redeeming grace was that, though the " hanging laws " were temporarily increased, the actual number of persons hanged was in the decrease : for, despite the revolutionary psychology of fear, spiritual and humanitarian values were still at work, and all that was best in the nation shrank from enforcing a blood-thirsty code.

Arthur Young, in his *Autobiography*, records a conversation he once held with Edmund Burke in which the political philosopher said that : " Gibbon was an old friend of his, and he knew well that before he died, he heartily repented of the anti-religious part of his work for contributing to free mankind from all restraints on their vices and profligacy, and thereby aiding so much the spirit which produced the horrors that blackened the most detestable of all revolutions."[1] When Gibbon came to feel thus, is it surprising that many landed squires and hireling lawyers, who cared little for spiritual Christianity, turned to the ceremonies of formalistic religion and to the repressions of a sterner criminal code, to combat the revolutionary spirit ? With the more robust humanitarian Radicals and with the thorough-going Evangelicals, such was not the case ; and as sanity gradually reasserted itself, these groups worked steadfastly, side by side, to rationalise the chaos and to remove the inhumanity of a vicious and tyrannical penal code. Nor was such co-operation limited to this particular issue. Both Professor Graham Wallas and Professor Halévy do well to remind us that for long there existed " the tradition of a working alliance between the two forces."[2] On doctrinal matters they agreed to disagree ; each recognised in the other admirable practical qualities ; and when pressing humanitarian work was to be done, both stripped off their coats and put their shoulders to the wheel. And so doing, they manifested characteristics which fortunately were becoming increasingly typical of Englishmen at their best.

In codifying, rationalising and humanising the criminal law the names of Bentham, Romilly and Mackintosh stand rightly to the fore. All were great lawyers and, what does not always follow, great hearts. For a generation they struggled valiantly to bring order, sanity, justice and mercy, into a bewildering jungle of legal entanglement ; and notwithstanding all hoary prejudice and die-hard resentment, their efforts finally were crowned with success. But what is commonly forgotten is that such philanthropic Evangelicals as Wilberforce, Thornton, Allen and Grant, despite their already wide range of

[1] *Op. cit.* (edited by Bentham Edwards), p. 258.
[2] See Halévy, *English People* (1815), pp. 507–11 ; and Wallas's Introduction to same volume, pp. vi, vii.

humanitarian interests, rendered them yeoman support. " The barbarous custom of hanging," wrote Wilberforce as early as June, 1787, " has been tried too long, and with the success which might have been expected from it."[1] " Every time Romilly brought forward in the Commons the abolition of the death penalty for an offence," says Halévy, " Wilberforce intervened in the debate to support Romilly's proposal with his influence."[2] In 1817, supporting Romilly's attack on the Game Laws, Wilberforce declared it " unjust " to punish so severely " an act, which it was contrary to the natural feeling of mankind to say was, in itself, a crime and which men could never be brought to think a crime merely because there were legislative provisions against it."[3] Repeatedly, Wilberforce inveighed against " our bloody laws " and " our murderous laws." After Romilly's tragic death, in 1818, he was urged to don his friend's mantle, but he pointed to Mackintosh as Romilly's most competent successor. He was a member of Mackintosh's Select Committee on " death penalty for felonies," and to Mackintosh he rendered as consistent and sincere support as he had rendered Romilly.[4]

In view of the incessant attempts to paint Wilberforce as a hopeless reactionary in " home " affairs, such facts should not be overlooked. He was representative of the Evangelical Revival in general, and of the Clapham Sect in particular. It was with the help of sons of the great Spiritual Awakening, that the " bloody criminal code " was at last swept into the limbo. But more pertinent, it was the new spiritual value which that Awakening attached to " man as man," which began to make inoperative, long before its deletion from the Statute Books, the blood-thirsty taint of the English criminal code. Nor was this truth altogether hidden from the great Radical legal reformers. Romilly's admiration and love for Wilberforce, we have already observed, and Bentham's feelings toward him were equally warm. But Bentham's admiration for the spirit of the Revival in general, is little known. " Townshend," he wrote, " was once what I had liked to have been, a Methodist, and what I should have been, had I not been what I am."[5]

---

[1] See *Life* of Wilberforce, by his sons, Vol. I, p. 131.
[2] Halévy, *op. cit.*, p. 397 ; Wilberforce's *Life*, Vol. III, pp. 440, 444, 504.
[3] Coupland's *Wilberforce*, p. 430.
[4] For Romilly, see his *Observations on the Criminal Laws of England* (1810), and his *Speeches in Parliament* (two vols., 1820).
[5] Bentham's *Works* (Bowring edition), Vol. X, p. 92.

(iii) *The Origin and Significance of Protestant*
Foreign Missions

Even when the Evangelical Revival was busy creating the spirit, the leadership, the organisation and the financial sacrifice, which finally redeemed the British Empire from the pollution of the slave trade and slavery ; when it was engaged in civilising a benighted populace, and laying the foundations of popular education throughout a nation ; when it was injecting mercy and sanity into a tortuous, revengeful prison system ; when it was helping gallantly to rationalise a chaotic penal code—even at the same time, it was mediating the international sympathy and vision, which mothered that remarkable series of Christian societies, whereby was established and nurtured the whole Protestant Foreign Missionary Movement, throughout the world.

It is a peculiarly poignant fact that, neither the Reformation in the sixteenth century, nor Puritanism, in the seventeenth century, was possessed of any real world outlook or foreign missionary zeal. The reasons are obvious. Both the Reformation and the Puritan eras, were times of ecclesiastical warfare, and, amidst the dust and passion of battle, vision and universal sympathy usually are shut out. Luther and Zwingli, Calvin and Melancthon, Knox and Cranmer, Latimer and Ridley, were too utterly absorbed with perplexing problems at their door, to see far afield. Theological controversies, national complications, the principles of religious liberty, the clarifying of the Reformed Faith and the organising of the Reformed Churches—these questions occupied their every waking hour. And if Loyola, Xavier and other leaders in the Jesuit Counter-Reformation, succeeded in initiating a mighty revival of missionary fervour within the Roman Catholic communion,[1] their very success enforced upon the Protestant reformers the necessity for consolidating their home-base. The same was largely true of Puritanism. A study of the lives of Milton and Bunyan, of Baxter and Fox, of Hampden and Marvell will reveal no urge to foreign missionary effort. Puritanism knew itself to be a determined minority, struggling desperately against weighty vested interests for its very life. During its brief tenure of power, it failed to convert the nation to its manner of thought and faith. As a movement, English Puritanism made an epochal stand for liberty, justice, equity and fraternity ; but it was at least as political as it was religious, and never did it rise to the vision of the Kingdom of God over all the earth.

---

[1] See " Missions (Roman Catholic)," in *Ency. of Rel. and Ethics* ; also in *Ency. Brit.*

Such generalisations, however, demand some modification. Erasmus, who himself represented a halfway house between Roman Catholicism and the Reformation, was an enthusiast for foreign missions. In his *Art of Preaching*, calling for men to address themselves with " fearless minds " to the glorious task of foreign missionary labour, he proceeds : " It is hard work I call you to, but it is the noblest and highest of all. *Would that God had accounted me worthy to die in such a holy work.* . . . No one is fit to preach the Gospel to the heathen who has not made his mind superior to riches or pleasure, aye, even to life and death itself."[1] Lord Bacon, a century later, referring to the inevitable preamble prefacing foreign trading charters, to the effect that merchants should seek to " spread the Gospel among the heathen with whom they traded," sagely remarked that, " what was first in God's providence, was but second in man's appetite and intuition." Bacon here was extremely urbane ; for such preambles were really a farce. Nevertheless Cromwell, with his penetrating plans and undoubted Christian zeal, did capture something of a missionary vision, for, in his later years, he was devising a scheme for Protestant missionary endeavour which, he believed, would rival that of the Congregation of Propaganda of the Roman Catholic Church. His scheme, however, was never completed, and at his death it fell to earth.[2] The *Mayflower*, of course, was destined to contribute powerfully to Protestant missionary achievement, but that contribution was wholly indirect. The Pilgrim Fathers established New England not as missionaries, but as refugees, prepared, for conscience sake, to face all the rigours of a wilderness, that they might establish new institutions according to their faith, in Liberty. To a Pilgrim Father, nevertheless, must go the honour of originating the first real Protestant foreign missionary endeavour ; for, when, in 1646, John Eliot began his Nonantum mission among the Indians, preaching to them in their own tongue, establishing settlements for them, and translating the Bible and other religious works, he was a pioneer indeed.[3]

Nor must the Society for Promoting Christian Knowledge and the Society for the Propagation of the Gospel in Foreign Parts, founded respectively by Dr. Thomas Bray in 1698 and 1701, be wholly overlooked. During the reign of Queen Anne, these High Church Societies flared into a feeble enthusiasm ; but under the chilly pressure of Deism, their zeal was quite quenched, and were it not for the ensuing Baptism of Fire

[1] See L. Creighton, *Missions, their Rise and Development*, pp. 47–8.
[2] See " Missions (Modern Protestant)," *Ency. Brit.*
[3] See Caverby's *Life* of John Eliot.

they soon would have died. As it was, the S.P.G. fell into " the unfortunate position of being a slave-holder " on two West Indian estates[1] ; while some of its representatives, being sheer adventurers, were anything but a credit to their profession.[2] In no real sense, can either of these Societies be reckoned a precursor of the Protestant foreign missionary movement. With the German and Danish Moravians, however, the case was different. Despised products of the despised Pietist Movement, they began in 1732 a foreign missionary effort which ever since has continued. First in Georgia, later in London, and finally in Germany, on the eve of his world-stirring crusade, Wesley was profoundly influenced by these humble, simple emissaries of the Gospel of Christ. Before the middle of the eighteenth century, the much maligned Moravian Brethren had missionaries labouring as far afield as among the slaves of the West Indies and the Eskimos of Greenland. They were the true harbingers of the Protestant missionary movement.

" When the eighteenth century opened, and for many years to come," says Professor Halévy, " there was not a single Protestant missionary in the entire world with the exception of the small German group of the Moravian Brethren."[3] That statement is substantially, if not absolutely, correct. The Moravians were the *forerunners* of Protestant missions, but their efforts were far too sporadic, too isolated, too ill-organised, and too ill-supported by any strong home base, to entitle them to be considered the *founders* of Protestant missions. Indeed, without the impact of the Revival, Moravian missions very probably would have been short-lived. That the Evangelical Awakening both founded and established the far-sighted world Protestant foreign missionary movement, is a fact no student of the period can doubt.

Nothing is more characteristic of Wesley's outlook, than his constant dictum, " The world is my parish ! " Yet never after his conversion, did he find time to cross the sea. Whitefield traversed the Atlantic thirteen times ; more than a third of his life mission was devoted to the American Colonists, and he died, at work, in New England ; but Wesley, the guiding spirit and genius of the whole Revival, exercised his world influence from English soil. Restoring to Britain her soul, and rekindling her spiritual vision, he became the centre of that Pentecostal renewal which not only created the basic missionary societies of Protestantism, but, through its heralds,

---

[1] W. L. Mathieson, *British Slavery and Its Abolition*, p. 216.
[2] See *Reporter*, I, p. 193.
[3] *The English People in 1815*, p. 389.

caused men and women of a thousand tongues to understand the common language of the Love of God, the Leadership of Christ, and the Brotherhood of Man. Not long after the arrival of Moravian missionaries, certain of Wesley's converts began preaching the Gospel among West Indian slaves, and when in 1786 Dr. Coke, who meanwhile had become Wesley's chief missionary lieutenant, officially established " Methodist missions " in those Islands, they soon grew to such proportions as, indirectly, to become the most vital *local* influence in the great Emancipation cause.[1] The " Methodist Societies " were from the beginning missionary institutions ; but with the expansion of the Revival, as its spirit began to possess Nonconformity, to leaven the Church of Scotland, to call forth the Clapham Brotherhood and to permeate whole strata within the National Church, the pulsing passion for world missionary endeavour demanded the creation of new vehicles of expression. And those new vehicles, became the parent missionary societies of the Protestant world.

Even as Dr. Coke, with indefatigable zeal, was establishing his Methodist missions in the West Indies, and as Francis Asbury, with apostolic heroism, was blazing the trail for a mighty Church, which finally was to affect profoundly the whole American Republic—simultaneously this Evangelical enthusiasm broke forth into a world illuminating flame. The *dates* of the pioneer Protestant foreign missionary societies, are themselves highly revealing. In 1792 William Carey and his associates founded the Baptist Missionary Society ; in 1795 came the interdenominational London Missionary Society[2] ; in 1796, the Scottish Missionary Society ; in 1799, the Church Missionary Society, which emphasised its desire for " cordial relations with Nonconformists "[3] : in the same year appeared the Religious Tract Society ; while in 1804, came the classic and interdenominational British and Foreign Bible Society, through whose agency more than seven hundred of the thousand different translations of Scripture have been achieved.[4] These Evangelical societies were the noble and heroic parents, from which sprang the whole Protestant foreign missionary world movement.

This Movement has made mistakes : but, taken for all in all, it has represented, perhaps, the most humane and most

[1] See Dr. Coke's *History of the West Indies*, Vol. II, p. 441f. ; and Mathieson, *op. cit.*, p. 111.
[2] This Society was later to come under the control of the Congregational Church.
[3] See Stock's *History of the Church Missionary Society*, Vol. I.
[4] See G. Smith's *Short History of Christian Missions*.

soulful of all the impacts of the West upon the East. The mercantile, military, political and imperial interests of the West in the East, have left much of which Christendom may well be ashamed. Loud, vulgar advertisement, crass materialism, duplicity and deceit, cupidity and profanity, stupid arrogance and swashbuckling assumptions of superiority, have far too frequently been the paving stones of their trail. Christian missionaries, contrariwise, have preached and lived a Gospel of Love ; they have proclaimed the Fatherhood of God and the Brotherhood of Man. For many primitive peoples, they have created both an alphabet and a grammar ; they have planted in their trail both schools and colleges ; they have translated not only the Bible, but many other of the finest literary and inspirational books of Christendom. They have established hospitals, which annually treat hundreds of thousands of needy patients ; they have introduced to many backward races the elemental laws of health and sanitation ; they have consecrated scientific, professional, industrial and agricultural knowledge to the needs of the most underprivileged peoples. Everywhere, they have raised the status and increased the dignity of woman, thereby enriching both home and community life ; whilst persistently, amidst colossal difficulties and much misrepresentation, have they striven to mediate the spirit of international co-operation and understanding, and to abridge the yawning gulfs of colour, caste and race. Their key emphasis has been, that God hath made of one blood all the peoples of the earth, and that in Christ all races are brethren.[1]

The purpose of Christian Missions, both Protestant and Catholic, has been to mediate the spirit and Gospel of Christ. This task, moreover, has generally been interpreted in a wide sense. Missionaries persistently and perseveringly have opposed the ravages of the opium and liquor traffics ; often at the cost of life, they have struggled against cannibalism, slavery and forced labour ; consistently have they toiled to put down tribal raids and wars ; while untiringly, have they kept in the van to protect the integrity of native lands, against encroachment or appropriation by exploiting interests, whether commercial, national or imperial. The causes of education, health, sanitation, co-operation and peace, have been greatly furthered by them ; while among the most backward and benighted peoples, they have been the supreme civilising force. No less critical an observer than Charles Darwin, after careful examination of the conditions prevailing in the Fiji Islands, before and after the

---

[1] See Robt. E. Speer, *Missions and Modern history* (two vols.) ; *International Review of Missions* (quarterly) ; J. C. Lambert, *The Romance of Missionary Heroism*.

work of emissaries of the London Missionary Society, says : "They had abolished human sacrifices and the power of an idolatrous priesthood, a system of profligacy unparalleled in any part of the world, and bloody wars, and had greatly reduced dishonesty, intemperance and licentiousness."[1]

[1] L. Creighton, *op. cit.*, p. 68.

BULWARKS OF SOCIAL LIBERTY

" The finest gentleman I ever knew was a working
miner in England, whose gentleness, absolute fairness, instinctive horror of anything underhand or
mean, or anything that was not the strictest fair-play,
gave him a character that enabled him to rise to the
position of Privy Councillor."

EARL GREY, as Governor-General of Canada,
concerning Thomas Burt.

(AARON WATSON, *A Great Labour Leader*, p. v.)

" The first fighters and speakers for unions, Co-op.
Societies, political freedom, and improved conditions,
were Methodist preachers. That is beyond argument. And the Gospel expressed in social terms has
been more of a driving power in northern mining
circles than all the economic teaching put together."

JACK LAWSON (M.P.), *A Man's Life*, p. 67.

BULWARKS OF SOCIAL LIBERTY

IN the centre of Piccadilly Circus stands one of the most beautiful and most remarkable memorials in the world. Most Londoners to-day know it only as the " Eros Monument " ; and that is unfortunate, for it has profound significance. Built chiefly by the tons of consecrated pennies collected in factory, workshop and mine throughout the kingdom, it depicts the deep devotion of the emancipated workers of England to their great friend and tribune, the Seventh Earl of Shaftesbury. It is the tribute of the freed operatives of Britain to their Emancipator—the British Lincoln. For Shaftesbury was as much the emancipator of England's " industrial slaves " as was Lincoln of America's negro slaves. That memorial, too, is a constant rejoinder to the gospel of class-hatred so solemnly, so ponderously and so vituperatively elaborated by Marx. It betokens the active affection of a liberated and liberty-loving industrial populace, for a gallant and godly peer.

But this Shaftesbury fountain has also a memorable mystic symbolism. Its famous sculptor, Sir Alfred Gilbert, was peculiarly fond of sprightly, allegorical elusiveness. So he conceived the idea of a play on the name Shaftes-bury. Taking the physical beauty of Eros, the Greek god of love, he strove to inject into it the essence of Christian love ($\alpha\gamma\alpha\pi\eta$), as expressive of the great reformer's soul. Hence, mounted on the pinnacle of the memorial, is the transfigured and now Christian Eros, bow in hand, " burying-the-shaft " of Christian love in the heart of the Empire, from the busiest spot in the Empire, the nerve-centre of the Metropolis. The pun, if scarcely obvious, is keenly suggestive. Shaftesbury profoundly influenced the social welfare not only of the British, but of all English-speaking peoples ; he was a thorough-going Christian ; yet his parentage was pagan.

Around the base of this Shaftesbury memorial is a raised inscription, composed by Gladstone, reading thus : " During a public life of half a century he devoted the influence of his station, the strong sympathies of his heart and the great power of his mind to honouring God by serving his fellow-men—an

example to his order, a blessing to his people, and a name to
be by them ever gratefully remembered."

(i) *The Emancipation of Industrial England*

What Wesley was to the dormant social conscience of the early
eighteenth century, what Wilberforce was to the negro slaves,
what Howard was to prisoners, what Carey was to the outcasts
of India, that Shaftesbury was to the " factory slaves " of
England. He, like his predecessors, in an epic succession of
humanitarian achievements, became an emancipator of his
fellows because he himself had been first emancipated by Christ,
and because having thus entered into the spirit of vital, practical
Christianity, he was a sincere lover of God and man.

Lord Shaftesbury, albeit, was raised in a godless home.
His father, though for forty years Chairman of Committees in
the House of Lords, was a haughty, hard-drinking remnant of
eighteenth-century Deism ; his mother, a descendant of the
proud Marlborough family, was a society worldling. Fortunately for the future of England, there was in the Shaftesbury
household a remarkable Christian nurse—Maria Millis. She
was Shaftesbury's spiritual mother ; and though she died when
the coming reformer was but a lad, she had moulded his
character for life. Till death, he carried the watch she left him,
and daily he repeated prayers learned at her knee. In the year
of Waterloo, when fourteen, and a student at Harrow School,
Shaftesbury witnessed a pauper funeral wherein drunken pall-
bearers, trying to turn a corner, tumbled in a heap, the coffin
crashing to earth and cracking. That ghastly spectacle was to
the Emancipator of Industrial England what the auction of
the negro girl in New Orleans was to the Emancipator of
America's slaves. There and then, before God, the young
peer pledged his life—to the uplift of the wretched, the degraded
and the oppressed. How well, was that pledge fulfilled ?

To understand the social problems Shaftesbury faced, it must
ever be remembered that both the Commercial Revolution,
with its insatiable monetary cupidity, and all the most revolting
exploitations of the Industrial Revolution, had already come
into being under the influence of the slave trade, and under the
impacts of colonial slavery. Following the Asiento concessions,
and for many years before the conversion of Wesley, every
economic perversion which later was to manifest itself on the
titanic stage of the factory system, was present in the economic
and industrial fabric of English society. The slave trade and
slavery had contaminated every branch of commercial and
financial organisation. The South Sea Bubble itself, was but

symptomatic of the pervasive and almost universal moral collapse. What with godless Deism and slave-trade economics, all human life had been cheapened and all ethical foundations undermined. The first imperative of social emancipation, therefore, was the renewal of spiritual life ; the second was the suppression of the slave trade which, by its manifold repercussions, defiled all trade. Without these preceding achievements, Shaftesbury's intrepid life-work would have been impossible. Nor is it any accident that his soul's awakening led him into the same spiritual succession, as his mighty forerunners in social reform. Repeatedly, he described himself as " an Evangelical of Evangelicals."

How well, then, did Shaftesbury fulfil his vow, made under the shadow of Harrow School, in 1815 ? When twenty-one, he came down from Oxford with a First Class in Classics ; when twenty-five, he entered Parliament ; when twenty-seven, under Wellington, he tasted the power of office, to find his independence largely curbed. Repeatedly, under Conservative and Liberal Governments, he rejected Cabinet portfolios, high posts at Court, and both the Lord Lieutenancy and the Chief Secretaryship of Ireland. For years, braving even the Queen's displeasure, he declined the exclusive distinction of being made a Knight of the Garter ;[1] and on his death-bed he refused interment in Westminster Abbey, though his name was first on Dean Stanley's List, among those most worthy of burial in the National Shrine. Fifty-seven of the sixty years of Shaftesbury's public career were given without a penny of pay. For long, though his tastes were simple and his habits abstemious, he had to borrow money to educate his ten children. Yet to the end, his father, who— most inconsiderately—lived till the great reformer was fifty, continued not only to oppose his reforming labours, but to embarrass him financially. At one period, for seven years on end, he refused him admission (even at Christmas) to " St. Giles," the family estate of which he was heir. The Sixth Earl blusteringly contended that his zealous Christian son was teaching the common people to aspire " beyond their station." He continued to cling to the aristocratic eighteenth-century assumption, that the poor should be left " ignorant, drunken and stupid " in order that they might be " kept under."

Had Shaftesbury during his long public career achieved nothing else than the famous Ten Hours Victory he would have merited historical immortality. That victory, however, requires a word of explanation. Popularly it is associated, almost exclusively, with the Factory Act of 1847. In reality, it includes

[1] When finally, in 1862, Shaftesbury did accept the Garter, his father-in-law, Lord Palmerston, paid all the expenses.

also the Factory Acts of 1833, of 1844 and of 1850 ; while the industrial Extension Acts, of 1864 and 1867, practically universalised the application of the principles and provisions of that epochal advance. Shaftesbury's dedication of life and ceaseless labours, provided the inspiring, impelling and sustaining force behind every one of these Acts. Albeit, they were among a score of important legislative enactments, which his ceaseless humanitarian endeavours placed on the Statute Books of Britain ; while, as for Royal Commissions of social investigation, he fathered more of them than any other private Parliamentarian in British history. Shaftesbury's revolutionary Mines and Collieries Act (1842), which henceforth freed all women and young children from underground " slavery " in British mines, is described by Hutchins and Harrison, in their classic *History of Factory Legislation*, as " perhaps the most high-handed interference with industry enacted by the State in the nineteenth century."[1] His Chimney Sweep Acts completely closed a barbarous chapter in our social history. The second of his Lodging House Statutes (1851) was pronounced by Charles Dickens " the best Act ever passed by an English Legislature."[2] His far-sighted Lunacy Acts transformed the whole status and treatment of the insane, from that of prisoners to patients. His Agricultural Gangs Bills protected the children of the countryside, from a thraldom scarcely less cruel than had been the lot of urban youngsters in factories ; while his labours on the first National Board of Health, and his repeated Parliamentary attacks on the mercenary entanglements of the liquor and opium traffics, had far-reaching effects.

Outside Parliament, Shaftesbury's labours were only less important than within. He it was, who both aroused in the Prince Consort his intense interest in social reform, and opened up for that interest wide avenues of service among the poor, thus creating a new tradition for British royalty. The " Shaftesbury Estate," with its many hundreds of neat working-class homes and gardens, laid out in what was the centre of Battersea's vilest slums, marks the initial move toward " decent housing " for the labouring populace. Shaftesbury, too, was the arch-promoter of public parks, playing fields, gymnasia, gardening allotments, workmen's institutes, public libraries, night schools, choral societies, debating societies and all manner of self-help media. He was President of the Ragged School Union, of the world Y.M.C.A., of the British and Foreign Bible Society, of the Religious Tract Society, of the Pastoral Aid Society, of the Protestant Alliance, of the National Refuges and Training Ships,

[1] *Op. cit.*, p. 82.
[2] E. Hodder's *Shaftesbury as Social Reformer*, p. 138.

of the Costermongers' Mission, and many other humanitarian associations. At the unique National Memorial Service in Westminster Abbey on October 8th, 1885, nearly two hundred social, religious and philanthropic institutions were *officially* represented, " with all of which Lord Shaftesbury was more or less directly connected."

Fully ninety per cent. of Shaftesbury's outstanding colleagues, in the epic effort to emancipate the " industrial slaves " of England, were as much products of the Evangelical Revival as he himself. John Wood, the great cotton-mill owner, who largely financed the Ten Hours crusade, was a keen student of the Bible, and gave unstintingly of his means, as to a holy mission. Richard Oastler, " the Factory Children's King," whose eyes were opened to factory cruelties by his friend, the said John Wood, was the son of a local preacher, who, " disinherited by his father for his Methodism,"[1] had become an ardent campaigner against slavery. On Wesley's very last visit to the Oastler home, he had taken the infant Richard in his arms and " blessed " him—a fact of which Oastler was always proud. In truth, it was Oastler's immediate connection with the Revival and with the anti-slavery crusade, that caused him to coin the phrases " factory-slave," " white-slave," " industrial-slave," etc. ; while, on his personal confession, it was his own Christian faith that sustained him in the arduous struggle to the end of his days.[2] The indomitable J. R. Stephens, who " had sworn allegiance to the Children's King," and who suffered eighteen months' imprisonment because of the unparliamentary character of his popular agitation, was an ordained Methodist preacher and the son of a President of Conference. Though dismissed from the Wesleyan ministry because of his too vitriolic politics, he remained till death a preacher of the Gospel in his own independent chapel.[3] Michael Sadler, instigator of the famous *Sadler's Report* on factory conditions (1831–32), was the superintendent of a large Sunday school in Leeds. So spiritual was his conception of his task, that he wrote religious poems, including *The Factory Girl's Last Day*, to stimulate popular sympathy. The intrepid Rev. G. S. Bull was an Evangelical Anglican. Philip Grant, the capable editor of the *Ten Hours Advocate*, was a fervent Bible Christian ; while Joseph Brotherton, Sir Andrew Agnew and Lord Kenyon, all of whom rendered

[1] *Dict. of Nat. Biog.* (" Richard Oastler "). A magnificent statue of Oastler, with two factory children, stands in the heart of Bradford. It was unveiled by Shaftesbury in 1869.

[2] See " Alfred " (Benjamin Kydd), *History of Factory System*, Vol. I, pp. 94–7.

[3] See Holyoake's *Life of J. R. Stephens*. In Stamford Park, Stalybridge, stands a noble public memorial commemorating Stephens's life work.

yeoman service, were staunch Evangelicals. John Fielden, too, in youth, had been a Sunday school teacher, and though later he became a Unitarian, who can study his life and fail to recognise that he was a gracious, zealous Christian to the end?

Such were Shaftesbury's principal colleagues in the valiant industrial struggle. Not all were possessed of his statesman-like sagacity and restraint, but all conceived the campaign as a sacred mission. And under Shaftesbury's sustained, sacrificial leadership, it came to be recognised as the accepted policy that the inevitably long struggle for the comprehensive Ten Hours Programme, should be conducted without violence of speech or action. Strikes, lock-outs, mob tactics, intimidation and threats, were to be avoided. Vituperative, provocative language was sternly discouraged. And if, at times, the volcanic energy, the burning sympathy, the infectious enthusiasm and the excited, though honest, passions of the great field lieutenants Oastler and Stephens overflowed these accepted bounds, never-theless, on the whole, balance, restraint, patience and good humour prevailed. The justice, the humanity and the essenti-ally Christian character of the programme, were always the cardinal emphases. Public opinion was educated and converted, not brow-beaten and coerced. The Faith of Shaftesbury and his colleagues endowed them with a sense of serenity, even tranquillity, in the midst of "utter warfare," for they were fighting with the Sword of the Spirit. They could endure passing rebuffs and apparent defeats, because they knew the final issue of their conflict was never in doubt, so vested was it in the justice of God.[1]

This same religious spirit, permeated even the humblest ranks of the crusade. Shortly after the passage of the 1847 Factory Act, a great national conference of operatives' delegates was convoked in London, and there this Resolution was unanimously passed :

"That we are *deeply grateful to Almighty God* for the success which has hitherto attended our efforts, and now that the object of our labours for the last thirty years is about to be brought to a happy consummation, *we pledge ourselves to promote by every means in our power* THOSE RELIGIOUS AND SOCIAL BLESSINGS *which it was the object of the Bill to extend to the factory workers.*"[2]

The Ten Hours Acts, together with Shaftesbury's celebrated Mines and Collieries Act, represent the *Magna Charta* of the industrial workers' liberty. They closed the factories at

[1] See Sir Josiah Stamp's Foreword to the *Cheap Editions* of Bready's *Shaftesbury*, pp. 5–6.
[2] See *Halifax Guardian*, May 22nd, 1847.

6 p.m. and kept them closed till 6 a.m., thus suppressing the guileful practice of "shifts" and "relays," stopping night work, and guaranteeing evening leisure. They established practical immunity from Sunday labour, and enforced a weekly day of rest ; they prohibited the iniquitous " Truck System " with its cruel exploitations, and suppressed the whole vicious practice of the " free " use of women and children as " fodder for industry." They initiated the practice both of compulsory education, and of State inspection of industry. Again, as early as 1850, and long before any other country had even dreamed of such a boon, they won for British operatives the Saturday half-holiday, thus providing a prolonged weekly period for recreation and sport. Indeed, by the provision of all this " Shaftesbury Legislation," the factories and mines of Britain were humanised, socialised and largely Christianised.

The indirect consequences of the Ten Hours Victory, how-ever, were not less epic in their significance, than were the direct consequences. That victory, by its humane, rational control of factories, workshops and mines, and by its encourage-ment and protection of human dignity, laid deep the founda-tions for a hundred self-help and co-operative movements which to-day are taken for granted like the air we breathe, but which, nevertheless, form the warp and woof of all that is most abiding in Anglo-Saxon democracy. The social-industrial legislation which resulted chiefly from Shaftesbury's leadership, and which was directly inspired by a Christian conception of the spiritual· destiny of man, prepared the way—especially through the Ten Hours Acts—for general education (juvenile and adult), for innumerable friendly and benefit societies, for recreation and temperance guilds, for literary and debating societies, for Workers' Institutes and for the sane, self-governing British Trade Union Movement, the like of which never before had been known in any land.[1] Was it not, indeed, futile even to dream of successful Democracy, till the soul of man had been awakened to its spiritual potentialities, till the curse of slavery had been abolished, till leisure had been provided for " self-help," and till at least the elementary lessons of co-operation and organisa-tion had been learned by the populace ?

Such truths, the industrial operatives, the Parliamentary legis-lators and the general population of England, came gradually to recognise. If the operatives showed their appreciation of Shaftesbury's life and spirit by raising the noble memorial in Piccadilly Circus, his fellow-legislators showed theirs, by erecting the superb statue at the west door of Westminster Abbey ; while the devotion of the general population, is reflected by the large

[1] See Halévy, *op. cit.* (Vol. 1895–1905), p. 212.

number of places, streets, districts, missions, institutions and schools—the Empire over—which bear his name. There is more than humour in the words of George Jacob Holyoake, the pioneer of the Co-operative Movement : " Should England one day be accounted among extinct civilisations, and some explorers arrive to evacuate its ruins, they will come upon so many stones deposited by Shaftesbury and bearing his name, that report will be made of the discovery of the king of the last dynasty." [1] Certainly no king has ever been so dear to the toilers of England as was " the People's Earl." [2]

Certain analogies in the lives of the two social emancipators of the English-speaking world, are highly revealing. The sterling characters of both, were early moulded by godly women ; both not only were deeply religious, but were life students of the Bible, which to them was a unique Revelation ; both experienced a " call " to their life-work in a soul revolt against spectacles of wretchedness, symbolising the misery of a multitude ; both, through their call, became men of unified personalities ; both, in supreme dedication, gave their all, without reserve, to liberate the oppressed ; both struggled with herculean endurance, in the teeth of slander, contumely and contempt ; both finally became mighty emancipators, who profoundly affected not only the destiny of a race, but the course of history.

Certain contrasts, nevertheless, are also revealing. Shaftesbury's life struggle was less dramatic, less spectacular than Lincoln's : yet, in a vital sense, the achievement of the Emancipator of Industrial England was even more majestic than was that of the Emancipator of America's Slaves. For without a civil war, without protracted strike or lockout, without, indeed, the loss of a single life, Shaftesbury freed his " slaves " entirely by constitutional and Christian means. The spread of knowledge and sympathy, the quickening of conscience, the conversion of public opinion, the persuasion of Parliament and the enactment of just, humane legislation, were the means of his conquest. No legacy of resentment, therefore, no smouldering hate, was left behind ; but rather a firm foundation, on which succeeding social attainments could securely be built. One pertinent fact, however, was all in Shaftesbury's favour. The previous abolition of British slavery, had made possible the quiet majesty of his far-reaching achievement.

[1] G. J. Holyoake, *Bygones Worth Remembering*, Vol. I, p. 148.
[2] For the detailed record of Shaftesbury's life, see the author's *Lord Shaftesbury and Social-Industrial Progress.*

(ii) *Religion and British Trade Unionism*

" The story of the trial and transportation of the Dorchester labourers," say Sidney and Beatrice Webb in their *History of Trade Unionism*, " is the best-known episode of early Trade Union history."[1] Popularly the victims of this " atrocious sentence " are known as " the Tolpuddle Martyrs," and so dear has been their memory to British Trade Unionists that, in 1912, there was erected by them in Tolpuddle village a memorial arch, unveiled by the Rt. Hon. Arthur Henderson.[2]

The thrice-told story of these six " martyrs " need not be here retold. Often, however, it is forgotten that three of them, George and James[3] Loveless and Thomas Standfield, were local preachers ; that John Standfield and James Hammett were active Christian workers and members of the Tolpuddle Methodist Chapel ; and that James Brine, who when transported had no religious conviction, was so influenced by the character of Thomas Standfield with whom he slaved in a " convict gang " in Australia, that, on return, he married his daughter and, migrating to Canada,[4] became an Enthusiast and " for many years a Sunday school superintendent." Often, too, is it forgotten that James Hammett, who himself had no connection with the formation of the Union and who was arrested by mistake for his brother John, heroically insisted on concealing the error, in order that his brother might not be torn away from his wife, who very soon was expecting the birth of a child.

These humble " martyrs " were all sober, intelligent, hard-working and respectable agricultural labourers. They and all their fellow " farm-hands " around Tolpuddle, because of an agreement among the local farmers, had found their wages gradually depressed to the bare subsistence level of seven shillings a week. So under the leadership of the able, sincere and godly George Loveless, they decided, for the protection of their families, to form an Agricultural Trade Union ; and following the prevailing Union custom in industrial areas, they bound all members by a *secret* oath. Here accordingly was a loophole through which the authorities entered to apply an antiquated law. These men had been guilty of no violence, no insurrection, no outrage, no intimidation. They had not so much as hinted, at a strike. They simply had dared to form a friendly Agricultural

---

[1] *Op. cit.* (1920 edition), p. 144.

[2] See Henderson's Foreword to Owen Rattenbury's *Flame of Freedom*.

[3] The Webbs, incorrectly, refer to *John* Loveless as the brother of George, instead of *James*.

[4] Five of these six " martyrs " finally settled in Southern Ontario, Canada. See Preface to second edition of Rattenbury's *Flame of Freedom*.

Union to counter the combined coercion of their employers, and, in so doing, they inadvertently had administered a " secret oath." That was enough ! The antiquated and long-dormant statute was called into play. Despite the fact that the magistrate in question, and the Home Office, in conjunction with which he laid his trap, knew well that Masonic and other Fraternal Lodges regularly administered " secret " oaths, at daybreak on February 24th, 1834, the said six labourers were all bundled from their houses and marched off to the Dorchester jail. After the " briefest of trials," conducted by a new judge, John Williams, who harangued against the labourers as though they were arch-conspirators, all were subjected to the " monstrous sentence of seven years' transportation."[1] Before March 30th, " the prisoners were in the hulks," destined for Botany Bay ; and Lord Melbourne, the then Home Secretary, voiced the opinion, that the law had " in this case been most properly applied."[2]

With the execution of this ferocious sentence, it was predicted by the forces of repression that the whole Trade Union cause would be stunned into inaction. Such was far from the case. In prison, George Loveless wrote his Hymn of Freedom :

> " God is our Guide ! from field, from wave,
> From plough, from anvil, and from loom,
> We come, our country's rights to save,
> And speak the tyrant faction's doom ;
> We raise the watchword ' Liberty.'
> We will, we will, we will be free !

> " God is our Guide ! No swords we draw,
> We kindle not war's battle fires,
> By reason, union, justice, law,
> We claim the birthright of our sires ;
> We raise the watchword, ' Liberty,'
> We will, we will, we will be free ! "[3]

Loveless's Hymn of Freedom was smuggled from prison to friends without. It was expressive of the spirit of the rising Trade Union movement. The London *Observer* (August 29th, 1937), paying tribute to that " monumental study of nineteenth-century England " by the French professor, Élie Halévy, says : " No one got so thoroughly under the surface of political labels or made a more telling demonstration of the interaction of economic, religious, and other forces. England has never found a truer interpreter." Yet this same penetrating interpreter, in the first volume of his " monumental " history, boldly avers :

[1] Sidney and Beatrice Webb, *History of Trade Unionism*, p. 146.
[2] *Lord Melbourne's Papers*, p. 158. See, too, Geo. Loveless, *Victims of Whiggery*.
[3] See Frontispiece to Rattenbury, *op. cit.*, for the music to this song.

" The majority of the leaders of the great trade union movement that would arise in England within a few years of 1815 will belong to the Nonconformist sects. They will often be local preachers, that is, practically speaking ministers. Their spiritual ancestors were the founders of Methodism."[1]

The purport of Halévy's observation, is apparent in this connection. Far from these transportation sentences intimidating Trade Unionism, they caused it speedily to prove to a lethargic Government that, already it was becoming a power in the land —a power inspired by high ideals, disciplined by self-control, and set on the attainment of Justice and Liberty by pacific, co-operative action. Scarcely had the cruel verdict been pronounced, when a strong petition of protest was circulated under Union auspices. Soon it contained " over a quarter of a million signatures."[2] And despite the disgruntled pronouncement of Lord Melbourne, that he would neither receive a deputation nor a petition from a procession, a great demonstration was arranged to bear the petition to the Home Office. On April 21st, 1834, on the admission of *The Times*, which feverishly opposed the procession, not less than 30,000 organised workers, bearing thirty-three trade banners, marched from Copenhagen Fields to Whitehall to present the petition.[3] It was the first great Trade Union demonstration England had seen, and it was thoroughly peaceful and orderly. At the head of the procession, wearing full canonicals, including the scarlet hood of a Doctor of Divinity, rode the " chaplain to the Metropolitan Trades Unions," Rev. Dr. Arthur S. Wade. Religion, sincerely and purposely, was symbolised as leading the union cause.

Nor did the petition and procession represent the end of this matter. A London-Dorchester Committee forthwith was set up, and, throughout the country, an unceasing agitation was maintained. Even in Parliamentary debates, the " Dorchester Labourers " became first familiar, then heroic, characters. Indeed, the day soon arrived when Lord Melbourne wished heartily that he had never heard of the village of Tolpuddle, or of its six Trade Union " martyrs." For if, as Home Secretary, he had encouraged their arrest and sanctioned their sentence, two years later, as Prime Minister, he was compelled by the pressure of growing public opinion to remit their sentence, to sanction their pardon, and to find public funds wherewith to effect their return. Though, owing to official blundering, both in England and in Australia, it was not till early in 1838 that

---

[1] *History of the English People* (1815 volume), p. 372.
[2] Webb, *op. cit.*, p. 148.
[3] *The Times*, April 22nd, 1834.   Trade Union accounts claim that fully 100,000 took part in the procession.

the transported men arrived home, where, to their surprise, they discovered that fellow-workmen had collected £1,300 to give them a fresh start in life.[1] Moreover, although the future of all save one of these " martyrs " lay in Canada, it is significant that their true successor, Joseph Arch, founder of the National Agricultural Labourers' Union, was also a local preacher.[2]

If, then, in the first great episode of the British Trade Union drama, the influence of the Evangelical Revival is so apparent, in the second, when Unionists found themselves directly represented by their own members in Parliament, the same permeating influence is scarcely less pronounced. The earliest Trade Union M.P.s were returned as Liberal-Labour members (" Lib-Labs ") with the General Election of 1874. They were but two in number, Alexander Macdonald and Thomas Burt. The former, and considerably the elder, was a typical product of thrifty, Puritan Scotland. When eight, he was initiated into the life of a miner, but by frugal, temperate habits and force of character, he prepared himself for Glasgow University, which he entered in 1846. While still at the University (though continuing work in the pit during vacations), Macdonald " became known as a leader of the miners all over Scotland." In 1863, on the formation of the National Union of Miners, he was elected president, and such he remained till death, in 1881. Alexander Macdonald, therefore, enjoyed but seven years of Parliamentary representation ; nevertheless, because of his devotion, sagacity and tenacity, those seven years proved a boon to the Trade Union cause. Emphasising always that essentially Christian principle, the " sanctity of personality over property," he insisted, as an axiomatic moral tenet, upon the " compulsory maintenance of the workmen's Standard of Life."[3]

The latter of these original Labour pioneers in Parliament, Thomas Burt, who continued to sit as " Lib.-Lab. " M.P. for Morpeth for forty-four years without a break, sprang from a family of Primitive Methodist local preachers and class leaders.[4] He himself was early enlisted as a Sunday school teacher, and honorary temperance lecturer. For eighteen years, Burt laboured

[1] The fullest account of the " Dorchester Labourers " is in Owen Rattenbury's *Flame of Freedom* (" The Romantic Story of the Tolpuddle Martyrs "). See, too, *A Narrative of the Sufferings of James Loveless* ; H. Brooks (J.P.), *Six Heroes in Chains* ; and George Loveless, *Victims of Whiggery*.

[2] Arthur Clayden, *Revolt of the Field*, p. 6 ; Howard Evans, *Radical Fights of Forty Years*, pp. 36–7 ; also F. S. Attenborough, *Life of Joseph Arch*, *passim*.

[3] Webb, *op. cit.*, p. 300 (note) and pp. 301–7 ; also Dr. Baernreither, *English Associations of Working Men*, p. 408.

[4] Aaron Watson, *A Great Labour Leader*, pp. 7–8.

as a miner. For forty-eight years (1865–1913), he was elected Secretary of the Northumberland Miners' Association. In 1890, he was sent, as a leading British representative, to the Berlin Labour Conferences. In 1891, he was elected President of the great National Trades Union Congress. From 1892 till 1895, he was Parliamentary Secretary of the Board of Trade. In 1906, he was made a Privy Councillor. When, in 1918, at eighty-one years of age, he retired from public life, he was the " Father of the House of Commons." Increasingly, during his long Parliamentary career, had he won the affection of his constituents and the respect of all parties in Parliament. Burt's winsome character, his open-mindedness, his capacity for toil and his unimpeachable honesty, had made him a true leader of men. He had proved conclusively that a Union miner, deprived of all youthful opportunities for academic attainment, could rise creditably to take his place among the legislators of an Empire. Never was he a pedant or a doctrinaire. His faith endowed him with a broad human sympathy, with boundless patience, with a passion for fairness, and with a deep understanding of men. Pride, jealousy and pettiness were foreign to his nature. He loathed the gospels of Class-Hatred and Class-War. His culture, which was both real and gracious, derived from the School of Life ; and his guiding texts in that school were the Bible, the great poets, and the great historians. Earl Grey, on a public occasion, as Governor-General of Canada, once said of Burt : " The finest gentleman I ever knew was a working miner in England, whose gentleness, absolute fairness, instinctive horror of anything underhand or mean, or anything that was not the strictest fair play, gave him a character that enabled him to rise to the position of Privy Councillor."[1]

Charles Fenwick, elected as " Lib.-Lab." M.P. for Wansbeck in 1885, was a man of similar mould to Burt, and, like Burt, was early a local preacher. For thirty-three years, till his death in 1918, Fenwick continued to represent the same constituency in Parliament. As with Burt, practical religion, rather than economic theory, was the source of his strength. From nine till thirty-five years of age, he himself toiled in the pit as a common miner, during which years, because of his strength of character, his fairness of mind and his genius for team-work, he was elected to various responsible posts by the Northumberland Miners' Association. Fenwick entered Parliament, therefore, a practical workman, a thorough-going Unionist, and a representative of Labour. But, like Burt, Macdonald and other early Labour Members, as a " Lib.-Lab.", his general political outlook—

---

[1] Aaron Watson, *op. cit.*, Preface. See, too, Thomas Burt's *Autobiography* (with supplementary chapters by W. Burt).

aside from complete independence on Labour questions—was Liberal. Fenwick was the first Labour M.P. ever to preside over the House of Commons in Committee. For years he was elected Secretary of the Parliamentary Committee of the Trades Union Congress. In 1911, he was made a Privy Councillor. Though a tireless advocate of the aspirations of the labouring world, his life was devoid of bitterness or shibboleth worship ; and, if in Parliamentary circles, he was first coldly tolerated and then stiffly patronised, long before his death, by his disinterested integrity, he had won the admiration and honour of all high-minded men. Halévy says of these " pious Methodists and local preachers," Burt and Fenwick, that they were " universally respected for their earnestness and virtues."[1]

From a dozen angles, the study of this much-neglected impact of the Evangelical Revival upon the Trade Union Movement of England, might be profitably pursued. Nowhere is it more dramatically conspicuous, than when British Unionists enter into international conference with the leaders of Organised Labour on the Continent. In 1910, for instance, 260 English Trade Union delegates visited the industrial city of Lille, in the north of France. Public parades, as well as conferences, were part of the arranged programme. The English deputation, like their comrades, carried the socialist flag and many trade emblems. They also carried a banner reading : " We represent 500,000 English workmen ! " This all was excellent. But one thing dumbfounded the Continental Labour leaders. They also carried banners, reading : " We proclaim the Fatherhood of God and the Brotherhood of Man ! " and " Jesus Christ Leads and Inspires us ! " In conference, moreover, some of the veteran English leaders, quoting freely from the Bible, declared stoutly that, their Christianity had made them trade unionists, co-operators and socialists.[2]

This same truth, from another angle, is emphasised by Mr. Lloyd George. " The movement," he says, " which improved the conditions of the working classes, in wages, in hours of labour, and otherwise, found most of its best officers and non-commissioned officers, in men trained in the institutions which were the result of Methodism. I never realise the effect which Methodism has had upon the national character so much as when I attend international congresses. It has given a different outlook to the British and American, from the outlook of the Continentals. . . . John Wesley inaugurated a movement that gripped the soul of England, that deepened its spiritual instincts,

[1] *Op. cit.* (Vol. 1895–1905), p. 214.
[2] See Professor Walter Rausckenbusch, *Christianizing the Social Order*, p. 109.

trained them and uplifted them ; and the result is that, when a great appeal is made either to England or to America, there is always the response, and it is due to the great religious revival of the eighteenth century. The same thing applies to peace. When you preach the Gospel of Peace and say, ' Let us have peace,' they say, ' What is England after ? Trade ? What is it ? She is after something.' The idea that she is preaching Peace because it is the supreme message of her Faith, never enters their head. That is why it is difficult to interpret the outlook and the appeal to those who have not had the same training, as those subject to the influence of the great Evangelical Revival."[1]

This leavening influence of practical Christianity upon the Trade Union movement of Britain, is not so strong to-day as once it was. Various doctrinaire groups and organisations, bidding strongly for the control of Labour, have striven subtly to undermine it. Nevertheless, it was during the years when that Christian influence was strongest, that the British workman's standard of life rose with a persistence never known before or since. Even Professor Bowley and G. D. H. Cole, admit that the " real wages " of the English worker were practically doubled, during the latter half of the nineteenth century.[2] And these were the years when the work of Shaftesbury, of Ruskin, of the Christian Socialists and of the Evangelical Trade Union leaders, were most vitally active. Yet, despite the efforts of all the theoretic and economic materialists, this spiritual heritage is by no means exorcised from British Trade Unionism to-day. Witness the first-hand account of the " stay-in " strike at the Nine Mile Point Colliery, Wales, in October, 1936. The strikers, " nearly a mile underground," had " no proper food for a week." Living " in the stables all the time," they slept on boards procured by " breaking up the stalls." For recreation, they organised quoits matches, played with " metal cones " stripped from blast pipes. But their deeper emotion, craved and found deeper expression. " Religious meetings," reports one of their number, " and concerts were held. Two miners conducted the religious meetings. One of them is being ordained next week. We sang hymns, ' Lead, Kindly Light,' ' Abide with Me,' and others. There were beautiful prayers—as good as any preacher in the land could give."[3] The day, too, has not yet passed when the tens of thousands gathered at

---

[1] From a speech made in London, June 20th, 1922. (Sir Kingsley Wood in the chair.)

[2] See " Charts and Figures " in Cole's *Short History of the British Working-Class Movement*, Vol. II, p. 196ff.

[3] *Observer* (London), October 20th, 1936, p. 21.

a great British football match—many of them Trade Unionists—will break spontaneously into the singing of a hymn. Nor has the day passed, when the National Trades Union Congress fails to appreciate the prayers offered for the guidance of its deliberations, in thousands of churches throughout the land.[1]

In striking contrast to the sour philosophy of Marx, and to the " pedantic fanaticism " of certain later theorists, who hope to superimpose their materialistic panaceas on Labour, stands that remarkable story, *A Man's Life*—the autobiography of Jack Lawson, M.P., a practical and leading Trade Unionist, who held office in the first Labour Government of 1924. Maintaining that the Evangelical Revival " saturated the industrial masses with a passion for a better life, personal, mental, moral and social," he pronounces the Chapel their " first social centre," where " they drew together, found strength in their weakness and expressed to each other their hidden thoughts and needs." " Here," says Lawson, " men first found the language and art to express their antagonism to grim conditions and injustice." To the modern " intellectuals " who " curl the lip " and sneer at " the Little Bethel," Lawson answers that, " the most powerful force for the mental and moral elevation of the workers during the industrial era, has been this contemptuously called ' Little Bethel.' " " The so-called intellectuals," he continues, " speak of these as ' reactionary.' In truth the gentlemen who speak so, know as much about the real living history of the people of this land, as pigs know of aeroplanes."[2]

Lawson's language here seems strong ; but as one who toiled in the bowels of the earth for twenty years, as a life-long Unionist and a practical Labour leader, he *knows* the influences of which he writes. " Methodism," he says, " took the ' nobodies ' and made the most humble and hopeless ' somebody ' " : while, recalling the warmth and fellowship of the particular Little Bethel in which his own spiritual life was inspired and nourished, he avers that there radiated from it, " a spirit of *camaraderie* among the young people *I have never seen equalled.*" Indeed, deploring the historical neglect of the influence of the thousands of Little Bethels throughout Britain, Lawson stoutly contends that, " the Gospel expressed in social terms has been more of a driving power in northern mining circles, than all the economic teaching put together."[3]

---

[1] See Halévy, *op. cit.* (Vol. 1895–1905), p. 211.
[2] Lawson, *op. cit.*, p. 66.
[3] *Ibid.*, p. 67. See especially chapters x and xx of this book ; but it is worth pondering throughout.

(iii) *The Independent Labour Movement and Workmen's Aspirations*

The early Labour M.P.'s., like Burt, Macdonald, Fenwick and Arch, were " Lib-Labs," forced by the pressure of Trade Union strength upon the reluctant Liberal Party machine. But the pioneer Trade Unions, like the effective Short Time Committees behind the Ten Hours campaign, had derived not only their moral virility but also their organising ability, through the Spiritual Awakening. Indeed Halévy, referring to the Anti-Corn Law League agitation, says : " Every Englishman since Wesley's time who had organised a campaign of propaganda, had copied intentionally or unintentionally the Wesleyan model."[1] In the case of the early Trade Union and Labour movements, the impact of this influence is inescapable. Scarcely is it surprising therefore, that the man who inspired and led the movement for the complete independence of Labour from both Conservative and Liberal parties—which respectively were almost dominated by the vested interests of Land and Industry —was an ardent product of the continuing Baptism of Fire.

Keir Hardie, is one of the most romantic and intriguing characters of modern history. The *Encyclopædia Britannica* refers to his " strong personality, his unquestioned honesty and his lovable character," as notably fitting him for his life work ; while the Webbs remind us, that his " kindliness and integrity of character endeared him to all who knew him."[2] Born in 1856, Hardie, when eight, began to earn his living as a " message boy " in Glasgow. Leaving Glasgow when ten, he laboured in the collieries at Newarthill, and for the next twelve years pursued the life of a miner by day and a student by night. " Brought up an atheist," in 1878, when twenty-two, he was " converted to Christianity." His conversion, due largely to the impact of Ruskin and the study of the Gospels, unified his every faculty, intensified his humanitarian zeal, and made him a dynamic leader of men. Henceforth he was to be an apostle, a crusader, an evangelist proclaiming a Message ; and that message centred in the Fatherhood of God, the Brotherhood of man and the things appertaining to the Kingdom of Christ *on earth*. Even the titles of his popular social pamphlets commonly assumed a religious mould as, for example, *Can a Man be a Christian on a Pound a Week ?* and *My Confession of Faith in the Labour Alliance*.

The year following his conversion, Hardie was elected Secretary of the Ayrshire Miners' Association. In 1887 he started the *Miner*, later to develop into the *Labour Leader*. The same year, on his first appearance at the Trades Union Congress,

[1] History of English People (Vol. 1830–41), page 340
[2] *History of Trade Unionism*, p. 681 (note).

he proposed the creation of an *independent* Labour party, maintaining that too frequently the workers had been " befooled and betrayed " by the old parties. A few months later, at a by-election at Mid-Lanark, he was nominated to run as a representative of Independent Labour against both Liberal and Conservative candidates. Despite an offer from Liberal Agents of a " safe seat " at the " first opportunity," if only he would wear the Liberal badge, Hardie never so much as wavered.[1] He polled only 619 votes, but he had begun a movement of far-reaching effects. Forthwith he established the Scottish Labour Party ; in 1892, he was elected M.P. for West Ham (London)—the first " Independent " Labour representative to sit in the House of Commons. Next year, at a small conference in Bradford, he founded the " Independent Labour Party," into which the " Scottish " was merged. In 1899, he induced the Trades Union Congress to authorise the formation of a Labour Representation Committee to work in conjunction with the " I.L.P." and other co-operating bodies, for the purpose of " promoting legislation in. the direct interest of labour." In 1906, he became the leader of the newly formed " Labour Party " in the House of Commons. Always he stood firmly for peace, temperance, education, justice and social equity, based squarely on what he conceived to be obvious Christian principles. His integrity, his perseverance and his humanity, were unassailable : but, the failure of " civilised peoples " to prevent the World War broke his heart, and hastened his end ; he died in 1915.[2]

Any man who rises to the dizzy height of being three times Prime Minister of England, will have many political foes; and if the circumstances surrounding his premierships be analagous to those experienced by J. Ramsay MacDonald, such foes will be peculiarly clamant and virulent. This is not the place to attempt judgment upon the conduct of the first Labour Prime Minister, in the various crises of his highly difficult and highly dramatic career. Around that subject, debate will long and furiously rage. But one thing is beyond debate. Moral and spiritual forces have been uppermost, in shaping all that is most attractive in the life of Mr. MacDonald. Born of labouring parentage in Scotland (1866), his latent abilities were discovered by the minister of the local kirk, who procured for him a post as " pupil teacher." When eighteen, he was a clerk in London earning only 12s. 6d. a week, but slaking his thirst for education by attendance at night classes and by incessant reading. In

[1] *History of Trade Unionism*, p. 682 (note 2).
[2] For Hardie, see D. Lowe, *From Pit to Parliament* ; and W. Stewart, *J. Keir Hardie.*

1894 he joined the I.L.P., where force of character, pronounced organising ability and high ideals, marked him for special leadership. When thirty, he married that noble, capable, Christian woman, Margaret Gladstone, niece of Lord Kelvin. In 1899 he was made Secretary of the Labour Representation Committee ; in 1906 he was elected M.P. for the industrial city of Leicester ; by 1911, he was leader of the Labour Party. His pacifism, during the war, caused him to refuse Office and made him the target of much vitriolic attack.[1] From 1918 till 1922, he was without a seat in the Commons ; but, returned again to Parliament in the latter year, he was chosen by his colleagues as Opposition Leader. In 1924, he became Britain's first Labour Prime Minister ; in 1929 he formed his second Labour Ministry ; in 1931, to grapple more effectively with the perplexing conditions of the world economic depression, he sank party interest and headed a National Government.

MacDonald's public career and his writings alike, show that consistently he has opposed the way of violence. War and revolution were equally repulsive to him. Though a thoroughgoing Socialist, the materialism, the economic-determinism, the class-hatred, the atheism and the final world cataclysm of Marx's doctrinaire dogma, have always repelled him. His books, *Parliament and Democracy* and *Parliament and Revolution* are vigorous, logical apologetics for Democratic government : but to him such government must always postulate freedom of thought, speech and institution, must be based squarely on moral principles, and must proceed from the untrammelled consent of the governed. MacDonald's " Foreword " to Dr. Belden's book, *George Whitefield*, reveals clearly his belief in the dependence of true Democracy upon vital Christianity. " The Free Churches," MacDonald pronounces, " one of the pure sources from which free Democracy came." " It was by the dynamic of free religion," he avers, " that the masses were inspired to escape from the quagmire of misery and injustice " ; while again, he maintains that the Christian faith " preserved the masses from becoming soulless things, obedient to the convenience and advantage of economic forces."[2]

" Democracy," in Britain and America, MacDonald contends, has already " conquered the foothills." The baffling summit towers challengingly before its view. " Can it afford ? " he asks, " now to dispense with that ardour and devotion which only profound religious belief and stern ethical principle can

---

[1] See C. W. Mullins, *The Patriotism of Ramsay MacDonald and Others* (1916) ; H. Tracey, *From Doughty Street to Downing Street* (1924) ; his biography by his wife (1912).

[2] *Op. cit.*, p. 11.

provide?" Then coming to that "Common Baptism in one Free Faith," mediated by those intrepid modern apostles, Wesley and Whitefield, he points out that it "gave men self-respect and pride, and did not merely arm them with claims for sharing in this world's goods." "The problem is still unsolved," MacDonald continues, "how to make man his own master. It never will be solved by rectifying difference in status, or in material possessions. Class conflicts will only mislead us, and give victories which will be barren of results. . . . The generation which loses the spirit of life loses everything worth having. Let us not pride ourselves that we are progressing, if we let go the interests and inspirations which brought the Free Churches into being."[1]

If Keir Hardie and Ramsay MacDonald were the central figures in making the Labour Party an independent force, the Labour leaders who have left the next deepest impress upon the popular mind are Arthur Henderson and George Lansbury ; the former a life-long local preacher, the latter a zealous Christian crusader combining in his own person many of the most attractive aspects both of the Evangelical and the Anglo-Catholic approach. Born of humblest parentage, in 1863, Henderson as a boy served apprenticeship as a moulder in Newcastle. Soon practical Christianity and constructive Trade-Unionism became his consuming interests. His education was self-acquired : his driving motive was the peaceful application of Christian principles to the solution of personal, civic, national and international problems. While yet very young, he rendered excellent service on the Newcastle city council. In 1903 he became Mayor of Darlington, and the same year at a by-election won a seat in Parliament. From 1908 to 1910, he was Chairman of the National Labour Party, a post to which he again was elected in 1914. In the Coalition war Ministries, both under Asquith and Lloyd George, he held Cabinet stations : in the Labour Government of 1924, he was Home Secretary and in that of 1929, Foreign Secretary. Always a man of peace, his labours after the war centred in that field, and he was chosen President of the Disarmament Conference, held at Geneva in 1932.

Lansbury, born in 1859, did not enter Parliament till he was fifty-one. His training for Parliamentary service, like that of Henderson, was through municipal experience. Till 1892, he had been an "ardent Liberal" ; then, converted to Socialism, he became a flaming apostle and ceaseless propagandist of "Labour" doctrines. Long and intimate contact with municipal

[1] *Op. cit.*, pp. xii and xiii ; see Professor Ernest Barker's *Oliver Cromwell* for a penetrating elaboration of this same theme.

VITAL BUILDERS IN THE NEW WORLD
Bishop Francis Asbury   Dr. Egerton Ryerson

affairs enabled him, in 1909, to render signal service as a member of the Royal Commission on the Poor Law. In 1910 he was elected M.P. for Bow, East London, and two years later resigned his seat, to vindicate his advocacy of women's suffrage. In 1912 be began editing the *Daily Herald*, thus giving " Labour " its first daily paper. In 1919–20 he was Mayor of the London borough of Poplar, and in 1921 his policy of " generous relief to the unemployed " won him a short term of imprisonment. In 1924 he refused Office in the first Labour Government. From 1925 to 1927 he published *Lansbury's Labour Weekly*, and from 1927 to 1928 was Chairman of the national Labour Party. First Commissioner of Works in the second Labour Government (1929–31), he vastly improved and expanded the parks and playing fields of the land, adapting them especially to the needs of children and to the requirements of wholesome games and recreations. Finally he rose to be Opposition Leader in the House of Commons, but, for conscience sake, relinquished that Office. The *Christian World* expressed but sober truth when, after suggesting that " often " he may have been " politically wrong," it continued : " Everyone feels that all George Lansbury's actions and decisions are inspired by an utterly unselfish and high-minded motive. Such men, whatever their party allegiance, are the glory of our public life. . . . Lansbury's career was crowned by an action which, in a sense, ended it. He resigned the leadership of his party because, as an absolute pacifist, he could no longer accept office in any Government committed to preparation for war."[1] After resignation, as an apostle of " Christian peace," Lansbury chivalrously carried his evangel to the private ears both of Hitler and of Mussolini ; while in September, 1937, presiding at a " National Convention of the Parliamentary Pacifist Group," he said : " We refuse to accept the ghastly doctrine that only massed force can bring peace to a distracted world."[2] Furthermore, dismissing *in toto*, as " absurd futility," the arbitrament of the sword, he frankly declared : " We should be willing to accept *international organisation* of the world's undeveloped territories and non-self-governing peoples."[3]

These Labour giants, however, stand not as isolated individuals. Despite all the efforts of Marxian atheists and ideological rationalists, to capture control of the British Labour movement, practical Christian influences have remained its saving salt. The historical backgrounds of the Movement, have made it wary of doctrinaire dogmatists and " cure-all " political

[1] See issue of September 2nd, 1937, p. 3.
[2] *Observer*, September 19th, 1937.
[3] *Ibid.* See Lansbury's *My Life* (1928).

2 C

adventurers. Continental organs often have dubbed the
Labour party " the Salvation Army of British politics " ; but
the country's working masses have not been perturbed by the
jibe. The very name of Labour's chief educational centre,
Ruskin College, Oxford, is indicative of the social-evangelical
forces that have inspired the Labour crusade. Moreover,
when the names of such characters as Will Crooks, Philip Snow-
den, Margaret Bondfield, James Hudson, Jack Lawson, Professor
Lees Smith and A. V. Alexander are placed alongside those of
Burt, Fenwick, Arch, Hardie, MacDonald, Henderson and
Lansbury, it will be seen how deep are the ethical-religious
springs at which this political movement, expressive of the
British workers' humane aspirations, has been fed.

Nor dare one suggest that the same spiritual influences have
been absent from the Conservative and Liberal parties. Both
have passed many measures of high humanitarian value. Both,
through the days of Wilberforce, Buxton and Shaftesbury, to
those of Gladstone, Lloyd George and Baldwin, can point to
many noble characters whose disinterested championship of
high causes, would have enriched the public life of any State.
The purging Baptism of Fire affected not only the personal,
educational and social life of the British people, but also its
political and national life. Even the pathetically meagre
application of Christian principles, has proven the chief inspiration and sustaining bulwark of that measure of social liberty
the British people already enjoy.

CHAPTER XXII

CREATIVE SOCIAL SERVICE

" HENCE freedom of association proved in the end the restriction of individual freedom and the authority of custom replaced and almost superseded the authority of law. And this is modern England. . . . In the vast work of social organisation which is one of the dominant characteristics of nineteenth-century England, it would be difficult to over-estimate the part played by the Wesleyan revival."

ELIE HALÉVY, *A History of the English People* (1815 vol.) p. 372.

CHAPTER XXI

CREATIVE SOCIAL SERVICE

In no previous age, and among no other peoples in the modern age, has the expression of *voluntary* benevolence, co-operation and social service reached such proportions or exhibited such virility, as during the last century and a half among the Anglo-Saxon peoples. This, moreover, is no accident. Nor is it the result of any superior natural humanity, or inalienable virtue, resident in the Anglo-Saxon character. Indeed, the deeper and more exhaustive the research into the earlier half of eighteenth-century Britain, the more inescapable becomes the conclusion, that the British people were in no degree exempt from what theologians once were wont to designate, " original sin." On the contrary, the wanton torture of animals for sport, the bestial drunkenness of the populace, the inhuman traffic in African negroes, the kidnapping of fellow-countrymen for exportation and sale as slaves, the mortality of parish children, the universal gambling obsession, the savagery of the prison system and penal code, the welter of immorality, the prostitution of the theatre, the growing prevalence of lawlessness, superstition and lewdness ; the political bribery and corruption, the ecclesiastical arrogance and truculence, the shallow pretensions of Deism, the insincerity and debasement rampant in Church and State—such manifestations suggest that the British people were then perhaps as deeply degraded and debauched, as any people in Christendom.

Whence, then, this pronounced humanity ?—this passion for social justice, and sensitivity to human wrongs ? There is but one answer commensurate with stubborn historical truth. It derived from a new social conscience. And if that social conscience, admittedly, was the offspring of more than one progenitor, it none the less was mothered and nurtured by the Evangelical Revival of vital, practical Christianity—a revival which illumined the central postulates of the New Testament ethic, which made real the Fatherhood of God and the Brotherhood of men, which pointed the priority of personality over property, and which directed heart, soul and mind, toward the establishment of the Kingdom of Righteousness on earth.

(i) *Christian Liberty in Action*

Nothing in modern Britain, perhaps, better illustrates the principle of Christian liberty in action than her extensive voluntary hospital system, wherein the poorest receive the best medical and surgical treatment free. The British hospital system is too well known to warrant any elaboration here. Nevertheless, it should be remembered that this is the only major hospital system in the world supported almost exclusively by the free-will gifts of an appreciative public.[1] And that phenomenal generosity is closely associated with the spirit of personal sacrifice and public service, engendered by the modern Baptism of Fire. Such hospitals as existed in England prior to the Great Revival, were used largely for healing the wounds, mending the limbs and maintaining the general physical fitness of soldiers and sailors of the Crown. The early eighteenth-century Charity Sermons and Reports, make that fact abundantly clear. Wesley it was who started the first free medical dispensary in England; he established the first centres offering free electric treatment to the poor; he emphasised constantly the sanctity of the human body as the temple of the living Spirit of God, urging the Christian duty of keeping it pure and healthy; while also, his widely circulated *Primitive Physic* helped largely to make the care of the body a matter of religious and social, as well as of personal, concern. As Sir George Newman has observed, an unprecedented improvement in public health accompanied the progress of the Revival; and the splendid voluntary hospital facilities of modern England (so generously supported by religious organisations) came to be more closely associated with a spiritual than a materialistic conception of life.

If, however, the voluntary hospital system is the best known of all the voluntary-humanitarian services of Britain, it is but symbolic of a unique heritage of modern social service organisations, in the creation of which nineteenth-century England led the world. Even the briefest survey of some of the characteristic humanitarian movements at work in Britain to-day, will evince their close relationship to the Baptism of Fire which purged and enlarged the soul of England. The spiritual awakening which abolished the slave trade, which laid the foundations of popular education, which humanised the prison system, which established a world missionary movement, which emancipated England's " industrial slaves," and which raised up a valiant leadership both in Trade Unionism and the Parliamentary Labour Movement—that same awakening inspired also the

[1] See *Encyclopædia Britannica* (" Hospital ").

modern philanthropic and social service movement, which extended its sympathy not only to all sorts and conditions of human beings, but even to the lower creatures of creation.

The Royal Society for the Prevention of Cruelty to Animals, founded in London in 1824, is not only the largest but the oldest animal protection society in existence. In Great Britain it has more than 2,000 branches and employs 230 full-time and well-trained inspectors. Every year it offers free veterinary service to over a quarter-million mute creatures. Not only has it promoted much animal-protection legislation and created an organisation which guarantees its effective enforcement, but, more important, it has circulated much knowledge regarding bird and beast life and has mediated kindness toward all dumb, defenceless creatures, particularly those domesticated as helpmeets of man. Prizes offered by this Society draw forth, every year, hundreds of thousands of competition essays from British school children, all dealing with the habits and rights of, or man's duties toward, the beast and bird world ; while also the Ladies' Committee of the Society, which specialises on child education, spreads influences which predispose the nation's children to kindness toward all the lower animal creation.[1]

Scarcely is it surprising to discover that Arthur Broome, founder of the R.S.P.C.A., which now has mothered " many hundreds of kindred societies all over the world,"[2] was an obscure Evangelical clergyman, who resigned his living that he might give all his time to conducting a mission for the Christian treatment of defenceless animals. Neither is it surprising, on examining the records of this Society, to find that at its inaugural meeting the great Evangelical emancipator, Sir Thomas Fowell Buxton, was in the chair, and that both William Wilberforce and Sir James MacKintosh were present as supporters[3] ; while all three of these humanitarians, along with Richard Martin, M.P., and other enthusiasts, were on the initial Committee of the infant organisation. Again it is pertinent that the Ladies' Committee of the R.S.P.C.A., was founded by that remarkable Evangelical leader· the Baroness Burdett-Coutts, while she it was also who, in 1869, laid the foundation stone of the present headquarters of the Society in Jermyn Street, London. Nor was this Evangelical manifestation of kindness toward animals, disassociated with the earliest teaching of the Revival. No one had more sternly opposed

---

[1] For a vivid historical record of the work of the R.S.P.C.A., see Edward Fairholme and Wellesley Pain, *A Century of Work for Animals* (second edition, 1934) ; also see Annual Reports and pamphlets of the Society.

[2] *Facts and Figures about the R.S.P.C.A.*, p. 2.

[3] Fairholme and Pain, *op. cit.*, p. 54·

the "sport" of baiting animals than Wesley. He made it a fixed rule moreover among his itinerant preachers, that never after a journey should they seek food or rest themselves, till they had seen to it that the horse, which shared their labours, had been properly fed, brushed, rubbed down, bedded and, if necessary, blanketed. So deeply interested in animals was Wesley, that he even believed they had souls : while Cowper, the classic poet of the Revival, wrote :

> " I would not enter on my list of friends,
> (Though graced with polished manners and fine sense,
> Yet wanting sensibility) the man
> Who needlessly sets foot upon a worm."[1]

The famous London City Mission, even more emphatically than the R.S.P.C.A., was conceived and nurtured in the immediate spiritual succession of the great Revival. David Nasmith, its founder, was born of poor but pious Glasgow parents, in 1799. At fourteen, he became secretary of the Glasgow Youths' Bible Association. When but sixteen, he was a most successful Sunday School teacher. When eighteen, his religious fervour impelled him to volunteer as a missionary candidate for Africa ; and sore was his disappointment when he learned that, for lack of sufficient educational background, his application had been unsuccessful. Nevertheless, if secular employment was still to demand much of his time, a missionary he had to be, wherever a door would open. When nineteen, he became honorary-secretary of the Glasgow Bridewell Association, giving unsparingly of his time to work among prisoners. When twenty, to his great delight, he was appointed, at £60 a year, to the assistant-secretaryship of Religious and Charitable Institution House, Glasgow, a post which sharpened his organising abilities and revealed to him the deeper needs of the slum-dwellers of his city.

When twenty-seven, Nasmith launched upon his real life work. Resigning his secretarial post, he founded the Glasgow City Mission, and having established it upon interdenominational foundations of service to the most needy, proceeded in 1828 to Dublin, where he founded a similar Mission. The year 1830 found him in North America, where he created not only the New York City Mission but also Missions in a score of the larger centres of the U.S.A. and Canada. In 1832, after much effort, he established a City Mission in Paris ; while in May, 1835, came the crowning success of his life, the founding of the London City Mission.[2]

---

[1] Cowper, *The Task*, Book vi, l, 560f.
[2] For Nasmith's life, see Dr. John Campbell, *Memoirs of David Nasmith* ; also *London City Mission Magazine* (January to September, 1935). " An Apostle of the People," by Baruck.

The co-operation of all willing Christians, of whatever denomination, upon which these Missions were founded, would have been unthinkable aside from the leavening influences of the Evangelical Revival. Sir Thomas Fowell Buxton became the first Honorary Treasurer of the London City Mission ; and the co-labours of " Enthusiasts," Anglican and Nonconformist, made possible its marked success. Within twenty-two months of its founding, the L.C.M. was commanding the full-time, paid services of sixty-three missionaries in the most neglected purlieus of London, together with the voluntary efforts of many helpers. From the beginning, it entered into fullest co-operation both with the British and Foreign Bible Society and the Religious Tract Society. No sooner was it on its feet, than it established its own Magazine, and never since has that organ missed its monthly publication. To-day the L.C.M. has 270 full-time missionaries, ministering to the most unfortunate strata of the World Metropolis, not only through the medium of the English tongue but through twenty other languages as well ; while this regular staff is assisted by some 2,000 Sunday School teachers and other voluntary workers. Every year, the L.C.M. missionaries pay more than a million-and-a-half home visits among those the Churches but slightly touch : to scores of thousands of struggling people—especially poor mothers—they act as guides, counsellors and friends. At the sick bed, in hospitals and lodging houses, among criminals and prisoners, they are ministering angels. In their own Halls, they care for 20,000 Sunday School children ; they conduct Temperance Guilds, Bible Classes, Mothers' Meetings and Young People's Societies of Christian Endeavour. They preach too in the open-air, distribute Bibles and Christian literature, provide thousands of free beds and tens of thousands of free meals, while also they annually send multitudes of poor children for a " day's outing," in the country or by the sea. And all this is made possible, by freewill gifts of about £75,000, which Christian people yearly bestow upon the Mission.[1]

Next, among the memorable permanent organisations that grew up in the spiritual succession of the Revival, was the Y.M.C.A., founded by George Williams in 1844. William's parentage, was as humble and obscure as Nasmith's. Following a schooling little above the average, he was apprenticed, when fourteen, to Mr. Holmes, a draper in Bridgwater. Holmes, being himself a regular attendant at the local Congregational Chapel, insisted that all his apprentices attend service there, on Sunday mornings. This at first, to Williams, was an irksome duty. But gradually, the quiet personality and earnest teaching

[1] See *Annual Report* of L.C.M., June, 1937.

of the minister, Rev. Evan James, grew upon him ; and he began attending the evening service also—by choice. When sixteen, on a winter Sunday evening in 1837, Williams experienced his soul's awakening. Sitting alone, in the back seat of the little Chapel, his being was pierced to the quick by the minister's sermon. Christ, he knew, was pleading for the lordship of his life. That night, he knelt in fervent prayer " at the back of the shop " and arose a " new creature." Henceforth, the one-time " careless, thoughtless, godless, swearing young fellow "[1] was a staunch disciple of Christ.

Shortly after Williams's conversion, he read two books by the then-famous American evangelist, Charles Finney—*Lectures to Professing Christians*, and *Lectures on Revivals*. These books fanned his new-found spiritual life into a consuming fire, and made him a ceaseless missioner among his daily associates. Before his apprenticeship was over, he had the joy of seeing the atmosphere of the Holmes Drapery establishment completely changed. Every one of his immediate business associates in that Bridgwater shop, he had led into a personal Christian experience and into active discipleship. Such was the youth who, when twenty, procured a post, at £40 a year, with the great metropolitan drapery house of Hitchcock.

When Williams came to London, in 1841, the working conditions of drapers' assistants were peculiarly bad. Already Shaftesbury's epic campaign had begun to restrict the hours and improve the conditions of *factory* operatives : but so far, " black-coated workers " behind counter and desk had found no relief, and the Short Time Committees were not yet. By common consent, the drapers' assistants were the worst " slavies " of all the white-collared toilers in London. Competition in their ranks was keen ; daily hours of labour, ranged from twelve to fifteen ; by ancient custom, they lived and slept over their master's place of business ; and none, had a bed to himself. In these circumstances it was difficult to nurture spiritual life, though profanity, smutty stories and scandal-mongering, found fertile soil. Among the one hundred and forty assistants in the Hitchcock firm, Williams, on arrival, found but one professing Christian. These two, immediately becoming friends, began a campaign of prayer and personal evangelism, inviting their closest associates, one by one, to come and hear their favourite preachers and attend a Bible Class of which they were members. It was all surprisingly ingenuous, and they at first were the recipients of many a jibe and rebuff ; but soon a prayer and Bible study group was meeting daily, in one of the bedrooms over the Hitchcock

[1] J. E. Hodder Williams, *Life of Sir Geo. Williams*, p. 17.

establishment. Finney's books were introduced to this tiny nucleus. Conversions followed ; and at the end of a year, about a dozen of the assistants were utterly committed to the service of Christ. Before the end of the second year, temperance, mutual improvement and missionary meetings, besides those for prayer and Bible study, were part of the regular programme. Even the head of the firm, now was one of the converts : the Enthusiasts were transforming the whole aspect of a great business house, while it, in consequence, was contributing workers to Sunday Schools, Missions, Temperance Guilds and Churches, throughout London.

George Williams's third year in London, marks the origin of the Young Men's Christian Association. The moral and spiritual influences started in Hitchcock's, spread to the West End drapery house of W. D. Owen, where the principal assistant, James Smith, supported by Mr. Branch, a London City Missionary, began similar efforts. Williams successfully co-operated with them. Then the thought began to possess him : Why not a comprehensive Association of Christian young men, to mediate spiritual and moral influences in all the drapery houses—indeed, in all the business firms—of London ? The zealot prayed and pondered ; he discussed the project with his most intimate helpers ; and finally, on June 6th, 1844, an inner circle of twelve young men assembled in Williams's bedroom, and formed themselves into an Association pledged to attempt this high purpose.

Thus, in " an upper room," over a great city business firm, inspired by the faith and vision of a mere stripling from the country, was born the Y.M.C.A. At that historical meeting, however, the name had not been determined, the immediate designation being " The Drapers' Evangelical Association." It was in a later consultation, that the now-famous name was agreed upon. Then, a carefully worded circular letter was sent to the leading business houses of London. This drew forth many encouraging replies. The mission spread. New zealots were forthcoming. Lord Shaftesbury, whom Sir George Williams was later wont to style " our Moses," was procured as President. And so from that Upper Room where twelve young clerks, aflame with missionary fire, bound themselves into a committee for definite Christian advance, evolved a movement which, spreading to every Continent, has affected millions of young men for good.[1]

[1] J E. H. Williams, *op. cit.* (*passim.*), but especially chapter v ; Sir Arthur Yapp, *The Romance of the Red Triangle* ; 1936 Y.M.C.A. Report (*Our Message is Christ*).

(ii)   *The March Continues*

Something of the work of the Ragged School Union, as a distinctive pioneer in the struggle for popular education in England, we have already observed. That Union was founded in the same year as the Y.M.C.A., and by persons who drank from the same spiritual springs. After the passing of the Board School Act (1870), the Union manifested no little genius in adapting itself to changed conditions. Relieved by the State of most of its secular educational tasks, it became under Shaftesbury's guidance more and more a medium for wider social service to childhood and youth. For decades now, this Union has been known as The Shaftesbury Society, Lord Shaftesbury being, from its inception in 1844 till his death in 1885, its active, devoted President. To-day the Shaftesbury Society has well over 6,000 voluntary workers who, together with 150 trained and paid Missioners, Deaconesses, Teachers, etc., labour in the most needy sections of Britain's industrial cities. It has almost 200 Local Branches and affiliated Missions, conducting most comprehensive programmes ; it operates a score of Seaside and Country Homes, Camps, humane Residential Schools and Hostels, Fresh Air Retreats and Sunshine Camps ; it has 440 Companies of Scouts, Guides and other Brigades ; it runs more than a score of Infant Welfare Centres, Medical Missions, Day Nurseries and Nursery Schools. For the Deformed, it affords 90 Cripple Parlours, thus engendering joy and fellowship in some 7,500 lives which otherwise would be lonely and bleak. Every year, this Society sends scores of thousands of underprivileged children for an outing by the sea, or in the country ; it distributes myriads of garments, toys and pairs of boots ; while also it lends out hundreds of surgical appliances and invalid carriages. The essence of its being, however, is represented by its Gospel Services, Sunday Schools, Bible Classes, Prayer Groups, Bands of Hope, Institutes and Clubs. Annually, apart from all local support, and all gifts in kind, the British people contribute more than £80,000 to the central funds of the Shaftesbury Society.[1]

Lecky, as we have seen, pronounced the eighteenth century liquor traffic " the Master Curse " of English Society.[2] A curse that traffic remains. But no mean campaign has been waged against it ; and the power and persistence of that campaign have derived chiefly from the unquenchable moral enthusiasm engendered by Evangelical Christianity. Wesley, his itinerant

---

[1] See *Two Cities in One* (Annual Report of Shaftesbury Society, 1937).
[2] See chapter viii (ii).

and local preachers, his class leaders and all his official standard bearers, were confirmed opponents of intoxicating beverages. Temperance in all the social, educational and moral endeavours of the " Clapham Sect " was a central plank. So pronounced too was the temperance emphasis of Whitefield, Asbury, Coke and their spiritual successors in America, that, by 1833, the United States alone had over one million members of Total Abstinence organisations, united in 6,000 local societies. In England, in 1831, inspired almost entirely by Evangelical zeal, the British and Foreign Temperance Society sprang into life. Four years later, the Independent Order of Rechabites was established, and spread rapidly to America. In 1853 came the powerful and interdenominational United Kingdom Alliance, which began to press the temperance cause in politics ; while in 1862, followed the Church of England Temperance Society. Such orders and organisations, moreover, as the Good Templars, The Women's Christian Temperance Union and the Band of Hope Union, are immediate products of the sustained Baptism of Fire ; and notwithstanding all " interested " ridicule, they have been the means of inestimable good. Nor can the Prohibition movement of the U.S.A. ever be understood apart from the same Spiritual Succession. If not the child, it unmistakably was the grandchild of the Great Revival. The " Noble Experiment " was fraught with not a few mistakes. It became too legalistic, too coercive, too intolerant, too politically-minded. Temporarily it is under a cloud. But the true temperance movement behind it, is not dead ; nor will it die, while high moral enthusiasm and the yearning for clean citizenship, survive.[1]

Again, the lives of the great temperance leaders no less than the origin of the great temperance movements, bespeak their common relationship to vital, vigorous Christianity. Who can explain the endeavours of John B. Gough, of Frances Willard and of Sir Wilfred Lawson, apart from the sustaining inspirations of their Evangelical Faith ? Nor is the case of that intrepid Roman Catholic temperance leader, Father Mathew, widely different. His burning moral and temperance enthusiasm of course expressed itself through the medium of his own Church, wherein he wrought inestimable good. But not a little of the vision, zeal and technique of his marvellous " Missions," he had learned from the impact of the world's greatest Protestant Revival.[2]

[1] See articles on " Temperance " in *Ency. Brit.*, *Ency. of Rel. and Ethics*, and *Daily Express Ency.*

[2] See Gough's *Life*, by C. Martyn ; Frances Willard's, by Florence White ; Mathew's, by F. J. Matthew ; also Lawson's *Law and the Liquor Traffic.*

Some sophisticated persons still sneer at the Salvation Army. Their sneer is the sneer of ignorance. Who can read Hugh Redwood's *God in the Slums*, without realising the unobtrusive efficiency of its Emergency Relief Corps ? Yet that is but one of a hundred vehicles through which these *Soldiers of the Cross* render vital service, amidst desperate situations. To-day the Salvation Army is organised and labouring in eighty-three countries. Its efforts are guided by 32,460 officers and officials, controlling 15,304 centres of activity. It commands the services of more than 35,000 bandsmen and over 63,000 songsters. Nevertheless, these represent but a fraction of its voluntary workers, consecrated to " the service of humanity, in the name and spirit of Christ." It seeks to form an unbroken chain of sacrificial love, throughout the shadowed places of the earth. " Sanctified sanity " motivates its toil.

Besides all its moral and spiritual teaching facilities, the Salvation Army conducts an amazing retinue of social services. Its Hostels and Shelters, provide scores of thousands of free beds for the homeless and forlorn. Millions of free meals are annually given to the hungry, through its Kitchens and Canteens. Employment is found for large numbers out of work. As for criminals, prisoners, and their dependents, the " Army " annually assists many thousands of these, with a tenderness and an understanding no state institution could emulate. It provides many companies of trained nurses and midwives, in quarters where their services are a " God-send." It runs Maternity Homes, Hospitals, Crèches, Industrial Homes, " Eventide Homes," Seaside Camps, Land Colonies, Migration Centres, Slum Sisterhoods, Prison Visitation Corps, and most winsome Rescue Homes for unmarried mothers ; for, uncompromising as is their morality, never do Salvationists look upon young unmarried mothers as prostitutes. Even educationally, the Army does " its bit." In India alone, it conducts 648 Day Schools and several Boarding Schools. Recently, the Punjab's Minister of Education, on opening a new Salvation Army School, said : " The Salvation Army in this country puts our own people to shame. The work that should be done by Indians, has too often been done by the European Officers of the Salvation Army. But for their great sacrifice, these children, who will be housed in one of the best school buildings the Province possesses, would probably have roamed about committing offences."[1]

William Booth, founder of this Christian " Army," was an ordained Methodist minister. In 1864, to reach " the hopeless,"

---

[1] *Glorious Quest* (Annual Report of some of the Salvation Army's Worldwide Work—1936), p. 27. The above facts are gleaned from fully a dozen different pamphlets and reports.

he created the East London Revival Society. That Society, in 1878, was re-organised and christened the Salvation Army. So it also, is a lineal descendant of the mighty Spiritual Awakening![1]

The National Society for the Prevention of Cruelty to Children is another voluntary organisation in the same succession. Throughout the country, it has some 300 Branches, supported by nearly 3,000 Ladies Committees and other auxiliary bodies. No district in the Kingdom is without a local Committee pledged to the guardianship of childhood. But as Rev. Benjamin Waugh, its first Director, often said : " The Inspector is the Society." Of these trained and uniformed inspectors (men and women), the N.S.P.C.C. has no less that 270, permanently stationed in allotted areas. With local clergymen, school masters, Sunday School superintendents, magistrates, policemen and others interested in child welfare, they keep in closest touch. Hence, with the backing of Committees, Branches and Headquarters, a salutary supervision of child life is always in progress. The purpose of the Society is protective, not punitive. True, in dire necessity, it does not shirk resort to the Courts ; but for one case of prosecution, it records several scores of conference, advice and warning.[2] Education, social illumination and the sensitising of conscience, are its chief avenues of expression. Not only does it help irresponsible parents to realise their duty towards their offspring ; it also helps refractory children to appreciate their duties towards their parents. The *Child's Guardian*, the Society's official organ, enjoys a circulation above 100,000 : its other publications render high service. Yearly, too, the N.S.P.C.C. sponsors thousands of public lectures, lantern talks and films, to further the home and community interests of the Child. To this Society again a grateful public annually donates about £150,000.[3]

The immediate British forerunners in this field, were Thomas Agnew and Rev. George Staite, both passionate lovers of children and both religious Enthusiasts.[4] By their efforts, a child protection society was founded in Liverpool in 1882. Local enthusiasts in Birmingham and Bristol, followed suit. Soon the Baroness Burdett-Coutts and Hesba Stretton, the religious authoress, investigated the Liverpool essay. The upshot was that Mr. Agnew was invited to London to confer with that noble zealot, Benjamin Waugh, a Congregational minister

[1] See *Life of William Booth*, by St. John Ervine ; also *Life* by Harold Begbie.
[2] *Annual Report of the N.S.P.C.C.* (1936–37) p. 3.
[3] *Ibid.*, p. 35. This is independent of Scotland, which has its own co-operating organisation.
[4] Already certain American cities, led by like enthusiasts, had formed Child protection societies.

who, as author of *The Gaol Cradle : Who Rocks it* ? as Editor of the *Sunday Magazine* and as a member of the London School Board, had wrought conspicuous service to children. They, forthwith, were introduced to Lord Shaftesbury, who at once advised the formation of a *National* society. In deference to the three local societies aforementioned, and mindful of precedents in certain American cities, this advice was not acted upon : but arrangements quickly were made for the establishment of a strong *London* Society.[1] On July 8th, 1884, at a packed meeting in the Mansion House, Lord Shaftesbury proposed the resolution which gave birth to that Society. Among his supporters, along with Waugh and Agnew, were the Baroness Burdett-Coutts, the Earl of Aberdeen and Dr. Barnardo. These all were avowed Evangelicals, but they had sought and won the co-operation of those representing other schools of thought ; Cardinal Manning was on the first Executive.

Inevitably Shaftesbury was elected President, and Waugh, Honorary Secretary. Shaftesbury then was 83, with but fifteen months to live. Waugh was 45, and only approaching the zenith of his powers. With crusading fervour, this parson threw himself into his task. His contagious enthusiasm soon bore fruit. Aid Committees sprang into being : in less than five years there were thirty-one, labouring in the larger cities of England and Wales. So in May, 1889, this London society was transformed into the *National* Society for the Prevention of Cruelty to Children. Waugh led it from strength to strength. He, too, belongs to that ageless and saving succession of practical saints, to which the modern " Baptism of Fire " added so valiant a band.[2]

(iii) *Opportunity for the Destitute Child*

Many are the voluntary Anglo-Saxon organisations and associations, through which pulse the power of Christian liberty in action. The foregoing, are but representative. What the French Revolution was to the moral, social and political development of half Europe, the Evangelical Revival was to the development of England and the English-speaking peoples ; it was the modern water-shed of Anglo-Saxon history. As Professor Halévy repeatedly has hinted, Wesley was the Napoleon of the English-speaking world ; and the fact that his weapons were Christian and spiritual, not pagan and carnal, has profoundly affected the whole subsequent development of the

---

[1] *Occasional Papers* of N.S.P.C.C. (edited by Sir Robert Parr), XV, p. 11.
[2] For a good survey of the history of this Society, see *Jubilee Report* (1933-4), pp. 10-19 ; also *Benjamin Waugh*, by Sir Robt. Parr.

British Empire and the United States. Democracy in these commonwealths became a spiritual ideal, closely associated with a hundred organised manifestations of social service and self-help : it became rooted moreover in a Christian conception of the meaning and purpose of life. The Evangelical Revival is more central to the understanding of the modern heritage of the English-speaking peoples, than is the Reformation : and the more exhaustively it is examined, the more inescapable becomes the conclusion, that it was infinitely less marred by human alloy. Though headed by an incomparable clergyman, it primarily was a religious awakening of the people : and through it the people found its soul.

Returning however to the observation of creative social service, it should be noted that the Boy Scout and Girl Guide movement, founded by Lord Baden-Powell in 1908, owes much to the same spiritual succession. Of the four million members of this world organisation, the great majority are in areas profoundly influenced by Evangelical Christianity. Protestant Evangelical Churches indeed have been the chief organising centres of the movement, while its pledges ; " I will do my duty to God and my country " ; " I will do my best to help others, whatever it costs me " ; and the commitment to do a " good turn " daily, are surely expressive of practical Christianity.[1] Numerous, too, are the Friendly Societies and Mutual Aid Fraternities, which owe their life to the new springs of fellowship and humanity, opened up by this unparalleled Revival. But of all its later humanitarian achievements, few are more beautiful than its creations on behalf of orphaned, homeless and destitute children. Müller's Homes, Stephenson's (" The National "), Quarrier's (Scotland), Spurgeon's, Fegan's, and the Homes of the Waifs and Strays Society[2] are all traceable to the same fountain head. The greatest and most romantic of all such remarkable Homes, however, are those established by Dr. Barnardo ; and their unique pioneering importance merits some detailed attention.

In his middle-teens, Thomas John Barnardo was a priggish and rather parading Agnostic. Five weeks before his seventeenth birthday, on May 26th, 1862, during a memorable Irish revival, he experienced a thoroughgoing conversion. The scoffer was transformed into a zealous Christian, who soon was devoting five evenings a week to voluntary service in the vilest Dublin slums. When twenty, Barnardo heard an appeal by

---

[1] For the origin and growth of the Scout and Guide movements, see S. K. Wade, *The Story of Scouting.*
[2] The Waifs and Strays Society (Church of England), was founded by E. de M. Rudolf, Waugh's associate secretary of the N.S.P.C.C.

Hudson Taylor, founder of the China Inland Mission ; and so searching was its effect upon him, that the same day he volunteered as a missionary candidate for China.

A few weeks later, the young enthusiast had resigned his Dublin business post and was settled in London, training for medical missionary service. But scarcely had he discovered his bearings, when he discovered also the missionary needs of East London's slums : so forthwith, at his own expense, he started the " Donkey Shed " Ragged School. And there it was, on a wintry night, in 1866, he confronted Jim Jarvis, his first homeless waif.

Barnardo, when closing his school for the night, heard a sound by the fireplace ; and there, curled up by the dying embers, but hidden by a box, lay a gaunt, tattered urchin, who pleaded piteously to be allowed to sleep in the school all night. The youngster had no underclothing, no cap, no shoes or stockings : his coat and trousers were ventilated by a score of rents ; and though he said he was ten, his appearance betokened a badly nourished lad of seven. Soon Jim Jarvis was seated at a " feast " in Barnardo's " digs." On cross-examination, he insisted that he had no home, parent or friend. He was one of a tribe of street urchins, living nowhere and sleeping anywhere—beyond the reach of the police ; and that tribe he maintained, was more numerous than he could count. The meal over, and the cross-examination concluded, a coin was placed in Jim's hand and the two sallied forth in dead of night, in search of a " lay " sleeping out. Well over an hour, they trudged, peered and peeped, in vain. Barnardo began to think his companion was hoaxing him. But the waif was persistent : " Don't stop, gov'nor ; we'll find 'em a'right ! " At last, in a blind alley, they climbed a wall ten feet high ; and there, on a metal roof, covered only with rags and tatters, lay *eleven* human waifs.

From that moment, China was challenged by East London. Before many days, other " lays " were discovered ; and the Ragged School teacher, with missionary intensity, bombarded all his Christian friends. Then an unexpected situation arose. Barnardo, as a foreign missionary candidate, was seated on the platform of a great missionary meeting in the Agricultural Hall. The speaker advertised, was an eminent public man ; but, at the last minute, came a message that he had been taken ill and could not appear. Dr. Thain Davidson, the chairman, was one of those to whom Barnardo already had related his discoveries. In his extremity, he turned to the missionary student, and warned him to " collect his thoughts " : he must speak in the great man's stead.

Without polish or rhetoric, Barnardo told of the waifs he had discovered, and challenged the Christian conscience on their behalf. He intended to speak only twenty minutes : but the response of the audience carried him on. Almost for an hour he electrified their interest. Among those who came up to him after the meeting, was a little servant-girl who timidly confided that she had been saving her farthings, to " help the missionaries abroad." Then, pressing a small bag into his hand, she explained : " Surely to help these homeless lads, is missionary work ! " The bag contained 27 farthings ; it was Barnardo's first " public " assistance.

Next day, Barnardo's speech was featured in the Press. Jealous defenders of London's social institutions published letters in reply, accusing the young Irishman not only of exaggeration but fabrication. Shaftesbury, as President of the Ragged School Union, at once determined to know the truth ; so he invited Barnardo, his accusers, and certain disinterested social workers, to a dinner party at his home. There Barnardo's whole story was challenged. So, at midnight, cabs were summoned ; and Shaftesbury's guests proceeded from West London to East End " dives." The upshot was that the young missioner showed his companions, not eleven, but seventy-three boys—sleeping out. That " find " Barnardo always considered providential ; it was the largest, by far, he ever discovered. His critics were utterly disarmed. The veteran reformer was dumbfounded. Before the party returned westward, Shaftesbury intimated to the foreign missionary volunteer, that " his China " probably would be East London.

With the good Earl's blessing, Barnardo forthwith established the East End Juvenile Mission, one aspect of whose endeavour was to find Christian homes for homeless waifs. Its founder never was to see China, the land of his dreams.[1] But out of this humble Mission evolved the world-famous Dr. Barnardo's Homes, which, since 1866, have mothered, fed, clothed, educated, industrially trained, placed out in positions and followed up with parental care, more than 120,000 once-destitute boys and girls. While, by provision of food, shelter and clothing, by discovery of interested relatives, by finding employment, etc., they have casually befriended nearly a half-million more.

The scope of Barnardo's work is amazing. Rightly is their fellowship pronounced, " the Largest Family in the World." Exclusive of all boarding-out centres, the Homes to-day have nearly 200 separate Cottages, Households and Branches, and

[1] The author's book, *Dr. Barnardo, Physician, Pioneer, Prophet*, has recently been produced in a *Chinese* version, and seventy thousand copies have already been circulated.

constantly they are rearing about 8,500 children. In any of their fourteen Ever Open Doors, situated in the largest cities of England and Northern Ireland, any destitute child will be received at any hour of any day or night. Their Girls' Village Home, in Barkingside, has been acclaimed by the famous artist, Sir George Frampton, " the most beautiful village in England " : while such centres as the Boys' Garden City, Woodford Bridge ; the William Baker Technical School, Goldings, Hertford ; the Watts Naval Training School, Elmham, Norfolk ; the Russell Côtes Nautical School, Parkstone, Dorset ; and the Babies' Castle, Hawkhurst, Kent, are scarcely less alluring— all of them located in charming country-side environments. Barnardo's, furthermore, have two excellent Children's Hospitals and several specialised Hospital Homes. They have Crêches, Cripples' Homes, Convalescent Homes, Isolation Homes, Musical Homes, Vocational Homes and Employment Offices, together with excellent Distributing Homes, both in Canada and Australia.

The success of the Barnardo " family " is phenomenal. Walter Reynolds, for many years Director of Music for all the London Parks, has affirmed that he " owed everything " to these Homes which reared him. The Hon. James Page, for long Chief Whip in the Federal Government of Australia, was a child thief on London's streets before Barnardo's received and transformed him. Two per cent. of all Canada's British stock are Barnardo children and their descendants,[1] among whom have been Cabinet Ministers, University professors, clergymen, school principals, doctors, dentists, engineers, managers of great businesses—men and women, in fact, who have adorned every art, calling, profession and craft. Not two per cent. of the Largest Family in the World have been failures.

These Homes, furthermore, have had a marked impact on legislation. Repeatedly, Barnardo fought his way through the Courts to protect " his children " from vicious exploitation. Most memorable of these legal struggles, were those of 1889 and 1890. In the latter year, acting as his own barrister, he pushed two separate cases through the Court of Appeal. And in one of these, pleading before three Lord Justices, and opposed by three barristers, he continued for three days on end. In both cases, on the letter of the Law, a legal verdict *had* to be given against him ; but in both the Judges went out of their way to pronounce a *moral* verdict in his favour. Indeed, certain of the Judges, after hearing all the evidence, sent first subscriptions

[1] This includes the children of the Marchmont Homes, which always co-operated with Barnardo's, and which long since became part of Barnardo's.

to his Homes. Barnardo further appealed to the House of Lords ; and meantime, public opinion became so stirred that the Legislature was spurred to action. Before the cases could come up for ultimate hearing, there was passed, in March, 1891, the famous *Custody of Children Act*, which thereafter made impossible the monstrous exploitation of children by depraved, designing parents. That statute, to this day, is commonly styled " the Barnardo Act."[1]

Not only have Barnardo's Homes affected legislation, they also have affected profoundly the Poor Law system of England. The memorable Local Government Committee appointed in 1894, to investigate the whole question of rearing Poor Law and Charity children, sat two years and published a Report of 1,200 quarto pages ; the Chairman was the Rt. Hon. Anthony J. Mundella and his chief deputy, the Rt. Hon. Sir John Gorst, both of whom—on their own confession—approached their problem with a bias for State institutions. After the investigation, Mundella declared : " I came to the opinion, *which was shared, I think, by all my colleagues*, that we could wish that in the Local Government Board there was a department for . . . the ' Children of the State,' and that we had a Dr. Barnardo to place at the head of them. . . . Most of the reforms that the Committee has recommended, Dr. Barnardo had anticipated and put into practice. . . . *We owe him much for what he has done . . . we owe him more for the example he has set us of how to do it*." Gorst, summarising his impressions, concluded : " In doing this public work, for the public and on behalf of the public, Dr. Barnardo did it in a manner which is an object-lesson, not only to the authorities in England, but to the whole world." Nor do such expert judgments stand alone. The Rt. Hon. Charles Booth, in his inimitable *Life and Labour of the People in London* (1902), said of Barnardo's work : " It is, beyond question, the greatest charitable institution in London, or, I suppose, in the world, and its success has been deserved."[2]

Barnardo always conceived his task as a missionary project. For many years, despite all other duties, he preached twice every Sunday to thousands in the Edinburgh Castle, a one-time burlesque hall and pub, which he acquired and transformed into a Church. When Barnardo died, in 1905, at sixty years of age, he had reared 60,000 once-destitute children. *London Opinion* but expressed a universal sentiment, when it said of him : " The man was great ; the milk of human kindness flowed

[1] See Bready's *Dr. Barnardo*, chapter xii : " Litigation and the Barnardo Act."

[2] See Vol. II, series 3, pp. 46–7.

from him as dews from heaven : nor creed nor colour, caste nor kind, had weight with him. His lofty soul reached beyond the bounds of nationhood, girding the world with love."

That same fervent Evangelical spirit animates Barnardo's Homes to-day. Many feared that with their founder's death they would decline. Instead they have increased in strength and fame. The Council of Christian gentlemen who now guide them are all voluntary workers who, in kindness and love, give of their best, as to friends. Nor does the British public fail them. Cheerfully it entrusts to them nearly £600,000 a year, for the support of their famous family. And so it is that their gracious charter—NO DESTITUTE CHILD EVER REFUSED ADMISSION—is steadfastly maintained.[1]

Most historians have quite ignored the origin, development and influence of such voluntary bodies as this chapter has outlined. In the author's judgment, a knowledge of them is essential to any balanced understanding of the working of the predominantly Anglo-Saxon Democracies. For in spiritualised tradition, custom and humanity—not in coercion and regimentation—is to be found the cardinal genius of the English-speaking peoples. That genius furthermore has been nurtured largely in voluntary organisations and associations which, though deeply religious, are in no sense ecclesiastical. And the creation, management and support of such bodies has not only kept sweet the milk of human kindness, but has engendered the abilities and adaptabilities without which so intricate and delicate an instrument as Democracy hardly could hope to succeed. It is the " voluntary principle," as reflected in such spiritual-humanitarian institutions, that has nurtured and sustained in the typical Anglo-Saxon a deeply-rooted abhorrence of all revolutionary methods, a pronounced sympathy with the underprivileged, and a profound respect for disinterested Religion, Law and Order—which he regards both as essential vehicles of Liberty and Justice, and as indispensable media of any Good Society.

---

[1] For the full history of Barnardo's work, see J. Wesley Bready's *Dr. Barnardo, Physician, Pioneer, Prophet*, fourth and cheap edition (Preface by A. A. Milne).

CHRISTENDOM—WHITHER BOUND?

" If the spiritual oxygen which has kept alive the attachment to Liberty and self-government in the minds of the people becomes exhausted, will not the flame burn low and perhaps flicker out? . . . Without Faith nothing is accomplished, and Hope is the mainspring of Faith. Throughout the course of history every winter of despondency has been followed by a joyous spring time of hope."

VISCOUNT BRYCE,
Modern Democracies, Vol. II, pp. 663 and 670.

" A century earlier John Wesley had defeated Voltaire. Would he defeat Karl Marx? "

ELIE HALÉVY,
A History of the English People
(1895–1905 Vol.), p. 360.

CHRISTENDOM—WHITHER BOUND?

THE mind and spirit of the transfigured Wesley are accurately mirrored in his oft-reiterated aspiration: "The World is my parish." Whitefield's catholicity of interest is reflected in his numerous Atlantic crossings and in his ceaseless journeyings up and down the wildernesses of the New World—sometimes in a state of such exhaustion, that he had to be lifted on and off his horse. Though a priest of the Church of England, Whitefield directly inspired the founding of many congregations within other denominations; for always unity of Christian spirit and service—not conformity of creed and ritual—was his guiding principle: and dying in America, he was buried, at his own request, in a Presbyterian Church in New England.[1] Again, it is significant that Dr. Thomas Coke, the first "Superintendent"[2] Wesley ordained, crossed the Atlantic eighteen times, and died in the Indian Ocean, on a missionary tour to Ceylon. But the Evangelical Revival not only overflowed particular denominational and national barriers; it was impelled by an aspiration to sow the seeds of the Kingdom of God all over the earth; and those seeds, it believed, could be sown by all groups and organisations of faithful souls, who strove diligently to fulfil the will of Christ.

(i) *The Revival and the United States*

As long as the origin and evolution of American institutions are studied by free men, so long the *Mayflower*, the Pilgrim Fathers and Colonial Puritanism will represent key influences, which no cynic or iconoclast can brush aside. Lord Bryce, Professor Ernest Barker and other balanced scholars, have repeatedly emphasised the close connection between the little

---

[1] Whitefield's body lies immediately beneath the pulpit in *Old South Church*, Newburyport, Mass.

[2] Wesley ordained Coke as "superintendent," while he, in turn, was to ordain Asbury to the same office. But this term was unfamiliar, and both men came soon to be known as Bishops. Hence the origin of the great Methodist *Episcopal Church.*

democracies of the New England Congregational (" Independent ") Churches, the winning of American Independence,
and the overthrow of the old, corrupt Monarchy of France.
Religious self-government among these Colonists, prepared the
way for political self-government ; and the success of the
American War of Independence probably achieved more than
all the writings of Rousseau, Voltaire and the Encyclopædists,
in nerving the French people to break the yoke of their Bourbon
oppressors. The contribution of the Pilgrim Fathers, moreover, to popular education was far-reaching. Puritanism was
a book religion, demanding a first-hand knowledge of the
Bible ; while autonomous government in Church and community,
demanded a trained intelligence : hence the necessity for schools.
From the first, therefore, the Pilgrim Fathers established a system
of " common schools."[1] And it is but emblematic of their
thirst for knowledge, that within sixteen years of the sailing of
the *Mayflower*, they had founded a College destined to world
fame. Within two years of its founding, came its first important
legacy. The Rev. John Harvard, dying childless (1638), bequeathed all his books and half his estate to this new college,
which thenceforth bore his name. Nor did these builders of
New England forget their debt to certain venerable institutions
of Old England. The community cradling the infant Harvard
University was called Cambridge, in memory of the *alma mater*
of several of its founders ; for not a few of the early Pilgrims
were University men, who cherished fond memories of youthful
days at Cambridge and Oxford.[2]

But not only did these fathers of a mighty nation lay the
rock foundations of liberty, self-government and universal
education. Though their existence was long threatened, both
by the Indians and the French, and though for many years
they forced a rugged soil for scanty bread, they finally conquered
a wilderness, and made it to bloom as a garden. They were
courageous, adventurous men—these pioneers ; men of vision
and moral rectitude, conscious of a destiny, and living for
to-morrow rather than to-day. Their task however was so
titanic and they were so staunchly in earnest, that they had
little appreciation of the subtler shades of life. Colours to them
were white and black ; moral problems, Yea ! and Nay !
As soldiers scaling a mountain citadel, they had little time for
speculation or debate. Their theology, too, though singularly
direct, vivid and sustaining, was over stern and legalistic ;

[1] Dr. John Fiske, *History of the United States*, p. 96 ; W. H. Hudson
and I. S. Guernsey, *The United States*, p. 164.
[2] See Tyler's *History of American Literature during Colonial Times*,
Vol. I, p. 98 ; Fiske, *op. cit.*, pp. 96–7.

at some points indeed it was grim, sombre and terrible. The blacker shadows of Calvinistic logic, long dominated their doctrinal outlook. Their conception of the Sovereignty of God tended to be rigid, predestinarian, overpowering, almost merciless ; for too often it was little influenced by the compassion and love of Christ. Hence the " witchcraft " obsession inflamed by Cotton Mather, and the persecution of Quakers. These New World Puritans had all the faults of their qualities. Occasionally they were as stubborn and Old Testament minded, as the later South African Boers. But this, despite the modern avalanche of cynicism and iconoclasm, must in fairness be added. For all the iron in their blood, never would their collective conscience permit them to countenance slavery ; and sufficient Christianity underlay their Legalism, to cause them—when once they perceived the horrors of persecution—to recant their cruel, mistaken attitude both towards " witches " and Quakers.[1]

Only against the backgrounds of Colonial Puritanism, can the amazing impact of George Whitefield on America, be fairly gauged. True, the thirteen weeks of his first American sojourn, in 1738, though confined to Georgia, were richly successful. But it was not till his second Colonial tour (October, 1739, till January, 1741), when he came into contact with Pennsylvania and New England, that he began to stir the New World. And how comparatively congenial he found the Promised Land of the Pilgrim Fathers, his own words made clear : " On many counts it certainly exceeds all other provinces in America ; and for the establishment of religion all other parts of the world. Every five miles or perhaps less you have a meeting house . . . I like New England exceedingly well."[2]

Admittedly, too, it was in Georgia, despite the protestations of Benjamin Franklin, that Whitefield founded his famous Bethesda Orphanage, which for so many years was to offer a home for from 80 to 140 destitute or abandoned children. That Orphanage, however, was located in Georgia, because Georgia was the centre of such need. Whatever the shortcomings of the Puritan settlements, they not only educated their children, but they left none of their orphans to suffer the pangs of starvation and nakedness. The neighbourliness of the Puritan parishes obviated such inhumanity. Nevertheless, all was not well with the Puritan commonwealths when Whitefield began his momentous mission. The influence of that great but awful theologian, Jonathan Edwards, radiating from Northampton,

---

[1] Lowell's treatment of American Puritanism in *Among My Books* (first series) is balanced and fair ; see, too, Tyler's *Provincial America*. Hawthorne's attitude is somewhat hostile and exaggerated.

[2] Dr. Belden's *Whitefield*, p. 100.

Massachusetts, was still considerable ; but already reaction was at work. The relentless predestinarianism of the man who could write, *Sinners in the Hands of an Angry God*, was certain to alienate many sensitive souls ; while those who concluded they were damned, concluded, with equal consistency, that they might as well earn their damnation, by indulging the pleasures of sin while yet opportunity remained. The gigantic physical exertions, moreover, of the initial Pilgrim Fathers, now no longer, were equally imperative ; leisure was less scanty ; and not a few of the characteristic vices of Old England had become all too apparent in New England. Drunkenness was on the increase ; cock-fighting was becoming popular ; gambling in some quarters approached an obsession ; material standards of success were undermining the earlier fraternalism ; and the tares of monetary cupidity were choking the wheat of spiritual attainment.

The protracted impact of Whitefield on America was the very thing needful, to save Colonial Puritanism from its legalism, its rigidity, its mounting individualism, and its increasing danger of self-righteousness. His gracious adaptability, his marvellous imagery and his spontaneous, overflowing eloquence went straight to the heart of the New World. The man whose pulpit appeal could extract from the then-hostile Franklin, all the copper, silver and gold in his pockets, was no ordinary preacher, no common mortal. Whitefield was not a little influenced by what was best in New England, and some aspects of Edwards's teaching left a permanent stamp on him ; but he brought to this dominant religious outlook in America a com-plimentary message which was invaluable. His enthusiasm and compassion, his universal charity and selflessness were as gentle, fructifying showers on parched soil. His central emphasis was not the majesty, but the Love of God ; he proclaimed not divine wrath, judgment and retribution, but divine mercy and patience, divine pardon and grace. It is peculiarly poignant that from Northampton, where so many souls were seared and scorched by the threatened fires of judgment, Whitefield reports : " I found my heart drawn out to talk of scarce anything besides the consolations and privileges of the saints and the plentiful effusion of the Spirit upon believers."[1] Whitefield's theology was cast in moulds of a mild Calvinism, but his ministry always was tender, healing, inspiring. In pushing the logic of theory, he soon learned where to stop, and if to the end his preaching implied " the decrees," that implication was merely an attempt to vindicate the omniscience of God. It was his friend John Wesley, the unflinching advocate of " free will,"

[1] Belden, *op. cit.*, p. 113.

whom he desired to preach his funeral sermon in his great Tabernacle, London. To him, the conscious unity of heart and spirit superseded all disagreements on doctrine.

Not yet, has the historical importance of Whitefield's labours been sufficiently appreciated. In Scotland, with its Calvinistic backgrounds, his influence was immense ; in America, the land of his special devotion, it was strategic. Sir James Stephen, in his famous *Essays in Ecclesiastical Biography*, says : " If ever philanthropy burned in the human heart with a pure and intense flame, embracing the whole family of man in the spirit of universal charity, it was in the heart of George Whitefield. He loved the world that hated him ; he had no preferences but in favour of the ignorant, the miserable and the poor." Again, the free-thinking Benjamin Franklin, who at first was annoyed with Whitefield because he could not persuade him to plant his Orphanage in Philadelphia, finally said of him : " I knew him intimately upwards of thirty years. His Integrity, Disinterestedness and Indefatigable Zeal in prosecuting every good work I have never seen equalled, and shall never see excelled."[1]

Whitefield not only awakened the existing Churches in America to a new enthusiasm, a new vision and a new tolerance. His missions, being instrumental in establishing scores of new congregations within half a dozen different communions, diffused a new consciousness of evangelical unity ; while thousands of those who, in religious things, could not previously " discern between their right hand and their left," began to hunger and thirst after righteousness and to seek diligently the things of the Kingdom of Heaven. Even provincial Governors embraced him in deep emotion as he departed out of their midst. Franklin, to satisfy his curiosity, made a mathematical calculation of the size of the Philadelphia multitude hanging on Whitefield's words, and, to his own amazement, determined that 35,000 souls were at one time listening to the Evangelist's message. The financing of Whitefield's Orphanage was itself, in those days of sparse money, no slight undertaking ; albeit this was but one of many Good Works for which Whitefield raised such voluntary collections as never before had been heard of on American soil.

Even in education, Whitefield's contribution to American development was phenomenal. With the origins of two now famous Universities, he was directly connected. Princeton University, wherewith the name of President Woodrow Wilson is so closely connected, issued from the " Log College " started

---

[1] This tribute is engraved on one of the panels of the magnificent statue of Whitefield in the dormitory triangle of the University of Pennsylvania.

at Neshaminy by Gilbert Tennent and his father. That humble institution, with the support of Governor Belcher, a warm friend and follower of Whitefield, soon was transferred to Princeton, New Jersey, where, as " Princeton College," it became the recognised centre for the training of Presbyterian ministers in six colonies, viz. New York, New Jersey, Pennsylvania, Maryland, Virginia and Carolina ;[1] and in Princeton it expanded into the now world-known university. In the nursing days of this centre of learning, Whitefield was to the Tennents and Belcher a tower of strength. Gilbert Tennent often accompanied Whitefield on his preaching missions, and on both sides of the Atlantic the evangelist raised for the struggling College—" the parent of every Presbyterian College and theological seminary in America "[2]—substantial support. Whitefield was one of the first men upon whom " Princeton " conferred its M.A. degree.[3]

With the origin of the University of Pennsylvania, Whitefield's connection was even more intimate. In 1740, his " New Building " was erected in Philadelphia by warm supporters, including Franklin. To it the " Awakener " insisted on adding a Charity School, for " the instruction of poor children gratis, in the knowledge of the Christian religion and in useful literature." That Charity School evolved first into an academy, then into Philadelphia College, and ultimately into the University of Pennsylvania. When, in 1914, on the Bicentenary of Whitefield's birth, a noble statue of the evangelist was raised by the University, this statement was read : " The inspirer and original Trustee of the Charity School of 1740, the forerunner of the University of Pennsylvania, he solicited the first donations to the Library of the University . . . guided the new school of learning by his godly counsel, heartened it by his masterful preaching, and inspired it with his noble life."[4] " Zealous advocate and patron of higher education in the American colonies," is one of the inscriptions on the pedestal of this memorial. But the man who, taking two continents under his wing, spent more than two years of his life upon the Atlantic, fostered education on *both* sides of the water. For Charity Schools in England, he raised such popular collections as never previously had been known ; to Dr. Dodderidge's Nonconformist Academy, he proffered yeomanly assistance ; Dartmouth College was equally indebted to him ; while, after

---

[1] Tyerman's *Whitefield*, Vol. II, p. 323 ; see also Hodge's *Presbyterian Church in the United States* (opening chapters).
[2] E. Ninde, *Whitefield—Prophet and Preacher*, p. 139.
[3] Belden, *op. cit.*, p. 209.
[4] *Ibid.*, p. 237.

the destruction of Harvard's Library by fire, he secured fresh gifts of books from England. Nor did he forget the American Indians. Notwithstanding prevailing prejudice against the education of that fierce people, the *Boston Gazette* reports a single occasion when he collected £120 for Mr. Wheelock's Indian School, in Lebanon, New England.[1]

Whitefield was a man of heart and soul too big, to be understood by the swarm of little critics, who buzzed so busily to besmirch his name. Franklin's unvarnished tribute will stand the tests of time. Dr. Abel Stevens, in his *History of the Methodist Episcopal Church*, says :

" The Congregational Church of New England, the Presbyterians and Baptists of the Middle States, and the mixed colonies of the South, owe their later religious life and energy mostly to the impulses given by Whitefield's powerful ministrations . . . the New England Churches received under his labours an inspiration of zeal and energy which has never died out. He extended the revival from the Congregational Churches of the Eastern to the Presbyterian Churches of the Middle States. In Pennsylvania and New Jersey . . . he was received as a prophet from God ; and it was then that the Presbyterian Church took that attitude of evangelical power and aggression which has ever since characterised it. . . . The stock from which the Baptists of Virginia, and those of the South and South West have sprung, was also Whitefieldian. And, although Whitefield did not organise the results of his labours, he *prepared the way* for Wesley's itinerants. When he descended into his American grave, they were already on his track. They came not only to labour, but to organise their labours ; to reproduce, amid the peculiar moral necessities of the new world, both the spirit and the method of the great movement as it had been organised by Wesley in the old."[2]

The post-Whitefieldian development of the Evangelical Movement in America is a subject too expansive in range, too epic in consequence, to permit even of outline here. Francis Asbury, Wesley's master-builder in America, was a characteristic product of the Revival. His " Theological College " as Dr. Curnock puts it, " was his Mother's Class Meeting."[3] From infancy he imbibed the Evangelical spirit ; when eighteen he undertook the labours of a local preacher ; when twenty-one,

---

[1] Belden, p. 212.
[2] Quoted in Belden, *op. cit.*, pp. 115–16.
[3] Wesley's *Journal* (Standard edition), Vol. VI, p. 2 (note).

he was appointed by Wesley as an itinerant, and for five years (1766–1771) he laboured zealously and effectively on four different circuits, in England. Then, when twenty-six, the year following Whitefield's death, he volunteered for America, where for forty-five years, till his demise in 1816, he toiled with a constancy and selflessness rivalling that of Wesley himself.

Asbury was endowed with none of Whitefield's dramatic, spectacular gifts ; but attaining a much riper age, he laboured nearly four times as long on American soil, and being *par excellence* a conciliator, an organiser and a builder, he was singularly adapted to follow the fiery Awakener. Scarcely had Asbury landed in America, when friends importuned him to confine his labours to the more populous centres.[1] They knew not their man ; Asbury, above all, was a trail-breaker, a frontiersman, a pioneer. From the first, he determined that even the most isolated settlers must enjoy the privileges and inspirations of an organised religious life : his passion, like that of Wesley, was to serve the most neglected. Hence, decade after decade, despite the perils of the Revolutionary War, despite extreme changes of climate and extreme fury of elements, despite the lurking dangers of untracked forests, quicksand bogs, turbulent torrents, bridgeless rivers and stern, forbidding mountains, he rode regularly some 5,000 miles a year[2] ; winning wherever he went devoted followers who became local leaders ; and creating wherever he went, Class Meetings, Societies, Sunday Schools, Circuits and finally Conferences.

This Staffordshire peasant became perhaps the most creative religious statesman the North American continent has yet known. Owing nothing to the schools of his day, he was entirely the product of religion : love, sympathy, vision, courage, faith and prayer made him great. For thirteen years before Dr. Coke arrived to ordain him, he had been to the wilds of America their chief shepherd of souls. His ordination therefore but proclaimed him what already he was—a superintendent, a bishop, over the far-separated flocks of Christ, which his own ministrations had so largely led into the fold. Other of Wesley's leaders, including Philip Embury, Barbara Heck and Captain Webb, were at work in America long before Asbury arrived. Dr. Coke, his fellow " Superintendent," with his scholarly and executive powers, rendered memorable service. But to the saintly Bishop Asbury must go the honour of being the " Father in God " to the largest and most indigenous Protestant Church the New World knows. His life was a marvel—almost a miracle—of consecration and attainment.

[1] Curnock, *ibid.*
[2] W. H. Fitchett, *Wesley and His Century*, p. 265.

Like Wesley, he rose habitually at four a.m. ; and like Wesley again, he strove to account for every moment of every day. Self-taught, without fixed abode, a man of the roads, he made it his rule to read one hundred pages of good literature daily. He taught himself Latin, Greek and Hebrew. Always his saddle-bags were packed with books which he himself had mastered ; and many of these he persuaded not only his preachers and Class-leaders but thousands of his humblest followers, to buy and read. House-to-house visitation, field-preaching, barn-preaching and countryside camp-meetings in vast tents, were among his chief means of establishing contact with new pioneer communities : and always his converts he organised into Classes and Societies, thus nurturing local leadership. Log schools and Churches, accordingly, reared by the co-operative " bees " of settlers who hungered for under-standing and righteousness, rose up as beacons of light wherever this holy man went.

The salary of this inimitable missionary, " for the greater part of his life was under £20 a year." [1] Money to him, like time and life, was a trust from God : and this spirit he breathed into the whole heroic band of his " co-workers in the Gospel."

In the formative days of the young Republic's life, these apostolic missioners outmarched the prospectors and gold-hunters ; they out-toiled the homesteaders and ranchers. What Lincoln came to mean to the social and political life of the United States, that, Asbury before him, meant to her moral and religious life. Indeed, aside from the Bible and spiritual influences mediated by Asbury and his fellow " Enthusiasts," there is no understanding Lincoln. Bishop Asbury could claim " Apostolic Succession " only through Wesley, the " Baptism of Fire " and the Gospel of Christ. Often his episcopal status has been ridiculed. Yet, if by their fruits they are known, he was a Bishop indeed ! In the single decade, 1780 to 1790, the American Methodist circuits increased from 20 to 114, and their Church membership from 8,504 to 57,631. [2] This amazing achievement represented the first harvest of Asbury's valorous sowing ; and it successively became the seed of mightier harvests ahead. [3]

The most obvious legacy of the Evangelical Revival to the United States is the Methodist Episcopal Church. Apart from its many vigorous adherents, that Church to-day has 4,670,000 active members. Its places of worship number 27,000, and its ordained ministers and missionaries 18,000. In its Sunday

[1] W. H. Fitchett, *Wesley and his Century*. 264.
[2] C. E. Vulliamy, *John Wesley*, p. 335.
[3] See Strickland's *Life* of Asbury.

Schools, staffed by 379,000 voluntary officers and teachers, it regularly imparts Bible, moral and religious instruction to 4,000,000 children. Its Epworth Leagues have 552,000 young people in various stages of training for Christian Endeavour. Its foreign missionary efforts—including medical and educational —reach out to every Continent; while within the United States, its influence is enormous. In the sphere of higher education, it controls famous universities, colleges, professional schools and vocational institutes, with a faculty, in 1936, totalling 4,378, and a student body of 76,524. The properties committed to this higher educational work are valued at over $85,000,000, and its endowments exceed $91,800,000. That Church's hospitals, old age homes, orphanages and co-related institutions, moreover, are hardly less imposing, representing, as they do, an estate of $64,000,000, and caring annually for some 750,000 persons. The entire properties of the Methodist Episcopal Church, including its "foreign field" equipment, are valued at $700,000,000 : while in 1936, notwithstanding the pinch of prolonged depression, $57,000,000 was bestowed by loyal supporters upon this great voluntary Christian Communion.[1]

Such, are certain of the tangible symbols of a spiritual, and therefore largely intangible, movement. The Methodist Episcopal Church, however, is but one of sixteen Methodist Churches in the United States.[2] It is quite distinct from the great Methodist Episcopal Church *South*, and from the Methodist Protestant Church; while also it is equally distinct from the strong *African* Methodist Episcopal Churches, organised and run by the American negroes. These Churches now are all taking steps towards union, and, when united, will make a mighty Methodist Communion. They all are direct children of the Evangelical Revival. Yet Methodism, strong as it is, represents but half the influence of that epochal Awakening upon the United States. The older Protestant Churches—especially the Baptist, Presbyterian and Congregational—derived from it a new vision and a new infusion of Christian vitality. They became, in fact, missionary and truly evangelical Churches. Nor did this influence stop there. The revivals of Finney and of Moody were later expressions of the same great Movement : and all the Communions now co-operating in the vigorous

---

[1] These facts and figures are drawn from long and careful analysis specially prepared for the author by Dr. Thomas P. Potter, Assistant Editor of the General Minutes of the Methodist Episcopal Church. See *Christian Advocate* (New York), December 2nd, 1937, pp. 14–15. (*The Church in Figures*, by Dr. Potter.)

[2] See *Ency. Brit.* ("Methodism in the United States").

Federal Council of the Churches of Christ in America[1] owe a priceless debt to the mighty Baptism of Fire. Indeed, even the Roman Catholic Church, little as it may recognise the fact, has not been untouched by this purging, democratising influence.[2] Lord Bryce's conclusion is deeply significant : " It is in English-speaking countries only, that the Roman Church has frankly embraced democratic principles, declaring that she has no complaint against popular government. . . ."[3] Enough, however, has already been said to suggest the debt of popular government, in Anglo-Saxon commonwealths, to the character-building influences of voluntary associations engendered by the Evangelical rebirth of vital, practical Christianity.

In the United States, as in Britain, popular charitable, benevolent and social-service organisations are very extensive, and have reached a creditable level of attainment : while, being of and for the people, they are loved by the people. Their close historical relationship to Evangelical Christianity, though unmistakable, is a subject beyond the compass of this study. In one sphere of social attainment, however, America easily leads Britain and all the rest of the world. Her great and numerous Colleges for the higher education of women are without a peer : yet the heralds of that extensive emancipation movement, such as Mount Holyoke, Oberlin and Elmira, Vassar, Wellesley and Smith, together with Bryn Mawr and Goucher, were rooted and grounded in the soil of Protestant Evangelical Faith.

(ii) Impacts on the British Empire

If the influence of the Baptism of Fire on the United States was thus pronounced, its influence within the British Empire was hardly less permeating. Professor G. M. Trevelyan, after pointing out that the strength of the Evangelical Movement, " like that of the earlier Puritanism, was always among the laity," says : " Evangelicalism brought rectitude, unselfishness and humanity into high places, and into the appeal to public opinion." " The strongest type of English gentleman in the new era," Trevelyan further avers, " whether Whig or Tory, was often Evangelical. The army knew them with respect, and India with fear and gratitude. Their influence on Downing Street and in the permanent Civil Service, through families like

---

[1] See *Biennial Report* (New York, 1936) for a masterly survey of the aims and scope of this Council.

[2] Maximin Piette, a Franciscan Father, in his careful, sympathetic study, *John Wesley*, practically admits this fact. His book recently was translated into English.

[3] James Bryce, *Modern Democracies*, Vol. I, p. 100.

the Stephens, gravely affected our Colonial policy on behalf of the natives of Africa and the tropics. . . . on the whole for the great good of mankind."[1]

In India, the names of such valiant pioneer missionaries as Carey and Martyn, will ever be associated with the development of all that is best in that great land. Charles Grant, the first avowedly Christian Chairman of the East India Company, backed by the great banker Henry Thornton and all other fellow-members of the Clapham Sect, succeeded in imparting even to that hardened commercial corporation, some sense of conscience and trusteeship. As for the Government of India, Lord Teignmouth, also a member of the Clapham Sect, and first President of the British and Foreign Bible Society, strove zealously, during his five years as Governor-General, to impress upon all Departments of the Administration their stewardship both to God and the people of India. Later, too, Shaftesbury and other Commissioners of the India Board of Control emphatically took the position, that unless Britain secured for the whole Indian people a fuller measure of happiness and education, a truer equity and justice, and a more abiding peace and prosperity, than they possibly could achieve for themselves, she then was but an intruder and a usurper within that country. The new sense of service and humanity injected into the British Administration of Indian affairs, was an immediate product of the new conscience, created by the Evangelical Revival.

As for the heart of Africa, the labours of those dauntless missionaries, Livingstone and Moffat, emblemise the highest contribution of Christian civilisation to the most primitive peoples. The name of " Gordon of Khartoum," too, is synonymous not only with selfless chivalry, but equally with uncompromising Christian opposition to the slave-trader, the tryant and the exploiter. Or follow the enthralled African to his new habitation in the West Indies, and there again the labours of such courageous missionaries as Knibb and Smith, together with the devotion of such dedicated laymen as Sturge and Sligo, were the harbingers of Hope and Life. In the self-governing Union of South Africa, furthermore, the Evangelical emphasis on the brotherhood of all mankind and the sanctity of all personality, has proven the most salutary and effective influence in restraining the Whites from over-reaching themselves in their relationships with the Blacks.

In the autonomous British Commonwealths of Australia and New Zealand, Evangelical Christianity has been too strong to permit the domination of any hierarchical or oligarchical factions or cliques. There, also, it has been a sobering, educating,

[1] G. M. Trevelyan, *British History in the Nineteenth Century*, pp. 53-4.

inspiring and democratising influence, which contributed bountifully to the formation of the character and institutions of the people. In Canada, the same was true. So vital, indeed, were certain impacts of the Revival in establishing the liberty and culture of that expansive Dominion, as to warrant some little detail.

At the American "Christmas Conference" of 1784, when the Methodist *Episcopal* Church was organised, a call was made for three volunteer foreign missionaries, to serve in Nova Scotia and the adjacent Maritime districts of Canada. At once, this challenge was answered by three sturdy young preachers, and a special offering of £50 was forthwith collected for their initial expenses. Thus began the organised impact of the Revival upon what then were the isolated Canadas. But a later step was destined to more far-reaching significance. In 1790, Asbury and Coke commissioned a youthful American preacher, William Losee, to "range at large" in Upper Canada, then the special preserve of those redoubtable Royalists and Tories, the United Empire Loyalists. Losee's task was far from easy, for none of the exiled Loyalists desired to learn anything either from the young Republic or her Citizens. His mission, nevertheless, was a pronounced success. Losee was a preacher of the Gospel, and in no sense a politician. Following the Asbury example, he rode constantly through the forest from settlement to settlement and homestead to homestead, praying with and exhorting the settlers, and establishing, in many rude cabins, family altars around which Bible reading, sacred-song and prayer became hallowed devotions.

When Losee arrived in Upper Canada, its population was about 20,000, and its whole vast area was served by only six ordained ministers, most of them Anglicans, who considered themselves State officials, and who were bent above all else on establishing a State Church within the Province. Nor was their ambition without political support. By certain notorious clauses of the Constitutional Act of 1791, *one-seventh* of all unoccupied lands was granted for the support of a " Protestant clergy," generally understood to mean Anglican ; while power was given " to erect parsonages or rectories according to the establishment of the Church of England."[1] In fact shortly after 1791, " lands to the extent of nearly 2,400,000 acres in Upper Canada, and approaching a million in Lower Canada," which was dominantly French and Roman Catholic, were thus set apart.[2] Yet, notwithstanding the vested power of

[1] George Bryce, LL.D., *Short History of the Canadian People*, p.329.
[2] *Ibid.*, pp. 329–30.

the Clergy Reserves and the expanding assumptions of the Family Compact, the despised " saddle-bag preachers " steadily gained ground. The names of most of them are now forgotten, but they were a heroic band ; and such of them as Losee, Case, Ryan and Torry were among the truest foundation builders of English-speaking Canada.[1] Thirty years after Losee first crossed the St. Lawrence, instead of six ordained ministers in Upper Canada there were ninety-nine, of whom a full third were Methodists, to say nothing of the 112 local preachers and exhorters who augmented their work. Already, the Methodists were the most numerous people in Upper Canada : yet, so great was the power of the ruling and assuming junto in Church and State, that their Conference had as yet no legal status ; and for another nine years, their ministers were not even allowed to solemnise marriage among their own people.[2]

Such, was the measure of religious liberty granted to Nonconformists in Upper Canada, in 1820. Presbyterians,[3] Baptists, Quakers and Lutherans felt the grievance as well as Methodists. Nevertheless, the smaller became the proportionate numbers of the Family Compact, the more obdurately and unscrupulously did they cling to the seats and symbols of power. With their political corruption and their Clergy Reserves, they were the immediate cause of the famous " Mackenzie Rebellion." The real hope and salvation of Canada, however, lay not in rebellion, but in deep, sane plans for the religious, educational and political freedom of the country. And before the decade, 1820 to 1830, had run its course, the most creative leader in that emancipating movement already was looming large on the public horizon.

Egerton Ryerson, " the recognised champion of religious liberty and equality in Upper Canada,"[4] was born on March 24th, 1803, in Charlotteville, Ontario. Of Dutch Huguenot descent, he was the sixth and youngest son of Colonel Joseph Ryerson, a fervid, militant Empire Loyalist, who after the American Revolution settled first in New Brunswick, but soon followed the trek to Upper Canada, where, as a Loyalist officer, he was granted 2,500 acres of land. Ryerson's mother was a deeply religious woman of warm heart and open mind. As the Methodist and Baptist itinerant preachers were the first to visit and labour in their community, she was glad to take her

---

[1] For the great saga of the early Methodist Societies in Canada, see John Carroll, *Case and His Contemporaries* (Vols. I and II).

[2] Sir J. P. Bourinot, *Canada*, p. 346.

[3] Presbyterians, as representing the Established Church of Scotland, were thrown a few crumbs. See Dr. Bryce's *Canadian People*, pp. 330–1.

[4] See Preface to Professor C. B. Sisson's *Egerton Ryerson, His Life and Letters*, Vol. I, 1937.

children to profit by their services, while she herself was not a little influenced by their Bible exposition, their sincerity and their devotion. But to his mother's own teaching, Ryerson owed his deepest boyhood debt. His *Story of My Life*, confesses that in " the religious instruction, poured into my mind in my childhood by a Mother's counsels, and infused into my heart by a Mother's prayers and tears,"[1] germinated the guiding aspirations of his career.

When twelve, in the year of Waterloo, Egerton Ryerson experienced a conversion which, crowning his mother's teaching, brought with it a vital " change of heart." When eighteen, he formally joined the Methodist Church : whereupon his peremptory father issued the command that he " must leave the Methodists or leave his house." Choosing the latter alternative, Egerton next day procured a post as " usher," or student teacher, in the Grammar School of the London district. When twenty-two—his father meantime being reconciled—he was accepted as a Methodist preacher ; and within the next four years the Rev. Dr. John Strachan, soon to be first Bishop of Toronto, together with all his satellites in the Family Compact, was compelled to take notice that a new, brilliant and highly-disturbing luminary had burst into the sky.[2]

As early as 1826, this " Boy Preacher " began powerfully to expose the inaccuracies and inconsistencies of Dr. Strachan's famous " Ecclesiastical Chart," and its supporting " sermons." But the first crying need of the colony was a free, just, upright and Christian press : and this Ryerson, backed by all the " saddle-baggers " of Methodism, determined to provide. Initial capital of $2,000 had to be procured. Undaunted, the preachers themselves raised a full half of that sum ; their followers, mostly backwoodsmen struggling resolutely for meagre sustenance, raised the other half. *The Christian Guardian* was born in 1829 ; its growth and evolution represent one of the most pleasing romances in the whole Empire's development. Within two years of its founding, it " had achieved a circulation greater than the combined circulation of the thirteen other newspapers at that time published in Upper Canada."[3] From 1829 till the formation of the United Church of Canada in 1925, *The Christian Guardian* never missed an issue under that title ; since Union, having coalesced with the papers of the old Presbyterian and Congregational Churches of the Dominion, it continues publication, in its previous home, as *The New Outlook*.

---

[1] *Op. cit.* (edited by Geo. Hodgins), p. 27.
[2] Sisson's *Ryerson*, Vol. I, pp. 5–9.
[3] See J. L. Rutledge, *Victoria's First Hundred Years* (in *New Outlook*, June 17th, 1936).

The Ryerson Press, now the property of the United Church, and by far the largest and best-housed of all the publishing companies in Canada, is the lineal descendant of the little press created well over a century ago by Egerton Ryerson and the "outback" preachers. With the origin of *The Christian Guardian*, the handwriting of religious, educational and political freedom for Canada was on the wall ; but so blinded by prejudice and self-importance was the Family Compact, that it was unable to read.

The second crying need of the young colony was an institution of higher learning, open to all. As far back as 1819, the " saddlebaggers " had appointed a committee to " take into consideration the important subject of a seminary " ;[1] but for ten years it had to be shelved by more pressing problems. Now, however, with the genius of Ryerson in an editorial chair, the matter soon was revived. Constantly did *The Christian Guardian* keep this matter before its readers. It called for an academy which would provide " a good English and classical education," and wherein " the stream of educational instruction shall not be mingled with the polluted waters of corrupt example." The dream of Ryerson and his supporters was liberal and truly catholic : they envisaged a college where " scholars of every religious creed will meet with equal attention and encouragement." And when finally their dream was realised, it was laid down in the governing rules that : " All students shall be free to embrace and pursue any religious creed, and attend any place of religious worship which their parents or guardians may direct."[2]

At the Upper Canada Methodist Conference of 1830 definite plans for the college were formulated, and the staggering problem of finance was faced. As with *The Christian Guardian*, the preachers themselves took the lead, and returned to their people for support. So encouraging was the response that on June 7th, 1832, the corner stone of *Upper Canada Academy* was laid, amidst beautiful wooded surroundings, in Cobourg ; and building proceeded apace. But unforeseen difficulties were ahead. Soon it transpired that the ambitious scheme would cost substantially more than $40,000, and meanwhile an economic depression had settled as a black cloud over the province. Market value of farmers' produce dropped to low levels, and many subscribers found themselves utterly unable to fulfil their commitments. When the 1834 Conference met, it was warned by its College Committee that the unfinished buildings were in

[1] Carroll's *Case and His Contemporaries*, Vol. II, p. 217.
[2] See Dr. Jesse Arnup, " The Old Ontario Strand " (in *New Outlook*, October 21st, 1936).

danger of being sold for debt. Then it was that the " saddle-baggers " made their superlative effort. Despite all they previously had done, and though their salaries averaged barely over $200 a year, fifty of them came forward and signed promissory notes for $100 each—more than some of them then possessed. Nor did even that half-year's salary represent the full measure of their devotion. Having won the right to solemnise marriages in 1829, they determined also, for the next four years, to throw all marriage fees into the College Fund. Against such devotion, Family Compact and clergy-reserve religion could never prevail. Here, 4,000 miles from England, and wholly unobserved by the Mother Country, the spirit of the Evangelical Revival was asserting itself against the lingering and stagnant assumptions of the eighteenth-century " Establishment," in Church and State.

A little earlier, when the Methodist Conference, through Ryerson, petitioned their Governor, Sir John Colbourne, on behalf of their educational plans, that gentleman in reply had the effrontery to jibe at " the limited views of the leaders of societies, who perhaps have neither experience nor judgment to appreciate the value or advantages of a liberal education."[1] Later, when it applied for a royal charter for the academy, the law officers of the Crown in Upper Canada replied tersely, that " the Methodist Conference was unknown in law."[2] A Royal Charter, nevertheless, these pioneer preachers were determined to have ; so Egerton Ryerson was despatched to England to plead their case. The difficulties Ryerson there encountered were numerous and colossal ; but ere he returned, the charter had been promised, and some little financial assistance through the Colonial Office as well.

On June 18th, 1836, Upper Canada Academy was officially opened with an initial enrolment of 120 students—both men and women. On October 12th, of the same year, its hard-won charter was formally granted. It was the *first Nonconformist College in the whole British Empire to receive a Royal Charter.*

More than 3,000 pioneer Methodists in Upper Canada subscribed to the building of this Academy, their subscriptions averaging about $16. And if the superior critics who so glibly assert that the Evangelical Revival was a benighted, retrogressive movement will condescend to learn anything from facts, they well might remember that on one of the preserved " Subscription Books " appear about 1,000 contributors, only one of whom was unable to sign his name in full. In the New

---

[1] See Chancellor Edward Wilson Wallace, " Methodist Cavalry " (*New Outlook*, September 23rd, 1936).
[2] See Dr. Jesse Arnup, article cited above.

World, as in the old, the Revival was an illuminating and educating, as well as a character-building, movement.

Six years after its founding, Upper Canada Academy changed its name to Victoria College, thus designating its loyalty to, and admiration for, the young Queen. When it opened Faraday Hall it provided the first building in Canada devoted " exclusively to the teaching of the sciences." On moving from Cobourg to Toronto, the rapidly expanding capital of the Province, its utility and its fame increased. To-day it is a great *University*, still holding it own Charter and granting its own degrees, though now under the control of the United Church of Canada, and affiliated with the great State University of Toronto. In October, 1936, Victoria University, before thousands of its *alumni* and friends, assembled from every continent, celebrated the Centenary of the reception of her Royal Charter. Among the eminent men upon whom she then bestowed her distinguished Doctor of Divinity degree was Canada's Governor-General, Lord Tweedsmuir, so well known and loved as John Buchan. Addressing Convocation on behalf of his fellow-recipients of that degree, and pledging " loyalty and devotion to the great University of which we are now a part," Lord Tweedsmuir observed :

" I find myself among eminent theologians who represent various communions of the Christian Church, an example of the ecclesiastical broad-mindedness which is so pleasing a feature of Canadian life. There is another feature of Canadian life which I heartily approve. I do not know any country where the Church and the world—or shall we say the better side of the world—walk together so harmoniously."[1]

During the continued celebrations of Victoria's Centenary, Canada's renowned Governor-General made this further declaration : " The Christian religion alone gives the warrant for that high evaluation of the human soul, which is the meaning of humanity."[2]

Far more than is commonly realised, did that " ecclesiastical broad-mindedness " and that leavening influence of Christianity upon Canada's work-a-day life, which Lord Tweedsmuir so warmly admires, derive from the saddle-bag preachers who rode the rough and often snow-drifted trails of Upper Canada. Over a century earlier they, as firmly as Canada's present Governor-General, believed that vital Christianity alone could inspire

---

[1] See " This is Victoria's Day " (Centenary Number of *New Outlook*, October 21st, 1936).
[2] *Ibid.*, p. 978.

and sustain " that high evaluation of the human soul," which brings to humanity meaning, vision, hope and power : and in that Faith they built. These trail-blazers established " the first Missionary Society in connection with any church in Canada."[1] By their struggle for liberty, their broad tolerance, their deep charity and their evangelical zeal for the things of the Kingdom of God, they were the initial forerunners of the great Church Union movement which, in 1925, resulted in the formation of the United Church of Canada.

The most eminent of those trail-blazers, Egerton Ryerson, not only founded and edited the most influential newspaper in Upper Canada ; he became first principal of Victoria College, and later " founder of the Educational System of Ontario."[2] " With the magnificent system of public schools now possessed by Ontario," says the French-Canadian historian, Sir J. G. Bourinot, " must always be associated the name of Dr. Egerton Ryerson, a famous Methodist, the opponent of Mackenzie's seditious action, and for many years the superintendent of education."[3] In 1844 Ryerson was appointed Chief Superintendent of Schools for Upper Canada. He visited the New England States, the British Isles, Germany and other Continental countries, and learned from them all—in some cases what *not* to do. The Education Acts of 1846 and 1860 were both drafted by him. His statue in front of the Toronto Normal Training College recalls the fact that he initiated Canada's excellent system of Teachers' Training Colleges. " During the thirty-three years of his superintendency," says the *Encyclopædia of Education*, " Dr. Ryerson built broadly and well the foundation of the present system of common school education in Ontario." That system has left an indelible impress on the whole educational structure of Canada, while its reflex on various other lands, within and without the British Empire, has not been small. It is a logical consequence of Ryerson's work that Ontario, for many years, has had *compulsory* public education till sixteen years of age. So this also is a product of the "Enthusiasm" engendered by the Revival of vital, experimental Christianity.[4]

Nor was the expression of inspiring, adventurous Christianity in Canada confined to the Methodist frontier-breakers. The heroism of Roman Catholic missionaries is inextricably woven into much of the romance of Canada's development. Moreover, the great English Revival which created Methodism and

[1] Dr. Arnup, " Old Ontario Strand."
[2] Professor Sissons, *op. cit.*, Vol. I, p. 9f.
[3] Bourinot's *Canada*, p. 368.
[4] See Dr. Nathaniel Burwash, *Life of Egerton Ryerson*, and *History of Victoria College* ; also *Nat. Dict. of Biog.* (" Egerton Ryerson ").

initiated the Protestant world missionary movement, affected profoundly all the pioneer Reformed Communions in the premier British Dominion. The frontier work of the early Presbyterians was scarcely less magnificent than that of the Methodists, and from the earliest times these churches learned to co-operate. The same harmonious spirit increasingly permeated the Baptist, Lutheran and Congregational Churches, though they represented much smaller numbers. As for the Anglican Church, it too, when once it freed itself from the shackles of the Family Compact and dropped its stiff, assuming airs, captured this missionary fervour and became a splendid pioneering force. The moral, social and educational history of Canada, is bound up with the heroic evangelising efforts of these *voluntary* religious bodies ; and what such missionary zeal accomplished in Canada, it accomplished also in other parts of the British Empire.

(iii) *Is Christianity Effete ?*

In the ponderous elaboration of his " economic determinism " and materialistic " philosophy," Karl Marx, to establish his case, assumes throughout that all religion is humbug—a priest-concocted anodyne, a pernicious opiate, designed to stupefy the masses into passive subservience, that they may the more easily be exploited by the usurping capitalist tyrant, as beasts of burden. Morality and law, Marx dashes overboard in the same grandiose style. " Law, morality, religion," reads the *Manifesto of the Communist Party*, are to him (the Communist) so many bourgeois prejudices, behind which lurks in ambush just so many bourgeois interests."[1] As for the ideal of the Christian family, Marx, for all his top-heavy learning, has no clearer conception of what it is, or means, than a Hottentot. So around it also, he thrusts his ever-present " bourgeois " blanket, and casts it contemptuously aside.

" Our bourgeois," he writes, " not content with having the wives and daughters of their proletarians at their disposal, not to speak of common prostitutes, take the greatest pleasure in seducing each other's wives.

" Bourgeois marriage is in reality a system of wives in common. . . ."[2]

The man who solemnly could prescribe to the " proletariat " such patent falsehood, such pernicious poison, as an inherent

---

[1] *Op. cit.* (first published in 1848), p. 19 of authorised English translation (1933 edition).
[2] *Ibid.*, p. 25.

part of his revolutionary " science," had great need to dismiss all religion as a soporific. That dogma, was essential to his purpose : his very hypotheses compelled him to beg the case. Consequently he will hear of no relation between Christianity and social justice. For instance, " Christian Socialism," avers the *Manifesto*, " is but the holy water with which the priest consecrates the heart-burnings of the aristocrat."[1] In Marx's monumental and belaboured work, *Das Kapital*, the same attitude is equally pronounced. Pride, hatred, jealousy, revenge and flagrant atheism parade through every chapter ; while, by inference, Marx substitutes his economic, materialistic and " scientific " omniscience for God. Much of his argument, moreover, Voltaire fashion, reduces itself to assumption, aspersion and innuendo, as when glibly he asserts that " The Anglican Church will more readily pardon attacks upon thirty-eight of its thirty-nine articles than upon one thirty-ninth of its income."[2] Yet this is but representative of many of the " facts " adduced in support of the economic-revolutionary " proposition," which Engels, Marx's collaborator, predicts " is destined to do for history what Darwin's theory has done for biology."[3]

Pure religion embodies the highest, most ennobling and most sustaining aspiration known to man. But that " the highest," if prostituted, may degenerate into an unlovely and nauseating thing, exhibiting many of the properties of an opiate, who will deny ? Furthermore, that religion, including certain expressions of Christianity, has, at some times and in some places, been so prostituted, is surely beyond dispute. It may be that the economic and atheistic " gospel of Communism," through its loud cry for social justice, will yet prove a thorn in the side of Christianity to spur it to greater unity, higher purpose and more Christ-like expression of its Faith. But such speculation is beyond our field. The backgrounds, origin and evolution of the Evangelical Revival, as well as certain of its fruits, we now have briefly surveyed. If the religion mediated through that revival is to be designated an opiate, then all relationship between cause and effect has departed, the meaning of words has gone, and logic is dead.

But sinister, revolutionary and devastating as have been the assaults of Karl Marx's Class-Hatred and No-God disciples, the barren, negative assumptions of those who have long been posturing as the *intelligentsia* of Christendom, have injected into current society a still more blighting and paralysing infection. Thus far, the twentieth century has been dominated by a

[1] *Op. cit.*, p. 30.
[2] Marx's *Das Kapital* (" Everyman " English edition), Vol. II, pp. 864-5.
[3] Preface to *Communist Manifesto*, p. 8.

soulless rationalism and an agnostic humanism which, conjointly having usurped the seats of authority, have striven to impose an intellectual dictatorship over the minds and spirits of men : and already their fruits are manifest. " Emancipated " man, in his worldly wisdom knowing not God, has endeavoured to establish himself " as God," and having mastered the laws of many scientific phenomena, has succeeded in conjuring into being many amazing gadgets, devices and " things." But now these " things " are threatening destruction to their maker. Increasingly, " civilised " society has been finding itself in the position of a reckless sorcerer—unable to control the powerful robots which, by the wand of science, it has called forth from space to do its bidding.

Secularism, rationalism and humanism have penetrated and mastered not a few mysteries of the physical world. Mechanisms they have enormously enlarged and improved. Man's reach, they have so extended as almost to make plausible the fabulous Magic Carpet and Seven League Boots ; but his grasp on ultimate reality, they have almost paralysed. Glutting the body, they have starved the soul : hence the inevitable Nemesis. As they pause and ask themselves : " Is not this great Babylon that I have builded ? " a taste of dust and ashes rises in the mouth. As they behold their unfinished Tower of Babel, whose top was to " reach unto heaven," they are becoming conscious not only of a confusion of tongues, but of a confusion of spirit. Already, they seem to hear a cracking in the foundations. Science, which they enslaved to their ambitions, to make them a name, is working overtime, not to create the means of happiness and culture, but the contraptions of fear and death. And paradox of paradoxes, all this is being done by rationalised, secularised, humanised peoples for the mutual defence of the " civilisation " which they have builded. When man denies God and sets about to exalt himself, he is but tugging at his boot-straps, and so sinks the deeper in the mire. Kant, having in his *Critique of Pure Reason* demolished all the " rational " arguments for the existence of God, later, as a *practical* man, *postulated* the existence of God, the immortality of the Soul, and the freedom of the human Will.[1] For these, spiritually, are the Bread of Life. Modern sophisticated rationalism, which, like eighteenth-century Deism, increasingly has issued in cynicism, frustration and failure, might well contemplate the insight of Cowper, the initial poet of the Evangelical Revival :

> " Learning itself, received into a mind
> By nature weak, or viciously inclined,
> Serves but to lead philosophers astray,
> Where children would with ease discern the way."[2]

[1] See Kant's *Critique of Practical Reason.*   [2] See Cowper's *Progress of Error.*

Contemporary humanistic Secularism, for all its once vaunted powers and lurid promises, has sailed a rudderless course. In its dashing youth, it quite failed to distil understanding from the *minutiæ* and experience of the past : now, facing a premature old age, it lacks the faith, hope, love and vision, without which men and nations perish. Communism and Fascism are its children, the one turning Left, the other Right ; and they are furiously at war. Secularism dislikes and disowns its violent, uncouth progeny : loneliness and disillusionment possess its household ; and it is bereft of hope beyond the grave. " Vanity of vanities " will be its epitaph. Yet, had it been teachable in its youth, it soon would have discovered that its brilliant " naturalistic " philosophy was none other than a revived, embellished and camouflaged edition of Deism. Denying God, it placed its trust in abstract, deified man ; and behold its " educated," " scientific " grandchildren are risen up to proclaim man—" a parasite, crawling on the vertebræ of the pigmy among the planets."

The seething disunity, animosity and strife ; the rampant hatred, distrust and fear ; the recrudescence of crass, tribal nationalism ; the ghastly, accelerating race in the production of the armaments of mutual destruction : these unsavoury current phenomena indicate not that Christianity is bankrupt or effete, but that the rationalistic ideologies which temporarily have pushed God, Christ and Revelation from the centre of cultural influence, are devoid of the spiritual vision and vitality which alone can save mankind. Reason, divorced from Faith, has afresh been proving itself but a critical, destructive faculty.[1] Modern Secularism, therefore, now faces the age-old dilemma : without God, whence cometh Hope, Unity or Purpose into the world ? Without Revelation, where are to be found the corner stones of morality ? Without Faith, where is man's guiding star ? " If the spiritual oxygen," writes Viscount Bryce, " which has kept alive the attachments of Liberty and self-government in the minds of the people becomes exhausted, will not the flame burn low and perhaps flicker out ? . . . Without Faith nothing is accomplished, and Hope is the mainspring of Faith." Hope, however, has survived many seemingly fatal assaults, for Bryce adds : " Throughout the course of history every winter of despondency has been followed by a joyous springtime of hope."[2]

* * * * * *

[1] For the development of this thesis, see Benjamin Kidd, *Social Evolution* (1894).

[2] Bryce's *Modern Democracies*, Vol. II, pp. 663 and 670.

In this year of Grace, 1938, two momentous Centenaries will be thankfully and reverently celebrated throughout the English-speaking world, and far beyond. One is the four hundredth anniversary of the official and general circulation of the Bible in their own tongue among the people of Britain, thus opening to them a vivid, direct and unique Revelation of the things of God and His Purposes for man. The other is the two hundredth anniversary of the Conversion of the priest, John Wesley, which transfigured him into the most vitally effective prophet, leader and saint the English-speaking world has yet reared.

To emphasise the influence of the English Bible upon the character and development of the Anglo-Saxon and English-speaking peoples, would be utterly superfluous. The richest and best in English literature has been fed from its springs. The noblest British and American poets have been inspired by its beauty and its imagery, by its prophecies, its aspirations and its ethics. The English Bible was the rock foundation upon which all that was most practical and most magnificent in English Puritanism was builded. It has been to Anglo-Saxon civilisation not only *the Biblos*, the "Book of Books"; it has been the chart and compass of their moral and spiritual life. He who would assume to interpret the achievements of British and American character and culture without an understanding knowledge of the Bible, is like a drunken man fumbling at a locked door, without the key.

The two hundredth anniversary, now to be commemorated, represents a development and a fulfilment of the four hundredth. It was as Wesley, the rigid sacerdotalist, listened in a Moravian meeting to the reading of Luther's preface to the Epistle to the Romans, that the central message of the *New Testament* broke with overpowering illumination and conviction upon his soul. Henceforth the Bible became to him a book of new inspiration, new revelation. But the later Centenary, though dependent upon the earlier and inextricably connected with it, commemorates an advance of more thorough-going and far-flung significance. When once Wesley's heart was "strangely warmed" and the divine sonship of Faith possessed his being, he initiated and moulded a movement which applied the central principles of the Reformation, as never before had they been applied. "Salvation by Faith" now became a vital and personal experience, not a doctrinal dogma; the "Priesthood of all Believers" once more, as in Apostolic days, constrained every faithful convert to become a missionary, which was not the case in the Reformation Century; while again, the "Open Bible," whose key was the Gospel, became a guide to daily life and conduct such as neither the Reformed Churches of the sixteenth century nor the Puritans of the succeeding century had quite dared to make it. " It is scarcely an exaggeration," says Lecky, the great rationalist historian, " to say that the scene which took place in that humble meeting in Aldersgate Street forms *an epoch in English history*. The conviction which then flashed upon one of the most powerful and most active intellects in England is the true source of English Methodism."[1]

Had Lecky been writing a history of nineteenth as well as of eighteenth century England, and had he investigated the deeper significance of the whole Evangelical Revival, he soon would have realised that Wesley's conversion resulted in something still greater than an " epoch in English history." It is highly dubious if any spiritual leader since that matchless Missionary to the Gentiles, has exercised such wide-spread, creative and beneficent influence upon the souls of men. In the seventeen centuries intervening between St. Paul and Wesley, the achievements of St. Francis of Assisi alone compare with those of the great Protestant Evangelist. But whereas St. Francis quickly won the approval of the Pope and the support of the whole Catholic Church, Wesley, in a then vulgarised, slave-trading, Deistic England, faced bitter ridicule and animosity—ecclesiastical and oligarchical—for more than three decades. He lived to an age however which doubled that of St. Francis ; his personal crusade was almost three times as long ; each succeeding year, his zeal and his influence increased ; and so solidly did he build, that by far his greatest victories were won after his death. But if the world achievements of St. Francis and Wesley are comparable, Wesley remains incomparably the greatest of all Protestant leaders, and the initial medium of the most powerful spiritual movement the English-speaking world has yet known.

That the Evangelical Revival developed the fairest flower and fruit of Reformed Christianity, is indubitable. In the early eighteenth century it seemed as though Protestantism was dying of sheer spiritual paralysis and moral anæmia. Puritanism, by iniquitous legislation, had been bullied, tortured and coerced. A priggish Deism had descended on England as a stagnant, poisoning atmosphere. In the name of " naturalism," men and manners were corrupted ; beneath a polished, tinsel surface, abysmal ignorance was rampant ; the slave-trade was flourishing and expanding ; the Bible, discredited and mocked at, was little read ; the Gospel was treated as a myth. Wesley, defying the " new philosophy," and penetrating to the heart of the *New Testament*, finally changed the entire scene. Dr. Johnson once said of the mighty evangelist : " The dog enchants

[1] Lecky's *History of England in the Eighteenth Century*, Vol. II, p. 558.

you with his conversation, and then breaks away to visit some old woman." It was just at this point, that both Dr. Johnson's "High and Dry" and Sydney Smith's "Low and Slow" schools of contemporary England, equally failed to understand either Wesley or the Evangelical Revival. The "Old Woman" had a soul; so too, had the humblest labourer; and so also had the worldling, the drunkard and the prostitute. The Revival sought to make them soul-conscious, through Christ, in God. It represented a new revelation of

> "Love to the loveless shown,
> That they might lovely be."

Furthermore, it made its converts co-labourers together with God, to bring nearer that

> ". . . one far-off divine event
> To which the whole creation moves."

The popular modern notion that the Evangelical Revival was an irrational, inhibitive, "joy-killing" movement, is but a sophisticated delusion. A constraining enthusiasm for righteousness imparts joy and gladness: and these, the Revival abundantly mediated. Wesley, from the day of his conversion, knew no depression of spirit. "Sour godliness is the devil's religion," was one of his favourite epigrams and a cardinal article in his daily creed. If certain pleasurable bypaths the Revival closed, it was that the Highway of Peace and Righteousness might be opened and maintained. In a hard, materialistic and individualistic age, to the outcasts of England, to those starved of spiritual religion, Wesley brought fellowship and love, joy and hope; he brought also vision, radiance, power and holy inspiration. The Revival led its followers first into peace with God, then into brotherhood with man. Individual and moral redemption, it used as a lever to social and humanitarian redemption. Inward holiness, it insisted, must express itself in outward righteousness; faith must be judged by its fruits. Yet, as the converts sought righteousness, even in the performance of the humblest daily duties, the blue bird of happiness sang in their midst. Wesley not only was one of the happiest of men; he also was one of the most truly rational. Sanity and faith he always combined, even as religion and joy. Reason he ever considered a priceless gift from God; and his interpretations of Revelation always were rational. But never did he permit reason to put on airs. Wesley triumphed because of the purity of his soul, the majesty of his message, the singleness of his purpose, and the sheer magnificence of his moral and spiritual stature. He won England again for Christ, for the Gospel, and for sane Biblical religion. His faith and vision compelled him to claim the world for his parish; and one of the rich fruits of the Revival was the creation of the whole Protestant World Missionary Movement. Another was the creation of the British and Foreign Bible Society. Hence, on this year of vital Quatercentenary and Bicentenary celebrations, it is pertinent to remember that this incomparable Society has translated the Scriptures, in whole or part, into over seven hundred languages and dialects, and has circulated hundreds of millions of copies. It was Wesley and the Evangelical Revival, therefore, that made the Bible a world-known Book.

In two brief, memorable sentences, Elie Halévy, the great French historian of modern England, points a poignant challenge : " A century earlier," he writes, " John Wesley had defeated Voltaire. Would he defeat Karl Marx ? "[1] In these words are focused the very essence of the world's elemental problem to-day. John Wesley and Karl Marx, unmistakably, are the two most influential characters of all modern history. The former revived and spread vital, practical Christianity ; the latter formulated and mediated the gospel of revolutionary Class-Hatred, based on economic materialism. The two men are at the opposite poles of human endeavour and social reform : they are as Love and Hatred ; they represent the thesis and antithesis of modern thought and action. Wesley was concerned with every aspect of man's welfare. Often he used the motto : " *Homo sum, humani nihil a me alienum puto.*"[2] But he believed that human welfare was attainable only by faith in God, and by the direction of all material powers toward the development of abundant spiritual life. Marx, contrariwise, denying God, denied the existence of the spiritual life, and incited the pro-letariat to world revolution, by bloody means. Wesley's crusade represented the epitome of spiritual power ; Marx's crusade, the epitome of material force. In the eighteenth century, as Halévy reminds us, the master Evangelist defeated the master iconoclast. In the twentieth century, will he defeat the master materialist ? Wesley *versus* Marx, is the crux of the modern problem : and progress no longer is deemed inevitable. Christendom—whither bound ?

[1] *A History of the English People* (1895–1905 Volume, English translation), p. 360.
[2] This motto, for instance, he attached to his famous medical treatise.

INDEX

Newton, John, 57, 173, 290, 299
New Zealand, 436
Nightingale, Florence, 306, 370
Nonconformist, 88, 94, 167, 278, 292, 302, 353, 365
Nonconformity, 58, 166, 185, 289; decline of, in early eighteenth century, 292
Nonconformity ("The New"), 292-3, 356; in Canada, 438
Non-Jurors; expulsion of, 24; 25, 53
North, Lord, 48, 122, 230
Northington, Lord, 178
N.S.P.C.C., history and work of, 415-16

O

Oastler, Richard, 215, 306, 318, 385
O'Connell, Daniel, 341
Occasional Conformity Act, 28
Oglethorpe, General, 130, 132
Old Sarum, 124, 246
Olivers, Thomas, 219
Ormonde, Duke of, 28
Orsman, 306
Ostrogorski, *re* Evangelical Revival in his *La Democratie*, 252
Overton, J. H., 19, 59, 75, 93, 124, 179, 180, 206
Owen, Robert, 273
Owen, W. D. (Drapery Firm), 411
Oxford, 22, 202-3
Oxford Movement, 61, 62, 296, 307
Oxford University, 54; St. Edmund Hall, 60; pictures of deaths of Charles I and Christ, 68 (note); 183, 185, 186-87; Lincoln College, 187; 258, 279, 383

P

Page, Hon. James, 420
Paine, Tom, 265, 268, 273, 304, 326
Paley, William, 54, 91, 95
Paris, Treaty of, 99
Pascal, 38
Pattison, Mark, 93
Pelham, 150
Pericles, 92
Perronet, 282, 290
Perry, Canon, 46
Petrie, Sir Charles, 43
Philip II, 231

Phillpotts, Bishop, 338
Pilgrim Fathers, 374, 426, 427
Pitt, William, the Younger; letter to Cornwallis, 51; 52, 150, 299, 300, 308; effect of French Revolution on, 370
Place, Francis, family history, 169; 273, 304
Plague (the Great), 22
Plato, 92
Plimsoll, 306
"Political Arithmetic," 94
Pope, Alexander, 19, 36, 125, 172
Potter, John, 45, 95
Pounds, John, 359
Presbyterians, 23, 63; in Canada, 444
Press Gangs, 107
Pretender, 28, 205
Price, Dr., 52, 88; *Love of Country*, 89-90
Priestley, Dr., 269, 325
Primitive Methodist, 392
Princeton University; Whitefield's influence on, 429-30
Pulteney, 123, 150
Puritan, 21, 126; strain in Wesley, 185
Puritanism, 61; Green on, 76; 93, 199, 222, 293, 337, 425f.
Puritanism ("New"), 298, 373
Puritans, 69, 366; in America, 425-27; 449
Pyle, Dr., 46

Q

Quakers, 229, 259, 292, 302; and the Evangelical Revival, 337; educational support, 356; in jails, 366; 438
Quakerism, 337
Queen Anne's Bounty, 29

R

Ragged Schools, 358-60; the Bible in, 360
Ragged School Union, 353, 358; extensive programme of, 359-60; 361, 419
Raikes, Robert, 58, 268, 308, 353, 354
Ranke, 19, 76
Rebellion of 1745, 129

CPSIA information can be obtained
at www.ICGtesting.com
Printed in the USA
BVHW071349250521
608094BV00001B/22